WIMPY

WIMPY

A DETAILED ILLUSTRATED HISTORY OF THE VICKERS WELLINGTON IN SERVICE, 1938–1953

STEVE BOND

GRUB STREET · LONDON

Published by
Grub Street
4 Rainham Close
London
SW11 6SS

A CIP record for this title is available from the British Library

ISBN-13: 9781909808140

Printed and bound by Berforts Group, UK

Grub Street Publishing uses only FSC (Forest Stewardship Council) paper for its books.

CONTENTS

DEDICATION

JD 'Dave' Paterson
1931–2013

FOREWORD

WING COMMANDER STUART LINDSELL RAF
OFFICER COMMANDING 99 SQUADRON
RAF BRIZE NORTON

The Vickers Wellington or Wimpy, as it is so affectionately known, is the unsung hero of Bomber Command operations. Just as the vast achievements of the Hurricane are often overlooked in deference to the Spitfire, so too the Wimpy stands in the shadow of the Lancaster. Indeed, the Lancaster's, and subsequently the Liberator's four-engine range and payload capabilities provided the strategic advantage to the RAF's bombing campaign. Yet until the Lancaster's introduction in 1942, it was the Wimpy that provided the backbone to that offensive and the aircraft, with its geodetic design, truly took the war to the Germans. The Wimpy proved to be a long and faithful servant of the Crown throughout the war and was produced in vast quantities (over 11,000). Nearly twice as many Wellingtons were built as Halifaxes and fifty percent more than the Lancaster. The Vickers Wellington's contribution to the war effort was phenomenal but came with a heavy price. High percentages of operational losses, particularly during the early years, saw nearly 2,000 aircraft lost with many of their crews either killed or seriously wounded in action.

Often, the historical narrative does pay a warm tribute to the Wimpy. However, this is usually in bit-part when recounting or analysing Bomber Command operations as a whole. In this book, Dr Steve Bond sets the record straight and seeks to tell the whole story of the Wimpy from its initial design on a piece of paper, through to its operational service and retirement. Steve has over twenty years of service in the RAF as a propulsion engineer and twelve years as an academic at City University London. He has a long-standing and unquenchable thirst for all things Wimpy, which was fired by meeting many veterans at squadron association dinners, who told him their stories and of their affection for this great aircraft. It was these meetings with veterans that drove Steve to write this book.

Steve's research is extensive, covering thirty-nine squadrons' operational record books as but a mere starter for ten. There is some fantastic information within these pages, which tells how the Wimpy was so much more than a strategic bomber of the German mainland. How many of us knew the Wimpy was responsible for twenty-five of Coastal Command's 220 U-boat sinkings? Or how in the desert environment the Wimpy needed an engine change after just sixty to seventy hours of operation when hunting armour convoys? Or that the French may just have been the last to retire the Wimpy in 1955? If you want to find any Wimpy fact then you will find it here. More important than fact, however, is the personal story this book tells us; Steve details what the Wimpy meant to those who operated and loved it.

99 Squadron has a long history and proud association with the Vickers Wellington. Today we operate a fleet of eight Boeing C-17 Globemaster III aircraft and provide the essential element of strategic outsized cargo airlift in support of UK operations. I am proud to say we were the first squadron to operate the Wellington in October 1938 and we are the longest serving Wimpy unit with five-and-a-half years of continuous operations. As the first squadron to operate the

Wellington I would dearly love for 99 Squadron to be able to lay claim to the nickname 'Wimpy'. Alas, I can find no proof (either way), but I suspect it was already known as that prior to its initial arrival at RAF Mildenhall. Our no-notice move to Newmarket's Rowley Mile Racecourse on 1 September 1939 was for force protection in the face of looming war with Germany and I particularly like the transcript of the interview with Norman Didwell in Chapter 1. The transcript details how the squadron landed unannounced on Newmarket Racecourse, much to the disdain of the course clerk, who ran at the ground crew shouting, "You can't park here this is a racecourse". Having known Norman for some years with the 99 Squadron Association, I can imagine exactly how he told Steve this story and the glint of humour in his voice.

Chapter 2 details the darkest day in the squadron's history; 14 December 1939. Twelve 99 Squadron Wellingtons set off in the morning as part of a larger formation on a reconnaissance mission to track enemy shipping around Heligoland Bight. The Met Office had advised there was only a low chance of mission success; the weather was poor with cloud base and visibility deteriorating across the channel to but a few hundred feet. During this mission the formation came under continuous air and naval attack for over thirty minutes in dire weather. Back at Newmarket that afternoon, only seven of the twelve Wimpys returned. The five missing aircraft and their crews were lost in action with the confirmed kill of one (but possibly up to three) German Me 110 fighters. An ill-twist of fate was yet to befall the returning aircraft when the final of the seven Wimpys crashed on approach killing three of the six crew; battle damage to the left flap was the suspected culprit. The squadron lost thirty-nine men that afternoon.

Perhaps the most interesting chapter for me is Chapter 6, which documents the Wimpy's role in the Far East. 99 Squadron's Wellington history is international: Mildenhall, Newmarket and Waterbeach in the UK and Ambala, Pandaveswar, Digri, Chaklala, Jessore and Dhubalia in India. The squadron relocated to the Far East in 1942 and spent most of the remaining war engaged in the fight against the Japanese. During this time the squadron's greatest Wimpy airmanship feat was achieved when Flight Sergeant Jim Cameron captained his single-engine Wimpy over the 10,000ft Chin Hills at night, losing altitude and using flares to light his way ahead and navigate around the mountainous terrain whilst 'scraping over the trees'. Jim and his navigator, Flight Sergeant Kearns, were each awarded the Distinguished Flying Medal for saving their aircraft and crew.

I walk past a painting of Jim Cameron's feat every morning as I head to my OC's office. Entitled simply 'Overdue', it brings a warm smile as part of the squadron's history and that of the Wimpy's. I met Jim at a 99 Squadron Association dinner in Newmarket some years ago, the same time I met Steve Bond (Steve was attached to 99 Squadron during 1975/6 when we operated the Bristol Britannia). As I now walk past that picture I think of what Steve brings us with his work and what has changed today. Some things are very different; the context of total war, national survival and 1,000-bomber raids in which the Wimpy operated simply cannot be compared to today's operations. Some things are the same, despite the passing of seventy-five years. Today RAF Mildenhall is a huge United States Air Force base and I'm pretty sure Newmarket Racecourse would not thank us for landing a C-17 there. But there is a golden thread in this book that rings true today just as it did back then – the people. Each chapter, indeed every page, tells a personal story or experience. Every one of these stories underpins a ground crew and aircrew community that is immensely proud of their aircraft and I believe that is exactly the same for all of us who proudly serve in the RAF today.

The real history of the Vickers Wellington is, to me, told here through the personal testimonies and squadron accounts in this book. What you get here and nowhere else is the story of the Wimpy as seen through the eyes of those who truly knew it and from the records of the squadrons that operated it. Steve has chosen now to do his book to ensure that the passage of time cannot silence the story of the Wimpy. The personal contributions of Norman Didwell, Peter Fotherby and Graham Harrison, to name but a few, give the amazing story from people who are now well into their nineties. The personal accounts from some who have sadly departed such as Jim Cameron, Lucian Ercolani and Gerry Tyack, add tremendous weight. The personal accounts of over forty Wimpy veterans and supporting documentation from countless families of those who have sadly departed provide the voices to these pages.

I commend Steve for his publication. I cannot imagine the time, the years, it has taken him to complete this work but I think it has been more than worth it. He truly gives us the Wimpy and its air and ground crews; bombers, trainers, sub hunters, ship hunters, minesweepers, armoured convoy hunters and desert and Far East operators. This is the service history of the Vickers Wellington and I commend it to you.

Quisque Tenax (Each Tenacious)

Wing Commander Stuart Lindsell
Officer Commanding 99 Squadron
January 2014

INTRODUCTION & ACKNOWLEDGMENTS

Of all the major combat aircraft types flown by the Royal Air Force during the Second World War, the Vickers-Armstrongs Wellington is notable for not having had the same amount of attention in the written word as some of its perhaps more illustrious brethren. With the war becoming ever more distant, those brave souls who flew in and maintained the Wellington in its many guises and theatres of operations are becoming few indeed, so I knew that now was the time to capture their stories first-hand before it became too late. Indeed talking to the Wimpy veterans they all shared this view, and their affection for the aircraft shone through virtually every conversation I had.

While people may automatically think first of the fabulously successful Avro Lancaster when the Bomber Command campaign is mentioned, it is fascinating to realise just how huge a part the Wellington also played, and how varied its operations became as the war progressed. Many too, probably think that when it was withdrawn from main force bomber operations in October 1943 it faded away quietly in training units, although some may be aware of its sterling bombing work with 205 Group in the Mediterranean, or with Coastal Command on convoy patrol and anti-submarine work. There was though, very much more to the Wellington than even these diverse roles, and as I got deeper and deeper into my research for this book, I was constantly surprised to discover yet more unexpected and previously unsung chapters in its story. Among the Wellington's many claims to fame are:

- It was the only Royal Air Force (RAF) bomber type to serve in its original role from the first year of the war to the last, and to serve as such in every major theatre of operations.
- It was the first type to bomb Germany (on the second day of the war).
- With some Whitleys it was jointly the first type to bomb Berlin.
- It was the first to drop the 4,000 lb 'Cookie' bomb.
- Over half the aircraft used on the first 1,000-bomber raid were Wellingtons.
- Sergeant (Sgt) 'Jimmy' Ward of 75 (New Zealand) Squadron was the war's first New Zealand winner of the Victoria Cross, awarded while flying a Wellington.
- Total production was 11,462, which far outstripped both the Avro Lancaster (7,366) and the Handley Page Halifax (6,176) and it served in the RAF longer than either of them.

The Wellington was credited with flying 47,409 operations for Bomber Command alone, dropping 42,000 tons of bombs for the loss of 1,727 aircraft, and at its peak in the autumn of 1942 sixty RAF squadrons and operational training units (OTUs) were equipped with the type. Bomber squadrons in the Mediterranean theatre flew fifty percent more operational hours than those in the UK, and added to these must be the many long hours flown by the white Wimpys over unforgiving seas and the almost countless other uses to which the type was put in its seventeen-year service career.

While the chapters that follow outline the origins and development of the Wellington, the bulk of the content comprises detailed accounts of its use in all roles, heavily supported by personal accounts and anecdotes. The period covered is from the first deliveries in 1938 until the final withdrawal from use in 1955, the post-war period having been almost completely ignored in print up until now. I have also endeavoured to include stories from both air and ground crew, and taken a look from the other side of the coin, when Luftwaffe men came across Wellingtons.

Deliberately, there is no attempt to analyse the morals of aerial warfare, nor is there any detailed discussion of the policies and strategies of operations, other than where some explanation is essential to facilitate the reader's understanding of why the Wellington squadrons were doing what they were at that time. Of necessity therefore, much of the operational detail includes overviews of the regional war situations prevailing to set the Wellington's part in context and provide some assessments of its effectiveness. First and foremost this is a book about people; those who designed, built, flew, maintained and supported the Wellington in so many different ways. As one of the veteran's relatives said: "There were so many ordinary young men with extraordinary stories." With each passing year the ranks of those brave men and women inevitably diminish, and it is the duty of succeeding generations to ensure their efforts are recorded and remembered.

The debate about the spelling of the aircraft's nickname continues. The correct version is Wimpy without the 'e', since the aircraft got the nickname from the Popeye cartoon character J Wellington Wimpy. All the veterans I have met also spell it thus, and so shall I.

Of course putting this book together would not have been possible without the enthusiastic support of a great many people and organisations with whom I have had countless hours of contact in researching this book. First and foremost amongst these must be the many Wellington veterans, both aircrew and ground crew, and their families who have contributed so much and to whom I will be eternally grateful; nothing was too much trouble and log books and precious photograph collections were enthusiastically made available to me.The following veterans – some of them sadly now gone from us – have kindly recounted their experiences and contributed so much to the final work:

Derek Allaway, Peter Ayers-Hunt, Flt Lt Eric Barfoot DFC, Plt Off Michael Bennison, Fg Off John Brennan DFC, W/O Jack Bromfield, Bob Clarke, Fg Off Aubrey 'Tommy' Coles DFC, Cpl Norman Didwell, George Dunn, Fg Off John Elliott, Wg Cdr Lucian Ercolani DSO & bar DFC, W/O David Fellowes, W/O Peter Fotherby, Flt Lt Harry Hacker, WOp Air II Ron Hall, Charlie Harris, Flg Off Graham Harrison, Flt Lt Fred Hill DFC, Flt Sgt Cliff Hobbs, Fg Off Lionel Horner DFC, W/O Dennis Jackson, Fg Off Harry Kartz, Sqn Ldr Jo Lancaster, Sqn Ldr Peter Langdon DFM, Dennis Mason, Flt Lt Ted Mercer DFC, Fg Off Bill Parr, Flt Sgt Geoff Paine, Ray Powell, Flt Lt Alan Richardson, Flt Lt Guy Sharp, Fg Off Alan Thomsett, Gerry Tyack, Sgt David Vandervord, W/O Jack Wade, Fg Off Jack Wakefield, W/O Les Weeks, Fg Off Graham Welsh, Andre Wesolowski, Flt Sgt John Whitaker, Arthur Williams, Wg Cdr George Williams CBE, W/O Calton 'Cal' Younger RAAF.

Others who have provided assistance and information, including many relatives of veterans who were no longer around to speak to, include: Roger Allton, Jeremy Ayers-Hunt, Sally-Anne Barrett, Simon Batchelor 24 Squadron Association, Dave Birch Rolls-Royce Heritage Trust, Elizabeth Bond, Rebecca Bond, the late Chaz Bowyer, Peter Briton-Jones, Ron Brown, Petr Bucha, Bill Burgess, Linda Burton, Rachael Casey Fleet Air Arm Museum, Mark Chandler, Stu Clay, Paul Couchman 99 Squadron, Viv Cunningham, Markos Danezis, Steve Darlow Fighting High

Publications, Dugald Davidson, Egil Endresen Flyhistorisk Museum Sola, Mark Evans Midland Aircraft Recovery Group, Michael Fisher, Sqn Ldr Richard Forder RAF (Ret'd), Nicola Gaughan, Keith Hayward British Airways Speedbird Heritage Centre, Keith Hawes, Elsie Henry, Nicholas Hill, Harry Hogben, Dave Homewood, Dennis Jackson, Peter Jackson 70 Squadron website, Sqn Ldr Dicky James IX(B) Squadron Association, Christopher Jary, Gill Kerslake Fleet Air Arm Officers Association, Goole Local Studies Library, June Leese, Andrew Lewis Brooklands Museum, Wg Cdr Stuart Lindsell 99 Squadron, David Lloyd, Geoff Mann, Steve McLean South African Air Force Museum, Jeremy Millington, Cliff Minney, John Mounce Royal New Zealand Air Force Museum, Dr Ray Neve, Roland Orchard 458 (RAAF) Squadron Association, Robert Owen 617 Squadron Association, Dave Page, Mark Postlethwaite ww2images, Diane Rickard, Peter Roberts 37 Squadron website, Hauptmann Heinz Rökker Knight's Cross with Oakleaves, Alan Scholefield, Joan Self Meteorological Office's National Meteorological Archive, Chris Sharp, Lyn Skells, Geoff Stayton, Heather Stonehouse, Richard Stowers, Cpl Rob Swanson IX(B) Squadron, Glen Turner 75(NZ) Squadron Association, Richard Vandervord, Leslie Watts, Tim Whitaker, Andy Wilson Brooklands Museum, Diane Wilson IX(B) Squadron, Graham Withers and last but by no means least, John Davies, Natalie Parker, and Sarah Baldwin of Grub Street Publishing for their enthusiastic support of this project.

Thank you all, and if I have missed anyone please accept my sincere apologies. I have also assembled a great many photographs mainly from private collections, but also from public and company archives. I have done my best to ensure that they are all credited correctly, but in this digital age where material is spread throughout the Internet, the original sources of a small number of photographs have been impossible to trace, since they appear on several websites credited to different sources. These have been credited as 'Unknown', but I have included details of the websites above and again, if I have inadvertently omitted anyone, I am sorry.

Steve Bond
Milton Keynes
2014

CHAPTER ONE

A NEW BOMBER FOR THE ROYAL AIR FORCE

"Air power may either end war or end civilisation"
Winston Churchill, 14 March 1933

At the start of the 1930s, the RAF heavy night-bomber force consisted of aircraft which were little removed in terms of performance from those it had inherited from the Royal Flying Corps in 1918; the Vickers Virginia formed the backbone of the fleet. This aircraft lumbered along at a stately maximum speed of just 108 miles per hour (mph), had a service ceiling of 15,530 feet and could carry a maximum bomb load of 3,000 lbs; hardly different from the Great War-era Vickers Vimy that it had replaced. The other principal types in use at this time were the Handley Page Hinaidi and Heyford, neither of which offered any significant improvement in performance, not least because they still followed the same basic biplane and fixed undercarriage configuration. Although both the Fairey Aviation Company and Handley Page had come up with monoplane bombers in the shape of the Hendon and Harrow respectively, neither presented a significant forward step in performance.

The day-bomber force was even worse off, consisting merely of 101 Squadron at Bicester in Oxfordshire equipped with the Boulton Paul Sidestrand, and later its development the Overstrand. Although the latter had a maximum speed of 153 mph and could climb to a relatively impressive 22,500 feet, it could still only carry a very modest 1,600 lbs of bombs over a range of 545 miles.

OPERATIONAL REQUIREMENTS

Despite, or perhaps because of, the failed Geneva Disarmament Conference in 1934, much behind-the-scenes planning was set in motion to modernise the RAF, a key figure in this activity being chief of the air staff (CAS), Marshal of the Royal Air Force Sir Edward Ellington. In recognition of the shortfalls in bombing ability, as early as 1932 Operational Requirement OR.5 was issued which called for a twin-engined day-bomber to replace the Sidestrand. On 20 October of the same year, the resultant Specification B.9/32 was issued to the aircraft industry with invitations to tender, the basic requirements including the ability to carry a bomb load for 720 miles, or up to 1,250 miles with auxiliary fuel tanks, have a service ceiling of not less than 22,000 feet, and a bomb load of 1,650 lbs; hardly a step-change in performance.

This specification was also in partial response to Scheme F of the RAF Expansion Plan which called for replacement of all light bombers such as Hawker Hinds and replacing them with what were termed medium bombers such as the Fairey Battle and Bristol Blenheim, and heavy-mediums which resulted in a variety of aircraft including the Armstrong Whitworth Whitley.

Two manufacturers subsequently tendered for B.9/32 and in February 1933 both were contracted to take their designs to the prototype stage. Handley Page with their type H.P.52 Hampden, and Vickers-Armstrongs at Weybridge in Surrey with the Type 271. The latter was originally called the Crécy after the 1346 battle in which King Richard III triumphed over the French army against considerable odds. No doubt deciding this was not exactly a politically-correct choice, the aircraft was renamed Wellington in September 1936 in order to continue the established practice of naming bombers after English towns. Under chief designer Rex Pierson, Vickers based their proposal on an aircraft that utilised Barnes Wallis's unique geodetic construction, which had first been used in the Vickers Wellesley single-engined general-purpose bomber in response to Specification G.4/31 issued in the previous year. A remarkably strong structure resulted which was to prove its worth many times during the coming war when Wellingtons frequently suffered substantial structural damage yet were still able to make it home. A side-effect of the geodetics was a curious flexing of the airframe which bemused many a first-time Wimpy flier.

Initially proposed to be fitted with either air-cooled Bristol Pegasus or liquid-cooled Rolls-Royce Goshawk engines, the B.9/32 design was refined during 1934 to offer either Pegasus or Perseus radials and, powered by 915 horsepower (hp) Pegasus Mk.Xs. The first prototype K4049 made its ten-minute maiden flight from the Weybridge factory airfield at Brooklands on 15 June 1936 in the hands of Chief Test Pilot Joseph 'Mutt' Summers. Some reports have stated that he was accompanied by Barnes Wallis and Head of Production Trevor Westbrook. However, Summers' log book entry records that he was alone. A second flight of twenty-five minutes was made the next day and then on 17 June, Summers took the aircraft down to Eastleigh near Southampton which was the centre of Vickers flight test operations and offered a larger flying field than that within the tight confines of the motor-racing circuit at Brooklands; on this occasion Summers was accompanied by Wallis.[1]

B.9/32 prototype K4049 at Brooklands in 1936. (*Brooklands Museum*)

After a week at Eastleigh, the aircraft returned to Brooklands on 23 June prior to being shown to the public at the Hendon Air Pageant just twelve days after its first flight. On 8 July it was also inspected among a line-up of many new fighter and bomber prototypes by their Royal Highnesses The Duke of York and The Prince of Wales at the Aeroplane & Armament Experimental

Time carried forward :— 1455 15.

Date and Hour	Aeroplane Type and No.	Pilot	Passenger(s)	Time	~~Height~~	Course	Remarks
24.5.36	Falcon	Self	K Quill		20		Brooklands to Eastleigh
5.6.36	"	"	-		20		Brooklands to Eastleigh
"	"	"	-		20		Eastleigh to Brooklands
15.6.36	"	"	K Quill		20		Brooklands to Eastleigh
15.6.36	B9/32 K4049	"	-		10	✓	FIRST FLIGHT
16.6.36	"	"	-		25		2ND "
17.6.36	"	"	B N Wallis		20		Brooklands to Eastleigh
18.6.36	"	"	-		15		Tests at Eastleigh
20.6.36	"	"	-		20		Eastleigh to Brooklands
23.6.36	"	"	F/O [illegible]		10		Local Handling
29.6.36	[illegible]	"	-		10		Local
17.6.36	Venom Proto.	"	-		15	✓	FIRST FLIGHT
19.6.36	"	"	-		10		2ND "
5.7.36	B9/32	"	-		20		Contractors Test
6.7.36	"	"	-		45		Brooklands to Martlesham
9.7.36	"	"			30		Martlesham to Brooklands
20.7.36	"	"	R. Handasyde		5		Local
"	"	"	"		25		Brooklands to Eastleigh
21.7.36	Falcon	"	"		25		" " "
"	"	"	" Quill		25		Eastleigh to Brooklands
22.7.36	B9/32	"	...		20		Tests at Eastleigh
"	"	"	...		15		"

Mutt Summers' log book for the first flight B.9/32. (*Brooklands Museum*)

Establishment (A&AEE) at Martlesham Heath, Suffolk. In September it was passed briefly to Royal Aircraft Establishment (RAE) charge prior to the manufacturer's heavyweight trials back at Martlesham Heath which commenced on 13 November 1936. The A&AEE then took over the aircraft for official performance and handling tests, their initial reports being critical in a number of areas. These included poor grouping of some cockpit controls, examples of poor workmanship, a very heavy rudder and excessive trim changes during an overshoot.

The trials had been largely completed when the aircraft came to grief on 19 April 1937 after its elevators broke off following horn balance failure and it was written off at Brightwell in Suffolk, killing the flight engineer Aircraftman First Class (AC1) George Smurthwaite; pilot Flight Lieutenant (Flt Lt) Maurice Hare was thrown out of the cockpit as the aircraft broke up and he parachuted to safety. To prevent a re-occurrence of the problem, part of the re-design of the aircraft for production included adoption of a new fin, rudder and elevator assembly already being planned for the later B.1/35 aircraft which eventually emerged as the Vickers Warwick.

CONTRACTS AND FLIGHT TESTING

On 15 August 1936, just two months after the first flight, the Air Ministry placed an order with Vickers for 180 aircraft under contract number 549268/36, with further contracts following two months shortly afterwards including one issued to Gloster Aircraft at Hucclecote which was sub-

B.9/32 prototype K4049 in flight, 1936. (*via Norman Didwell*)

The wreckage of B.9/32 K4049 after its fatal crash on 19 April 1937 at Brightwell, Suffolk. (*via Norman Didwell*)

sequently cancelled in favour of Vickers-Armstrongs. All the aircraft were to be constructed to Specification B.29/36 which had been issued on 29 January 1936, and among the updated detail requirements were the need to carry up to 4,500 lbs of a wide variety of bombs of sizes up to 500 lbs, and the aircraft were to be fitted with Pegasus Mk.XVIII or Mk.XX engines.

To cope with the expected scale of orders and to disperse production under the 1935 shadow factory scheme, work was put in hand to prepare additional production lines at Broughton/Hawarden, near Chester and Squires Gate, Blackpool. Work at Broughton began in November 1937 and the government-owned, Vickers-managed factory produced its first Wellington Mk.I L7770 largely assembled from parts delivered from Weybridge. The aircraft made its first flight on 2 August 1939 to start satisfaction of a May 1939 contract for 750 aircraft, with a target production rate of fifty a month. Somewhat later, Blackpool's first contract was for fifty Mk.ICs, with the first X3160 not flying until August 1940; rather fortuitously just a month before the Weybridge factory was bombed. The Blackpool factory had an even more ambitious production target of no less than 100 Wellingtons every month. It had originally been planned to establish a third Wellington shadow factory at de Havilland's Hatfield site in Hertfordshire, but the idea was abandoned in 1940 and the factory focused on producing the Mosquito.

Wellington Mk.XIVs in production at the Broughton shadow factory near Chester, with Lancasters in the background. (*BAE via 99 Squadron*)

During early flight testing, the original aircraft had been criticised for some undesirable trim characteristics resulting in it being nose-heavy in a dive, and the cockpit layout was considered to require improvement. Nonetheless, lessons learned from the short flight test programme were rapidly applied to get another aircraft into the air as quickly as possible. Other major design changes at Vickers were also incorporated into the production aircraft, which was a very different looking aeroplane from the prototype, and included a more angular fuselage with a much deeper rear section to make room for a rear gun position and the revised tail unit. [2]

Following some preliminary fast taxi tests, the first production Wellington Mk.I L4212 flew on 23 December 1937 to check general handling and controllability, again flown by 'Mutt' Summers accompanied by Trevor Westbrook. The aircraft took off at 12:50 hours local time and flew for twenty minutes. The flight test reports[3] in this case state that there were no adverse comments apart from the aircraft being slightly left wing low, with the trimming tab movement being insufficient to correct this. Summers also noted that the racks in which the cockpit windows slid were most unsatisfactory, and the windows had to be held in position in order to prevent them being sucked out.

The first production Mk.I L4212 during a test flight in the winter of 1937-38. It was written off in a crash on 1 January 1942, when in charge of the RAE. (*Brooklands Museum*)

A second flight of thirty minutes followed at 15:30 hours that afternoon, the port side cockpit window having been removed, with Summers this time accompanied by Flight Test Observer Bob Handasyde and Barnes Wallis. A general inspection of the fuselage interior exposed quite a number of bad air leakages, especially at the gun turrets. However, more serious were severe oscillations of the control column which increased with speed.

Thereafter testing continued at an increasing pace with fellow Vickers test pilots Mike Hare and Jeffrey Quill helping the effort. Barnes Wallis frequently joined the crew, and by mid-January 1938 the control column oscillation problem was showing marked improvement following static balancing of the elevators with lead weight plus the addition of elevator horns (referred to as 'antlers' in the flight test reports). Subsequent lateral stability tests using the second aircraft were able to demonstrate the complete elimination of the problem, and the lateral behaviour of the aircraft was now described as extremely good.

On 18 January, observation of the opening and closing of the bomb doors was performed for the first time and on the 20th of that month passengers included Bristol test pilot Bill Pegg and a Mr Green from the Aeronautical Inspection Department (AID). The AID was an engineering organisation consisting of both civilian and RAF personnel with the task of ensuring that equipment manufactured or repaired by contractors and RAF maintenance units was done to approved designs and was fit for operational use; the first RAF pilot to fly in a Wellington, Squadron Leader Haines, was also on board and may well have also been from the AID.

In July and August 1938 L4212 (which had by this time completed around seventy test flights) was joined by the second production aircraft L4213 for a series of trials at Eastleigh. These included take-off and landing performance at a relatively modest load weight of 22,355 lbs, with the aircraft requiring a remarkably short average run of just 333 yards to become airborne (obviously far greater with a full bomb and fuel load), and a landing speed of around 79 mph. There was still criticism of the aircraft's longitudinal instability, and this was addressed by the fitting of ballast weights in the tail to control the centre of gravity. Testing of the Pegasus Mk.XVIII engines proceeded in parallel and it was found that the indicated air speeds attained at high-power settings were lower than expected due to the inability of the engines to maintain boost.

The first aircraft was handed over to A&AEE in September for handling and operational trials. Here again the longitudinal instability was commented on and the aircraft was seen to tighten during turns and could get close to the stall. It was also noted that the nose and tail gunners were not able to rotate with their guns, and this was improved. Armament testing, which later included the tenth aircraft, L4221, noted that carrying the maximum bomb load of 4,500 lbs necessitated a reduction in the fuel load. This same machine was also used for radio and electrical trials.

Other aircraft in the A&AEE Wellington fleet during the pre entry into service period included L4213 for performance, fuel consumption and oil cooling tests and L4217 which trialled cockpit dual-controls. It is believed that one or two Wellingtons were briefly attached from squadrons to Boscombe Down for trials in support of airborne gas equipment known as smoke curtain installation (SCI). Flt Lt Guy Sharp flew a trial with this equipment on 3 March 1941 in conjunction with the army to simulate dropping mustard gas on troops:

> "We were going to use it, if they wanted to walk into it. They'd [The Axis] used it in Eritrea and Abyssinia; luckily it didn't happen. That was the only time we did it, we had to wash everything down afterwards of course."

FIRST DELIVERIES

September 1938 had brought the Munich Crisis and a rapidly deteriorating political situation. An agreement was signed between the major European powers that permitted Germany to annex those parts of Czechoslovakia along its borders that were largely inhabited by German-speaking people, the annexed area to be known as the Sudetenland. This was an act of appeasement towards Germany that brought into sharp focus the gathering threat of conflict. It became apparent that the speedy introduction of the planned new aircraft types for the RAF was essential and thus the Wellington was considered ready to enter service even before all the testing had been completed.

The only known photograph of the first Wellington delivered to the RAF, Mk.I L4215 in the background of a 99 Squadron group photograph at Mildenhall in November 1938. (*Norman Didwell*)

Since December 1933, 99 Squadron, motto *Quisque Tenax* – Each Tenacious, had been flying the Handley Page Heyford night bomber, initially from Upper Heyford in Oxfordshire, moving in November 1934 to Mildenhall, Suffolk. On 10 October 1938, Wellington I L4215 was flown in from Brooklands to begin re-equipping the squadron which was under the command of Acting Wing Commander (Wg Cdr) John Griffiths. The replacement process was essentially complete in just two months when the Heyford was officially no longer on strength, although at least one aircraft was still at Mildenhall the following May. The initial production Mk.I Wellington represented a considerable advance over the Heyford, with a maximum speed of 245 mph compared with 142 mph, a service ceiling of 21,600 feet (only some 600 feet higher in fact), a bomb load of 4,500 lbs (3,500 lbs) and a range of 3,200 miles (900 miles) at a cruising speed of 180 mph.

Defensive armament was provided by a single Vickers K gun in the nose, two Browning 0.303 guns in the tail and a further single machine gun in a retractable ventral 'dustbin' position, although it appears that in service some may have been fitted with twin Brownings in all three positions. Initially the aircraft carried a crew of five comprising pilot, observer, two wireless operator/air gunners and one air gunner. Later on it became common to carry a sixth man as a second pilot.

Cpl Norman Didwell was ground crew on the squadron from its early days with the Wellington, arriving just a few months after the first aircraft.

> "I went to 99 Squadron as an under-training (U/T) flight rigger fitter's mate in May 1939. I did all the odd jobs you get when you're a sprog on a squadron. The first job I was ever given was on a Heyford, lacing-up the side panel, because it was all fabric. It

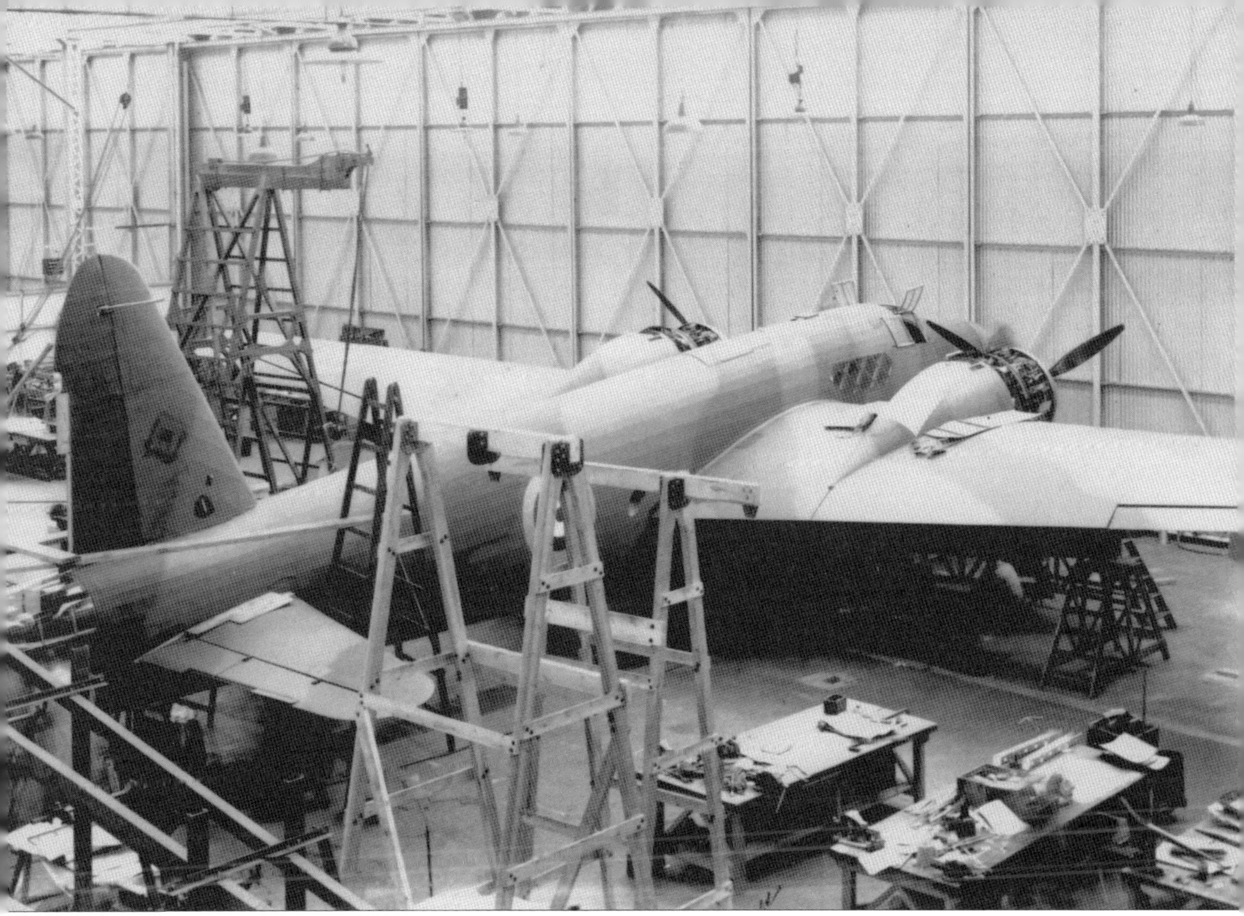

Mk.I production at Brooklands in 1937. (*Brooklands Museum*)

A formation of 9 Squadron Mk.Is in 1939. L4261 is nearest the camera. The unit moved from Stradishall to Honington that July. (*IX Squadron*)

had a big panel on the fuselage on the starboard and port side, where they could check the airframe itself, and that was all laced-up, a right old job that was I'll tell you; beeswax and lacing-cord. There were only two Heyfords still there, and they went to Number 4 Bombing and Gunnery School at West Freugh. Our pilots went down to Brooklands and converted on to the Wimpy. I think it was Squadron Leader 'Pussy' Catt who went down there and collected one. Most of the original pilots in November 1938 were NCO [non-commissioned officer] pilots, most of them ex-Halton apprentices in the early days. Just before the war I saw two civilians walking around and wondered who they were; it turned out they were 'Mutt' Summers and Barnes Wallis.

"Wellington Development Flight at Mildenhall was part of 99 Squadron with three aircraft, and they were all 99 Squadron pilots. I can always remember, there was Flight Sergeant Bill Williams AFM who had come from flying Harrows, Gerry Blacklock who was a sergeant pilot in those days, Flying Officer Kirby-Green, and Flight Lieutenant Hetherington, he was a New Zealander; they were on Wimpy Flight. They were just doing duration tests, and fuel consumption tests; they used to go up to nine-hours duration. I think one of the aircraft was the original one delivered, L4215, a Mk.I Wimpy which had Parnall turrets and a cupola. Later on we started getting Mk.IAs with Frazer Nash turrets.

Cpl Norman Didwell served as ground crew on 99 Squadron at Mildenhall from 1939. (*Norman Didwell*)

"If you were doing a DI [Daily Inspection] sometimes we had fitter 2, or flight mech engines, then you'd have a flight rigger, you got an armourer who was usually responsible for two aircraft – armourer guns and armourer bombs – you'd have an electrician, and an instrument basher. But sometimes the ground crew had two aircraft to look after. There were a lot of oil leaks in those days. You were forever washing the undercarriage down from an oil leak on the port side or the starboard side. You washed it down with paraffin, and then you had to get going again with the grease gun on all the grease nipples. Eventually they brought out covers for the tyres, for the leaks, because the oil was ruining so many tyres by soaking into them. That was mainly with the Pegasus engines.

"Otherwise they were reasonably serviceable in many ways, you didn't get many problems, not like some aircraft. The only thing was you got a lot of fabric damage, which you had to repair. If they lost a bit of it, the chaffing strips on the geodetics, you had to replace all of them; it was a bit of cord with the fabric wrapped round. You had to crawl up between the wing top surface and the bottom surface; you could get in so far, you know. The other thing was putting the engine covers on and the cockpit and turret covers. You had to crawl over it and that was tricky, especially when you were trying to get the front turret cover on, while the wind was blowing and you were on a rickety old set of steps. We had to have a pit dug for the ventral dustbin turret to be lowered on the ground so that the guns could be harmonised at 600 yards. On one occasion, after we had moved to Rowley Mile, gunner Dennis Sharp was doing this and decided the Salvation Army tea wagon, which was manned by stable boys, was about the right distance away so pointed at it. Unfortunately, he let a couple of rounds go which went through the van roof! He didn't half get a ticking off for that.

"We had twenty commissioned ranks and nineteen NCO pilots. Most of the Group 1 fitters 1 and 2 were ex-Halton apprentices, and the Group 2 flight mechanics were engines and airframes. We also had WOMs [wireless operator mechanics], wireless operators, cooks and butchers, admin clerks and a parachute packer. From pre-war the air gunners were mainly wireless operators and ground crew technicians until April 1940, when direct air gunner recruitment was introduced and on qualifying, they were given the rank of sergeant. I seem to recall pay was eight shillings [forty pence] a day prior to April 1940. Ground crew technicians were AC2, AC1, LAC [leading aircraftman] and corporal, and on passing out as an air gunner, they were paid an extra six pence a day flying pay. They wore a brass winged bullet to denote their rank on the right sleeve of their tunic.

"On the squadron we had eighteen aircraft in two flights, A & B (I was on B Flight). We had about 110 ground crew, but then at any one time there would be duty crew (four blokes), fire crew, flarepath crew – that was seven including the duty sergeant pilot who manned the flying control (which was in a caravan when we moved to Newmarket in '39). Then there was the chance light crew and guard duty, which came round twice a week, so there wasn't a lot of you left to look after eighteen aircraft really."

Flt Sgt John Whitaker had been a wireless operator with 38 Squadron on Fairey Hendons before moving on to Wellingtons, and he particularly recalls some of these duties:

"One of the less popular duties for pilots and wireless operators was flarepath duty. We had no concrete/tarmac runways and the aircraft landed on grass. So, when there was night flying in progress a crew had to go out into the middle of the airfield and lay an illuminated flarepath. This crew consisted of a pilot, a wireless operator equipped with an Aldis lamp and battery to work it, and a few aircraft hands to lay the flares out. The flares were known as goose-necks and were like oil cans with long necks and a bit of rag or tow stuffed in. This can was filled with oil and the tow was lit to give a crude lamp. The lamps were spaced out according to the wind direction and were in a double line; it was crude, but effective.

"When an aircraft wanted to land its wireless operator sighted his Aldis lamp on the beginning of the flarepath and flashed his identification letter in green, i.e. asking for permission to proceed. The duty pilot on the ground then told the operator to respond with the aircraft's letter in green if he could go ahead or in red if he was being told to overshoot. Then the fun began: the pilot aligned his aircraft on the flarepath and began his descent but he had to keep correcting his approach angle as the wind varied, even slightly. So, the aircraft was aimed at exactly where the ground crew were standing who scattered as they saw the airscrews getting closer and closer. The problem was to decide whether to go to the left or to the right as the aircraft was continuously making small corrections. I did hear of one flarepath airman who did not scatter correctly at Mildenhall and was picked up by the lower wing of a Heyford and then fell off as the aircraft came to a standstill. He recovered."

The next Wimpy variant to arrive was the Mk.IA (referred to by at least one squadron as the 'Battleship' Wellington), which was first flown in 1939, standardised on the Pegasus X and introduced Frazer-Nash hydraulically-powered nose and tail turrets to overcome the limitations in coverage of the Mk.I armament. It also had soundproofing in the cabin, an astrodome for the navigator, a fuel jettison system, and strengthened landing gear with larger main wheels which were no longer fully enclosed when retracted. Cpl Gerry Tyack, who established the Wellington Museum at Moreton-in-Marsh – which was opened officially by Air Marshal (AM) Sir Ivor Broom in 1990 – recalled an issue for the ground crew with the Mk.IA:

"I was an engine man at Bassingbourn, on 11 OTU. One thing I can tell you is about putting out engine start fires with my forage cap. The Pegasus had a bottom carburettor and if the pilot over-primed the engine fuel would pour out and as he started it it then caught fire. The only thing to do was to stuff your cap down the carburettor air intake, and that would put it out. Then you'd have to go to the clothing stores and get another cap."

Other Wellington variants to fly before the war included the Mk.II on 3 March 1939, for which engine availability considerations led to the fitment of Rolls-Royce Merlin Mk.X engines, this mark actually pre-dating the Mk.IA in the design process. The Mk.II initially exhibited an alarming tendency to swing to the left during the take-off run, counteracted with full use of right rudder and a technique of staggered throttles. This was followed by the Mk.IC fitted with 1.050 hp Pegasus Mk.XVIII engines; the other major change with this variant was the deletion of the ventral turret which was replaced by two Vickers K or Browning beam guns amidships; it also had improved hydraulic and electrical systems. Finally, the Mk.III flew on 16 May 1939 and was fitted with 1,375 hp Bristol Hercules Mk.III engines and a Frazer-Nash 20A four-gun rear turret as standard.

Although one can never be sure who first used the term 'Wimpy' by which the Wellington became universally known by that name, Norman Didwell believed it to have been originated in 1938 by fellow ground crew 'erk' twins Ernie and Les Evans ['erk' was a term commonly used to describe ground trade airmen]. "When I joined the squadron in May '39 they were all calling them Wimpy then."

One month after 99 Squadron received its first Wellingtons, 38 Squadron at Marham under the command of Wg Cdr Ernest Spencer Goodwin AFC, became the next to receive the type to replace its unique fleet of Fairey Hendons; its first Mk.I L4230 arriving on 24 November and its last Hendon departing on 12 January 1939. Thereafter the pace of re-equipment continued to accelerate and by the outbreak of war the following squadrons, all part of 3 Group headquartered at Mildenhall, also had the new type and had been declared operational for daylight only:

January '39	9 Squadron Stradishall, replacing Heyfords
May '39	37 Squadron Feltwell, replacing Harrows
March '39	115 Squadron Marham, replacing Harrows
March '39	148 Squadron Stradishall, replacing Heyfords
January '39	149 Squadron Mildenhall, replacing Heyfords
May '39	214 Squadron Feltwell, replacing Harrows
April '40	215 Squadron Honington, replacing Harrows

Of these units, John Whitaker remembered 115 Squadron as being rather different from the others:

> "115 was an unlucky squadron as it had been chosen by the Air Ministry to do experimental flying, so on a cold windy night while we were comfortable in the canteen a flight of 115 was sent up to try de-icing using a pulsed attachment fixed to the leading edge of the wing. It must have been successful as nobody ever crashed. It was also chosen to test blind-approach landing using the Lorenz system, nerve-wracking I would guess."

A further addition to the force was a New Zealand flight formed on 1 June 1939 at Marham. The Royal New Zealand Air Force (RNZAF) had ordered thirty Mk.I and IA Wellingtons to equip two squadrons of their striking force to be based at Whenuapai and Ohakea. RNZAF crews

Mk.Is L4367 and L4370 of 75 (NZ) Squadron Stradishall during the air defence exercises held in August 1939. Note 'Eastland' cross markings on the rear aircraft. (*ww2images*)

were sent to the UK to be trained and prior to the outbreak of war six aircraft had been received. At that point the aircraft and their crews were offered to the United Kingdom and the Marham flight became part of 75 Squadron which was formed in July 1939 at Stradishall in Suffolk tasked with continuing the training. All six RNZAF aircraft and the remainder of the ordered batch reverted to RAF serials for service with the unit which became 75 (New Zealand) Squadron in April 1940, commanded by Wg Cdr Maurice Buckley RNZAF. Cpl Colin 'Toddy' Knight RNZAF (later Sqn Ldr DFM) was in the first group of New Zealanders to arrive in England:

> "December 1938. Arrived in the UK and was posted to 99 Squadron at Mildenhall to do development trials on the Wellington. Did those duties, but then Britain declared war on Germany and we simply carried on. We were just very green sprogs from the RNZAF and I will never forget how the RAF blokes took us in, gave us all the gen, and looked after us."

During the eleven-month pre-war build up of squadrons, much emphasis was placed on crews learning the skills of close formation flying since, at that time, the strategy was for aircraft to rely on mutual defence during daylight raids, a policy that would all too soon prove to be based on woefully misplaced optimism. Training on the new type was not without its hazards and by 3 September 1939 six aircraft had been written off in accidents.[4] First to be lost on 15 May 1939 was 38 Squadron's L4243 which caught fire following an engine failure while practising shallow dive attacks on Marham aerodrome. Sgt E T Summers AFM attempted a landing in an adjoining field, crashed into a hedge and suffered undercarriage collapse, the aircraft burning itself out, fortunately with no casualties. This accident resulted in a modification to the flexible unions of fuel pipes to all Wellingtons in service.

Two months later on 21 July the crew of 148 Squadron's L4290, captained by New Zealander Fg Off David Jobson, lost control of the aircraft in cloud and dived into the ground at Milbourne Port near Yeovil in Somerset, sadly with the loss of all four on board.

August 1939 was a particularly bad month. On the 9th it was the turn of 149 Squadron, when L4258 went missing over the North Sea at night in bad weather, taking Fg Off Thomas Darling and crew with it. Two days later 38 Squadron's Plt Off John Hopkins (later Wg Cdr DFC) in Mk.I L4240 overshot in mist while force-landing at Debden with a failing engine, and hit a parked Hurricane (L1832 of 87 Squadron) before running into trees.

Two aircraft were lost on 29 August 1939. L4217 of A Flight 99 Squadron crashed on take-off from Mildenhall following an engine failure immediately after lifting off. Still with the wheels down all Flt Sgt James Healey could do was put the aircraft down straight ahead as it was immediately turning towards the dead engine. As it descended the aircraft hit the roof of a barn, slewed round and slid past a house, fortunately without hitting it, before ending up astride the Beck Row road. It had taken off with full fuel for a duration test, so the ensuing fire was intense but fortunately all the crew escaped, although two were slightly injured including a gunner who broke his ankle.

Sadly, a far worse fate befell Sgt Olaf Pitt and his crew in L4257 of 149 Squadron which also flew into the sea in bad weather five miles south east of the Happisburgh light vessel, the crash being witnessed by the skipper of a trawler who saw it dive in, leaving no trace. A sad day for the squadron was compounded by the death in sick quarters of observer Acting Sgt Anthony Freeman who succumbed to injuries received in an earlier forced landing of L4214 at Brandon in Norfolk.

On 8 August 1939 a bizarre ground accident took the life of Air Commodore (AC) Arthur

Mk.I L4217 of 99 Squadron following an engine failure on take-off from Mildenhall 29 August 1939. (*Norman Didwell*)

Thomson MC and bar AFC, the air officer commanding (AOC) of 3 Group, who was carrying out live-bombing practice by 115 Squadron aircraft operating from Larkhill on Salisbury Plain. F H 'Eric' Cummings was on 99 Squadron at the time:

> "The way I heard the story was that a bomb hung up, and to save hand pumping the bomb doors open the engine was left ticking over. As the doors opened, Thompson saw that the bomb had dropped onto the doors and leapt back into the turning propeller. I cannot vouch for the story as I was not detailed to fly, but I saw his blood-soaked parachute harness unloaded at Mildenhall."

PREPARATION FOR WAR

There were many varied activities for the squadrons in the build up to war, and 38 Squadron's operations record book (ORB) gives an indication of just how busy they were. In February 1939 they sent a detachment of four aircraft to 7 Armament Training Camp at Acklington in Northumberland for a month to train air gunners. From 14 to 17 March they were involved in a dispersal exercise at nearby West Raynham, with the crews living under canvas, which cannot have been much fun for them as the ORB records: 'Little flying was possible owing to the weather conditions.'

In April 1939 nine Wellingtons and their crews under the command of Sqn Ldr John Whitley AFC were sent to Northolt just outside London for fighter affiliation exercises with the Air Fighting Development Establishment (AFDE) which was based there. The exercises were carried out in two phases, day and night, the latter being primarily intended to test and train searchlight crews. Night operations were initially carried out within a twenty-mile radius of Blackdown

Camp near Aldershot and involved flying pre-determined courses for mock bombing attacks, with patrolling fighters attacking any aircraft illuminated by any of the twenty to thirty searchlights positioned in the area. The fighters were under direct radio-telephony (R/T) control from Northolt. Other targets attacked included the town of Berkhamsted in Hertfordshire.

Daylight exercises involved the fighters flying various attack profiles on a variety of bomber formations in order to assess the potential effectiveness of the mutual-protection policy. A maximum of six Wellingtons were flown at any one time, either in two 'vics' of three or in a close box formation. Evasive tactics used were described as follows:

> 'Rotation, sliding section, acceleration and deceleration, turns and skidding, all handled by R/T by a controller in the leading machine. Fighter attacks were made from every direction but nearly all developed into attacks from astern which appeared to be the only position from which good results (from the attacker's point of view) could be obtained.'

The first time Wellingtons were shown to the public in any numbers was at a display for Members of Parliament and invited guests, which was held at Northolt on 23 May 1939, when no fewer than twenty-four flew past. Exactly a week later the last Empire Air Day was held on Saturday 30 May with seventy-eight RAF stations open to the public who could clearly tell, from the sombre colours in which all the aircraft were now painted, that the service was well advanced in its war preparations. Wellingtons featured in the static or flying displays at many stations, with the 38 Squadron ORB noting that it was a 'successful programme...despite the poor visibility which was experienced. The attendance this year was 13,744 as compared with last year's 6,774.' Clearly the public were looking for comforting signs of readiness. In July 1939 9 Squadron (usually written as IX [Bomber] Squadron) flew a number of their Wellingtons over to Evére airfield, Brussels, in a show of strength at the International Aeronautical Exhibition, with a solo aircraft L4320 displayed by Flt Lt L S Lamb. 149 Squadron got in on the act by sending a formation of Mk.Is over Paris on Bastille Day 14 July.

That same month saw two regional exercises to test squadron readiness, one on the 7th and 8th, with the second on the 13th and 14th. 99 Squadron participation on the first day consisted of a formation of three Wellingtons flying over an unnamed 'designated target' and releasing Sashalite photo flashes. On the 8th five Wellingtons repeated the exercise over Salisbury. For the second exercise the flying clearly became rather more exciting:

> '13.7.39 Second Regional Exercise. Two sub-flights of three aircraft carried out a flight across England at 50 feet, from the east coast to Leicester and Cheltenham respectively. All aircraft reached their allotted targets.'

On 3 August 1939, orders were issued to all units to raise the state of readiness to 'C' with effect from 11:00 hours on the 7th. This required all fuelling and bombing equipment to be prepared and for all serviceable aircraft to be available for operations at twelve-hours notice. On the 4th the state was raised again to 'D' which required all serviceable aircraft to be ready for operations and loaded with pyrotechnics and ammunition. All aircraft were to be dispersed around their aerodromes by 10:20 hours and personnel were required to wear anti-gas clothing.

As a final test of readiness, a major home defence exercise was held over the United Kingdom between 8 and 11 August to assess and train forces engaged in both air and ground defences in combating air attack. A very large area of southern and eastern England was involved and the premise was that this was 'Westland' and its forces were to defend against and repel aerial onslaughts from 'Eastland', an imaginary power located somewhere across the North Sea. This was the largest such exercise held up to that time, around 60,000 personnel and 1,300 aircraft took part, with 'friendly' Westland aircraft being identified by white crosses applied over their roundels. This force was commanded by Air Chief Marshal (ACM) Sir Hugh Dowding, air officer commanding-in-chief (AOC-in-C) of Fighter Command, and was made up of 800 aircraft including nearly 500 fighters and fifty reconnaissance aircraft. In addition there was a force of 'friendly' bombers under the command of ACM Sir Edgar Ludlow-Hewitt, AOC-in-C Bomber Command, these aircraft being included 'for their nuisance value'. Clearly there was still much to learn about the strategic value of the bomber.

'Eastland' squadrons – also commanded by Ludlow-Hewitt – had 500 bombers including Battle, Blenheim and Wellington units, which overflew France at night before turning back towards England as an attacking force, with others approaching from across the North Sea. The symbolism was obvious. In preparation, Wellington formations had twice flown down to Marseilles and back, not least as a learning aid for future navigation performance. A contemporary newspaper article in *The Canberra Times* said, 'Throughout the bank holiday week-end, training preparatory to the main exercise has been in progress, and holiday crowds in many places have witnessed thrilling displays of low- flying and diving.'

The squadrons were allowed considerable freedom of action in both the planning and execution of their attacks in order to gain as much training value as possible. If a fighter felt it was in a good attack position it would indicate this by flashing its recognition lights continuously for one minute; the bomber was then supposed to reply with a similar signal; it would be interesting to know how many did. Bombers in their turn would indicate a bombing run by the use of recognition lights.

24 Squadron played their part and recorded that: 'London and Southampton were raided successfully, London being blacked out in the final raids.' On 26 August 1939 they added that one 'Acting Flt Lt M Nolan visited the Group Stations and gave short lectures on the lessons learned. Later that day he led a section to Feltwell, Mildenhall and Honington demonstrating the SCISSORS and ROTATION movements as a practice run for the planned wartime dispersal of the bomber force; time was running very short.'

In parallel with the development and introduction into service of the new aircraft types, Bomber Command planning had been focusing on how best to use the renewed force once hostilities began. After the 1937 Munich Crisis the air staff had drawn up a list of targets in Germany to be considered for attack. These were known as Western Air Plans (WAP) and were numbered according to specific groups of targets as follows (many had more specific sub-sections)[5]:

WA1	Attacking German Air Force
WA2	Reconnaissance of Home Waters and East Atlantic
WA3	Convoy protection in Home Waters and East Atlantic
WA4	Attacking German military communications
WA5	Attacking German manufacturing resources

WA6	Attacking Italian manufacturing resources
WA7	Attacking enemy naval forces and bases operating against trade
WA8	Attacking German depots and stores
WA9	Attacking Kiel Canal
WA10	Attacking German shipping and ports in the Baltic
WA11	Attacking forests
WA12	Attacking German fleet at sea
WA13	Attacking German headquarters and ministries in Berlin
WA14	Dropping propaganda leaflets
WA15	Operations against enemy shipping by 'M' mine
WA16	Mining of German waterways

Of these, the Munich Crisis resulted in WA1, WA4 and WA5 receiving top priority for concerted action. WA1 was to concentrate on the Luftwaffe's western bases and its supporting industry, WA4 on canal, rail and road communications to delay any German army advances in the west, and WA5 would focus particularly on the Ruhr valley and the enemy's oil supplies. In the event, as will be seen later, the early operations of the Wellington force did not really follow this pattern at all.

THE FINAL DAYS OF PEACE

The German invasion of Poland on 1 September 1939 finally precipitated the RAF moving onto a war footing, and the Wellington squadrons reacted immediately. Norman Didwell was caught up in 99 Squadron's frantic activity at Mildenhall:

> "Chiefy Darling in B Flight said 'Right lads, drop everything you're doing, gather round the flight commander's office'. We gathered round and stood there, and Sqn Ldr Catt said 'Right lads, go over to your billets, get all your kit, and get back here within half an hour.' So we thought hello, it looks like the balloon's going to go up, we shall be going to France. Anyway, we all assembled there and set off for Newmarket; some came over in the aircraft, some came by coach. I was on the coach; I never flew over with a kite. So where did they fly into? – Newmarket Heath, not above ten miles as the crow flies. I don't think many of them even dragged their undercarriage up.
>
> "After the fifth aircraft landed, a bloke came running down [Major Marriott, clerk of the course], waving a stick, wearing a deer-stalkers hat and hacking jacket: 'You can't put these aeroplanes here, go!go!' The CO said, 'There's a signal from the War Office, to take over this location, to operate my squadron from here for the duration of the war. I want all the keys for that building down there.' Now, he wouldn't hand over all the keys, so some of us were sleeping under the canopy [of the grandstand] in the outside as it were, you know. I mean if the rain blew in, we got soaked. Fortunately, it was a good summer.
>
> "Somebody must have blown the whistle and immediately they were ordered to open up everything, because we had to be put under cover. Now, the kitchen, he still wouldn't allow anyone to be given the key to the kitchen, this old bugger, Major Marriott. So we had what they call a field kitchen, the old cook and his assistant, a couple of

blokes, had to do it out in the open; bloody good wasn't it?

"Some of the officers were married, they had to move out of married quarters in Mildenhall, and they got digs in the town with people. Such as Kirby-Green, who was one of the fifty officers shot. [Sqn Ldr Thomas Kirby-Green was shot down in a 40 Squadron Wellington on 16 October 1941, twenty-first out of the tunnel in the Great Escape, and was murdered 29 March 1944.] There were two of them, Flt Lt Jim Brough and I forget who else, but they had digs in the town while the others had to sleep in the grandstand, until they found out the aircrew weren't getting enough sleep. We had eighteen aircraft, doing the daily run-ups which disturbed us, so they moved the officers into the Jockey Club headquarters. That's how we started off."

Newmarket Heath was one of the most famous horse-racing courses in the country and had been designated as a satellite aerodrome due to its reasonable proximity to Mildenhall to facilitate ground support, lack of obvious indications to prying Luftwaffe eyes that it was an airfield at all, and the fact that in the part of the course known as Rowley Mile, it was blessed with a well-maintained length of grass more than adequate to accommodate a fully-laden Wellington. Mike Bowyer was just a lad in 1939, but he recalled his surprise at finding 99 Squadron on Newmarket Heath:

"It was 3 September 1939, time 16:00 hours, and the war five-hours old. Braving the expected Luftwaffe onslaught Dad and I took a short tour of the local airfields. Judging by the road leading into Newmarket many folk out for a Sunday stroll were on the Heath. Parked cars suggested something unusual so ours joined them. Just over the grass brow rested the centre of attraction – a squadron of Wellington Is sheltering behind rolls of hastily-placed barbed wire with real, live bombs on trolleys[6]."

Over at Marham, 38 Squadron's ORB outlines their situation on 1 September 1939:

'Advance information received of General Mobilisation of the Royal Air Force. 38 Squadron commanded by Wg Cdr G B Adams and consisting of two Flights, A Flight commanded by Squadron Leader C N Amison, and B Flight commanded by Squadron Leader J P Selby.

'The strength of the squadron consisted of seventeen flying officers and pilot officers, ten sergeant pilots, sixteen sergeant observers, sixteen wireless operators, one W/O [Warrant Officer], fifteen flight sergeants and sergeants, seventeen corporals and 145 airmen.

"Equipment – eighteen Wellington aircraft fitted with Pegasus Mk.XVIII engines, twelve being serviceable for operations. The war establishment of aircraft was twelve."

By 10:30 that morning the squadron had dispersed twelve aircraft around the aerodrome and at 17:00 the CO addressed all the aircraft crews. Half an hour later the twelve aircraft previously dispersed were scattered to a satellite aerodrome at Barton Bendish, which was in fact little more than a large field, described as 'serviceable but with damp patches' five miles to the south west of Marham. Guards were dispatched from Marham and arrangements made to erect tented accommodation. The next day a series of briefings; no flying was carried out in order to conserve aircraft for operations; in any event an overnight thunder storm had rendered the surface at Barton Bendish boggy. Gas clothing, identity discs and small arms were issued.

With war being declared at 11:15 am on Sunday 3 September 1939 the squadron's first action was to remove all the aircraft to South Cerney in Gloucestershire. In the early afternoon skeleton crews took off with orders to fly below 1,000 feet, in formation in line astern, and avoid aerodromes. One aircraft had engine trouble and force landed at Little Rissington.

The other Wellington squadrons went through similar actions and dispersals; the war everyone had dreaded for so long had finally come.

CHAPTER TWO

INTO THE ABYSS – EARLY BOMBER COMMAND OPERATIONS

"The bomber will always get through"
Prime Minister Stanley Baldwin 1932

The start of hostilities found Bomber Command ready to support Western Air Plans 1, 4 and 5, all aimed at the German military and its manufacturing resources, and in order to achieve these aims it prepared six operational squadrons of Blenheims; five with Whitleys, six with Hampdens and six with Wellingtons. The Wellington units were 9, 37, 38, 99, 115 and 149 Squadrons, with 214 and 215 working up but not yet available for operations. All the Command's Fairey Battle light bombers had been moved to France on 1 September 1939, so were not available for any major bombing campaign.

The detailed bombing campaign planning was also thrown into disarray by an appeal from President Roosevelt to all the combatant nations to refrain from carrying out any bombing operations which might cause civilian casualties. This effectively meant that there was to be no bombing at all of mainland Germany. The only legitimate targets remaining were naval vessels at sea or moored in harbours (but not tied up alongside). Britain, France and Germany all gave assurances that this would be honoured, meaning that although Bomber Command could fly over German territory they could only do so for the purposes of reconnaissance and leaflet dropping. This began what came to be known as 'The Phoney War' which was to last until April 1940 when all restrictions on bombing mainland Germany were lifted following the German invasion of Norway and Denmark.

OPERATIONS BEGIN

The Wellington force commenced operations on the opening day of the war when aircraft including twelve of 149 Squadron at Mildenhall, were detailed to locate and attack the enemy fleet in the North Sea. The squadron ORB records that they were instructed to drop their bombs into the sea if no ships were spotted before dark; the record continues:

> '18:35 flight of three aeroplanes led by Sqn Ldr H I Dabinett took off to commence operations.
> '18:45 take-off of remaining aeroplanes cancelled on orders from HQ No.3 Group.'

In the event nine Wellingtons reached the search area but found nothing and all returned safely. In the afternoon of the following day the squadrons were again sent out against the fleet with an order to proceed to Brunsbüttel to attack two battleships reported to be entering the Kaiser Wilhelm Canal (the Kiel Canal). Fourteen Wellingtons were dispatched; the first section, led by Sqn Ldr Lamb, included Flt Sgt Borley and Flt Sgt Turner and the second, under Flt Lt Grant, included Sgt Purdie and Sgt Bowen. Sqn Ldr Lamb's section was met by nine German fighters, while the other section met anti-aircraft fire, but a ship was set on fire by Sqn Ldr Lamb who, after the raid, was received in audience by the king. A number of the crews reported bombing successfully, but due to poor navigation in adverse weather conditions and approaching darkness (a common problem in the early stages of the war), the formation split up and some bombs fell on the Danish town of Esbjerg. This attack also marked the first Wellington losses; 9 Squadron despatched six aircraft of which L4268 (Flt Sgt Ian Borley) and L4275 (Flt Sgt Albion Turner) fell victim to German defences, one of them being shot down by an Me 109 flown by Feldwebel (Fw) Alfred Held of II./Jagdgeschwader (JG)77. All the crew members in both aircraft were lost. The action was not totally one-sided for 9 Squadron as a 109 was claimed shot down by Fg Off Leech, a member of Sqn Ldr Lamb's crew.[1]

This operation was the only one flown by 9 Squadron with the fixed-turret Wellington Mk.I, as from 6 September 1939 the squadron started re-equipping with Mk.IAs. Eighteen were received by Christmas completely replacing the earlier version; from January 1940, the number of aeroplanes on the squadron was maintained at about twenty-four. Following the raid, the squadron was evacuated to Boscombe Down but this lasted for less than a fortnight and training on the new aircraft with its increased firepower continued from base. Every sortie included a period of air firing but the training programme was delayed by the necessity of returning aircraft to Vickers for the fitting of armour and self-sealing tanks.[2]

A Mk.I with early 99 Squadron VF- codes after a flare ignited in flight Mildenhall early 1939. (*Norman Didwell*)

In between operations, the squadrons were kept busy with a series of exercises to test their preparedness, and for the first two or three months of the war there were frequent short-term deployments to airfields away from home base under the Withdrawal Scheme. For example, on 5 September 1939, 99 Squadron was told to prepare for activation of the Withdrawal Scheme and eleven of the twelve aircraft at Newmarket were made ready to leave (the last one being unserviceable). Early the following morning the air raid sirens sounded in Newmarket and the ORB reported:

> 'The camp air raid warning system was sounded immediately by the duty look-out whose post was on top of the grandstand building. All personnel turned out immediately in varying stages of undress and were dispersed in an orderly manner. As only one shelter trench was available, this dispersal was necessary.'

Ten minutes later the squadron was instructed to put the Withdrawal Scheme into effect forthwith and at 09:00 all eleven aircraft took off for Upper Heyford in Oxfordshire. On 7 September 1939, four aircraft were recalled to Newmarket to carry out a leaflet raid while the rest of the aircraft made use of their time away by conducting air firing practice at Carew Cheriton airfield near Tenby in south-west Wales (which later that year was used as a bolt-hole for several months by 75 [NZ] Squadron). On the 9th, it was decided to evacuate Newmarket and move all aircraft, including those at Upper Heyford to Elmdon airport, Birmingham; five days later the whole unit was back at Newmarket. Training accidents continued and on the 19th, L4232 flown by Flt Sgt J W Brent suffered an engine failure on take-off at Carew Cheriton, and in an attempt to land again immediately, it collided with a Hawker Henley target-tug.

Once it became apparent that there was unlikely to be significant Luftwaffe raids on bomber airfields, these deployments tended to cease, thus allowing the maximum support for operations provided by the permanent stations. Another unit which benefited was 38 Squadron which was recalled back to Marham from its rearward station at South Cerney on 15 September 1939. Other diversions included a small number of aircraft being briefly detached to A Flight of St.Athan's Special Duty Flight, which was located away at Martlesham Heath, for experimental identification friend or foe (IFF) work. L4298 was allocated to the unit in December 1939 but never arrived, being replaced by L4213 and L4229, the latter being flown in from Kemble, Gloucestershire on 2 April 1940; both were disposed of the following month. 99 Squadron also sent four aircraft to Leuchars for radio direction-finding trials.

A 38 Squadron pilot, Marham 1940. (*Eddie Hancock*)

The next significant operation by Wellingtons took place on 3 December 1939 when twenty-four aircraft again went after German warships, claiming a hit on a cruiser. Me 109s got in amongst the formation, this time without any Wellington losses, but in return a single 109 was claimed shot down. However, the most notable fact about this raid was that a 115 Squadron aircraft suffered a bomb hang-up and this was subsequently accidentally dropped on the island of Heligoland to become the first bomb of the war to drop on German soil.

THE BATTLE OF HELIGOLAND BIGHT

The Wellington's luck as an unescorted, daylight bomber, relying on close formation for mutual defence, was about to run out in a spectacular fashion that was to change the whole of Bomber Command's strategy. In what came to be known as The Battle of Heligoland Bight, over two disastrous days the Wellington force suffered a major set-back which exposed its vulnerability to concerted enemy fighter attack.

On Thursday 14 December 1939, twenty-three Hampdens, twelve Wellingtons, and seven Whitleys were sent out on shipping searches. The Wellingtons, all from 99 Squadron and led by Sqn Ldr Andrew McKee, found a convoy including a battle cruiser, a cruiser and three destroyers steaming in a southerly direction in the Schillig Roads, north of Wilhelmshaven. Weather conditions prevented them from getting into the optimum position for bombing, flying at just 200 feet due to low cloud. The bombers continued to loiter in the area for some time and came under sustained and determined attack from both anti-aircraft fire and the fighters, one of which was claimed by a Wellington gunner. Five of the Wellingtons were shot down, and no German shipping was hit.

Norman Didwell watched the 99 Squadron aircraft leave Rowley Mile:

> "It was a frosty, cloudy morning. The aircraft took off at 11 o'clock in threes and turned south west towards Cambridge. When all twelve were airborne they formed up and then turned back right over the top of Rowley Mile at 800 feet as they headed east; people in Newmarket High Street saw them go. Then by three o'clock the news came through that it had all gone badly wrong."

Of the twelve Wellingtons just seven came back to Newmarket. Under the guidance of an experimental early version of the Freya early warning radar, large numbers of German fighters fell on the formation off the Island of Wangerooge, the formation having been spotted on radar when it was still seventy miles out over the North Sea. Flt Sgt James Healey in N2886, and Fg Off John Cooper in N2956 succumbed to Me 109 and Me 110 attacks and crashed into the sea, while Sgt Richard Brace in N2986 was brought down by fire from enemy warships; in each case all crew members were lost. Pilot Officer (Plt Off) Norman Lewis in N2870 collided with N2911 flown by Flt Sgt William Downey while desperately trying to take evasive action from fighter attacks; both aircraft fell into the sea, again with the loss of all lives. Wireless Operator/Air Gunner (WOp/AG) AC2 Bill Simmonds flew on that fateful day:

> "Squadron Leader Catt's aircraft N2912, in which I was the WOp, was the only aircraft which suffered no damage that day. Considering I saw aircraft hit and go down all around us, this was I think, a miracle. It is something which will remain a vivid memory until I die – we lost many friends that day."

'Toddy' Knight was the WOp/AG with Sqn Ldr McKee's crew in the lead aircraft, Mk.IA N2958:

"I remember sitting for hours in a bus outside the ops room, then being told to stand down. Then the final word to go, with the awful result. I can still see the tracer flying around the aircraft as I was sending the sighting report and, when we got back, to find the petrol pouring out of punctured tanks! I saw aircraft of our squadron with wings blazing, falling out of the sky."

Newmarket Grandstand 1940, Bill Shankland rear gunner in Jack Hatton's crew, Sgt Jim 'Ginger' Ware, AC F G Quibble, all 99 Squadron. (*Norman Didwell*)

Even after all this, 99 Squadron's troubles were not over. Flt Lt Eugene Hetherington in N2957 survived an attack from an Me 110 which had caused the loss of one wing flap, and when he prepared to land at Newmarket by selecting flaps down, the aircraft rolled uncontrollably and crashed into a field close to the race course, killing Hetherington, WOp/AG AC1 Ronald Entwistle and rear gunner Cpl Andrew Sharp.

Norman Didwell:

"I was filling up a bowser, and it was just dark then, it was about five o'clock; the other aircraft had landed and Hetherington's was the last one. I watched it – it had its navigation lights on – and as he came round, over from the Soham area, all of a sudden as he put his flaps down, down went the red light up went the green light. I thought 'he's going to crash' and he did. I was one of the nearest there, because it was just over the other side of Devil's Dyke. With it going in, Wg Cdr 'Butch' McKee came charging down in his little Ford van. He said 'airman, where did that aircraft go down?' I pointed and he said 'keep pointing and jump in'.

"We got there just about the same time as the fire crew and the ambulance, and we saw what a mess it was in. There was a smell of fuel and I thought 'one spark and this lot'll go up'; little did we know there was a bomb hung-up. We got Tony Payne out [second pilot], he was wounded in the foot and leg, Parton [observer] was in a terrible state with geodetics stuck into him, saying 'let me die, let me die'. (He did eventually recover but I don't think he ever flew again.) Lofty Craig was still in his turret; the tail section was right up in the air, so we had to get him out with a ladder; he was wounded in the arm. We got Parton out, Jock Sharp the front gunner was killed outright and so was Ron Entwistle the wireless op. We found Hetherington's body and got him out and that was it. About eight o'clock they wanted crash guards. I was amazed, Collins-Campbell and Fred Calcutt, flight mech air gunners who had been on the raid, went on crash guard. What was the air force thinking? The old flight mech air gunners (replaced when sergeant air gunners came in in 1940) got 3/6d a day, with six pence a day on top as a qualified air gunner."

Four days later on 18 December, the same target was attacked again, this time with a force of twenty-four Wellingtons which were ordered to stay above 10,000 feet in an attempt to avoid the worst of the flak. A number of German vessels were spotted off Wilhelmshaven and were bombed from 13,000 feet. Once again, the fighters were directed on to the bombers by a ground controller using information from the Freya radar station on Wangerooge Island. The formation was spread out by individual pilots' attempts to evade flak, and when the fighters of IV./JG2 got in amongst them, twelve Wellingtons were shot down for the loss of two Luftwaffe aircraft. The twelve aircraft lost and their captains were:

Wilhelmshaven from 149 Squadron MK.IA N2960 flown by Wg Cdr Kellett, 18 December 1939. (*TNA*)

9 Squadron
N2872 Sqn Ldr Archibald Guthrie
N2941 Fg Off Douglas Allison
N2939 Fg Off John Challes
N2940 Plt Off Eric Lines
N2983 Sgt R Hewitt

37 Squadron
N2904 Sqn Ldr Ian Hue-Williams
N2889 Fg Off Oliver Lewis
N2935 Fg Off Arthur Thompson
N2888 Fg Off P Wimberley
N2936 Sgt Herbert Ruse

149 Squadron
N2961 Fg Off M Briden
N2962 Fg Off James Speirs

Of the sixty-five aircrew on board, Sgt Hewitt and three of his crew were rescued after ditching off Cromer, Fg Off Wimberley, Sgt Ruse and three other crew members were taken prisoner, and fifty-six perished.

Over the next few days, ACM Sir Edgar Ludlow-Hewitt visited Mildenhall and Honington to interview crews who had participated in the operation. At the latter station DFCs were recommended for Flt Lt Ian Grant (skipper of N2964) and Fg Off Donald Macrae (skipper of N2871), while Sgt John Ramshaw and gunner AC1 Ronnie Driver were both recommended for the DFM. Sgt F G Petts (skipper of N2873) and LAC D J Conolly were recommended to be Mentioned in Dispatches.

BOMBER COMMAND POLICY CHANGES

The greatest repercussion of The Battle of Heligoland Bight was to come shortly afterwards at the start of the New Year. Air Vice-Marshal (AVM) Arthur Harris, who was AOC 5 Group at that time, still clung to the belief that three or more bombers sticking together were capable of taking on anything in terms of enemy defences. On 2 January 1940, three aircraft from 149 Squadron were again sent out on a daylight reconnaissance of Heligoland Bight. Eighty miles out the Wellingtons were attacked by Me 110s of I./Zerstörergeschwader (ZG)76, one of the units that had decimated the formations on 18 December. Two aircraft were shot down, Fg Off Hugh Bulloch in N2943 and Sgt John Morrice in N2946 – there were no survivors; only Plt Off Sandy Innes succeeded in making it back to Mildenhall. The AOC-in-C of Bomber Command Charles Portal immediately issued orders that all Hampdens and Wellingtons were to perform night operations in future; the notion of assured mutual defence in daylight operations had proved to be a failure.

After this edict, Wellington operations followed a familiar pattern of leaflet raids – known as Nickelling – the first such by night being on 4/5 January 1940. Compared with what had gone before, these operations suffered a much lower casualty rate, and over the next three months just three Wellingtons were lost on leaflet raids. Nonetheless, navigation still proved to be a major problem, as shown by an entry in 99 Squadron's ORB following a reconnaissance of the River Elbe east of Hamburg by just two of their aircraft on the night of 15/16 March 1940.

> 'Navigation throughout the operation was carried out by DR [Dead Reckoning] in the case of aircraft N2999. Loop bearings from neutral countries were of no value. In the case of aircraft N3008 two 2nd class fixes were obtained on return, but proved to have been very inaccurate.'

The radio navigation and wireless aids available to Wellington crews at that time were described by Sqn Ldr R A Pink of 149 Squadron at Mildenhall:

> "I was a flight sergeant wireless operator mechanic and air gunner and some of the radio aids available and the wireless installation in the Wellington were quite interesting. Airfields of Bomber Command were being supplied with Lorenz standard beam approach (SBA) and with high frequency direction finding stations (HFDF). At Orford Ness a medium frequency radio beacon provided a bearing service, the aid being interpreted by the WOp making use of a calibrated stop watch; Direction Finding (DF) loops had not been fitted to early Wellingtons. There was also available a network of Marconi DF stations, each individually capable of providing a bearing service, and

collectively of determining an aircraft's position. The Wellington wireless installation, as delivered to squadrons, comprised a standard W/T transmitter and receiver capable of operating on medium frequency and high frequency, the equipment being installed adjacent to the wireless operator behind the pilot's position."

On the night of 20/21 February 1940 an attempt was made to find and attack German ships without success. As a result, and given the high priority placed on the German fleet, a further daylight operation was attempted on 12 April, when thirty-six Wellingtons joined a force of Blenheims and Hampdens for another reconnaissance over Heligoland Bight; yet again fighter and flak opposition was intense with three Wellingtons and six Hampdens being lost against five German fighters. The Wellingtons lost were N2951 Fg Off Noel Hawxby (presumed lost at sea) and P2526 Flt Lt M Nolan both of 38 Squadron, plus P9219 Flt Lt James Brough of 99 Squadron. Thankfully, Nolan and Brough both managed to get back to England and, despite a bale out and crash-landing respectively, both crews survived. This proved to be the last daylight operation for both bomber types and resulted in the cancellation of the pre-war bombing policy not to bomb the European mainland, thus releasing the hand that had been tied behind Bomber Command's back. Attention also turned to causing problems for the German fleet by extensive minelaying operations, known as Gardening. Flt Sgt Frank Tricklebank DFM was a pilot with 38 Squadron :

"We were very nervous of mines, kept well away whilst they were loaded, and flew the aircraft with great care until we were rid of them. On the first mining op our aiming point was 1,000 yards off the entrance to the harbour. We did a glide approach and in our case had no opposition until after dropping the mines. My flight commander chose to make a very long low-level run and was shot down by flak."

With the freedom to carry out unrestricted bombing operations, much attention was paid to bombing German-occupied aerodromes supporting the Danish and Norwegian campaigns, including those at Aalborg, Fornebu, Stavanger and Sylt. Following one such raid on 2 May 1940, a 99 Squadron aircraft again suffered a single flap failure when landing back at Newmarket. John A Francis RCAF was the WOp:

"I was one of several Canadians who made their way to Britain to join the RAF in 1938-39. I enlisted 7 December 1938 as a wireless operator, volunteered for an air gunner's course when war began, flew on my first operational sortie 18 March 1940 and completed my tour on 29 October 1940. The OC of 99 Squadron asked me to stay on as wireless leader which I did until returning to Canada in July 1941 as an instructor of wireless and gunnery. I was a crew member of a Wellington that came a cropper on a return flight to Sylt on 2 May 1940. As we made our approach to the field at Newmarket and activated the flaps, only one lowered. We made an abrupt change of course, landing in a farmer's field and leaving a trail of several 250 lb bombs and flares; one of the flares ignited close to the aircraft just as it skidded to a stop. Thinking the aircraft was on fire, we wasted no time scrambling out; one crew member sustained a ruptured spleen, the rest of us just cuts and bruises, only the aircraft was a write-off."

The first attack on an enemy land target by 9 Squadron was against Stavanger aerodrome by six aircraft on 20 April 1940 but due to cloud cover only one crew, captained by Flt Lt T S Rivett-Carnac, found the target; they dropped five 250 lb bombs with delayed action fuses. A further attack was made on this airfield ten days later when bombs from all three aircraft hit the target. All aircraft were again successful on 23 April and 2 May 1940, when negligible opposition was encountered. An interesting trip at the beginning of May was completed only by the two aircraft that had failed to receive a recall message; they flew round the North German coast looking for enemy minelaying aircraft returning to base; none was seen.[3]

INVASION OF FRANCE AND THE LOW COUNTRIES

10 May to 26 June 1940

Germany's invasion of Belgium and Holland, then on into France in the spring of 1940 prompted a rapid re-think of Bomber Command strategy and the ending of all remaining constraints on bombing the European mainland. Primary targets became airfields, major road networks and German communications in an attempt to slow down their advance and, on the first night of the invasion, thirty-six Wellingtons attacked Waalhaven airport at Rotterdam, fortunately without loss. This set the pattern for the Battle of France, with repeated efforts on a similar scale over the next few weeks.

In addition, night bombing of major targets in Germany commenced on the night of 15/16 May 1940, with an attack on a number of industrial targets in the Ruhr Valley. John A Francis was with 99 Squadron at that time:

> "On 19 May we did what was for the most part an uneventful sortie to Hal; because of 10/10 cloud we saw very little and hardly any anti-aircraft activity. We were on the way home and I left the centre [ventral] turret for a moment. I stopped to look out of the astrodome and plugged into the intercom just as there was an explosion as we were hit by a shell – but no sign of a hole. The pilot wanted to know where we were hit so I started looking. Through the foot-well of the centre turret was a hole four or five inches in diameter, the metal bent back over my flying gloves in the footwell. What was left of them was shreds – my time hadn't come! The electrical wiring and hydraulic lines were severed, but I was able to crank the turret back into the fuselage by hand so we made an uneventful landing.
>
> "Another episode took place on 29 May, a disastrous night and certainly the most memorable in which I was involved during three-and-three-quarter years of wartime flying. We were ordered to abandon in the vicinity of RAF Watton, Norfolk. I followed the second pilot out of the front hatch, since he had gone out head first I did the same. I was brought up with a jerk when somehow, my foot was trapped and I was hanging from the aircraft upside down. I was being battered by the slipstream but managed to pull myself up my leg and get my hands over the edge of the hatch, but failed to free my foot and had to let go and hang once again. I felt someone tugging at my ankle, looked up and there was the navigator looking down at me and trying desperately to free my foot. Thank God he had the presence of mind to untie my boot lace and I slipped free. As soon as the aircraft was clear I pulled my ripcord, stowed the ring in my jacket and

started to massage my leg which I thought was broken; actually it was only bruised, but a bone was broken in the top of my foot – thanks to the navigator it wasn't my neck!

"I landed in some gorse bushes but couldn't walk so I started crawling. I couldn't see much in the darkness and fog and stopped every few yards to shout, hoping someone would hear me. You can imagine my delight when I heard an answering shout from across the moor. It was the rear gunner, and since he had crossed a road to get to me we decided to stay where we were until dawn. We wrapped ourselves in our 'chutes and slept fitfully until daylight. The fog had cleared considerably and shortly an RAF lorry came along the road looking for us. We were taken to Watton and after being temporarily patched up (the rear gunner had wrenched his back), we joined the rest of the crew and returned to Newmarket. After a spell in hospital I returned to the squadron on 1 September with an op over the Black Forest dropping Razzles." [Razzles were incendiary devices used in several unsuccessful attempts to cause large-scale fires in German forests.]

The target had been the airfield at St. Omer in northern France, and the Wellington abandoned with low fuel was Mk.IC P9241. After the rest of the crew had baled out, the pilot Plt Off James Young force landed at Kilverstone Hall near Thetford, sadly losing his life in the process. 99 Squadron lost two more Wellingtons that same night, both after running out of fuel due to poor weather. P9282 was abandoned over Chrishall near Saffron Walden in Essex, and R3196 at Brettenham near Thetford. One of the men who baled out was never found. Norman Didwell remembered:

"The fog was very bad. They said three of the kites had gone missing, and the next thing we knew they'd crashed."

By late May 1940 the battle in France had become increasingly desperate and Hampdens, Wellingtons and Whitleys in increasing numbers were fully occupied attacking German troop concentrations, airfields and lines of communication. By the time the Battle of France was over, the Wellington force had lost sixteen aircraft, six from 99 Squadron, three from both 37 and 115 Squadrons, two from 149 Squadron and one each from 38 and 75 Squadrons.

Perhaps the most unfortunate of these crews were three members of 37 Squadron's L7793 which force landed at Stene, near Ostend, on 26 May after being hit by anti-aircraft fire during an attack on road and rail targets near Brussels. All the crew were safe, but the pilot Sqn Ldr Arthur Glencross, observer Plt Off John Cameron and WOp/AG Sgt Raymond Parkhouse were drowned along with thirty-eight other RAF personnel when *SS Aboukir* taking them back to Britain from Ostend was torpedoed and sunk.

The battle was also notable for the death of the oldest bomber crew member to be lost on operations during the entire war, Plt Off Sir Arnold Wilson, who was fifty-six years old. Previously a lieutenant colonel in the Sikh Pioneers, Wilson was also the Member of Parliament for Hitchin, Hertfordshire from 1933 until volunteering to join the RAF Volunteer Reserve (RAFVR) as an air gunner. His 37 Squadron Wellington L7791 was brought down south of Dunkirk on 31 May, together with the pilot Sgt James Brown.

On 10 June 1940, Italy entered the war and on the following night Whitleys flew an operation against Turin, refuelling in the Channel Islands. A few days later, the RAF sent a Wellington detachment code-named Haddock Force, comprising three aircraft from each of 9, 37, 99 and 149 Squadrons to Salon, Provence to attack Italy. They successfully flew two operations, the first against Milan and the second against Milan and Genoa, both without loss. However, when a third raid was attempted, the French blocked the runway with vehicles, so further operations had to be abandoned and the aircraft brought home. One Plt Off Page reported the experience when he was later posted to the Central Gunnery School (CGS), who recorded it thus:

> 'A member of a Wellington squadron sent to Salon before France capitulated. The conditions there were described. The French created a very poor impression; they were not in the least helpful. Food was difficult to get. Lorries were run across the aerodrome by the French because they were afraid of reprisals.'

One of Bomber Command's most notable wartime pilots was Group Captain Percy 'Pick' Pickard DSO and 2 bars DFC. He began his illustrious operational flying with 99 Squadron and was eventually lost on the renowned Operation Jericho attack on Amiens prison on 18 February 1944 while flying a 487 Squadron Mosquito. On the night of 19/20 June 1940 his 99 Squadron aircraft R3200 was one of thirty-seven Wellingtons attacking a number of oil and railway targets between Hamburg and Mannheim and became the only one not to return. Having been damaged by flak, Pickard was eventually forced to ditch about thirty miles off the Norfolk coast. Sgt Len Ambler was the coxswain of RAF High Speed Launch 112 which was sent out from Felixstowe to try and locate the crew[4]:

> "We headed out at about 13:00 hours, absolutely certain we would pick up this aircrew who by now, had been adrift in the North Sea for something like twelve hours. Well ahead an aircraft was sighted, later identified as a Wellington. No doubt it had spotted our wake and began orbiting and firing off Very light signals. Then the dinghy appeared on the crest of a wave and disappeared into a trough; eventually we had it alongside and the aircrew were taken below to dry out. From their reported ditching position and where we found them, we realised that they had drifted through a minefield overnight! The observer, Sgt Alan Broadley, told me 'The ditching was a good one and as the dinghy inflated it became fouled in the aerial, so with my penknife I sawed through it and freed the dinghy which we then launched from the still floating aircraft; having first gone back onto the Wellington and collected the signal pistol and cartridges. In launching the dinghy the paddles floated away and could not be retrieved. The aircraft remained afloat for about two-and-a-half minutes and as it settled beneath the sea all the lights came on. Through the hours of darkness and into daylight the dinghy shipped water and with the spray we got very wet; the only way to bale out the sea water was to use our shoes.'"

TARGET GERMANY

Operations once again turned towards strategic targets within Germany and occupied Europe. By mid-July the OTU set up for training bomber crews was sufficiently well-established to permit the limited use of crews under-training for operations, with leaflet raids being the most

Plt Off Frank Denton RNZAF and his 75 (NZ) Squadron crew at Feltwell 1940. WOp/AG Len Hayter, later DFC, third from the right. (*June Leese*)

common at this stage, although some limited bombing was also carried out. Flt Lt Len Hayter DFC flew as a WOp/AG:

> "On qualifying late July '40 I was posted to 20 OTU at Lossiemouth; my stay was brief due to a crew member on the senior course falling sick and I volunteered to replace him. So on 17 Aug '40 I became the sixth member of the Wellington crew captained by Plt Off Birch. Our training was over and we were posted to Feltwell to join 75 (New Zealand) Squadron. There was a crew change to provide us with a captain having operational experience, a New Zealander Plt Off Frank Denton. We also had a change of rear gunner to Plt Off Edward Jelley who was also the squadron gunnery officer.
>
> "We had our first night flight in a Wellington and after landing and closing down in dispersal I heard a ground crew member murmur 'only bats and fools fly at night'. I knew I was not a bat – so I reckoned I must be a fool. On 1 September we took off at 13.00 hours for local flying gunnery and bombing practice on a nearby range, then to Soesterberg in Holland, now occupied by German forces. On leaving the target area we had a fire in one of the engines, which was extinguished by diving steeply towards the North Sea and returned to base after four hours and thirty minutes. Further sorties were flown with various successes until returning from our tenth raid on 29 September [Leipzig] when due to a combination of events we had to abandon our aircraft over North Devon – miles from our base at Feltwell. The captain broke an ankle on landing

and the rear gunner lost his life. After a brief break of three days ordered by the local doctor, we were returned to Feltwell by rail."

Wellington Mk.IC R3168 had taken off at 19:30 and by 05:00 the next morning it was out of fuel and came down near Simonsbath on Exmoor. Although only Plt Off Jelley was killed, all the remaining crew members were injured.

The wreckage of Plt Off R Willis's 99 Squadron R3170 shot down over Haarlem while on operation to Kiel 6 July 1940. (*Norman Didwell*)

Among the many colourful characters who found themselves crewing Wimpys at this time was a former Danish speedway rider Jens 'Morian' Hansen, who happened to be in England at the outbreak of war and immediately volunteered to join the RAF as a pilot, having held a private pilot's licence in his native country. At the age of thirty-three he was considered too old and instead accepted to train as an air gunner and was posted as a pilot officer to 99 Squadron at Newmarket. On the night of 25/26 July 1940 Hansen was the front gunner in a Wellington during a raid on oil installations north east of Dortmund. On the run in to the target another aircraft ahead of him, Mk.IC P9275 flown by Plt Off Bruce Power, was coned in searchlights and shot down by an Me 110, the first and only victory for Lt Wilhelm Pack of Nachtjagdgeschwader (NJG) 1. Hansen was immediately in a position to fire at the enemy fighter and succeeded in shooting it down, killing both crew members and it was for this action, the first night fighter to be shot down by a British bomber, that he was awarded the DFC. All P9275's crew baled out and were taken prisoner, except Power who was killed.

Hansen was also awarded a George Medal for his efforts in rescuing the crew of another 99 Squadron Wellington that came down on 18 December 1940 immediately after take-off from Newmarket and hit the earth embankment of Devil's Dyke. This was Mk.IC R1333, 'The Broughton Wellington' which was subscribed by contractors, sub-contractors and employees of the Chester factory to the tune of £15,000 and became the subject of a good deal of public-

'The Broughton Wellington' Mk.IC R1333 on 7 November 1940. Delivered to 99 Squadron on 1 December, it was written off seventeen days later. (*Brooklands Museum*)

ity when it was ready for delivery in November 1940. It had only been with the squadron for seventeen days when it crashed. The pilot Flt Lt Glencairn Ogilvie, second pilot Plt Off Arthur Pritchard RNZAF and rear gunner Sgt Bill Boast were killed, but front gunner Sgt George Lee and WOp Sgt Cliff Hendy were rescued by Hansen, who was on flarepath duty at the time. Hansen went on to rise to the rank of squadron leader.

Flt Lt Alan 'Jock' Richardson was a WOp/AG on 38 Squadron at Marham as the major raids on Germany began:

> "My first op was to Hamm, then Hamburg. On 16 August 1940 we attacked Bernberg, dive bombed to 2,000 feet then force landed in Kent. Sgt Lewin was the pilot; he was a mad bugger – a very good pilot but mad. I can't remember if we got hit or not, we landed at West Malling because there was something wrong with the aircraft. We had a lot of engine trouble on the Mk.I Wimpys. We hated it when we had to bring the bombs back. In the end, of course, we didn't bring them back, we jettisoned them. In those days if you couldn't find your target you had to bring your bombs back and land with the buggers on board. Sometimes we had fourteen 250 pounders and some aircraft came back, landed and blew up."

BERLIN

On the night of 24/25 August 1940, the Luftwaffe dropped bombs on central London for the first time; a case of navigational error as the intended targets were the oil refineries at Thameshaven.

Winston Churchill immediately ordered a retaliatory attack on Berlin (which city Bomber Command code named Whitebait), for the following night with a force of about fifty Hampdens and Wellingtons. Although the city was obscured by thick cloud and subsequently bombing accuracy was poor, no aircraft were lost. Berlin was attacked again in force twice more during August. The pattern of repeated strategic targeting of major German cities was beginning to emerge. Jock Richardson remembered the feeling of seeing Berlin on the target map at briefing:

> "We didn't worry when we knew the target was going to be Berlin, we all thought 'Great stuff' it was going to be wonderful; because at that time it hadn't been attacked much, so we didn't know how well it was going to be defended – nobody knew that. On 9 September 1940 with Plt Off Robinson the target was Berlin, but we turned back because of the weather and attacked Barnsfeldt which was a fighter 'drome."

WOp/AG Sgt Alan 'Jock' Richardson of 38 Squadron Marham after his trip to Berlin, September 1940. (*Viv Cunningham*)

Plt Off Lucian Ercolani (later wing commander DSO and bar DFC) flew to Berlin with 214 Squadron on the night of 7/8 November 1941 and had a lucky escape when his Wellington Mk.IC X3206 was hit by flak, setting fire to the incendiaries:

> "We had a rough trip and got damaged over Berlin; we had a big chunk knocked out of us. We headed home and found ourselves over the sea somewhere off the Channel Islands. We were supposed to have coasted in at Southwold, so we had drifted way off track somehow. Anyway, we eventually saw a coast ahead, but we had no option but to ditch. We got down all right and got into the life-raft, all six of us. The aircraft had broken in half; the tail was round by the cockpit! After drifting for three days we awoke to find we were just off the beach at Ventnor on the Isle of Wight and just waded ashore. Not long afterwards the rescue launch came out to us, but we didn't need them."

Throughout the remainder of the Battle of Britain period, Bomber Command continued its parallel efforts to disrupt German industry while attempting to thwart Hitler's Operation Sealion invasion plans with repeated attacks on the Channel ports, principal targets in the latter case including the invasion barges. Major raids took place on the nights of 14/15 September (the 15th becoming known as the turning point – Battle of Britain Day) when a force of 157 aircraft was despatched which included forty-three Wellingtons, and 18/19 September with a force of 174 aircraft including Blenheims, Hampdens, Wellingtons and Whitleys. Eight aircraft were lost, including two Wellingtons and their entire crews, one each from 99 Squadron (P9242 Plt Off Michael Linden) and 149 Squadron (R3160 Fg Off John Pay). No trace of either was ever found and they were believed to have come down in the English Channel.

Flt Lt Jack Wetherley DFC flew with 214 Squadron as second pilot to Plt Off Hartford during an attack against the Channel ports on the night of 17/18 September, part of a force of 194 aircraft. They took off before midnight and reached Ostend a little over an hour later. Over the target there was no flak and, even before G-George bombed, the port and railway sidings were ablaze. In the outer harbour the crew saw four large ships which looked like destroyers and in Avant port, they spotted twenty barges. All ten Wellingtons from 214 Squadron bombed and suffered no losses. Jack subsequently went on to fly a second tour on Halifaxes with 76 Squadron, losing his life during a raid on Kiel in March 1943.[5]

Once Hitler's attention had turned to Russia, the Wellington force continued to expand rapidly to cope with the anticipated increased demand for scale and intensity of operations against German-held territories. In the final few months of 1940 the rate at which new Wellington squadrons appeared on Bomber Command strength increased significantly:

Oct '40	103 Squadron Newton replacing Battles
Oct '40	150 Squadron Newton replacing Battles
Nov '40	12 Squadron Binbrook (Mk.IIs) replacing Battles
Nov '40	15 Squadron Wyton replacing Blenheim IV
Nov '40	40 Squadron Wyton replacing Blenheim IV
Nov '40	57 Squadron Feltwell replacing Blenheim IV
Nov '40	142 Squadron Binbrook replacing Battles
Nov '40	218 Squadron Oakington replacing Blenheim IV

Mk.IA L8899 KX-E 'Eekloo' of 301 Squadron force-landed in Holland during an operation to Berlin 24 September 1940; Flt Lt K Trokacek and crew were taken prisoner. (*Dave Underwood*)

In addition to all these regular RAF units, the first Czech and Polish-manned squadrons were formed, with 311 Squadron at Honington in August followed by 301 at Swinderby in October,

Mk.IC T2501 LN-F of 99 Squadron intact at Vitry-en-Artois on 5 December 1940 and test flown by the Luftwaffe. (*via Petr Bucha*)

304 and 305 at Bramcote in November and 300 at Swinderby in December. To cope with this expansion, the OTU system also began to pick up pace in order to provide a steady flow of fully-trained bomber crews. The first such units to have Wellingtons were 11 OTU at Bassingbourn and 15 OTU at Harwell, which started work in April 1940 and, by the year's end, they had been joined by 12 OTU at Benson, 18 at Bramcote, and 20 at Lossiemouth.

An incident on 18 November 1940 served to illustrate just how confusing and perilous these times could be for bomber crews, even when flying over home territory. Wellington Mk.IC L7817, on the strength of 4 Ferry Pilots Pool at Prestwick and being flown by Plt Off W E J Lunn, was attacked by an unidentified Hurricane three times over Long Eaton near Nottingham, in broad daylight. The rear of the aircraft was damaged, resulting in the collapse of the tailwheel on landing, a very fortunate outcome given the determined nature of the fighter's onslaught. The Wellington crew escaped injury and Lunn at least survived the war.

Bombing operations were now beginning to range much further afield, with raids on Italy now being included. Guy Sharp was a pilot with 9 Squadron at Honington:

"In November '40 I went to Honington. It was a grass airfield, and on my very first op I cocked things up. I selected flap, but I couldn't have put the thing back into the neutral position, so when we took off we had full flap on a wet grass airfield. We were going to Mannheim, which I knew very well because I'd been there before the war in '34/'35, I'd swapped with a German family to learn the lingo.

"On 22 December 1940 9 Squadron bombed the docks just outside Venice and one of our chaps [Sgt R N Harrison and crew] flew across Switzerland and they had to steer across mountains and in cloud they overshot Venice by about 200 miles and bombed somewhere near Fiume. Coming back they hit headwinds and crossed the Swiss frontier in broad daylight. They only saw two fighters, nowhere near them, no-one expected to see a lone Wellington. They debated whether to bale out or crash in the sea, and they had enough height so that when the engines cut with no gas at all, they were over the Channel, and glided down until they saw a field at Pevensey. They put the wheels and flaps down, but they didn't know there was a ditch going across the field. They weren't hurt, and had been in the air for eleven hours and twenty minutes."

With many more squadrons at its disposal, Bomber Command again turned its attention to the previous pattern of attacks on major German cities and industrial targets, plus continued minelaying, albeit at a much reduced scale for some months. The main reasons for the lull in operations, which lasted until February 1941, included the onset of bad winter weather resulting in many more turn-backs and navigation issues than previously experienced, plus a need for the squadrons to take stock and re-energise after the hectic summer months. There was also the arrival of a new C-in-C Bomber Command, Sir Charles Portal, being replaced after just six months in post by AM Sir Richard Peirse who immediately sought clarification of a confusing number of target priorities coming from the Air Ministry.

Although the slowdown in operations was in place for the remainder of the first full year of the war, the Wellington had already started to display its versatility with what was without doubt the most unusual variant of them all, the DWI.

DWI – THE WEDDING RING WIMPY

From the earliest stages of the war it was recognised that there was a considerable threat to shipping from German magnetic mines and late in 1939, Weybridge's Experimental Department was tasked with modifying a Wellington with the purpose of exploding German magnetic mines from the air by use of a large de-gausing ring mounted under the airframe. Department manager, George Edwards led the project and the modified aircraft was code named the Directional Wireless Installation (DWI) Wellington to conceal its true intent, but in the workshops it was known as 'Down With 'Itler'!

After the aircraft had entered service they were known in some circles as 'Wedding Ring Wimpys'. The ring was energised by a 30 hp Ford V8 engine (later replaced by a de Havilland Gipsy Six Mk.II) driving a 35 kW (310 Amp) Mawdesley generator situated aft of the main spar inside the fuselage, and the magnetic field thus could be focused by adjusting its angle relative to the aircraft's fore-and-aft datum. The detonation of a mine would be caused by the effect of the magnetic field and the aircraft had to fly low enough to ensure the triggering effect without jeopardising the safety of the aircraft from the water spout that would follow a successful detonation. The calculations to determine the optimum height were conducted by Dr C S Hudson at the RAE.

A DWI 'Wedding Ring Wimpy' of 1 GRU landing at Manston in November 1939. (*ww2images*)

The first aircraft modified was P2518, a Mk.IA straight off the Weybridge production line. In addition to the 48 ft diameter aluminium ring, the aircraft had both turrets and bomb doors replaced by streamlined fairings and the inboard landing flaps were deleted to avoid changes of trim due to propeller downwash striking the ring section aft of the wing trailing edge. The first flight took place on 21 December 1939 flown by 'Mutt' Summers accompanied by Barnes Wallis, Bob Handasyde and Squadron Ldr John Chaplin. The flight test report notes that the ring had little effect on the take-off run, but acceleration and climb performance were markedly reduced. However, by the time of the third flight, Summers was able to report that the stability in roll and pitch was more positive than for a normal Wellington.

On 19 December 1939, 1 General Reconnaissance Unit (GRU) was formed at Manston in Kent and, following aircrew detachments to 214 Squadron at Feltwell to convert to Wellingtons, the first attempt to explode a mine was made over the ground mine unit at Boscombe Down on 2 January 1940 by Squadron Ldr Harry Purvis at a height of 50 feet without success. The following day thirty-one further runs at various heights over a mine were made in two flights, but the report does not discuss the results. The aircraft was then flown to Manston to continue the trials, the first operational flight and sea trial taking place six days later again flown by Sqn Ldr Purvis with Lt Cdr A S Bolt Royal Navy (RN) observing and Sqn Ldr Chaplin operating the generator motor. The Wellington was accompanied by two Avro Ansons from Detling for photographic purposes and an escort of three Hurricanes, all meeting up over Margate.

The first success came on 9 January 1940 when the aircraft flew a series of runs in the Thames estuary between the Tongue light vessel and a mark drifter at a ground speed of 170 mph and at varying heights. The achievement came on its seventh run, just past the wreck of the cargo ship *SS Sheaf Crest*, which had itself been sunk by a mine on 30 November 1939, and was described in a 1 GRU test report:

> "After four runs a signal was received from the monitoring boat that the aircraft was too high. Conditions for estimation of height were not easy as there was no defined horizon and the only mechanical arrangement for indicating a too low height was out of action. Run six was carried out at a much lower height about 25-30 feet and on run seven, when the aircraft was just passed the wreck of the *Sheaf Crest* a slight tremor was felt and an explosion heard indicating that a mine had been exploded."

Trials continued at an increasing pace, and it was noted that the aircraft's magnetic compass was of no use when the magnetic ring was energised. The second and third successful detonations were achieved in dramatic fashion on 13 January, flying between the North Goodwin light vessel and the wreck of the liner *MV Dunbar Castle*, another victim of a German mine sunk only four days previously. Escorted on this occasion by Blenheim fighters, the results were described in the unit's ORB thus:

> 'DWI sweeping on line 120 to 300 degrees through *Dunbar Castle* on the eighth run a mine was exploded. Sweeping was continued at 180 mph and on the eleventh run a second mine was exploded. A very considerable shock was felt and the accelerometer was off the scale exceeding 10G. It was decided to stop sweeping and examine the aircraft.'

The unit test report gives some additional detail:

> 'The attitude of the aircraft was not affected and the pilot felt no movement of the controls. The effect on personnel was a kind of shock which temporarily made one senseless and at the same time removed the air from the lungs. The observer, who was not strapped in, left his seat but was not thrown forward at all. A powerful pressure wave seemed to strike the aircraft and move it a very short distance vertically upwards.'

Already considerable thought was being given to how the DWI fleet could be used to full effectiveness in actual operations, particularly trying to balance the use of several aircraft together to increase the possibility of detonating mines against the risk from the violent results of explosions:

> 'Flying in formation of any sort at the height at which we have so far operated would be precarious, if possible at all. Line astern is out of the question, the rear aircraft would be blown up. 'V' formation would endanger the outside aircraft if the mine exploded to one side. Echelon is only safe if the mine explodes on the side opposite to the formatting aircraft.'

A shallow vee formation was subsequently adopted for operations, and on 15 January 1940 a second DWI arrived for the unit. Operations began in earnest in February, with a heavy concentration of effort in the areas of the Shipwash light vessel off Harwich harbour and the sunken light vessel in the Thames estuary, where a mine was exploded on the 22nd. Such successes were not common however, although mines were often spotted and reported to naval vessels for action.

The aircraft suffered from problems with the generating motor, with loss of cooling and overheating being quite common. This was largely overcome with the arrival of the fifth DWI which was fitted with the alternative Gipsy VI engine, later to become standard. On 4 April 1940 it was decided to bring the total DWI fleet up to fifteen aircraft, comprising four conversions of Mk.IAs as DWI Mk.I plus eleven Mk.ICs as DWI Mk.II; there were also some additional field conversions in the Mediterranean theatre.

In the early evening of 9 May 1940 three aircraft (L4356 Sqn Ldr Chaplin, L4374 Sqn Ldr Purvis and L4358 Flt Lt John Gethin), together with three Blenheim escorts from 235 Squadron at Bircham Newton, were flown over to the Dutch harbour at Ijmuiden where they were met with some tracer ground fire. Despite this, mine-sweeping runs were commenced covering the approaches to the harbour and, following some light signal exchanges, the ground firing ceased, enabling the Wellingtons to sweep right up to the harbour entrance. The ORB continues:

> 'Several Dutch soldiers, waving, were seen on the breakwater and on the surrounding hillocks and there was a British destroyer in the harbour. Nine more full runs were carried out and a signal was received by lamp from the destroyer that magnetic mines were being laid between the lighthouse and the buoy. The sweeping was carried out at a height of 45 feet and it is estimated that a channel 3 cables wide [3/10ths of a nautical mile] from the harbour entrance to three miles 285 degrees from the buoy was swept. No mines were exploded.'

It would appear that the principal aim of this operation was an attempt to clear a passage out of Ijmuiden harbour, from where the Dutch royal family was evacuated by *HMS Hereward* just a few days later. The ORB further notes that the aircraft were now fitted with tail magnetic compasses which worked satisfactorily. By this time it had already been decided that there was a more urgent requirement for the DWI force in the Mediterranean theatre and consequently 1 GRU

Mk.IC P9265 HD-F 'Jane' of 38 Squadron Marham August 1940 was destroyed in an air raid at Luqa on 25 November that year while en route to Egypt. (*Eddie Hancock*)

flew its final operation on 15 May 1940 and began flying its five aircraft out to Egypt on the 20th.

One of its original DWIs left behind in England, P2521, was converted to operate as a message relay aircraft and in 1942 was issued to 138 Squadron at Tempsford, Bedfordshire. This squadron worked for the Special Operations Executive (SOE), ferrying agents, weapons and supplies to occupied Europe, and was co-located with similarly-tasked 161 Squadron to whom the Wellington was passed. Its role was to orbit off the French coast to relay messages to and from agents in the field.

BOMBER OPERATIONS IN 1941

Despite the comparative lull in major operations at the turn of the year, the Wellington force was still engaged in a number of significant operations, with German naval forces in particular coming under heavy attack. The port of Wilhelmshaven was visited no fewer than six times in January, the first being on the night of 8/9 January when crews reported straddling the battleship *Tirpitz* and starting a number of fires without loss. Further attacks followed on 11/12, 13/14, 15/16, 16/17 and 29/30, but it was only on the fifth and least effective raid that any Wellingtons were lost, with Sgt Arthur Jones of 40 Squadron in T2912 and Plt Off Antonin Kubiznak of 311 (Czech) Squadron in T2519 both failing to return.

Mk.IC T2888 LN-R of 99 Squadron under protective engine tents at Rowley Mile Newmarket January 1941, a month before it was lost. (*Norman Didwell*)

An attack by twenty-five Wellingtons on the ports of Boulogne and Dunkirk was noteworthy for two reasons. Firstly, the force attacking Boulogne included one of a small number of aircraft operated by 3 Photographic Reconnaissance Unit (PRU) at Oakington near Cambridge, and used to photograph targets for damage assessment. R F Chandler was an air gunner on the unit, late undergoing pilot training:

> "3 PRU had three operational Wellingtons at Oakington from October '40 to February/March '41. We crashed T2707 at Binsey, Oxon, but it was salvaged and flew at Lossie-

mouth [20 OTU] finally to be abandoned in flight by its crew and crashed into the sea near Inverness. Another, T2706 went in to the North Sea with us [on 17 April '41 following an engine fire] and its remains were trawled up in 1986. After my second prang I was sent to Central Gunnery School at Warmwell, Dorset and as a gunnery leader, posted out to 115 Squadron at Marham, where I experienced my third Wimpy prang returning from Cologne on 24 June '41 in T2963."

The second reason for particularly noting this raid was that 311 Squadron's L7842 was force landed intact in France, with Plt Off F Cigos and his crew being taken prisoner. Their aircraft was taken to the Luftwaffe experimental station at Rechlin for evaluation (see Chapter Seven).

Early in February 1941 Bomber Command resumed its attacks on German oil production, industrial targets and major cities, a pattern which initially included major raids on cities approximately once a month. The first of these was Hanover on the night of 10/11 February, when a force of 222 aircraft included no less than 112 Wellingtons of which four were lost including a 115 Squadron Mk.IC R1084 flown by Sgt H H Rogers, which was shot down over West Raynham, Norfolk by a Ju 88 flown by Hauptmann (Hptm) Rolf Jung of NJG2; all the Wellington crew successfully baled out.

A raid on Bremen by seventy-nine aircraft on the following night ended in disaster. Although no aircraft were lost to enemy action, no fewer than eighteen crashed on return to England due to dense fog preventing them from finding anywhere to land and their crews having to bale out when their fuel was exhausted. Of these aircraft, eight were Wellingtons, one from 99 Squadron, three from 115, two from 149 and two from 218, with the loss of three crew members. Most of the aircraft came down in East Anglia, but others were as far afield as Gloucester and Kendal in Westmorland. Sgt David Vandervord was a second pilot on 218 Squadron that night in Mk.IC R1135 flown by Fg Off Agar:

"We came back with our bombs because we couldn't see anything over Germany or over here and we had to decide what to do. Should we climb, set the aircraft on George and parachute out over the sea. We could see little gaps in the cloud and the ground underneath so Fg Off Agar decided to dip down to get under the cloud and the next thing I recall is that there was a tree just in front of him. He lifted up over the tree and there was a ploughed field and he made a wheels-up belly landing. Oh, I should have mentioned that we first had to drop our bombs live over this country. We didn't know where we were, so we walked along a nearby road and found a little house, knocked on their door and they were as scared as sin to see us. They must have thought the Germans had landed. They told the police and we soon had transport back to Marham."

The Wellington was repaired only to crash in the North Sea with the loss of Sgt Alan Cook RAAF and his crew during an attack on Kiel on 15/16 November 1941. During a raid on Hamburg on the night of 13/14 March 1941 David was in Mk.IC R1448 and was wounded in a very close encounter with German fighters:

"We went up the coast of Holland and then round to the River Elbe and then to Hamburg. We dropped our bombs and it was decided to come back over land, I don't know

Painting the name on Mk.IC R1448 HA-L 'Akyem-Abuakwa' 218 Squadron Marham. (*Leslie Watts*)

why. We got as far as the Zuider Zee in Holland, got caught in searchlights and then two Me110s attacked us. I don't know how the aircraft survived. I think we shot down one of them and then Fg Off Agar dived right down to ground level. I was standing in the astro-hatch, and it was amazing just how close the German aircraft came. I was the only one who got wounded but the aircraft was shot to pieces and still kept on flying; I think we were quite close to the coast at the time. We went out over the sea, heading for Marham, one engine on fire and the petrol gauge was showing zero. I think the fuel supply to one of the engines had been severed and it was on fire every now and again; the speed of the engine blew it out and then it started again. I think most aircraft couldn't have survived the punishment that aircraft took. I was wounded in the leg and went straight to hospital.

"When we went to Berlin most of the aircraft had Pegasus, but one aircraft had Merlin engines and the squadron leader had that. He was already in his bed when we got back, because he had the better engines. [The first Mk.II Wellingtons arrived on the squadron in May 1941 but Mk.ICs continued until the following February.] I got to thirteen missions without flying the aircraft so I then asked to come off Bomber Command; I think I asked for fighters. I was offered the choice of either coming off flying or carrying on as I was. I had to make a quick decision so I decided to come off flying and that was the end of my flying career."

One of the attacking Me 110s was flown by Fw Hans Rasper of 4./NJG1 who claimed the Wellington as shot down over the North Sea.

Maintenance work on the port Pegasus of a Mk.I Wellington. (*Richard Stowers*)

Merlin-engined Mk.II W5461 EP-R of 104 Squadron Driffield 1941. It was lost over Berlin on 13 August that year. (*Brooklands Museum*)

A diversion from allowing the full weight of the bomber force to concentrate on German industrial targets came in March 1941, when the ever-increasing U-boat and Focke Wulf Condor threat to convoys resulted in an urgent directive to concentrate on the enemy aircraft and U-boat bases, plus the factories and shipyards building them. On the night of 31 March/1 April six Wellingtons went to Emden with one aircraft each from 9 and 149 Squadrons carrying the 4,000 lb 'Cookie' bomb for the first time, which necessitated the removal of the aircraft's bomb doors.

Other principal targets included Kiel (visited many times), Brest and Lorient and this effort continued for almost four months until early July when a perceived lessening of the threat allowed attention to turn once again to the wider industrial targets. Flt Lt Jo Lancaster arrived on his first squadron during the anti-U-boat period:

> "We were posted to 40 Squadron at Wyton and when we turned up we were told we shouldn't be there, and that we should be at Alconbury. So we got the service bus round and were immediately put on a charge for turning up late! [The squadron had moved to Alconbury in February.] We had Wimpy ICs and we were given a skipper called Jim Taylor, a Scot, he was a professional swimming instructor. We did eight trips with him and then we were off on our own, the five of us, and of course we were given a second pilot then. We proceeded on our tour, successfully, finished it in October and went our separate ways."

Jo Lancaster served as an apprentice with Armstrong-Whitworth Aircraft before enlisting and flying tours with 12 & 40 Squadrons. (*Jo Lancaster*)

Jo's regular aircraft was T2701, and their first op was to Calais on 9 May 1941. On 27 May they were involved in a sweep search looking for the German capital ship *Prinz Eugen* in the Bay of Biscay.

Jo Lancaster flew most of his 40 Squadron ops in Mk.IC T2701 BL-S seen at Alconbury in July 1941. A year later it was lost in a mid-air collision. (*Jo Lancaster*)

"Ops that stand out – I can't put them into chronological order. We went to Berlin and had our only night-fighter attack on the way back. We were all diverted in cloud because we had been shot at for hours and we suddenly saw though a gap in the clouds, the causeway across the Zuider Zee. While we were looking at that, a ruddy Me 110 turned up, but missed us fortunately. As soon as I saw it I went into a very steep spiral dive. He came round again and tried to follow us and apparently he showed his belly to Keith in the rear turret, and Keith reckoned he got a good score. We both eventually went into cloud and I don't know what happened to him. We survived unscathed and I think we went well over the limiting speed of the Wellington because they gave me a new one which was rather good.

"We did a daylight raid on Brest, 24 July; that was a reasonable experience. There was supposed to be a fighter escort but we never saw a British fighter at all; they were probably down low I don't know. We saw one or two Me 109s and one went past behind our formation, all the Wimpys were shooting at him and he pulled up and baled out; who shot him down nobody knows. Our squadron sent six aircraft, two vics of three, and the first vic lost one, shot down. [Wellington IC T2986 BL-A flown by Sgt M Evans RNZAF was hit by flak and came down in Brest town, killing all the crew.] Our three came through unscathed. We were very short of fuel and landed at St. Eval; so did a lot of others, it was pretty chaotic there.

"We got iced up and lost both engines coming back from Cologne one night [30 July]. I got out of the seat and let the second pilot have a go; I went back to the astro-dome and he promptly flew into cloud. It turned out to be an electrical storm. I told

Gordon to do a one-eighty to get out of it, and to put the carburettor heaters to hot air. Then we got St.Elmo's fire started, so I thought I'd better go forward and take over, and as I squeezed past the navigator, the wireless operator Jack Crowther was standing up with all his equipment glowing, I think he'd left his trailing aerial out, and he was standing up looking at all this. I eventually got there and changed places with Gordon, and found that he hadn't put it to hot air and he hadn't done a one-eighty, which was uncharacteristic.

"By this time it was far too late to provide the hot air because the starboard engine started to do a bit of surging and then it petered out. Not long after, the other one did the same. I stayed on the same course by that time, I thought I might as well carry straight on; routinely if you got into a cu-nim you got out of it as soon as possible. The thing was flying very heavily, obviously loaded with ice, and then there was an enormous bang and flash and we had been hit by lightning. I had to turn the cockpit lights right up – you had a little rheostat and normally had them turned right down – but even then it was quite a while before I could see the instruments properly. We got the gunner out of the front turret because he couldn't do it very easily on his own and he and the other three all got their parachute packs on and we opened the hatch under the nose; you could do that in flight, you didn't get an awful draught in there at all.

"We were down to about 5,000 feet, or perhaps a little bit lower by the time we got the parachutes on. We could see searchlights playing on the bottom of the clouds and we heard the occasional 'crump' of a shell, then one of the engines picked up again. Then the other one did, and we actually didn't break cloud, we recovered before we broke cloud and were able to climb away. We shut the door and took the parachutes off, then we called Keith in the rear turret and there was silence; we thought he'd gone. He did the same, he called us and heard nothing. He had an oxygen regulator with a little min-altimeter on and he was sitting ready to go and then he saw 4,000 feet and it seemed to be stable, and then he heard the engines going again. He looked round and saw Jack Crowther, I had sent him back to see what had happened and Jack discovered he had pulled his intercom plug out while putting his parachute on, so we hadn't lost him after all."

On this trip, Jo's aircraft (R1168) was hit by flak thirteen times, including in the engines and windscreen, and the hydraulics were out of action. The rear gunner was accredited with the destruction of an Me 109F.

During the first large raid of the war on Nuremburg (152 aircraft, with seven out of the eighty-two Wellingtons despatched being lost), C W Carson found himself part of what was thought to be the longest flight home on one engine:

"I was WOp/AG on Wellington IIs with 12 Squadron at Binbrook, Lincs in 1941. On 12 October our squadron was detailed to attack Nuremburg. The captain was Plt Off Colin Barnes and our aircraft was W5611. Over Nuremburg the starboard engine overheated and had to be switched off and the captain decided to try and make it back to base. We threw out everything which was jettisonable, including the front guns. After about four hours we finally crossed the English coast with no identification or navigation lights and landed at a night-fighter base at Tangmere in Sussex, having set off an air raid alert which despatched several Beaufighters to look for us (without success I'm glad to say). Colin Barnes got the DFC."

The official report of this event in Headquarters Bomber Command Routine Orders mentions a number of interesting additional facts about the crew's struggle to make it home.

'Immediately after bombing Barnes noticed a sudden and increasing rise in the temperature of his starboard engine. He made his way out of the area and searchlights and attempted to lower the temperature by reducing the output of the defective engine. All attempts to do this were unsuccessful and the engine was feathered and switched off. In view of the extreme distance from home, the possibility of making for Switzerland was discussed, but the pilot discovered that the navigator had not brought with him any of the maps necessary to plot a course for Switzerland, so that option was rather ruled out! A wireless message was sent to base reporting the engine failure but the wireless could not be used again as a result of the failure of the generator and exhaustion of the accumulator. When jettisoning equipment the front turret guns were dismantled and scattered in pieces to render them useless; the guns in the rear turret were kept in order to provide some measure of self-defence.'

Expansion of the Wellington force had continued primarily with the arrival of Commonwealth crews. By the year's end the following new units had been established:

Apr '41	101 Squadron West Raynham replacing Blenheim IVs
Apr '41	405 (RCAF) Squadron Pocklington
Aug '41	458 (RAAF) Squadron Holme-on-Spalding-Moor
Nov '41	460 (RAAF) Squadron Molesworth

Even when arriving back over England after a raid, crews had other perils to face, including yet more encounters with the balloon barrage intended to deter low-flying enemy aircraft.

John Leeuwin-Clark RAAF was a pilot with 405 Squadron:

"On the night of 20 September 1941 we took part in a raid on Ostend; it was my first op as captain. Everything went well over the target area – the fun was yet to come! After crossing the English coast somewhere near Felixstowe on the homeward journey I handed over the controls to my second dickey and then went back to the astrodome. Subsequently, the navigator gave the second dickey a change of course. Trouble began when instead of setting his compass red and red, he put blue on red and began flying a reciprocal course.

"Suddenly there was a severe shuddering – the aircraft had hit a balloon cable and balloons were all around us! I raced back to the cockpit where the second dickey handed over the controls with eager alacrity. Balloons were looming up like ghosts out of the darkness, nonetheless I decided to fly ahead and weave past the remaining ones. To try turning back would be to risk colliding with a balloon hidden from view. After negotiating the balloon barrage we went on and landed at base without any further ado. The next morning the damage to the Wimpy was examined. The balloon cable had first struck the spinner making a large dent. It then slid onto the propeller blades leaving them all serrated like a bread knife. The cable had then moved onto the leading edge of the wing where it left a tell-tale mark in the anti-freeze paste as it slid to the wing tip and parted company. At the instant of impact I cannot recall if the Merlin Mk.X engine involved faltered, but I can say that for the rest of the flight it ran smoothly, as did the rest of the aircraft."

One potential solution to the problem of hitting balloon cables was the installation of cable-cutting equipment on the wing leading edges, and this was tested by an RAE Farnborough Wellington Mk.IA P9210. Operating from Culmhead, Somerset on 24 March 1942 the aircraft was deliberately flown into a balloon cable and, although the Type J cutter successfully severed it, the cable end then fouled one of the propellers rendering the aircraft uncontrollable. The Wellington disintegrated throwing the pilot Sqn Ldr Charles Hawkins DFC clear and able to parachute to safety.

Roaming Luftwaffe intruders were also ready to catch out the tired crews as they made their landing approaches after a long operation. A report issued by the vice chief of the air staff on 25 May 1941 detailed the extent of aircraft losses due to enemy action against RAF aerodromes, and revealed that during the first twenty days of that month alone, twenty-five aircraft had been destroyed or damaged beyond repair, fifty-one were damaged but repairable and 100 were lightly damaged. Fg Off Harry Kartz, a front gunner with 9 Squadron, had a very close encounter with a Ju 88 coming home from Dieppe on 11 May in R1763 piloted by Flt Lt Edwards:

Fg Off Harry Kartz flew his ops as an air gunner with 9 Squadron. (*Harry Kartz*)

"We did a trip to bomb the two battleships *Scharnhorst* and *Gneisenau* and on the way back, it was the night that the Germans were raiding over England and our pilot was an ex-fighter pilot. He was shot down over the Channel and transferred to bombers and instead of going back to Honington, he wanted to land at Tangmere to see his pals. We asked Flying Control for permission to land and they said 'OK, do you want the flare path on?' 'Oh yes, please.' So they said 'Well, fire your colours of the day and we'll put on'. He did that, and when he fired his colours of the day, a Junkers 88 was sat at the back of us! Fortunately, they switched off the flarepath and the Junkers took off and dropped a fire bomb behind us. Fortunately we had taken off...I was in the astrodome because to take off and land, you couldn't do it in the turret. As I stood there, they got very close and I saw the pilots and their instruments as plain as could be, but of course I couldn't shoot at them! Eventually we landed at Middle Wallop."

JAMES WARD VC

Discussion of Wellington operations cannot be complete without telling the story of the sole recipient of the Victoria Cross while flying the type, Sgt James Ward, the son of Percy and Ada Ward of Wanganui, New Zealand. Enlisted in the RNZAF in 1939 and, after pilot training, he joined 75 (New Zealand) Squadron at Feltwell. On the night of 7/8 July 1941 he was flying as second pilot to Sqn Ldr Reuben Widdowson in Wellington Mk.IC L7818. The contemporary account that follows comes from 75 Squadron's ORB:

'On the night of 7 July 1941, Sgt Ward was the second pilot of a Wellington returning from an attack on Münster. When flying over the Zuider Zee at 13,000 feet the aircraft was attacked from beneath by a Messerschmitt 110 which secured hits with cannon shells and incendiary bullets. The rear gunner was wounded in the feet but delivered a burst of fire which sent the enemy fighter down apparently out of control. [No night fighters were lost that night, but two which had been in the area returned to base with battle damage.] Fire then broke out near the starboard engine and, fed by petrol from a split pipe, quickly gained an alarming hold and threatened to spread to the entire wing. The crew forced a hole in the fuselage and made strenuous efforts to reduce the fire with extinguishers and even the coffee in their vacuum flasks, but without success. They were then warned to be ready to abandon the aircraft.

Sgt James Allan Ward VC of 75 (NZ) Squadron. (*75 [NZ] Squadron Association*)

'As a last resort Sgt Ward volunteered to make an attempt to smother the fire with an engine cover which happened to be in use as a cushion. At first he proposed to discard his parachute to reduce wind resistance, but was finally persuaded to take it. A rope from the dinghy was tied to him, though this was of little help and might have become a danger had he been blown off the aircraft. With the help of the navigator he then climbed through the narrow astrohatch and put on his parachute. The bomber was flying at a reduced speed but the wind pressure must have been sufficient to render the operation one of extreme difficulty. Breaking the fabric to make hand and foot holes where necessary, and also taking advantage of existing holes in the fabric, Sgt Ward succeeded in descending three feet to the wing and proceeding another three feet on and off the wing.

'Lying in this precarious position he smothered the fire in the wing fabric and tried to push the cover into the hole in the wing on to the leaking pipe from which the fire came. As soon as he removed his hand however, the terrific wind blew the cover out and when he tried again it was lost. Tired as he was, he was able, with the navigator's assistance to make successfully the perilous journey back into the aircraft. There was now no danger of the fire spreading from the petrol pipe, as there was no fabric left nearby, and in due course it burnt itself out.

> 'A safe landing was made despite the damage sustained by the aircraft. The flight home had been made possible by the gallant action of Sgt Ward at the risk of his life.'

Immediate awards of the DFC and DFM were also made to Sqn Ldr Widdowson and Sgt Allen Box the rear gunner, and Sgt Ward's VC was promulgated in the *London Gazette* on 5 August 1941. Just a few weeks later on 15 September he lost his life, together with all but two of his crew, when their Wellington (X3205) was hit by flak over Hamburg and crashed in the target area. He was twenty-two years old.

Mk.IAs and ICs of 75 (NZ) Squadron. (*75 [NZ] Squadron Association*)

AIRMEN'S THOUGHTS

Another New Zealander serving on 75 (New Zealand) Squadron as a navigator, Plt Off Eric Lloyd frequently wrote home to let his family know how he was getting on, and his letters give a unique insight to his thoughts as he started his operational tour:

> 'Tuesday 11:30 am.
> 14 October, 1941.
> Feltwell
>
> Dear Family,
>
> 'We are still flying the same type of machines as we did at our last station and they are wonderful old crates. We have our own machine, of course – 'O' for Orange. She was a brand new job when we got it, and are we proud of it. Paddy and Tommy spit & polish their guns until they shine like the fittings of a battleship. It makes a big difference flying

in the same machine every night as you know just what she will climb at, at different heights, all of which helps the navigation tremendously. Also having swung the compass and loop oneself, one knows just how accurate they are. Each 'plane has its own ground crew, and they are just as proud of their 'F' for Freddie or 'O' for Orange, or whatever it is, as the aircrew are. Whenever we go up for a test flight, our ground crew hop in with us to see how she runs – we must look a bit like a travelling circus at times. There were eleven of us in the machine this afternoon – still that's only the weight of one decent bomb.

'I was fortunate in getting into a crew who wanted a navigator, on the third day I arrived here, and so got started on the job right away. The little white horse has been for four rides over Germany and likes it very much. Ray has done five, so I think I have just about caught up with the boys who left Canada before us. My crew are a great lot – all sergeants – three Englishmen (Tony, our captain, Tommy, front gunner, Jimmy, wireless operator) two New Zealanders (Jack, 2nd Pilot, and myself) and Paddy, our Irish rear-gunner. Paddy is a born humourist, and keeps us in fits of laughter. Tony completed his 'ops' on our last trip, so Jack will be taking over, and we will be getting a new 2nd Pilot. We had a snap taken the other day, and I will send you one if I can get a copy.

'By the way, if you should see Target for Tonight (I think I mentioned seeing it) you will see our CO. He takes one of the leading parts – a tall, well-built, good looking blighter, with fair wavy hair.

Your loving son/brother,

Eric'

Eric and his crew lost their lives just over three weeks later on 8 November when Oberleutnant (Oblt) Helmut Lent of 4./NJG1 shot down their Wellington X9976 over Oldeboorn on their way home after bombing Berlin; it was their ninth op. Eric's letter was not received by his family until four days after his death. The names of the rest of the crew, carefully disguised in Eric's letter, were:

Flt Sgt John Black RNZAF, pilot
Sgt Trevor Gray RNZAF, 2nd pilot
Flt Sgt Leslie Green, WOp/AG
Sgt Jack Thompson, WOp/AG
Sgt Charles Black, air gunner

The CO he refers to in his letter was Wg Cdr 'Pick' Pickard. During the last two weeks in March and the first two weeks in April 1941, 149 Squadron aircraft and crews were used as background for the Ministry of Information film, Target for Tonight, and Pickard was seconded from 311 (Czech) Squadron to play the part of the pilot using 149 Squadron Wellington P2517 'F' for Freddie.

The sentiments Eric expressed about the ground crew were echoed by many others, including 'Toddy' Knight when he was with 99 Squadron (the first of his four tours):

"It was all very well for us, all we had to do was deliver the goods, but nothing could have been done without all the effort that went into making it possible for an aircraft to get away by the ground crew chaps. I know one night when we came back from Stavanger, we found the ground crew sitting on the chocks out in the cold. We had a crook captain on that trip, and the boys knew it and were worried about us. I suppose I get a bit sentimental about these things, but I wept real tears when I saw these chaps sitting on the chocks."

An unknown 12 Squadron airman penned a poem[6] which rather neatly summed up the general feelings amongst bomber crews at this time of ever increasing effort.

SIGNAL FROM GROUP
or How it appears to us

The day dawns warm and sunny,
The forecast – clear and bright,
Although this may sound funny
There'll be no 'ops' tonight

An Air Vice-Marshal, by his fire,
Looks out, one foggy morn,
Runways thick with mud and mire
And a bloody great thunderstorm

He rubbed his hands with a fiendish sneer,
From his eyes shone a baleful light,
He shook with glee, and was, I fear
A really most horrid sight

He woke his minions from their sleep
And from the carpet took a bite
"There's rain and hail and snow and sleet,"
"BINBROOK FLIES TONIGHT!"

CHAPTER THREE

BOMBER COMMAND MAIN FORCE

"They sowed the wind, and now they are going to reap the whirlwind"
Air Marshal Arthur T Harris 3 June 1942

On 14 February 1942, the Air Ministry issued the Area Bombing Directive informing Bomber Command that it had priority over all other commitments and directed it to prioritise targets in Germany and factories in occupied France. That same month AM Sir Arthur Harris – better known as 'Bomber Harris', or 'Butch' to his crews – became AOC-in-C Bomber Command, charged with putting the directive into practice. Harris recognised that bombing performance had previously suffered from poor navigation over long distances, poor bombing accuracy and often insufficient weight of bombs on target to achieve the desired results. For example, on the night of 28/29 January 1942 fifty-five Wellingtons and twenty-nine Hampdens attacked Münster in very poor visibility, as a result none of the aircraft were able to positively identify the target and German records indicate that no bombs at all fell in the city. Developments including the new four-engined bomber types which were expected to achieve better bombing results, and the up-coming improved navigation equipment such as GEE and the H2S ground-mapping radar meant that the usefulness of earlier aircraft including the Wellington was reappraised.

Thus 1942 marked both the Wellington's peak in Bomber Command operations and the decline of its fleet size. While new squadrons continued to form, mainly substantial numbers of Canadian units, as the year progressed eighteen RAF Wellington squadrons either transferred to the Mediterranean theatre (a process which had begun as early as 1940 when three were lost to the force, with a further two going in 1941), or re-equipped with the Halifax, Lancaster or Short Stirling. The new squadrons arriving during the year were:

Feb '42	156 Squadron Alconbury
Feb '42	158 Squadron Driffield (Mk.II)
Aug '42	420 'Snowy Owl' (RCAF) Squadron Skipton-on-Swale
Aug '42	425 'Alouette' (RCAF) Squadron Dishforth
Oct '42	424 'Tiger' (RCAF) Squadron Topcliffe
Oct '42	426 'Thunderbird' (RCAF) Squadron Dishforth
Oct "42	466 (RAAF) Squadron Driffield
Nov '42	199 Squadron Blyton
Nov '42	427 'Lion' (RCAF) Squadron Croft
Nov '42	428 'Ghost' (RCAF) Squadron Dalton
Nov '42	429 'Bison' (RCAF) Squadron East Moor
Dec '42	196 Squadron Leconfield
Dec '42	431 'Iroquois' (RCAF) Squadron Burn

During the first half of the year, the size of operations continued to build in line with the new directive, and the main force principle of large scale co-ordinated waves of bombers was proving to work well, and a number of raids stand out from this time. On 3/4 March 1942 the target was the Renault factory at Boulogne-Billancourt which was known to be producing lorries for the German army. 235 aircraft, including eighty-nine Wellingtons, were despatched in three waves. Much to the crews' surprise, there were no flak defences and 223 aircraft bombed the target achieving excellent results for the loss of two Wellingtons, one Halifax and a Stirling. The Wellingtons were 158 Squadron's Sgt Dennis Webb in Z8441 which crashed after take-off, and 311 Squadron's Sgt Bohuslav Hradil in Z1070; the same unit losing Sgt Karel Danihelka in Z1167 without trace on a parallel minor operation to Emden. The Billancourt attack saw the largest number of bombers over a single target in the war so far, with a concentration over the target of 121 bombers per hour and a record tonnage of bombs dropped.

A 75 (NZ) Squadron Wellington taxiing out at Feltwell for a night operation. (*Norman Didwell*)

The Wellington force was less fortunate against the Deutsche Werke U-boat yards at Kiel on 12/13 March. Although the bombing was successful, of the sixty-eight Wellingtons sent out, five failed to return with the loss of all thirty men. It was a particularly bad night for 75 Squadron. Twenty-one-year-old Sgt John Parnham in X3282 came down in the target area and Fg Off John Sandys RCAF was lost without trace in X3585, the same fate befalling Sqn Ldr Peter Kitchin DFC in X3588. Polish units again accounted for the other two losses; 301 Squadron's Fg Off Stefan Zakrzewski in Z1257 and 311 Squadron's Sgt Jiri Fina in R1802 also being lost without trace. One more returning Wellington X3603 crashed short of the runway at Bodney, Norfolk while attempting to land with engine trouble, but 9 Squadron's Sgt Webb and his crew all escaped serious injury.

Exactly two weeks later on the night of 26/27 March, 104 Wellingtons and eleven Stirlings attacked Essen with the loss of ten Wellingtons, two each from 12, 115 and 301 Squadrons, and one each from 57, 142, 214 and 300. Flak in the target area was intense and there were many night fighters covering the route, helped considerably by the clear starlit conditions. Oblt Egmont Prinz zur Lippe-Weissenfeld of NJG2 shot down four of the Wellingtons in less than fifty minutes; 12 Squadron's Flt Sgt Francis Lowe RCAF in W5371 and Wg Cdr Albert Golding DFC and bar W5372, 300 Squadron's Fg Off Bogumil Zelazinski Z1269 and 301 Squadron's Flt Sgt Franciszek Porada R1590. There were single victories each for Oblt Herbert Lütje (214 Squadron Plt Off Eric Creed RAAF Z1143), Fw Richard Launer (115 Squadron Sgt Harry Taylor X3589) and Lt Manfred Meurer (115 Squadron Plt Off Geoffrey Soames X3604). The other aircraft lost, almost certainly all to flak, were 57 Squadron's Flt Sgt Ronald Snook RNZAF X3665, 142's Plt Off John Tillard Z1283, and 301's Plt Off Witold Jaroszyk Z1262; none of the crews in any of the ten aircraft survived.

On 1/2 April 1942 there was yet more tragedy for the Wellingtons; thirty-five aircraft were sent to attack railway targets at Hanau and Lohr and no less than twelve were lost, with 57 Squadron losing five out of twelve despatched; Sqn Ldr G de L Harvie in X3140, Sgt T Roper X3425, Flt Sgt J Nevill RCAF X3607, Flt Sgt R Knobloch RNZAF X3748, and Sgt W Paterson RNZAF Z1565. 214 Squadron lost half its fourteen aircraft; Sgt S Burtwell R1789, Plt Off J Baker X9979, W/O W Page RCAF Z1052, Sgt A Ferguson Z1156, Sgt E Dixon Z8805, Flt Lt E Baker DFC RCAF Z8842, and Fg Off R Hayes Z8979.

Exactly a week later another Wellington crew that failed to return was particularly notable for including what was possibly the youngest member of any bomber crew to be lost in the entire campaign. Mk.III X3757 of 57 Squadron, Feltwell in the command of Plt Off Noel 'Bill' Morse RNZAF took off at 22:05 hours on his twelfth op to attack Hamburg and was never heard from again. The rest of the crew, all now commemorated on the Runnymede Memorial, comprised second pilot Flt Sgt Jim Linehan, observer Flt Sgt George 'Larry' Vogan RNZAF, WOp/AGs Sgt Graham Lakeman and Sgt Norman Naylor, and rear gunner Sgt Roland Richards. Richards was officially recorded as being aged eighteen at the time of his death, but extensive research by

Only 220 Mk.IVs were built and this 460 (RAAF) Squadron example at Breighton shows the distinctive cowlings for the Twin Wasp engines. (*Australian War Museum*)

one of Jim Linehan's relatives has established that he changed his name and lied about his age in order to enlist.

These were tough times indeed for the Wimpy boys, who were all being worked very hard with minimal breaks in between operations. Navigator Sgt Calton 'Cal' Younger RAAF knew just what it was like to be forced to abandon an aircraft over enemy territory, when his 460 (RAAF) Squadron Wellington Mk.IV Z1391 was shot down on the night of 29/30 May during a raid on the Gnome-Rhône factory at Gennevilliers near Paris:

"I had a premonition as we flew over a moonlit Northampton. As we approached the target, we could see we were expected. A fiery web of tracer of various colours and a cone of searchlights made for a beautiful sight but the low-level attack now seemed like a suicide mission. As we began our bombing run, we were hit amidships and lost our intercom. I got up from the bombsight and told Russ [pilot Fg Off Russ Jones RAAF] that I would use the red and green lights to give him directions. At that moment a red streak shot in front of us, travelled along the starboard wing and set it ablaze.

9 Squadron observer Fg Off Graham Welsh, whose aircraft was shot down by Hptm Werner Streib on the first 1,000 bomber raid. Welsh was taken prisoner. (*Graham Welsh*)

"The flames streamed far behind us and Godfrey [rear gunner Sgt Godfrey Loder RAAF], who had been firing down the blue master searchlight, baled out. It was now a matter of seconds. I had time while we were still straight and level to grab Russ's parachute and dump it on his knees, release [Sgt] George Houghton from the front turret, hand him his parachute, clip my own on, then go back to Russ and clip on his. 'Is there any hope Cal?' he asked. I told him no and just then the Wellington went into a steep dive. It was screaming. Russ sat with a serene smile on his face, resigned to going down with the stricken 'plane. I too, felt calm and happy to stay with him. He shouted over the noise 'Jump Cal'. I thought it was futile but had nothing to lose, so I jumped. George might have jumped a second or two earlier, but in his cumbersome gunner's kit, may have had trouble clipping on his parachute or simply thought there was no point. I felt the hot flames over my head then the jerk as my parachute opened, at the same moment as I heard the crash. I brushed a tree and hit the ground. Ken also died [WOp/AG Sgt Ken Mellowes]. He was probably killed or wounded when we were first hit, otherwise he would have come forward to see what was happening."[1]

Both Cal and George Loder were captured and spent three years as prisoners of war. Fg Off Graham Welsh was an observer with 9 Squadron and his crew was feeling the pressure of intense operational flying:

"On 29 May we were about to take off on our tenth operation in twenty-two days [Dieppe]; this was the last straw. The typical operation involved over twelve hours from briefing to reports and breakfast; after breakfast sleep usually ended at noon. As I entered the aircraft I felt there was something very wrong; our pilot Sgt Ian Pearson [ex-Imperial Airways and later Flt Lt DFC] was extremely exhausted. I had also noticed ominous symptoms with our W/Op and rear gunner. I climbed back down again and demanded to be taken to the CO, Wg Cdr Inness. I explained the situation and called for the medical officer [MO]; Inness agreed. The MO concurred with me and the three of them were sent on leave. I awaited arrest on a charge of mutiny. The MO had, however, brought group into the matter. The result was that the CO was removed shortly afterwards (he had not flown on any operation with the squadron). I was not court-martialled but was commissioned two weeks later!"

Don Bruce recalled another little known aspect of work on 9 Squadron at that time:

"On arrival at 9 Squadron in May 1942 I was immediately introduced to two things, one was GEE, which was then in its early stages of operational use and the second was SCI (smoke curtain installation), which sprayed 'smoke' or gas by compressed air. Apparently 9 Squadron was designated as one of the retaliatory squadrons to drop gas in the event of the Germans carrying out such a raid on the UK."

Little did Don or Graham know at the time that they were just a few days away from the first of three operations that were arguably the Wimpy's finest hour and for which it is perhaps best remembered – the 1,000-bomber raids.

OPERATION MILLENIUM

On 3 June 1942, three days after the first 1,000-bomber raid, Air Marshal Harris stood before a group of newsreel cameras in London and said:

"The Nazis entered this war under the rather childish delusion that they were going to bomb everybody else and nobody was going to bomb them. At Rotterdam, London, Warsaw, and half a hundred other places, they put that rather naive theory into operation. They sowed the wind and now they are going to reap the whirlwind. Cologne, Lübeck, Rostock – those are only just the beginning. We cannot send a thousand bombers a time over Germany every time, as yet. But the time will come when we can do so. Let the Nazis take good note of the western horizon. There they will see a cloud as yet no bigger than a man's hand. But behind that cloud lies the whole massive power of the United States of America. When the storm bursts over Germany, they will look back to the days of Lübeck and Rostock and Cologne as a man caught in the blasts of a hurricane will look back to the gentle zephyrs of last summer. It may take a year. It may take two. But for the Nazis, the writing is on the wall. Let them look out for themselves. The cure is in their own hands. There are a lot of people who say that bombing can never win a war. Well, my answer to that is that it has never been tried yet, and we shall see. Germany, clinging more and more desperately to her widespread conquests and even seeking foolishly for more, will make a most interesting initial experiment. Japan will provide the confirmation. But the time is not yet. There is a great deal of work to be done first, and let us all get down to it."

Mk.III X3662 KO-P 115 Squadron Marham June 1942 with thirty-seven ops to its credit. It was then passed to 20 OTU. It ditched out of fuel off Skye 8 October 1943. (*IWM CH16994*)

The 'Thousand Plan' had been in Harris's mind since he took over at Bomber Command, the intention being to demonstrate to both the public at home and in Germany that Bomber Command was now powerful enough to deliver devastating blows to the German war machine, not least by exceeding the psychologically important 1,000-aircraft mark. CAS Sir Charles Portal approved the plan on 18 May 1942 and it was then presented to the Prime Minister Winston Churchill who approved it two days later.

The first of three such raids would be on Cologne on the night of 30/31 May, under the code name Operation Millennium, with the second to Essen on 1/2 June and the third to Bremen on 25/26 June. Not least among the many challenges to achieving success was locating the requisite number of aircraft and crews by drawing on training units to bolster the front-line squadrons, which meant that there would be trainees as well as experienced crews taking part. An innovation used for the first time was the bomber stream, with all aircraft flying a common route and speed both to and from the target, with each individual aircraft allocated a specific height band and time slot to minimise the risk of mid-air collision.

COLOGNE

Code name Trout

A total of 1,047 aircraft were dispatched, this number being made up as follows:

1 Group – 156 Wellingtons

3 Group – 222 aircraft comprising 134 Wellingtons, 88 Stirlings
4 Group – 147 aircraft comprising 131 Halifaxes, 9 Wellingtons, 7 Whitleys
5 Group – 153 aircraft comprising 73 Lancasters, 46 Manchesters, 34 Hampdens
91 (OTU) – 257 aircraft comprising 236 Wellingtons, 21 Whitleys
92 (OTU) – 108 aircraft comprising 63 Wellingtons, 45 Hampdens
Flying Training Command – 4 Wellingtons

Mk. II W5361 12 Sqn Binbrook winter 1941. (*via Richard Forder*)

Thus 602, or well over half the force, were Wellingtons, the largest number ever used in one operation, and included some GEE-equipped aircraft in the leading formation. Every Wellington squadron was involved, with perhaps the best effort coming from 12 Squadron which managed to muster no fewer than twenty-eight Wellington Mk.IIs (losing five), a figure probably only beaten by 22 OTU who fielded thirty-five (losing four). In the event, 868 aircraft reached and bombed Cologne, inflicting considerable damage on the city and putting a number of factories completely out of action. A further fifteen aircraft bombed secondary targets. Wg Cdr Lucian Ercolani:

> "This was at the time when Bomber Command was trying to get all the support they could, and they wanted to prove to the powers that be that if they'd only help them, let them have enough aircraft, they couldn't half do a hell of a lot of damage. And so he [Air Marshal Harris] made sure every aircraft that he had any control over at all (quite a lot of which were on training), were concentrated to main bomber stations and we all took off with as many bombs as we could, and got as many aircraft into the air as we could and we were all rather excited about it. We knew that something rather special was happening and knew you had more company! You actually became more spread out in the air, you don't see all that number; unless you got one that came a bit too close."

In total Bomber Command lost fifty-three aircraft either during or on return from this raid, including thirty-four Wellingtons; nineteen from squadrons, fourteen from OTUs and one from

Flying Training Command (N2894 from the Central Gunnery School, Sutton Bridge piloted by Plt Off David Johnson and shot down by Oblt Emil Woltersdorf of NJG1 near Apeldoorn, Holland). Honington's 9 Squadron, which had recently re-equipped with the Hercules-powered Wellington Mk.III, was typical of the front-line units called to action. The ORB records that sixteen aircraft took off between 22:50 and 23:56 hours and there was one early return when Sgt Laurance Goalen brought X3332 back with a defective rear turret (he and his crew were lost four months later on a minelaying op). The remaining fifteen continued to the target and of these thirteen returned, with the first to land being Sqn Ldr Turner in X3372 at 02:57. There was then an agonising long wait until the last one back came in nearly two hours later at 04:46. The two that failed to return were Sgt S A Langton in X3469 which ran out of fuel and crashed near Turnhout in Belgium on the return leg, and Fg Off Michael Hodges in BJ674 which was shot down near Venray in Holland and crashed on the west bank of the River Maas, also while on its way home. The successful Luftwaffe pilot was Hptm Werner Streib of NJG1 and this was his twenty-sixth victory and the first of two that night. Graham Welsh was the observer in Langton's crew:

> "The first 1,000-bomber raid May 30/31 1942: As part of the Pathfinder group, 9 Squadron and five others had the job of lighting up the various target areas. Half our squadron were equipped with loads of flares to light up the general areas. We, equipped with loads of incendiaries, were able to identify the target from flares that lit up as we approached. I congratulated myself on completing my thirtieth op according to the record board in the crew room. Naturally we did not wait around to see how the main force was doing. We followed the Rhine south west for a time, then turned north for home.
>
> "At that time our port engine stopped with a loud bang. I was not aware of enemy action at the time; I believe lack of oil was the problem. The pilot, Sgt Langton, lost control and, trying to regain control lost most of our height. On attaining stability (under 3,000 ft) I gave him a course for Manston. Shortly after I noticed that he had changed this by about 7 degrees to the north. His explanation was that he was allowing for distance covered while bringing the aircraft under control. These were the last words he spoke.
>
> "Soon afterwards, he was huddled over the control column, airspeed just above stalling point but keeping an approximate course. I warned him he was 'mushing' but he was completely unresponsive. I had already let Sgt Johnson out of the front turret and warned the gunners to jettison guns and other equipment. By now we were close to the ground and heading toward a large farmhouse.
>
> "I reached over and grabbed the control column against the weight of the pilot. The aircraft stalled immediately and a wing dropped...I picked myself up, then noticed Sgt Howarth the WOp walking towards me (about 40 ft from the wreckage). He was followed by Johnson. The three of us and the wreckage were less than 20 feet from the house, a door opened and the farmer let us in and let us clean up our minor abrasions.
>
> "A language problem ensued; I recognised Dutch and I did the talking mostly in German and sign language. Anyhow the farmer (and neighbours who had arrived) would not allow us to go out in search of Langton and Sgt Pexman, the rear gunner, in

case we might set the plane alight. It was agreed that one of the men should go out and search. He returned shortly, indicating by running his hand across his throat, that both were dead. Pexman had expected we would crash land and turned his turret for easy exit. There had been no time to warn him of our action and he was thrown out, colliding with a tailplane. He survived the crash but died in hospital soon after.

"After our crash we set off to find the 'Underground'. This proved difficult. We soon found we were in a Flemish area of Belgium. A Roman Catholic priest warned the Germans where we were. After a few days we were captured by a German infantry regiment while seeking medical help for Howarth. We were turned over to the Luftwaffe who sent us off to Stalag Luft 3. During preparation for The Great Escape I provided a kitbag for the tunnel air pump and scanned Berlin, Frankfurt and Hamburg newspapers daily, occasionally Vienna, for data on transport and communications for the intelligence committee. I was awarded a space as an escaper and although I was carrying papers as a Dutch worker my number was too high (about 130), so I did not get out."

In fact Sgt Langton had also survived with head and arm injuries and was repatriated a few months later after a long hospital stay while the rest of his crew spent the remainder of the war as prisoners. In June Langton wrote to his parents in London saying 'I was trying hard to get home...we stayed with the kite and hit the deck in Belgium'. His crash landing was witnessed by the crew of a 92 Group Wellington whose observations were included in a Bomber Command intelligence report issued on 6 June 1942[2]:

> 'Twenty miles east of Antwerp at 02:05 hours. Wellington seen flying slowly west at 500 feet. Our aircraft followed and overtook it then turned calling it on R/T. No reply received. When next seen aircraft was pancaking in field and crew were seen to be flashing torches. Aircraft was not seen to catch fire. It is thought that crew were OK.'

Visibility over the target was excellent with little or no cloud, although as the raid progressed considerable ground haze built up, and there was only spasmodic flak and searchlight activity. The same intelligence report identified three flak batteries located within the city boundaries, a total of just twenty-three searchlights and barrage balloons in and around the target up to a height of 10,000 feet. Comments during crew debriefing concerning the attack indicated that it had achieved its aims, with crews remarking 'bombs fell in town centre', 'the whole town was ablaze', 'fires visible from Antwerp on return'. One crew who must have been extremely frustrated with one of their number, was that of Sgt Trustum in X3666; the ORB records their remarks:

> 'Cologne reached but bombs not dropped as selector switch was not selected by the bomb aimer. 2 x 1,000 and 4 x 500 lb bombs brought back.'

Polish 300 Squadron was at Ingham, Lincolnshire with Pratt and Whitney Twin Wasp-engined Wellington Mk.IVs and completed the raid without loss. Their ORB rather colourfully describes their involvement thus:

> 'Operations were ordered with Cologne as the target and fifteen crews were briefed.

The crews were informed that this raid would be the biggest ever attempted to date. Approaching the target seemed to be a mass of flame and smoke rising to a height of 10,000 feet. Lübeck was nothing to this spectacle. The fires burning prevented results of bombing being observed, but all captains of aircraft state that the target area was well and truly plastered and describe the trip as perfect.'

Typical of the many OTUs taking part, often with trainees as well as staff, was No.15 at Harwell, Oxfordshire, which despatched twenty aircraft from Harwell plus a further ten from their satellite aerodrome at Hampstead Norris also in Berkshire. Of these, twenty-three reached Cologne and again achieved good bombing results. Of those aircraft that failed to get to the primary target, owing to failure to reach sufficient height, W/O Herriott in X9789 bombed a night-fighter airfield despite being attacked by four fighters, W/O Fletcher in N2816 jettisoned his bomb load near Flushing, and the remainder returned with their bombs, apart from two aircraft from whom nothing more was heard. W/O J Hatton in W5586 had been taken prisoner along with all his crew except WOp/AG Sgt R Collins RAAF who lost his life, and Sgt D Paul DFM in R1791 who fell victim to the NJG1 night fighter of Lt Helmut Nilas on the outskirts of Charleroi, Belgium and was taken prisoner. Paul survived also to become a POW; his rear gunner Flt Sgt B Evans DFM successfully evaded and returned to England on New Year's Day 1943, while the other members of the crew were lost.

Fg Off Bill Parr was an air gunner crewing up at 15 OTU Harwell and when he arrived he discovered he had already been detailed to go to Cologne:

Fg Off Bill Parr was an air gunner under training at 15 OTU Harwell when he was detailed for Operation Millennium. (*Bill Parr*)

"I don't think I had even been teamed up with my Wimpy crew or I would have flown with them. We were all in a mass briefing, and as a spare air gunner, I was allocated to a crew I did not know. I thought this could be it, a one-way trip, but without any previous operational experience I could only play it by ear. As we accelerated down the runway, the pilot was soon remarking over the intercom. that it was not fast enough to take off, so slammed the throttles shut with only just enough runway to stop. I suppose it was a clapped out training aircraft that could not take a full bomb load. To say I was hugely relieved not to go is a big under statement – I think that it saved my life."

Bill subsequently went on to complete forty ops with 70 Squadron in 1943. Fg Off Jack Wakefield was a gunnery instructor at 23 OTU Pershore, Worcestershire when he found himself called for the raid:

"One day the 'phone rang and Sqn Ldr Warner, the CFI said 'I am taking off for an air

Fg Off Jack Wakefield was a gunnery instructor at 23 OTU Pershore called tot operations for the first 1,000 bomber raid. (*Jack Wakefield*)

test. Meet me out on the runway with your flying gear, pyjamas, toothbrush, etc.' I tested the turret for him and he said 'I cannot tell you anything but briefing is at 4 o'clock'. On 30 May we took off, instructors with instructors, and crews who had finished their operational training as crews, the aircraft at the OTUs were fairly tired. We were climbing off the English coast heading for Cologne – the sky was full of aircraft in every direction, it was a sight to stir the blood."

26 OTU at Wing in Buckinghamshire contributed twenty aircraft and crews. Flying training was suspended towards the end of May and staff instructed to form their men, including pupils, into crews. On 27 May 1942, twenty aircraft were positioned at newly-constructed Graveley, Huntingdonshire, of which eight would be crewed by 26 OTU and the other twelve by crews from 22 and 27 OTUs. Sqn Ldr Ralph Edwards recalled the pre-raid move in his book *In The Thick Of It*:

"We were to be accommodated in Nissen huts. Crews arriving in the later hours were not so fortunate; they had to sleep on floors and store their clothing and equipment in the chicken huts of a nearby farm. We settled in as best we could under the cramped circumstances still wondering what was in the wind."

At briefing the next day they were told: "Gentlemen, you are privileged to take part in a special operation tonight, a momentous occasion. 1,000 bombers will be attacking a single target. The target is Cologne."

In the event, four wing aircraft would be lost; Fg Off William Whiting in W5704, Flt Sgt Edwin Ford DFM DV707, Sgt John Dixon DV709 and W/O F Hillyer DV740. Of the twenty crew members, fifteen were killed, three injured and two, including Hillyer, taken prisoner. Dixon's aircraft crashed during an emergency landing at Soham near Cambridge, the others all fell to the prowling NJG1 night fighters; Whiting to Oblt Reinhold Knacke, Ford to Ofw Wilhelm Beier, and Hillyer to Staffel Feldwebel (St.Fw) Gerhard Herzog, with all the Wellingtons coming down in Holland.

The Germans did not have everything their own way however. 20 OTU's W/O Fortier in Z8843 was attacked by a night fighter which gunner WOp/AG Plt Off Gerry Stone claimed as shot down. This must have been a Bf 110G of NJG1 that came down near Kaldenkirchen/Rheinland and was the only fighter lost. Gerry and the rest of the crew flew again on the second 1,000-plan raid but returned early with engine trouble; just two months later on 156 Squadron he was lost to a night fighter.

Ken Law RCAF W/AG (WOp/AG) flew to Cologne with a 22 OTU crew from Wellesbourne Mountford, Warwickshire:

Mk.III Z1572 VR-Q of 419 (RCAF) Squadron Mildenhall 27 May 1942. It survived to be scrapped in April 1945. (*RAF Museum*)

"I was posted to 22 OTU in March 1942. After circuits and bumps, local flying and cross countrys in Ansons and Wimpys I was crewed up with a Canadian navigator and bomb aimer, and RAF pilot and tail gunner. The pilot was ex-flying instructor Flg Off Plunkett, promoted to flight lieutenant. We finished OTU with the 1,000-bomber raids; 30 May '42 to Cologne in L1711 with six containers of incendiaries and leaflets, and bombed from 13,000 feet.

"On 1 June we went to Essen, again in L1711, with the same load and bombed from 14,000 feet. On this trip we were holed by flak and lost some fuel, causing the skipper to order an SOS signal sent while over the North Sea; but this was later cancelled and we made it safely to base. We were then posted to 218 Sqn at Marham where Flt Lt Plunkett went missing on his first second-dickey trip."

Flt Lt Desmond Plunkett was taken prisoner after his Stirling was brought down over Holland on 20 June 1942, returning from a raid on Emden. He was the thirteenth man out of the tunnel in the March 1944 Great Escape from Stalag Luft 3 in Sagan, Poland but was recaptured and survived in another camp until the end of the war.

1483 (Target Towing) Flight at Newmarket, with an establishment that included eight Wellingtons and twelve Lysanders, contributed aircraft and crews to all three 1,000-bomber raids. For the first, three aircraft were despatched; Flt Lt Barratt in X9754 with Sgt Albert Mann as second pilot; Flt Lt Ercolani in Z1080 (who would later become OC of 99 Squadron in India); and Plt Off Masters in R3232. All three successfully reached and bombed the target, returning safely, although Masters' aircraft was described as being 'slightly shot up'. Flt Lt Ercolani then took part in both the second, when he stated his bombs were dropped on fires and searchlights, and third raids in the same Wellington. He was joined on the third raid by Flt Sgt Birch in R3232 (with Mann as second pilot) and the ORB records that his navigator W/O Binns, made an excellent effort with DR navigation, with the aircraft on track and estimated time of arrival (ETA) all the way, although no pinpoints were obtained after leaving base. Once again though, this unfortunate Wimpy was slightly shot up. The flight went on to then participate in operations to Hamburg on 28 July 1942 and Düsseldorf on 31 July.[3]

ESSEN (Code name Stoat)

Essen was chosen as the target for the second 1,000-plan raid on 1/2 June 1942, the principal aiming point being the large Krupps works, and the attack followed much the same pattern as the first, although the total of aircraft available was down somewhat at 956. This included 545 Wellingtons, with a leading flare force of twenty-four Wellingtons drawn from Feltwell, Honington, Marham and Oakington. These were to drop twelve bundles of three flares at eight-second intervals at the designated point from zero hour to zero plus twenty-three minutes, with the first following wave to bomb at zero plus two minutes and all aircraft to have bombed by zero plus one hour thirty minutes. The route out was from base to north of The Hague and thence to the target, returning via Krefeld, south of The Hague and home.

The weather was much poorer than for Cologne, with the result that the bombing was very scattered, and thirty-one bombers were lost, fifteen of them Wellingtons. The OTU aircraft came off particularly badly this time, accounting for nine losses while 57, 115, 142 and 305 Squadrons each lost a single aircraft, and 460 (RAAF) Squadron two; once again the German night-fighter force took a heavy toll, downing the following:

16 OTU DV763 Plt Off Ron Robinson DFC	Hptm Walter Ehle NJG1
21 OTU W5618 Sgt Fred Albright RCAF	Oblt Reinhold Eckhardt NJG3
23 OTU Z8867 Flt Lt William Ewart	Oblt Jakob Bender NJG1
23 OTU R1266 Fg Off William Mawdesley RAAF	Oblt Hermann Reese NJG1
25 OTU DV434 Fg Off R Jessop (POW)	Oblt Kurt Loos NJG1
460 Sqn Z1311 Sgt John Walsh RAAF	Oblt Reinhold Eckhardt NJG3
460 Sqn Z1344 Fg Off A Holland (POW)	Oblt Horst Patuschka NJG2

Two of the squadron losses occurred over England. 142 Squadron's Z1410 flown by Plt Off Donald McDonald RCAF, a US citizen, was forced to turn back with engine trouble and crashed an hour-and-a-half after take-off at Thoresby Bridge; only the rear gunner survived. The loss of 305 Squadron's Z8583 took the lives of the entire six-man crew including Wg Cdr Robert Hirszbandt OBE DFC who had served in the Polish air force before the war and had also been a test pilot at Farnborough. Having been damaged over the target, his aircraft stalled and crashed while attempting a single-engine landing at Billingford near East Dereham in Norfolk.

BREMEN (Code name Salmon)

Although Harris had planned to mount these very large-scale operations once or twice during each moon period, he abandoned the idea, largely due to the considerable disruption to crew training brought about by the heavy involvement of the OTUs. Thus the final 1,000-bomber raid took place on the night of 25/26 June 1942 when the target was Bremen, which was referred to by 3 Group at least as Operation Millennium 2. As with the Essen raid, the force assembled was just short of four figures, with 960 aircraft including 472 Wellingtons. The 5 Group target was the Focke-Wulf aircraft factory, while the remainder of the main force was detailed to concentrate on the town and the docks. Cloud cover again stepped in to reduce accuracy, but 696 aircraft claimed to have bombed the target causing considerable damage.

In return, the force lost forty-eight aircraft, with the heaviest toll falling on 91 Group's OTU aircraft probably due to the greater distance to the target in cloudy conditions being more of a challenge for the many trainee crews involved. No fewer than 21 OTU Wellingtons failed to return, plus examples from 115, 156, 301 and 305 Squadrons and 1481 Target Towing and Gunnery Flight from Binbrook. The night fighters found themselves in ideal conditions and again exacted a heavy toll claiming:

11 OTU R1078 Plt Off S King RCAF (POW)	Lt August Geiger NJG1
12 OTU R1349 Flt Sgt Alan Wilson	Lt Robert Denzel NJG2
12 OTU R1410 Sgt John Shapcott	Maj Kurt Holler NJG4 or Lt Hans-Georg Bötel NJG2
12 OTU DV951 Plt Off E Cooper (POW)	Oblt Herbert Lütje NGJ1
15 OTU DV935 Sgt James Leather	Oblt Hermann Greiner NJG2
18 OTU T2612 Plt Off Maksymilian Niemczyk	Hptm Helmut Lent NJG2
20 OTU T2723 Sgt N Levasseur RCAF (POW)	Oblt Egmond Prinz zur Lippe-Weissenfeld NJG2 or Lt Hans-Georg Bötel NJG2
23 OTU X9875 Sgt D Lord RCAF	Lt Hans-Hermann Müller NJG2
23 OTU DV475 Sgt J Crossing RCAF	Oblt Werner Rowlin NJG1
1481 Flt X9812 Sqn Ldr Matthew Atkinson	Maj Kurt Holler NJG4

Of the squadron aircraft, Sgt W Thompson of 156 Squadron in BJ594 had to abandon the sortie forty-five minutes after taking off from Alconbury due to an electrical failure and on his third attempt to land back at base, the aircraft hit a pillbox, tearing off the rear turret and killing the gunner Sgt Henry Young, who at thirty-three was the 'old man' on board. The rest of the crew escaped unscathed.

THE FINAL MONTHS OF BOMBER COMMAND OPERATIONS

With the 1,000-bomber raids at an end, Bomber Command's efforts continued much as before with a mixture of substantial raids on major industrial centres, shipyards and harbours, while continuing the minelaying effort. The major operational development around this time was the formation of the Pathfinder Force (PFF) in August 1942. Wellington units had begun to suffer a higher loss rate on some operations as the increased sophistication of German defences and the type's relative performance vulnerability began to show. For example, a raid on Duisburg on 21/22 July saw ten Wellingtons lost out of 170 despatched and five nights later fifteen out of 181 failed to return from Hamburg; these loss rates being noticeably higher than for other aircraft types. Accordingly, Wellington units continued to re-equip, both to address this issue and to satisfy an increasing demand for bombers in overseas theatres.

A 214 Squadron crew fly an end-of-tour beat-up at Stradishall.
(*Elsie Henry via Richard Forder*)

By the end of 1942, 103, 158, 405 and 460 (RAAF) had re-equipped with Halifaxes, 9, 12, 57, 101 Squadrons with Lancasters, 75, 214 and 218 with Stirlings, while 40 and 150 had moved to the Mediterranean, with 99 and 215 going to India. In addition, under pressure from the Admiralty to tackle the serious U-boat threat, Harris reluctantly released 304 and 311 (Polish) and 458 (RAAF) Squadrons to Coastal Command. Against the flow of this run-down, May 1943 saw the formation of 432 'Leaside' (RCAF) Squadron at Skipton-on-Swale within Bomber Command, but its Wellingtons only lasted for a few months before Lancasters replaced them. One of the other late-forming units was 466 (RAAF) Sqn with Wellington Mk.X at Driffield, East Yorkshire from October 1942. H E Dickson served with them as an armourer:

"The aerodrome had been heavily bombed the previous year and was still bomb scarred when we formed the squadron. We then moved to Leconfield to become operational and operated for several months with considerable success and very few losses. The front gun turret was blanked off and occasionally we mounted free standing .303 Browning guns amidships, although this was soon phased out. The rear turret was an FN20 four-gun type with ammunition tanks in the fuselage. Mounted on the leading edge of both wings were cable cutters – a double towards the wing tips, singles either side of the engines and one close to the main fuselage. These cable cutters contained shortened 12-bore type cartridges with a high tensile steel cutter set in the cartridge, and again these were soon phased out. They had to be armed and de-activated before and after each op. The squadron laid mines, dropped 500 lb HE bombs, and 4 lb and/or 30 lb incendiaries.

"The pilot of Y-Yorker was a Plt Off Young, and he and his crew completed their tour. Young had the bearded-Scotsman mascot of Younger's beer on the side of his 'plane and foaming half pints of beer to denote ops completed. [At least fourteen ops were marked in this way.] He was allowed to send a photograph to Younger's brewery, who in turn sent 144 gallons of best beer for a squadron booze up.

"Flg Off Sampson RNZAF was the pilot of V-Victor and I flew with him over the North Sea near Flamborough Head and Scarborough to test the guns and turret. He always flew on ops wearing civilian clothes under his sheepskin coat and trousers – how I never found out – but he swore he would never become a POW. He was shot down after a number of raids and we heard that the crew had managed to escape the crash and were POWs, all except Fg Off Samson, of him there was no news.

"A sergeant pilot joined the squadron and on his first day was put on circuits and bumps to familiarise himself with the aircraft and the surrounding countryside and landmarks. However, on his second or third 'bump' he careered across the grass and smashed the Wellington into the side of a hangar, demolishing the flight commander's office. Not long after that he was on ops laying sea mines; he and his crew were unable to locate the correct position and so returned with both 2,000 lb sea mines still aboard. He made a hash of landing, overshot the runway and the undercarriage collapsed. The aircraft burst into flames from wing tip to wing tip and nose to tail in seconds. The duty crew, of which I was a member, rushed to help get the crew, who miraculously all got out, albeit the navigator broke his arm. Meanwhile, the ammunition and signal cartridges were exploding as everyone ran from the blaze. Fortunately the fire engines and crash wagons were still on their way when the mines exploded, extinguishing the fire."

Minelaying remained an activity that many pilots disliked, including Graham Welsh describing one such operation shortly before he was shot down and taken prisoner:

"Mining in the Baltic: Being averse to surprises we managed to provoke a flakship into revealing its position by firing; this told us that it was close to our dropping point. Our gunners were briefed on action when we neared the flakship. The moment we dropped our mine all hell broke loose. Within seconds our pilot flew over the flakship at 400 ft. Our gunners disorientated the flak gunners, we flew off with only minor damage and returned home. Our fellow miners did not return."

One of the most disastrous raids for the Wellington took place on the night of 28/29 August 1942 to Nuremberg (code name Grayling). The 159 aircraft attacking force included forty-one Wellingtons and fourteen of these failed to return, a loss rate of thirty-four percent. 57, 75 and 101 Squadrons lost two each, while 156, 301 and 305 each lost a single aircraft, but the biggest blow came to 115 Squadron with five of their aircraft going down. Plt Off J Duffy in X3464 was seriously damaged by flak and force landed, the crew being taken prisoner. Flt Sgt William Allen X3647 came down near Rethel in France with the loss of all but WOp/AG Sgt W Haddleton RCAF who was captured. W/O John Smith X3675 was shot down by Hptm Ludwig Bietmann of NJG1 killing Smith, one of the WOp/AGs and the rear gunner, the observer evading and the second WOp/AG being captured. And Plt Off J Berry Z1607 crash-landed on return near Swaffham, Norfolk with all the crew escaping. Plt Off Clifford Pafford RCAF BJ688 was shot down by Lt Ludwig Meister NJG4 with the loss of all crew members.

Flt Lt Marian Wlodarczyk's Mk.IV Z1407 BH-Z of 300 (Polish) Squadron back at Hemswell from Bremen 5 September 1942. It was repaired. (*www.polishsquadronsremembered.com*)

The sole 57 Squadron aircraft to be brought down was BJ619 flown by Sgt L E Brooks, which crash landed near Wahlenau in Germany, the entire crew being captured unharmed. On 5 September 1942, Brooks wrote a letter from the Dulag Luft interrogation centre at Frankfurt in which he said:

> 'We were unfortunate enough to get our starboard engine hit by flak, and we tried to get home on one engine. Luck was against us however, and we got picked up by searchlights a bit later and they belted hell out of us. The other engine caught fire and we started to go down. I got all the rest of the crew out at 1,000 feet, and then the 'plane went into a dive with me still in it. At the last minute I managed to flatten her out a bit and the crash was not so bad.'

THE BATTLE OF THE RUHR

In March 1943 Harris unleashed what he called The Battle of the Ruhr (known as 'Happy Valley' to the bomber boys), which lasted until the end of July and was intended as an all-out effort to destroy Germany's manufacturing capabilities built around the extensive Ruhr coalfields. Following this the most significant event in Bomber Command's strategy was the issue in May 1943 of the Operation Pointblank directive, which coordinated the United States Army Air Force (USAAF) 8th Air Force day-bombing effort against German industrial targets with Bomber Command attacking by night. By this time Harris was able to call on 600 bombers a night (rising to 800 by July) and accuracy was becoming much better as the Pathfinder Force found its feet. Although the Wellington force continued to play its part, it did so to a lesser extent, with increasing numbers of operations not calling in the type at all.

Re-equipment and transfer continued to take its toll during this year, and although 166 Squadron at Kirmington, Lincolnshire was added to the ranks in January it had switched to Lancasters by September. Other units to go included 425, 427, 428, 429, 431 (all RCAF) and 466 (RAAF) Squadrons going over to Halifaxes, 156, 426 (RCAF) and 432 (RCAF) Lancasters, 196 and 199 Stirlings, and 305 (Polish) to Mitchells marking a complete change of role. 301 (Polish)

Squadron disbanded completely in April, and 420 (RCAF) Squadron was sent to the Mediterranean theatre.

Mk.III BJ668 ZL-X of 427 (RCAF) Squadron Croft shot down during a raid on Lorient, 5 February 1943. (*RAF Museum*)

Having flown his first tour as a captain on 99 Squadron in late 1940/early 1941, Acting Sqn Ldr Cyril Earthrowl DFC started his second on 427 Squadron in their last few weeks with Wellingtons before completing the tour on the Halifax. His log book comments provide an insight into some of the targets and challenges being faced at that time:

> 'February 16 – Wellington III BK137, Lorient (U-boat pens). 1 x 4,000 lb, no cloud, excellent visibility, no flak.
> March 3 – Wellington X HZ264, Hamburg. High explosive and incendiaries, no cloud, hit by Ju 88.
> April 4 – Wellington X HZ264, Kiel. 9 cans of incendiaries, 10/10ths cloud.
> April 10 – Wellington X HZ264, Frankfurt. Overload tank, 1 x 1,000 lb, 3 x 500 lb. 10/10ths cloud. Bad PFF. Wasted effort.'

In their final months of main force operations, the Wellingtons continued to visit such targets as Wuppertal on 29/30 May 1943, considered to be one of the most effective attacks of the Battle of the Ruhr. They also targeted Düsseldorf, Mülheim, Krefeld, Gelsenkirchen and Aachen before joining in the Battle of Hamburg which commenced on 27/28 July, continuing with more raids on 29/30 July and 2/3 August. By this time Wellingtons made up a much smaller percentage of the attacking force, for example seventy-four out of 787 aircraft on the first Hamburg raid, with just one lost. This was 429 Squadron's Mk.X JA114 captained by Wg Cdr James Piddington DFC on only his third sortie since taking command. He was shot down near Neumünster and only the WOp/AG and the rear gunner survived.

THE DIARY OF AN OPERATION

Early in the morning, on every day of the war, ground crews all over Bomber Command were starting their DIs to ready the aircraft for the day ahead. Any defects reported by the last crew to fly them were being attended to, and careful checks were made of all the aircraft systems; including engines and controls, hydraulics, pneumatics, wheels brakes and tyres, radios, lights and any battle damage. Engines were ground run to check for 'mag' (magneto) drops, fuel or oil leaks, vibration and temperatures. Once the aircraft had been signed off as serviceable on the Form 700, the next step was for the aircrew to conduct a night-flying test (NFT) for up to half an hour, following which preparations could start for the next operation. The fitters, riggers and armourers were rightly proud of keeping 'their' aircraft on the line regardless of the conditions under which they had to work, for as far as they were concerned it was theirs, and was only lent to the aircrew on the promise that they must bring it back! Flt Lt Eric Clarke was a WOp/AG and flew his tours on Hampdens, Manchesters and Lancasters, but the principles were the same regardless of the aircraft type:

> "The NFT involved a ten to fifteen-minute flight, usually with the pilot with whom you would fly that night, but this did not always happen. Later in the morning, we could see from our crewroom window a tractor towing a string of bomb trolleys and we might just get an inkling of the type of operation that night. Ruhr, 'Happy Valley' or gardening, but we just speculated."

At lunchtime on Monday 30 August 1943 the teleprinters at Bomber Command stations started clattering out the Form B Operation Order for the coming night. Clerks at stations across the country including 1 Group, 4 Group and 92 Group Wellington units at Kirmington, Leconfield, Silverstone, Wing and Bruntingthorpe hurried to pass on the instructions to the waiting senior station staff; there were two 'targets for tonight'. Main force consisting of 297 Lancasters, 185 Halifaxes, 107 Stirlings, fifty-seven Wellingtons and fourteen Mosquitoes were responsible for the first major attack on the towns of Mönchengladbach and Reydt; a maximum effort was required from the participating squadrons and training units.

A second force of 33 OTU Wellingtons drawn from three stations and supported by six Mosquitoes fitted with the Oboe navigation aid and six Halifaxes from 8 (PFF) Group, was to target an ammunition dump in the Foret d'Éperlecques near St.Omer in northern France. This was the first occasion in 1943 that OTUs had been called upon to supply aircraft and crews for a bombing operation. Both forces were to be ready at 22:00 hours for take-off at around midnight.

Once the number of serviceable aircraft was known, lists went up in the various messes of those crews detailed to fly that night, and in the late afternoon they attended briefings. The main briefing was when the target was revealed for the first time – accompanied by much groaning if it was deep into Germany or a well-known heavily-defended one – and details were provided such as take-off time, time over target, the weather expected en route, over the target and on return.

On this occasion the crews were briefed to bomb at the red target indicators (TI) if visible, otherwise at the centre of all green TIs seen; if none were seen the bombs were to be brought back. The met man sounded optimistic as a ridge of high pressure extended over most of the UK and the Continent as far as the two target areas. At zero hour there was expected to be a force 2 or 3 north-westerly wind, with a temperature on the ground of about 55 degrees Fahrenheit and little or no cloud. There was a weather front approaching from the Atlantic, and on their return to England, crews were expected to find a cloud base of 7/10 to 8/10 at around 3,000 to 4,000 feet and a moderate south-westerly wind to contend with.

There were various specialist briefings for navigators and other crew positions, depending on the type of aircraft and type of operations; for example gunners might be briefed separately by the gunnery leader to discuss ammunition quantities etc.

> "You just reported to the briefing, if there was a seat, you would sit there and tried to take notes but nothing else. The squadron commander pointed out the target and the reason for the operation, and the route out and back and followed by specialist officers, meteorologist, navigator, signals and intelligence and take-off times were also announced. Then the individual crews got into a huddle over the navigator's chart after which we returned to our messes for a night-flying supper."

Loading a 1,000 lb bomb with a 250 lb bomb on the ground, 214 Squadron Stradishall. (*Elsie Henry via Richard Forder*)

An anonymous aircrew member of 9 Squadron wrote an article explaining the daily routine and about the briefing noted:

> 'On our initial entry into this sanctum sanctorum, our eyes, ears and sensitive nostrils are assailed by;
>
> 'The soothing hubbub of sixty or more men conversing quietly together. The kaleidoscopic glaring colour scheme provided by multi-hued socks, scarves, and miscellaneous equipment of this cosmopolitan crowd of aviators.
>
> 'The combined odours of tobacco fumes and perspiring jovial humanity. Acclimatisation is fortunately a rapid process, so do not be over-critical, for this rare atmosphere actually embodies and personified the spirit of flying and true comradeship.'[4]

Now the ground crew could load the aircraft. Bomb load, weight, and range required were calculated to ensure the correct uplift of fuel, not the easiest of tasks in a Wimpy. The Mk.III had two sets of three wing tanks forward and aft totalling 150 and 167 gallons respectively on both sides, a 58 gallon tank in each engine nacelle plus overload tanks of various capacities up to 185 gallons which could be fitted in the bomb bay (and a small one in the centre fuselage) for the longest range operations or ferrying. Bombs had to be winched by hand into the bomb bay using the integral winch built into the aircraft, with each bomb needing to have its fuse set for the

Loading 250 lb bombs 149 Squadron Mildenhall 1940. (*via Norman Didwell*)

correct timing, its detonator and tail fins fitted, the safety wire attached to the bomb carrier, and the final load distribution passed to the bomb aimer so that he could set up the bombing panel in the aircraft's nose. The required bomb load could vary between squadrons and, for this particular operation, the Wellingtons going to France were to carry a minimum of four, maximum six, 500 lb general purpose (GP) bombs, which were to be fused as soon as the aircraft crossed the English coast outbound, and this was to be noted in the navigator's log.

There were very specific orders concerning what to do about any bombs that were not dropped on the target, with jettisoning only being done if absolutely necessary and then only with the bombs made safe first. Otherwise bombs were to be made safe immediately it was intended to return, and brought back to base, and once the aircraft was on the ground the bomb doors were only to be opened by an armament officer.

Time to go. Engine starting was supervised by the ground crew 'Chiefy' in communication with the pilot. An airman was needed to prime each engine via a priming pump in the wheel well, and to connect and disconnect the 'trolley acc' battery set to provide the considerable electrical power required to turn the engines over.

Thus fifty-seven Wellingtons started getting airborne shortly before midnight, and joined up with the rest of the bomber stream before heading off over the North Sea, but sadly, two aircraft were lost almost immediately. 466 (RAAF) Squadron despatched fifteen Wellingtons from just before to just after midnight and ten minutes after take-off two of them collided over the town of Goole, Yorkshire just a few miles from their base at Leconfield. There was a new moon in the sky, and the air was very clear so it is highly likely that other crews may have seen the collision as they all set out en route to the target at 5,000 feet together with more Wellingtons from 166 and 300 Squadrons to join up with the rest of the main force.

Wellington Mk.X HZ531 came down at 00:25 hours on the bank of the River Ouse at Skelton, two miles north east of Goole without causing any damage on the ground, although a considerable quantity of petrol ran into the estuary and was carried away by the tide. The bulk of the other aircraft LN292 crashed into Carlisle Street in the centre of Goole town between the Tower Theatre and Robinson's furnishers, with another section coming down on top of The Peacock Hotel. All ten crew members on the aircraft were killed. Those lost are listed below, all being RAF Volunteer Reserve (RAFVR) crew men unless stated otherwise:

HZ531 (total flying time 120 hours fifteen minutes)

Pilot Flt Sgt Mervin Smart RAAF (21) from Somerton, South Australia
Navigator Flt Sgt Newton Fuss RAAF (23) from Prospect, South Australia
Air Bomber Flt Sgt James McLachlan RAAF (30) from West Wyalong, New South Wales
Wireless Operator Flt Sgt Edwin RAAF (26) from Northcote, Victoria
Air Gunner Sgt John Eccleston (20) from Halebank, Cheshire

LN292 (an almost brand new aircraft that had only flown twenty-eight hours and fifty minutes)

Pilot Sgt John Harwood (29) from Earlsfield, London
Navigator Sgt Geoffrey Payne (19) from Bushby, Leicestershire
Air Bomber Sgt Joseph Noar (27) from Salford, Lancashire
Wireless Operator Sgt Peter Elliot (age unknown) from London
Air Gunner Sgt Thomas McCann RCAF (24) an American citizen from Allston, Massachusetts

The accident was front page news in *The Goole Times* on 3 September 1943, which reported that three people had been killed on the ground. Damage was extensive in the town with a large fire in Carlisle Street and another which gutted The Peacock Hotel in North Street. A twelve-year-old boy was burned to death in the hotel and a woman was killed when an engine fell on her house in North Street and penetrated the bedroom where she was asleep; the third fatality was a twenty-six-year old man. The paper reported that, despite the hour, many people in the town saw the collision, and hundreds were evacuated from their homes. Shortly after this accident, 466 Squadron was taken off operations until it had converted to Halifaxes.

Meanwhile, the main force arrived over the primary targets to find that the weather was indeed as good as predicted and the target marking by the Oboe-equipped Pathfinders had been good. On the approach to the target each bomb aimer set the wind speed and direction on his bombsights and confirmed these to the pilot, indicating that he was ready to bomb. When ready for the final run in the pilot said "attack", the bomb aimer repeated this back and confirmed that they were fusing bombs; the pilot then operated the appropriate fusing switch. The bomb aimer checked the sight and corrected for drift by giving instructions to the pilot until the line of sight entered the danger area when he told the pilot to select the bombs. The pilot operated the selector switch and the bomb aimer continued to direct him, releasing the bombs when the sights came into line, confirming the number of bombs gone. The pilot confirmed this back to him and then continued on course until the bomb aimer reported "bombs plotted" once the target photograph had been taken by the vertically-mounted F24 camera. Getting a good bombing photograph required the pilot to maintain an accurate and constant course, height and airspeed; it was a very tense time for all on board who just wanted to get away from the target area as quickly as possible.

Ten minutes was allowed for the force to transfer between the two towns and the bombing was good, reports indicating that approximately half the area of each town had been destroyed. German reports later stated that 1,059 buildings were destroyed and 117 people killed in Mönchengladbach, plus 1,280 and 253 respectively in Reydt. The defences were strong and the attacking force lost thirty bombers (3.8 percent), of which four were Wellingtons:

166 Squadron HE988 was shot down by Oblt Heinz-Wolfgang Schnaufer NJG1 and crashed at Limburg, Belgium. All crew members were lost:

Pilot Sgt Henry Heron (25) from Ayr, Scotland
Navigator Plt Off Clifford Musto (31) from Dartford, Kent
Air Bomber Sgt James Smith (33) from Liverpool
Wireless Operator Sgt Thomas Betts (22) from Rothley, Leicestershire
Air Gunner Sgt Leslie Wakerell (20) from East Grinstead, Sussex

166 Squadron LN397 missing without trace:

Pilot Flg Off Eric Cook (21) from Edmonton, Middlesex
Navigator Plt Off Albert Freeman (21) from Moseley, Birmingham
Air Bomber Sgt Stanley Baber (21) from Hayes, Middlesex
Wireless Operator Sgt Philip Davies (20) from Llanybri, Carmarthenshire
Air Gunner Sgt Ronald Blood (21) from Wythenshawe, Cheshire

300 Squadron JA116 was shot down by Lt Friedrich Potthast NJG1, and crashed at Kethel, near Rotterdam. All crew members lost were Polish citizens and no details of their ages or places of origin are available:

Pilot Flt Lt Leon Osmialowski PAF
Navigator Flt Lt Aleksander Steininger PAF
Air Bomber Plt Off Stanislaw Swiech PAF
Wireless Operator Sgt Jozef Zabal PAF
Air Gunner Sgt Franciszek Buda PAF

432 Squadron JA118 was shot down in the target area by Hptm Hans-Dieter Frank NJG1, all crew members were lost:

Pilot Flt Sgt James Pendleton RCAF no further details known
Navigator Sgt Derek Collins (21) from Scarborough, Yorkshire
Air Bomber Flg Off George Jarvis (30) from Shipley, Yorkshire
Wireless Operator Flt Sgt Raymond White no further details known
Air Gunner W/O Bland Pierce RCAF no further details known

The force attacking the St. Omer target took off much earlier than the main force, with the first away being four 30 OTU aircraft which departed from Seighford, Staffordshire, the most westerly station involved, between 20:35 and 20:38. Other units got away over the next forty-five minutes before routing base–Clacton–Gravelines–St.Omer, returning via Le Touquet and Beachy Head shortly after midnight. This raid too was successful, with crews reporting that the weather was clear with no cloud and eight to ten miles visibility. Bombing from 16,000 or 18,000 feet, some bomb bursts were seen to be overshooting the TIs, but a large explosion was reported, presumably of the ammunition dump that was being targeted. Two Wellingtons were lost.

26 OTU Mk.X HE500 crashed at Rubrouck near Cassel with the loss of all the crew:

Pilot Sgt Kenneth Knaggs (22) from Skelton-in-Cleveland, Yorkshire
Navigator Plt Off Ronald Durne (21) from Shepherd's Bush, London
Navigator Sgt Louis Lewis (22) from Holborn, London
Air Gunner Sgt Patrick Hogan no further details known
Air Gunner Sgt Clifford Hayhurst no further details known
Air Gunner Sgt Ernest Pursell (28) from Milton, Cambridgeshire

This was a very unusual crew make-up with no air bomber aboard, and it must be assumed that at least one of the air gunners listed was actually a WOp/AG.

29 OTU Mk.III BJ967 (one of four aircraft despatched by this unit) ditched at 22:30 while home bound with a fire in the starboard engine. The pilot managed to get into a dinghy and was rescued the next day, but the rest of the crew were lost:

Pilot Sgt T A Wilder no further details known
Navigator Sgt Alexander Trotter (22) from Felton, Northumberland
Air Bomber Sgt John Scott (21) from Lossiemouth, Morayshire
Wireless Operator Sgt Albert Raggett (19) from Tottenham, Middlesex
Air Gunner Flt Sgt Albert Oakes (21) from Hanley, Staffordshire
Rear Gunner Sgt William McDonald RAAF (20) from St.Arnaud, Victoria

As the aircraft gradually returned to their bases, the ground crew were waiting to receive them, and the sadness for some of finding themselves waiting in vain by an empty dispersal must have been intense, while those whose aircraft had come back now had the job of inspecting them for any damage that would need addressing before the next operation. The tired aircrews all faced a debriefing session with an intelligence officer prior to getting a hot supper and then drifting back to their billets to sleep. When they awoke and went for breakfast, they would cast a glance at the empty tables laid out for the crews who had not returned. Overnight a signal arrived at the 92 Group stations from their AOC Air Commodore Harold Haines CBE, DFC, MA:

> "I wish to congratulate you all upon the excellent results achieved on the night of 30/31 August. An examination of the night photographs received shows quite clearly the ground details in the vicinity of the target and the TI markers. In one other case the TI marker is clearly visible although no other ground details are apparent. It is clear from these results that the crews you are training are fully capable of carrying out a bombing task allotted to them. It is regretted that two aircraft are missing but I ascribe this to the fortunes of war. One aircraft failed to take off through getting bogged and one returned early through an engine defect. Whether the operation was a success or not must remain to be seen but there is no doubt that your part was carried well. The excellent results achieved so far will no doubt spur OTUs on in an endeavour to achieve 100 percent success."

The next day, the whole cycle would start all over again.

FINAL OPERATIONS

The last Wellington to be lost to enemy action while participating in a Bomber Command operation was 300 Squadron's Mk.X HF490 on the night of 7/8 October 1943 during a Gardening operation in very poor weather conditions. The aircraft had taken off from Ingham at 23:13 on the 7th and was never seen again, the crew being commemorated on the Polish Air Force Memorial adjacent to RAF Northolt in Middlesex. They were:

Pilot Sqn Ldr Stanislaw Morawski PAF
Navigator Fg Off Antoni Moskwa PAF
Air Bomber Flt Sgt Edward Gastol PAF
Wireless Operator Flt Sgt Wladyslaw Kordys PAF
Air Gunner Sgt Roman Zukowski PAF

The final Bomber Command raid in which Wellingtons took part was on the night of 8/9 October 1943, when twenty-six of the type from 300 and 432 Squadrons joined 282 Lancasters, 188 Halifaxes and eight Mosquitoes in an attack on Hanover. Although the German fighter controllers correctly identified the target and as a result twenty-seven bombers were lost, none were Wellingtons. After this date the use of Wellingtons in support of bomber raids was limited to the specialised role of 100 Group. Thus the Wellington had completed four years and one month on Bomber Command operations, a record for any RAF medium or heavy bomber. Its nearest rival, the Stirling, clocked up three years and seven months, with the Halifax reaching three years and two months, a month longer than the Lancaster.

BOMBER SUPPORT UNITS

The whole Bomber Command effort relied heavily on a wide range of support units including, on the training side, the OTUs which are discussed in more detail in Chapter Seven, while a number of the Bomber Groups maintained their own training flights. Also involved with Bomber Command was the Central Gunnery School at Sutton Bridge, Lincolnshire which, in addition to improving gunnery standards for fighter pilots, maintained a flight of Wellingtons for advanced training of bomber squadrons' gunnery leaders, who were senior air gunners. This mix of students frequently brought the bomber and fighter boys together during exercises as Norman Nava recalled:

> "During June 1943 George 'Screwball' Beurling, the Canadian fighter ace, blacked out during a camera-gun attack on a Wellington, due to the latter's well-timed climbing tactic. He baled out subsequently from a perfectly serviceable Spitfire."

Flt Lt George Beurling DSO DFC DFM and bar RCAF, was Canada's most successful fighter pilot of the war and was best known for having shot down twenty-seven Axis aircraft in fourteen days over Malta in 1942.

Other support units of particular note include a wide range of independent flights providing a number of different facilities including target towing for gunnery training, ferry training, and specialised crew training such as 1429 (Czech) Operational Training Unit/Flight.

One of the most interesting support units was 109 Squadron, formed at Boscombe Down in December 1940 out of the Wireless Intelligence Development Unit for the purpose of developing radar aids and identifying German methods of using radio beams for bomber navigation, which had first been identified in June 1940. In July 1942 109 Squadron split into two independent Special Duties flights. 1473 Flight at Upper Heyford (under the command of Flt Lt George Grant DFC) was based on A Flight (Radio Countermeasures), while 1474 Flight at Stradishall was based on B and C Flights and was primarily focused on German radar wavelength detection. Using a fleet of four or five Wellingtons, their tasks included Window trials, homing flights, and trials relating to the Benito, Ruffian and Knickebein systems which allowed German bombers to home onto their targets using a system of radio beams. They also used their wideband receivers to track Freya and Wurzburg early warning radars and due to the nature of their operations the aircraft were referred to as 'ferrets'.

On the night of 2/3 December 1942 one of 1474 Flight's was operating aircraft in the Frankfurt area on its eighteenth investigation of enemy AI radar, during which it was hoping to attract the attention of a night fighter to check identify its radio and radar frequencies. The Wellington was attacked several times by a Ju 88 whose AI radar transmissions had been picked up by Plt Off Jordan, the Wellington's special operator. Despite being severely wounded several times during the attacks, he was able to check the night fighter's radar frequencies three times to provide excellent intelligence data on the then-new Lichtenstein BC radar. After ten or twelve attacks the night fighter broke off, by which time the Wellington was down to about 500 feet, but the pilot was able to get it back to England where he ditched in the sea just off the Kent coast at Deal.[5]

In April 1943, 1473 Flight, now based at Finmere, Oxfordshire, commenced trials of the Jostle jammer, first used to interrupt German tank communications in North Africa (see Chapter Four), and later employed to great effect by 100 Group to disrupt German radar and night-fighter communications. The two flights later regrouped to form 192 Squadron. Fg Off Alan 'Tommy' Thomsett was a pilot on both 1473 Flight and 192 Squadron:

> "We had a mixture of ICs and IIIs. The main job there was to locate the beams coming out of Holland and France in particular and track them. Then a plot could give an indication of what was likely to happen that night, what the Germans' target might be. How helpful that really worked out to be I don't know but I think it was of some use, and it was quite tricky actually locating it. The other part of the job which I did was to come in with the German bomber stream and check the efficiency of the ground jamming. As their bombers came across the Channel we got a telephone call saying 'there's a radar image of a gang approaching from France, get up there quickly'.
>
> "We tracked them in from our base at Ford, and then we just rushed into the sky at an enormous rate of knots, clambered up there and then followed the beam. I remember it was unreadable at Crawley, but of course from Crawley you could see London so it would only require one incendiary or one flare and then of course they had the target illuminated. Three aircraft went up to Turnhouse for the winter and we did trials of our jamming which meant going way out and gradually climbing up to maximum altitude to check the efficiency of the jamming transmitter which was based in the aircraft. While we were there it merged into 192 Squadron, and that was the beginning of 100 Group."

A single 192 Squadron Wellington was operating on the night of 30/31 March 1944, when Bomber Command lost ninety-four four-engined bombers in a raid on Nuremberg, their biggest ever loss in one attack. Although not directly connected with the raid, the Wellington took off from Ford to investigate the effectiveness of countermeasures against German navigational aids Knickebein 8 and Knickebein 10. The beam was flown on to a point twenty-five miles south of the English coast after which countermeasures became effective and beam-flying was impossible.

One further unit involved in unusual activity against German raids against England was the Fighter Interception Development Squadron (FIDS) based at Ford, Sussex with a variety of aircraft. In late 1944 the Luftwaffe began air-launching V1s from He 111s as the ground launch sites were being over-run by the advancing Allies. FIDS planned to operate an Air-to-Surface Vessel (ASV) Mk.II-equipped Wellington orbiting off the Dutch coast at 4,000 feet to search for any such He 111 coming from the Continent, and send an accompanying Mosquito fighter to attack it. Tried for the first time on 13 January 1945, the radar operator successfully identified a large, slow-moving blip and the Mosquito was directed on to it only to discover it was another Wellington! This was the last time the Germans tried the air-launching method, so the FIDS idea was abandoned before it had a chance to prove itself. The basis of this plan had been work carried out in 1942 at the TFU, during which Wellington Mk.IC R1629 was fitted with a rotating aerial on top of the fuselage in an attempt to aid detection of Fw 200 Condor maritime reconnaissance aircraft, but the work was not pursued at that time.

First prototype high-altitude Mk.V R3298 first flown from Brooklands in late summer 1940. (*Brooklands Museum*)

HIGH ALTITUDE VARIANTS

In response to Operational Requirement OR.94 calling for a bomber capable of operating at a cruising height of 35,000 feet over 2,200 miles, Vickers proposed the Mk.V and Mk.VI variants of the Wellington, around which Specifications B.23/39 and B.17/40 were written. The aircraft were fitted with a pressurised cabin in the forward fuselage and ultimately a 12 feet increase in wingspan. The two variants differed mainly in their powerplants, with the Mk.V having the Hercules Mk.VIII and the Mk.VI the Merlin 60; prototypes of both were built at Vickers' Experimental Section site at Foxwarren, Cobham, a few miles from Weybridge. They first flew in 1940 and 1941 respectively, but a change in air staff policy led to second thoughts about the value of high-flying bombers and consequently only the Mk.VI was ordered into limited production, with sixty-four being built at Weybridge between May 1942 and January 1943 and assembled at Smith's Lawn temporary airfield in Windsor Great Park. Testing at A&AEE Boscombe Down commenced with W5795 but on 12 July 1942 the aircraft dived at high speed from altitude, breaking up before it reached the ground, with the loss of Sqn Ldr Cyril Colmore and his crew. The probable cause was the failure of a propeller blade which penetrated the pressure cabin and hit the pilot. In December 1942, a production Mk.VI DR484 was used to demonstrate its true performance and included a cruising altitude of 34,000 feet (which the aircraft took fifty minutes to reach), an estimated range of 1,100 miles, and a height over the target of 37,100 feet.

The aircraft was operated by a crew of four; pilot, navigator, bomb aimer and wireless operator, all housed in the forward pressure cabin. The need for air gunners was removed as the turrets were to be operated remotely from the cabin and sighted via a periscope. In the event the only service use was with one flight of 109 Squadron which received four aircraft (W5801, W5802, DR480, DR484) as GEE trainers and for Oboe trials in concert with Mk.ICs T2513 and X9678 of the Telecommunications Flying Unit (TFU) Defford, Worcestershire with trials also being flown from Tempsford. The remainder of the Mk.VI fleet was struck off charge and scrapped between March 1943 and August 1944.

CHAPTER FOUR

THE MEDITERRANEAN THEATRE

"The defeat at El Alamein was a turning point in the war...due to the stoppage of supplies from Sicily to Africa...and to the new system of carpet pattern bombing which the already shaken troops could stand no more"
General Maximilian Ritter von Pohl Luftwaffe Commander, central Italy, April 1945

Wellington operations in the Mediterranean theatre can be broken down into three main areas; the entry of Italy into the war and the consequent reinforcement of RAF strength in the region, the bombing campaign against Rommel's Afrika Korps and the campaign against southern European targets and the retreating German forces following the successful invasion of Italy.

When Italy entered the war on 10 June 1940, RAF bomber units located in the region were limited to Bristol Blenheims, Vickers Wellesleys, 216 Squadron equipped with obsolescent Bristol Bombay bomber-transports, and 70 Squadron with even older Vickers Valentias. With an urgent need to provide an improved bombing capability to help counter the Italian threats in

A well-worn 70 Squadron Mk.IC at Kabrit, Egypt autumn 1941. Pilot Guy Sharp is pictured second from left in this photograph. (*Guy Sharp*)

both East and North Africa, in August, 70 Squadron began receiving Wellingtons at Kabrit on the south shore of the Great Bitter Lake in Egypt. To further strengthen the force, 37 and 38 Squadrons were transferred in November from Bomber Command and flew their aircraft out to Luqa, Malta and Ismailia, Egypt respectively. These were not the first Wellingtons in the area though, as 1 GRU had arrived in May with its DWIs to protect Allied shipping lanes and harbours from the threat of mines.

FERRYING THE AIRCRAFT

The first challenge facing the aircrews involved in the transfer of all these aircraft was the ferry flight itself. Initially flights departed from the squadron's home station, but later that changed to a starting point in south-west England, most typically Portreath, Cornwall. The flight immediately involved a long over-water stage across the Bay of Biscay, with the attendant risks of both its inclement weather and roaming German aircraft. Sgt Robert Withers' aircraft DV454 was attacked by two Me 109Fs off Cap Bon on 4 February 1942, but Sgt Garbutt, the rear gunner, successfully saw them off and claimed as probably destroyed. Unfortunately, the Wimpy was destroyed in an air raid on Malta just eleven days later.

The coasts of neutral Portugal and Spain then needed to be avoided before reaching the first possible refuelling stop at Gibraltar. Others would be able to bypass Gibraltar and continue on to Malta in one hop. Jock Richardson noted that his flight took eight hours and five minutes direct from Marham to Luqa. He took off at 00:20 on 29 October 1940 in Mk.IC T2743 and routed over Maidenhead, Berkshire coasted out at Worthing, Sussex, overflying Marseilles and finally the Cap Bon peninsular in north-east Tunisia before reaching the island. Jack's log book simply noted 'Everything OK'.

Mk.IC X9889 BL-D 40 Squadron at Gibraltar en route to its new base at Luqa October 1941, where it was destroyed two months later. (*IWM GM263*)

Plt Off Eric Laithwaite, a navigator on 40 Squadron:

> "I was a sprog navigator engaged upon the task of directing the course of a brand new Wellington from the UK to Gibraltar, en route for Egypt. At the conclusion of training with 15 OTU at Harwell, our crew was issued with 'A' for Apple DV645 [they were now part of 1443 Flight and this aircraft was allocated to 37 Squadron on arrival in

theatre]. On Monday 18 May 1942 Harwell was very anxious to see the back of us, so they pushed us off to Lyneham. We were expecting to have the next day off due to bad weather, but we were surprised to be sent off to Portreath after lunch; a lovely trip down the Cornish coast arriving at 16:00 and told to report the next day at 06:30 for an 08:30 take-off. That morning, with two overload tanks, we staggered off at 06:57 and set course across The Bay. The weather was very dirty and we edged east to try and avoid it, making landfall north east of Coruna. From there down the coast to Gib was a beautiful trip, the colouring of Portugal was absolutely unbelievable. We saw very little, a ship or two and a civilian Whitley. Navigation was not too hot, as little as necessary, but on account of headwinds we landed at Gib in nine hours twenty-five minutes, actually no trouble at all. The other two legs from Gib to Egypt were rather more eventful.

"On Thursday 21 May we were briefed in the morning and rushed off at 3:45 pm. The winds were very favourable and we achieved unbelievable ground speeds. We followed the coast again, but well clear this time until just before dark we attempted to get closer to the coast and get a pinpoint, but Harry, the skipper, did not like the idea. Then we hit La Galite, which we were supposed to avoid – panic – and Harry is found steering for the African coast; we got clear and turned on DR for Malta.

"We saw Cap Bon flashing, then Pantelleria and soon saw searchlights. After two circuits we landed OK with no air raid in progress. The skipper was whisked off on the back of a motorbike to some underground intelligence room, because the enemy had evidently been putting out signals suggesting we were about to land at Pantelleria. We had a hectic briefing by the kite with tea and sandwiches, extra freight and less petrol, then off again after fifty-five minutes on the ground. Soon after take-off the front entrance hatch blew open and half my maps and charts disappeared down the fuselage. Then there was a great concern up front about a bright light ahead which got bigger and brighter, and which turned out to be the morning star!

"We had to be east of 24 degrees east before daylight, and we just made it after a long trip across the Med. We were fired at off the coast north of Benghazi, altered course and used DR then QDMs [the magnetic direction of a navigational aid] from Mersa, after finding the pilot was steering ten degrees out. We hit Mersa and crossed the coast dead on time. Desert flying was not much fun, the distances were very deceptive, and everyone got very tired and fed up. We finally reached the Nile Delta, saw the pyramids at Giza and on to the landing ground where we arrived at 6:30 in the morning. For a crew just out of training it was a great experience and at the end of it we were credited with three ops and twenty-five operational hours, a good start to one's tour."

These testing flights were not without their casualties. For example on 9 December 1940, two Wellingtons were lost after leaving Stradishall headed for Luqa. Fg Off J W Collins in R1246 crashed near Rouen in France with the entire crew being taken prisoner, and Fg Off Cecil Brain DFC in R1250 force landed at Bougie in Algeria after suffering engine failure; he and his crew were interned. Once the route over France was closed and all transit flights were forced to go the long way round to the Mediterranean. Ferry training units were established from 1941 to help prepare aircraft and crews for their long delivery flights, and as the system developed the responsibility for ferrying aircraft transferred from the squadrons to ferry units with crews being attached to these for the duration of their time between England and their final destination. Each crew was allocated an aircraft to deliver which had been prepared with the addition of overload fuel tanks and which may or may not be the aircraft they ended up using in anger. Guy Sharp also flew out from Stradishall:

Flt Lt Guy Sharp and his navigator Ben, 70 Squadron, 1941. (*Guy Sharp*)

> "Six of us left Honington, then went to Stradishall – they had concrete runways there – and took off for Malta on 8 April '41. The only one who didn't arrive was Carton de Wiart who was a passenger with the only officer captain. The bastards sabotaged his 'plane in Malta by putting water in the fuel, both engines cut out and they came down in the sea just short of the African coast, he swam ashore and was taken prisoner – they all were. But as he was the senior man in the prison camp, he was released to negotiate the Italian surrender. He was an incredible-looking man; a lieutenant-general, one arm, one eye; had the Victoria Cross."

Wellington Mk.IC W5677, nominally on the strength of 3 Group Training Flight and piloted by Flt Lt J W Bridger, took off from Luqa for Abu Sueir in Egypt on 9 April 1941 and ditched off Apollonia on the North African coast. This proved not to be the only example of aircraft fuel systems being deliberately contaminated with water. On 3 June 1943 a 70 Squadron crew in Mk.III DF689 captained by Sgt Sykes was returning from a raid on Messina when it suffered engine failure, rear gunner Fg Off Leslie Page noting in his log book:

Incendiaries loaded in a 70 Squadron Wellington 1941. (*Guy Sharp*)

> 'Operational sortie – railway buildings, ferry and marshalling yards – Messina. 7 x 500 lbs, 4 x 250 lbs, 480 lbs incendiaries, Engine failure, crash landed. Petrol watered – sabotage. Landed fifteen miles from base, on nose, 'plane damaged, crew OK.'

Having carried out endurance test flights at Harwell to check fuel consumption, Fg Off Bob Stowers DFM flew Wellington Mk.III HF750 out to North Africa from Portreath in January 1943, first stop Gibraltar.[1] The runway crossed the narrow neck of land which connected Gibraltar to the mainland. Since it was only 1,200 yards long, Bob had to touch down at the extreme end, otherwise risk a dunking at the other. They made a low approach over the water from the Atlantic side, touched down in the first few yards of the runway and pulled up well before the end. They had been eight hours and five minutes in the air, half of those in daylight. Bob stated, "It turned out to be a relaxing flight with no problems." They hung about Gibraltar the following day then, having been briefed for their next flight, they took off before dawn with extra fuel on board and pointed the nose towards Africa.

Fg Off Bob Stowers 70 Squadron, taking off at Kairouan, Tunisia. (*Richard Stowers*)

> "The briefing was a bit of a joke. If we encountered any trouble en route, then it was up to us to find a place to land. They didn't really know what was going on in Africa. We headed south over the Atlas Mountains into the Sahara to avoid the fighting in Tunisia, then turned east towards Libya, Thorn, the rear gunner keeping an eye out for enemy aircraft."

At the right time they transferred fuel by hand pumping from the auxiliary tank to the wing tanks. After ten hours and thirty minutes, they finally lined up and touched down at Benina airfield, inland from Benghazi, and taxied to where other Wellingtons were parked. As the two flights from Portreath to Benina were through hostile airspace, they were considered operational. So fifteen hours and thirty-five minutes were added towards their tour total, although the two flights were combined as one operation. After waiting two days under the hot sun, they flew the short distance to El Magrun and 70 Squadron.

> "The odd thing is, before we left England we were all issued with a revolver and twelve rounds of ammunition. What the hell we would do with that I had no idea."

W/O Geoff Stayton, who completed a tour as a front gunner with 70 Squadron, had a particularly hair-raising arrival in North Africa at the end of his ferry flight. Having left Portreath on 8 January 1942 in brand-new Mk.IC DV419 flown by Sgt Bill Gunning and made a successful arrival in Gibraltar, they then found themselves the subjects of an experiment to extend the ferry range of their aircraft:

"Someone at Ferry Command had a bright idea, why not send the next aircraft for the Middle East direct to Benghazi instead of staging at Malta? We were quite excited by this; as we would be blazing a new trail to Africa and at the same time not have to land at Malta in the middle of a perpetual air raid. So they fitted a long, fat, cylinder down the centre of the aircraft which was to hold our extra fuel, 250 gallons. Our skipper made the take-off of a lifetime. When we ran out of runway he just raised the wheels willy-nilly and kept on flying straight and apparently level because we never hit the sea and kept going.

"Hours later the wing tanks were getting a bit low and it was thought this would be a good time to see if we could get the spare fuel from the inside tank we were carrying into the wing tanks. If any problem arose over the transfer of fuel we would have an hour to decide what to do as we would by then be passing Malta to port. By mutual consent of the rest of the crew this turned out to be my job. I clambered over the main spar and sat down beside the thing with my torch. It was cold down there and dark and rather draughty. There were valves to be opened and closed in the right order. The skipper read out over the intercom from the written instructions he had been given. Then I had to pump the handle backwards and forwards. I pumped for a while. There was no comment from the second pilot who was watching the fuel gauges. I kept pumping. After a bit he said, 'I think the needle's moving skipper'. There was a faint and disembodied 'Thank goodness for that' in a Scots accent, presumably from the rear turret. 'Keep pumping' said the skipper. I kept pumping. There are many things I have forgotten but I have never forgotten that tank and those valves and the pumping and sweating and feeling cold at the same time and being out of breath. Later the navigator reckoned we might not make Benghazi and the skipper went and checked the auxiliary tank for himself and found no more could be squeezed out of it.

WO Geoff Stayton, 70 Squadron front gunner. (*Geoff Stayton*)

"After eleven hours and fifty minutes flying the sun had come up and we were still over the sea and the fuel gauges showed zero. It was quiet with both engines now throttled back so far that we just about hung in the air, slowly losing height. Five minutes later we saw a low coastline ahead with what appeared to be a sandy beach. Bill Gunning did not mess about. He just put the wheels and flaps straight down and drove us onto the beach with assurance born of desperation and we made a surprisingly good, if bumpy, landing on a reasonably hard surface and parallel to the tide line. I would say that this was indeed the landing of a lifetime and airmen sometimes tell these dubious stories about not having to switch off the engines because they just stop – but never, with a straight face to another flyer and expect to be believed – but this did actually happen to us. We had landed. All in one piece. And presumably in Africa.

"It was decided by the skipper that he and I should go inland and see what we could find. We found a track going more or less east and kept on all day. We had no compass but judged our direction reasonably well by the sun. We had no food or water. About four in the afternoon we had been on the go for about thirty-two hours and had just about reached that state of tiredness of body and mind when it becomes easier to keep plodding along than to make a rational decision and I do not think we had yet appreciated that it would soon be dark. Any decision of what we should do, knowing that we seemed not to be getting anywhere, was taken from us when a truck appeared, coming slowly in our direction. When it was about 400 yards away we could see there were two soldiers in it. They had a machine gun mounted on the bonnet and fired two shots over our heads. We put our hands up as we had seen it done on the films, and stood still. We had been shot at. This was where the real war was. My heart, I remember well, was beating very rapidly. As they came up close we could see that they were wearing khaki battle-dress and khaki turbans. They were Sikhs, quite obviously, even to us. We had just been rescued, in fact, by the 4th Indian Division of the 8th Army.

"We found ourselves in Barce, Libya for a week. A main street of tall imposing Italian-looking buildings, undamaged, no water, no electricity, occupied by our army this week, two weeks ago by the German army, and, not that we knew it at that particular moment, soon by them again. The main street of Barce was thick with two lines of army vehicles all heading towards Alexandria. We watched this for a while and gathered there was a retreat going on. This raised the question; do we get a lift and join it or get back to the aircraft (somehow) and burn it (not that it probably would burn, there was no fuel in it). In a temporary traffic jam in the bottleneck of Barce's main street we spotted a small tanker with 'SAAF' [South African Air Force] written on it. There was only the (South African) driver. We asked him if he had any aircraft fuel? 'Certainly,' he said. He had about 200 gallons and would be pleased to be relieved of it. He had come from Benina airfield near Benghazi from where his squadron's own aircraft had long since gone and from where he himself had got away just in time. 'Jerry can't be all that far off', he said. However, he was more than willing to postpone his personal retreat and accepted our story that we had an aircraft thirty miles away on the coast which might be coaxed off the ground. We all got onto the tanker and with more luck than judgement, found it just as we had left it, a slightly incongruous object in that particularly remote setting — and rather extraordinary that a patrolling Jerry fighter hadn't seen it as it was sitting there on the beach presumably visible for miles.

"We could only fill the aircraft tanks on each wing by using a funnel and putting four gallons in at a time from a can. This was slow going and by early afternoon we had only put about 30 gallons in each tank. The two pilots decided, as it would be dark before long, to try to take off as things were, land at Barce and the rest of the crew go back on the tanker. The take-off had to be seen to be believed. Personally, I had rated their chances as nil. But after some fierce revving of the engines to pull itself out of the ruts it had dug for itself in the sand, it was able to be turned round to take off in the opposite direction to which we had landed and then, with about 20 degrees of flap and given full throttle it swayed this way and that way, hit bumps, bounced violently several times, and quite incredulously became airborne.

"We met up again on Barce and the next morning we got off the ground and headed easterly for Cairo via Mersa Matruh. We landed, taxied to where there was another Wellington parked and got out. Our Wellington had been delivered. We had become quite fond of it and looked upon it as our own and flown it about 3,500 miles in twenty-eight-and-a-half hours spread over twenty-four days. It was still in one piece, still as good as new. We felt quite proud of ourselves. We found somebody. The skipper said that we had just brought this aircraft from England and here was the log book. 'Right, mate,' he said, 'I'll take that.' And that was that."

DV419 was to have a short operational life. Issued to 38 Squadron, it went missing during an anti-shipping sweep off Salamis on 5 April, exactly two months after arriving in Egypt with the loss of Plt Off Reginald Langley and crew. Four days later, Geoff Stayton flew his first operation with 70 Squadron, to Benghazi.

MINESWEEPING

Movement of 1 GRU (which had absorbed similarly-equipped 2 GRU) commenced on 20 May 1940 and the aircraft flew in groups of two or three, making refuelling stops at Luqa and Mersa Matruh before all safely reaching their new base at Ismailia three days later. In view of the local conditions, it was considered necessary to equip the aircraft with additional generator oil coolers which delayed the start of operations, and in this they were aided by 38 Squadron aircrew who had recently flown out from England and were awaiting the arrival of their ground crew by sea. Local flying finally commenced on 13 June 1940 and the first sweep of Alexandria harbour took

DWI L4356 flew the sweep of Ijmuiden harbour on 9 May 1940. It is seen here with 1 GRU at Ismailia in Egypt. (*ww2images*)

place the following day at a height of 40-50 feet. Trials were also carried out to ascertain the optimum method of sweeping the Suez Canal and it was decided that, although all eighty-seven miles could effectively be swept by a single aircraft, two operating a few miles apart would be more effective.

In January 1941 four aircraft were detached to Capuzzo in Libya to concentrate on sweeping the approaches to Tobruk harbour, but were recalled after a few days due to an urgent need to sweep the Suez Canal following an enemy mining operation. The canal was swept on 1 February and on the first sortie that morning two mines were exploded, the ORB stating: 'Judging by the bump and slight concussion effect they were not large mines.' Later that day, the ORB also recorded a spectacular success proving the value of the DWI:

A DWI of 1 GRU over Tripoli harbour. Its position is too high to be mine-sweeping. (*Brooklands Museum*)

'Then took place one of the greatest moments in the annals of the proud history of this unit. The large liner *Dominion Monarch*, filling the canal with its bulk of over 25,000 tons, proceeded slowly, gropingly, as if feeling its way through dangerous waters, down towards Great Bitter Lake. Both aircraft were sweeping up and down in front of her. Flt Lt Butler in aircraft L7771 was on a return sweep heading towards the ship. At a speed of 130 mph and 50 feet above the water the aircraft swept as near as possible to the oncoming ship. Just when the pilot was pulling his stick back to clear the ship's masts there was a violent explosion. The aircraft took a severe bump, the DWI opera-

> tor being knocked off his seat. A large mine had exploded in front of the very bows of the *Dominion Monarch*. But the ship was safe, the canal was saved. One of the Canal Company later told this unit that if the ship had sunk at that place, the canal would have been closed for three months.'

On 9 February 1943 the unit suffered its only aircraft loss, when P2518 had an engine failure while sweeping. The pilot had to belly-land immediately since it was known that a DWI on one engine could only remain airborne as long as its forward inertia lasted! Although the aircraft could not be salvaged due to the soft ground, sections of the solenoid ring were saved. Routine sweeping of the Suez Canal continued unabated for the remainder of 1 GRU's existence, intermingled with repeated deployments to sweep Tobruk harbour as the land battle ebbed and flowed along the North African coast, despite periodic negative comments from the Admiralty to the effect that their own minesweepers could do a better job. The unit was finally disbanded in March 1944, the surviving aircraft being struck off charge in situ during July.

70 Squadron bombing up in the Western Desert. (*Richard Stowers*)

EARLY BOMBING OPERATIONS

The newly-arrived Wellington bombers lost no time in starting operations with the main focus of attention being the Italian army which had invaded Egypt on 10 September 1940 from its bases in Libya, with their supporting airfields and supply ports also coming in for a lot of attention. The first night attack was flown on 19 September by 70 Squadron against the port of Benghazi. At the end of October Jock Richardson arrived for what he thought was a short stay:

> "They asked for volunteers to go out for a month to Malta, because they wanted to hit the Germans and the Italians where we couldn't bomb them from England. It was all meant to be hush-hush, but when we got there we found we were stuck there. Then we joined 148 Squadron."

The naval base at Naples was home to much of the Italian fleet; Jock flew there twice during December, his pilot, Plt Off Day, recording a direct hit on the jetty and a battleship on the 14th, and making three attempts at 5,000 feet, before hitting the dockside on the 29th. He tried again on 8 January 1941 but the target was under 10/10ths cloud so they flew to Palermo and attacked cruisers in the dock, and one further time on the 14th 'no results being seen except two small fires and a red lava stream down the side of Mount Vesuvius'!

> "At Naples the flak was terrible, hellish, coming up from the ships and the shore. We were getting it from three sides; it wasn't all that accurate. They were like strings of different-coloured onions – we called them 'flaming onions'. You could see them – though that didn't help you much because they still hit you! On 20 December we attacked the enemy aerodrome at Castel Benito at 200 feet. The Italians had their aircraft laid out, they didn't bother, and you could go down to low level and machine gun them all the way along. It was very good, quite exciting.
>
> "In January we went for the power station, customs houses and oil farm in Tripoli. That was a great big installation, you couldn't miss it because it was right next to the desert. We dive bombed at 310 mph to 1,000 feet over the town, missed the power station, and hit stores and the railway. On the 15th we went to Catania aerodrome. That was the place we hated; it was the place where the Germans gave us trouble. First of all it was just the Italians; we didn't worry much about the Italians, their fighters used to come up and wave their wings at you; not the Germans however!"

On 28 January 1941 Jock was injured at Luqa by a bomb dropped from a Ju 87 Stuka. In June, following his recovery, he joined 70 OTU to convert to the Blenheim prior to joining 211 Squadron. Another lair for elements of the Italian fleet was in Albania. Having only recently converted from the Valentia, Sqn Ldr Clive Stanbury (later group captain DSO DFC) flew to the port of Valona with 70 Squadron on 7 November 1940 as second pilot to Wg Cdr Webb, when the Wellingtons encountered determined opposition from Italian fighters and recorded the encounter in his log book:

> 'Daylight raid on Valona, carrying 10 x 150 lb and 8 x 120 lb bombs. Brian and Brooks shot down.'

Flt Lt Alan Brian in T2731 and Sgt George Brooks in T2734 were both shot down by Fiat CR.42s. The only crew members to escape were Brian's second pilot Plt Off G Rawlings and his WOp/AG Sgt W Mitchell, both of whom were taken prisoner.

For a few weeks the Wellingtons arriving in Malta were pressed into immediate operations from Luqa under the title of Wellington Attachment (also referred to as Wellington Flight). Among the aircraft operated by this unit was T2743, the same one that Jock Richardson had flown out to the island on 29 October 1940. On 1 November Jock flew this aircraft on a fruitless operation to Naples which was totally obscured by cloud. Two days later it was lost when it failed to gain height after take-off and hit the ground at Tal-Handaq. The pilot on that occasion was Sgt R M Lewin who, despite being injured, managed to drag his unconscious second pilot, Plt Off David Allen, clear before the bomb load exploded; sadly Allen, who was a member of the yet to re-form 148 Squadron, did not survive. An almost identical fate befell another Wellington Attachment aircraft. Mk.IC R1094 failed to gain height after take-off and hit houses at Qormi, killing Sgt Philip Forrester and the rest of his 148 Squadron crew with the exception of WOp/AG Sgt D Palmer.

Worse was to come for Wellingtons on the island following the reforming of 148 Squadron there on 1 December 1940. Italian and German air forces were starting to hit Malta hard and on 25 February 1941 they succeeded in destroying seven Wellingtons on the ground at Luqa, one from 70 Squadron and no fewer than six from 148 Squadron. John Leeuwin-Clark was a RAAF pilot on the squadron:

> "During 1941 Malta was subjected to relentless bombing. In April 148 Squadron based in Egypt sent a detachment of its Wimpys to Luqa. The plan involved each Wimpy flying three raids per night on Comiso aerodrome in Sicily with a view to neutralising the German attacks on Malta. On the night of 23 April I and my crew were briefed to bomb Comiso using fragmentation bombs. As we flew north over the Mediterranean towards Sicily we ran into cloud when, unbeknown to us, we crossed the Sicilian coast and were approaching Comiso without taking any evasive action. As the cloud started to clear we could see black puffs of smoke – we were in the middle of a box barrage – the flak was bursting all around us and getting close. The Germans had obviously picked us up as we crossed the coast and now had a good fix on our position.
>
> "Flak was now bursting perilously close. I asked the navigator for our position and he said we were over the aerodrome. Anxious lest a hit in the bomb bay might set off the fragmentation bombs, I opened the bomb doors and pulled the jettison toggle. No sooner had the bombs gone when a shell exploded on the starboard side of the Wimpy's nose. The aircraft shook, the cockpit filled with a strong smell of cordite and all the instruments ceased to function with the exception of the compass. The trip back to Malta was uneventful, the Pegasus XVIII engines didn't miss a beat, there was no apparent structural damage apart from numerous shrapnel holes and fortunately there was no cloud, so a landing in the dark without instruments was not a problem.
>
> "The next morning after a sleep, the crew went out to Luqa and oh! What a sorry sight! The Wimpy had been peppered with shrapnel, and so extensive was the damage that repairs would not have been justified. Our beloved Wimpy became another addition to an already crowded aircraft graveyard at Luqa."

Following his arrival in Egypt, Guy Sharp joined 70 Squadron:

> "I think it was Derna on one of our raids, there was low cloud so we had to be underneath it. All these searchlights came up, just like daylight it was. We were down at 2,000 feet and we had machine-gun bullets going into the bomb bay, which cut the leads to the Mickey Mouse [a bombing panel consisting of a clockwork distributor, so named because it was like a cheap Mickey Mouse watch] which was clockwork; so the bombs were released on top of ones that weren't released. We'd lost our hydraulics too, and we landed at Fuka, the satellite aerodrome. We got away again and we had the wheels down but of course we couldn't open the bomb doors, and then one engine packed up, so we managed to do a flapless landing at Heliopolis which was very nice, for a three-day holiday. They didn't realise there was a war on there, and when they found we had bombs on board, we were made to taxi to the far end and they eventually managed to lower them.

"There was a much nearer do when it was the only time we decided we wanted to give the gunners some practice; they were getting fed up with not doing anything. So went out below 2,000 feet and found machine-gun convoys going along. Of course their machine guns were much better than ours, and I was in the astrodome looking out to see if there were any fighters about. Then I don't know how many hundreds of incendiary bullets just missed us by inches; so we never did that again.

"We saw Bombays [216 Squadron] dropping off the first Long Range Desert Patrol and paratroopers; they were all training at Kabrit where we were. On some of our trips we dropped 50,000 lbs of ammo from the bomb bay. When it came to leaflet raids, the silly arses had put a hole in the fuselage that was too small for the bundles, we tried for about twenty minutes but couldn't get them out."

All was changing dramatically since in March 1941 Hitler had sent a small Panzer force under the command of one General Erwin Rommel, to support the faltering Italian campaign and the Luftwaffe bomber and fighter units in the region had been greatly strengthened. This was the beginning of what would grow into the Afrika Korps campaign and lead to bitter fighting to and fro across the desert lasting well over two years until the successful conclusion of Operation Husky, the Allied invasion of Sicily in July 1943.

A further complication for British forces came in May 1941 when a coup by pro-Nazi sympathisers in Iraq led to a direct threat to oil supplies. The RAF station at Habbaniya was surrounded by Iraqi troops and the response included detaching Wellingtons of 37 and 70 Squadrons to the second British base in the country at Shaibah, from where attacks were made against the troops surrounding Habbaniya, various Iraqi barracks and the airport at Baghdad. The emergency was brought to an end before the month was out.

THE WESTERN DESERT

As far as the overall RAF organisation in the area was concerned, an early change was made to the control structure for bomber operations with the formation of 205 (Heavy Bomber) Group at Shallufa, just north of Suez on 23 October 1941. This group had all the Wellington bomber squadrons under its command right through to the end of the war, by which time its headquarters had moved to Foggia Main in Italy.

As Rommel's desert campaign developed, bombing operations quickly became very fluid, with a need to react quickly to changing fortunes as the front line could and did move rapidly both eastwards and westwards over the coming months. In addition to attacking front-line areas, other major targets included the cities of Tobruk (Geoff Stayton attacked Tobruk no fewer than eight times in fourteen nights in August 1942) and Benghazi, with raids on the latter becoming so frequent that they became known as the 'mail run' as exemplified in a 70 Squadron drinking song (to the tune of 'Clementine'):

'Down the flights each ruddy morning
Sitting waiting for a clue
Same old notice on the flightboard
Maximum effort – guess where to
Though we say it with a sigh

We must do the ruddy mail run
Every night until we die'

A pilot on 70 Squadron, Plt Off Gordon Orchard, completed thirty-seven ops during which he had a few close encounters with the Luftwaffe, including on one occasion over Tobruk:

"The whole crew were looking down at the 'fireworks' after we had dropped the bombs. I glanced up only to see a rather large wing of another aircraft directly above me. This one had a big black cross on it, though. I yelled at the front gunner just as the enemy pilot spotted me. We were close enough and lit up enough due to the 'fireworks', for me and the German pilot to actually see each other. The Luftwaffe pilot banked sharply away, too late for the front gunner to train his guns.

"In June 1942 the squadron had been bombed by He 111s and were lucky enough to have shot one down. I got a souvenir of a small part of the aileron fabric, clearly showing the green paint (mainland Europe camouflage) on the upper surface. I wrote on it, 'Fabric taken from the aileron of a He 111K shot down by AA, LG 60, June 1942'."

The intense activity necessitated the extensive use of desert landing grounds (LG) by squadrons in order to keep in reasonably close touch with their prospective targets to enable raids to be mounted in short order; although it also increased the risk of attacks from the air.

Mk.IC Z8787 J of 37 Squadron at Landing Ground 60, 20 miles south of Qasaba, Egypt 1941. It survived a further year in service. (*via Richard Forder*)

OPERATING CONDITIONS

Living conditions in the desert were basic and challenging for both air and ground crew as Bob Stowers recalled:

"It was pretty grim. The conditions were almost as bad as the ops themselves. We went from the comforts of England straight into tents out in the sand. Beds were made from bomb fin cases, planks or whatever else men could scavenge on the airfield. Parachutes

> served as pillows and flying jackets became the blankets. Every time you went to get a meal it would be covered in flies, you couldn't get away from them. We each got a gallon of water a day. That was for everything – drinking, shaving and washing. There was never enough; we soon learnt to bathe with a drinking mug of water! My crew kept together. We ate, slept and flew together. We went off camp together, we drank together. I felt sorry for the ground crew. They had to work inside the aircraft in the heat of the day when the outside temperature must have been 120 degrees Fahrenheit. It must have been stifling inside the fuselage."

The effect of not just enemy action but high temperatures and sandy or dusty conditions proved quite a challenge to the serviceability of the aircraft. The repair and servicing capabilities at squadron level were generally minimal, especially when away from major stations and operating from LGs. H A Jones was a WOp/AG with 38 Squadron:

> "We flew a Wellington from Malta to Cairo towards the end of October 1941. That was the routine when the aircraft had reached the number of flying hours that required a level of service beyond the capacity of the ground staff at Malta. I note from my log book that we landed wheels up at Heliopolis so it would appear to have been a wasted effort."

Winston Churchill at 70 Squadron Abu Sueir 22 August 1942. On his left, ACM Tedder AOC-in-C Middle East and behind him, General Alanbrooke. (*Lyn Skells*)

One slight advantage of the North African terrain was the ability to put a disabled aircraft down almost anywhere with a reasonable chance that both it, and more importantly the crew, would stay in one piece. Sgt Withers flew a tour with 37 Squadron and his log book for 9 July 1942 flying Wellington IC DV457 contains a fascinating story to illustrate this point:

> 'Abu Sueir – operational bombing on Tobruk. Heavy and light flak, visibility good but dark. Flares dropped. Load 4 x 500, 1 x 250. Encountered low cloud in base area at 200 feet. Force landed at 29° 45' N 29° 15' E shortage of fuel. Aircraft slightly damaged. Sent nine SOS messages. Rescued by 216 Squadron Bombay 35 hours later. All crew OK.'

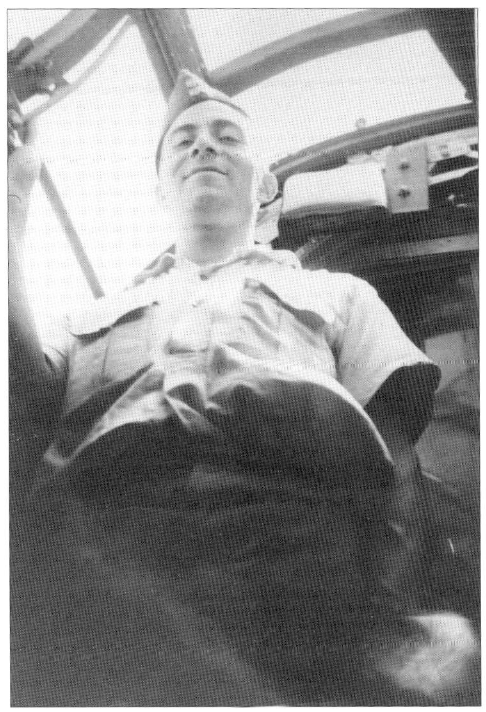

Bob Withers in a Wellington.
(*Graham Withers*)

Thus on 11 July 1942, Bombay L5831 piloted by Flt Lt Douglas Ruston (later DFC) duly arrived to pick up the crew from behind enemy lines and return them safely to Abu Sueir, leaving a salvage team to repair the Wimpy. The Bombay pilot later sent a letter to Sgt Withers congratulating him on a successful landing, which had enabled the salvage team to repair the aircraft in less than four hours and fly it out. They were also able to find three other Wellingtons in similar circumstances within a few days of this one. Sadly, however, DV457 would only fly on until the night of 7/8 September 1942 when, flown by Sgt Henry Shepherd RNZAF, it flew into a hill at Gebel Abu Shama in Egypt on its way back from a raid on Tobruk, killing the second pilot and one of the gunners. Shepherd later moved to 40 Squadron before losing his life just over a year later in September 1943.

Bob Withers with 216 rescue.
(*Graham Withers*)

Clive Stanbury of 70 Squadron was awarded his DSO that same year for another daring rescue of a downed Wellington when he was a flight commander. On the night of 27/28 May 1942 Mk.IC Z8787 lost its port propeller while being flown by Sgt L Holliday during an operation against Benghazi, leading to a belly-landing in the desert which tore away large sections of the lower fuselage. With a team of volunteers, Stanbury loaded a captured German lorry with a new propeller and replacement undercarriage parts and drove 200 miles behind enemy lines to find the Wellington. Having carried out emergency repairs sufficient to get away, he then successfully took off just as enemy troops were approaching and flew the aircraft back to LG 104 Qotafiyah II.

The previous November Stanbury had flown an operation to locate a crew who had baled out of their 38 Squadron Wimpy and drop food and water to them. Sgt Swingler RCAF and his crew had become lost and ran out of fuel; they were fortunate to be spotted and picked up after two days. The desert was indeed a vast and unforgiving place for any lost crew to find themselves in.

Sqn Ldr Clive Stanbury DSO DFC, 70 Squadron. (*Sally-Anne Barrett*)

'FISHINGTONS' AND 'STICKLEBACKS' OPERATIONS AGAINST AXIS CONVOYS

While tremendous work was being put into harassing the Afrika Korps in the desert and in their reward bases such as Tobruk, it was essential to do everything possible to disrupt the supply convoys upon which they relied for almost everything, especially fuel and ammunition. In 1941 torpedo bombing capability in the region mainly rested with the Bristol Beauforts flown by 69 Squadron from Malta, to be joined later by 39 Squadron. The Beaufort was able to carry a single 18-inch torpedo and it was recognised that a type with greater load carrying and range performance was urgently needed.

In December 1941 the Torpedo Development Unit at Gosport, Hampshire began trials with a Wellington Mk.IC modified to carry two Mk.XII 18-inch torpedoes enclosed within the bomb bay. Initial trials were disappointing, with torpedoes routinely diving to the sea bed on release, and the problem was traced to the horizontal surfaces of the triangular tail intended to guide the torpedo in the air and which were not being released on entry into the water. A hinged tail had the problem solved by March and the aircraft cleared for torpedo operations; later in the year

clearance for 'stick dropping' of both

221 Squadron 'Stickleback' JA270 S makes the unit's first trip to Grottaglie, Italy 1943. Geoff

Cook is pictured leaning on prop. (*G Cook-M Chandler collection*)

torpedoes was also achieved, thus considerably improving the chances of hitting the target ship.

Accordingly in January 1942, 38 Squadron at Shallufa became part of 201 Group and commenced training for a new anti-shipping role involving both minelaying (as Plt Off Knowles' loss described earlier) and torpedo bombing against Rommel's convoys, which would remain its primary task until late in 1942 when attention switched to the Balkans and shipping off the Italian coast. The torpedo-carrying Wellingtons were Mk.ICs and later Mk.VIIIs and were universally known as 'Fishingtons' (some crews also referred to them as 'Torpingtons'). R Oliver was a WOp/AG on the squadron:

> "Based at Shallufa, Egypt 38 Squadron was actively engaged in both high and low-level minelaying. The need arose for a night-operating torpedo aircraft to attack Rommel's supply convoys. 38 Squadron pilots were familiar with low-level flying over the sea at night, so they were assigned this task. After some trial and error the aircraft were modified. The front turret was removed and a rounded fairing fitted in its place. The regular bomb carriers were removed from the bomb bay and two tubular booms fitted to carry two torpedoes. To get the torpedo to enter the water at the correct angle, wood and canvas airfoils were clipped to the elevators and rudder of the torpedo; these broke away on entry into the water. Because of the size of these airfoils the bomb-bay doors were cut away at the rear, creating a distinctive 'V' cut-out in the belly of the aircraft. By these means the two torpedoes were enclosed within the bomb bay. A sight was developed to fit on top of the nose in front of the pilot. A curved tube had small electric lamps fitted at set intervals along the tube. They were painted black with a small opening of clear glass facing the pilot. Pilots and crews under the supervision of Fleet Air Arm instructors, practised drops in Suez Bay using the yacht *HMS Sagittarius* and the monitor *HMS Roberts* as targets.
>
> "For an op against a convoy an ASV Liberator [or Wellington] would shadow it and

A 38 Squadron 'Fishington' loading 18-inch torpedoes at Luqa, Malta. (*ww2images*)

transmit a homing signal which the Wellingtons homed on to. Generally half the aircraft carried two 1,000 lb bombs and half torpedoes. The bombing aircraft would bomb in turn at defined times to draw the flak. The torpedo aircraft would attempt to line up a ship in the moon's path and attack as the bombing aircraft distracted the flak."

The first torpedo attack was attempted on the night of 22/23 February 1942 to intercept a convoy attempting to reach Tripoli. Six bombing Wellingtons accompanied two torpedo carriers (a third being unserviceable), but the convoy was sighted only by a single bombing aircraft and the torpedoes were carried home. After a number of aborted operations, the squadron tried again on the night of 9/10 March and Wg Cdr John Chaplin DFC (previously involved with the DWI) flying Z9099, was attacked by two Bf 109s. Unable to manoeuvre to the usual extent due to the two torpedoes on board, the aircraft was badly damaged and crash landed in the desert. Second pilot Plt Off John Lister and navigator Fg Off Basil Fryer died in the landing, and the remaining four crew members (including a torpedo fitter) were picked up by officers of the 4th Indian Division and returned to the Allied lines.

On the night of 27/28 March 1942, the squadron finally undertook their first torpedo attack against shipping off the port of Patras. Locating a single 8,000-ton cargo vessel, Sqn Ldr John Gilliard in AD597 attacked first, releasing a torpedo at a range of 1,000 yards, but no results were seen. Plt Off John Swingler in Z8983 then released at a range of 500 yards, hitting the ship just aft of the smoke-stack and causing a large flash. However, observations over the area an hour after the attack failed to locate the ship, but it was uncertain whether it had been sunk or not.

From the outset of torpedo operations 38 Squadron were able to make use of the shipping search capabilities of the Wellington Mk.VIII equipped with ASV Mk.I radar. These aircraft were widely referred to as 'Sticklebacks' due to the four very large pole-type radar aerials mounted

'Stickleback' Mk.XIII JA416 L of 221 Squadron over Malta 3 January 1944. Transferred to Armée de l'Air 9 May 1946. (*G Cook-M Chandler collection*)

Mk.VIII W5731 R of 221 Squadron somewhere in North Africa. Transferred to SEAC, it caught fire on start-up at Mauripur and was burnt-out. (*SAAF Museum*)

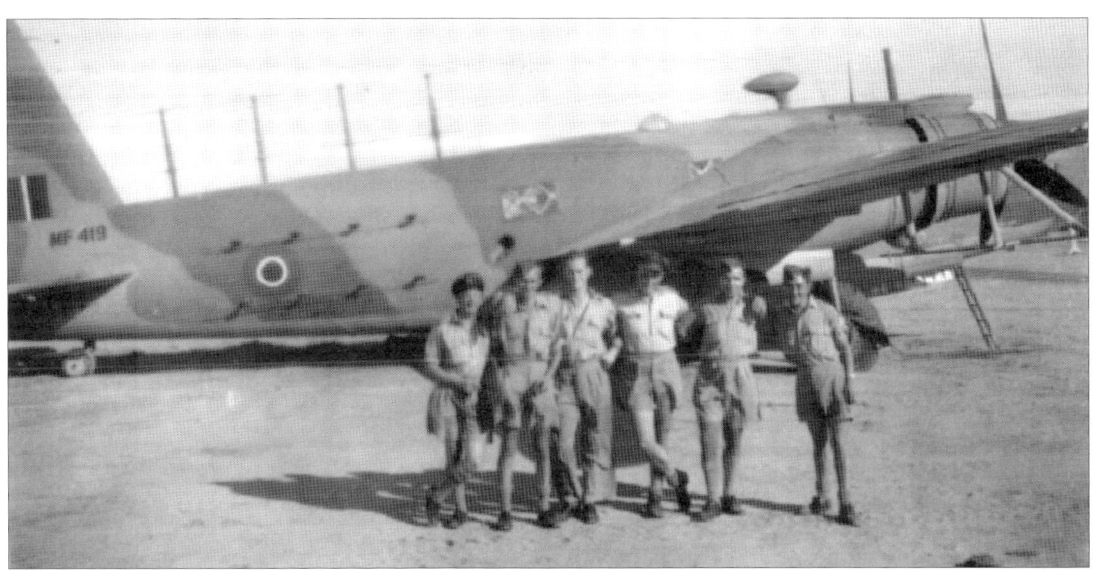

Desert-camouflaged 221 Squadron Mk.XIII MF419 with Bash, Roy, WO Peter Ayers-Hunt pilot, Neil Ogilvy RCAF pilot, Bob and Des. (*221 Squadron Association*)

above the rear fuselage, and due to the nature of their work they were also known as 'Goofingtons'. The use of this radar had been pioneered by 221 Squadron at Bircham Newton in January 1941 using modified Mk.IC aircraft as described in Chapter Five. In January 1942 the squadron flew sixteen 'Sticklebacks' out to the Middle East from Portreath via Gibraltar to Luqa. All painted in the white Coastal Command scheme, they were very unpopular at Malta as they presented an easy target on the ground and, most if not all, were repainted in night-bomber camouflage, although at least one is known to have been in the standard desert scheme. They initially operated from LG 39 (Burgh el Arab South) south west of Alexandria, borrowing ground crew from

47 Squadron while their own were travelling from Liverpool aboard *HMT Otranto*.

By February 1942 they had moved to LG 87 a little further to the east and were flying intensive anti-shipping patrols and on 26 April had their first success when Flt Sgt Nixon located and attacked an enemy convoy. The unit frequently operated in conjunction with 38 Squadron and others, to enable an increasing pace of night anti-shipping strikes. A typical operation would find the ASV aircraft locating the target and passing position information on to the attacking force, on the approach of which they would then illuminate the shipping by means of flares if necessary. From January 1943, 221 Squadron acquired its own 'Fishingtons', while 38 Squadron added its own 'Goofingtons'.

Former 221 Squadron CO Wg Cdr Thomas Vickers DSO wrote an excellent account of the unit's activity at this time[2]:

> 'At first we met with little success. The ships were there, we found and reported them, but the practice of night torpedo attacks on shipping was in its infancy, and no satisfactory method had been evolved. Slowly plans were made, theories put into practice and improved and by September some encouraging results were achieved with 38 Squadron and various others, all engaged on the task of hitting Rommel's supplies by sea. Our main trouble at this time was technical. The operating conditions in the heat and sand were really cruel on engines. The normal life per engine was sixty to seventy hours, before excessive oil consumption forced an engine change. Aircrews were taking up with them as many as six four-gallon tins of oil to recharge the auxiliary oil tank. Often three gallons per hour or more had to be pumped into each engine tank, and many were the blisters from pumping ninety strokes per gallon, six gallons per hour, during the course of nine and ten-hour trips. Sticky valves were also a bugbear, and how often the symptoms entirely disappeared on the ground, so that it was difficult to convince the ground crews that anything was wrong!
>
> 'In the month before the battle at El Alamein we were kept extremely busy and in spite of German attempts to jam the radar, the joint efforts of all the anti-shipping squadrons really stopped the enemy's sea-borne supplies. It was said that every attempt to run a tanker through to the Afrika Korps in the three or four weeks before Alamein, was frustrated. By the time the 8th Army had won their magnificent victory, Rommel had no fuel to either fight or retreat.'

A typical combined operation took place on the night of 25/26 May 1942, when the operation was to attack a convoy north west of Benghazi. The action by two torpedo carriers – Sgt Youens in DV542 and Sgt Flanagan in AD597 – is described in 38 Squadron's ORB:

> 'At 01:30 hours Sgt Youens in aircraft "A" received a revised position for the convoy from ASV aircraft. He set course, repeatedly checking by bearings on the ASV aircraft. At 02:15 he sighted the convoy consisting of two destroyers and two MVs, one large about 8/10,000 tons and the other 2/3,000 tons. The convoy was in echelon 1,200 yards apart with the destroyers on the flanks. He attacked the large MV, approaching past the stern of the starboard destroyer. The destroyer opened fire with 12/14 Bofors-type

> guns, hitting the aircraft and causing damage. As the aircraft came round to the north east of the convoy, Sgt Youens saw smoke screens beginning centring on the target ship. He could not see whether there was smoke coming from the stack or whether it was the result of a hit. Accurate observation was not possible due to preoccupation with intense flak.
>
> 'The ASV aircraft reported that clouds of smoke were pouring from the ship and the next day a reconnaissance aircraft reported a large MV beached some thirty miles north of Benghazi with a gaping hole in its side. It is therefore claimed that Sgt Youens hit the ship.'

The Wellington had suffered considerable damage to the starboard wing and fuselage and the port engine but succeeded in reaching LG 05. Sgt William Youens was awarded the DFM for this action. On 21 August that year Sgt Harry Clark had confirmed success against a submarine he found on the surface while escorting *HMS Coventry*, part of the Robertsbridge convoy; he was awarded the DFM for this action:

> "Sgt Clark ran in to attack at a height of about 20 feet. He dropped a stick of six depth charges, one of which hit the deck of the submarine abaft the conning tower, the others dropping to port and starboard of the stern. The stern was blown out of the water and the submarine slid under. She soon surfaced and attacked the aircraft with her guns. Sgt Clark ordered fire from his front and rear turrets and side guns and silenced the submarine's fire. She continued on the surface circling as if out of control and sinking perceptibly lower in the water. At 07:10 she sank quietly, i.e. not at a diving angle but horizontally."

The strain on the aircrew of continued lengthy searches and the aircraft's vulnerability during attacks certainly took its toll. In 1944 one of W/O Peter Ayers-Hunt's crew lost his nerve and could not face going on another trip. The crew were clearly very tight-knit as they got him extremely drunk and ensured that he finished his tour (as it was so shameful for an airman to lose his nerve), by which time he had gone from having dark hair to white. The same crew found themselves flying alongside a German aircraft on one occasion; they saw each other and both turned away for home.

BOMBING OPERATIONS EXPAND

Bombing became ever more in demand as the land campaign swung to and fro, and crews found themselves flying hard with little chance of much rest in between ops. Fg Off William Slack, 70 Squadron:

> "Benghazi was our first op with our new 'plane, Wellington IC T2842. This took us everywhere until we were taken off ops as 'time expired' and posted home. Another trip to Benghazi, then a very interesting trip was our next one. The instructions were very simple:
>
> 'You will take off at a time to be decided. You will be one aircraft on the raid.
> You will make as much noise as you can. Do as little damage as possible. Single

bombs would be appreciated but hit nothing that may endanger life. Keep clear of the following buildings. Your target – Beirut. Fly round until you see your

End of tour beat-up by a 70 Squadron crew. (*Sally-Anne Barrett*)

relief then come home."

"Trip number 13, unlucky for some, but Benghazi again. The harbour, as usual, was the target. From base back to base I noted a flying time of nine hours twenty minutes; doesn't time fly when you are flying? Two days later we were off to Eleusis, a round trip of eleven hours five minutes and a notable trip for me for it brought my operational flying past the magic 100 hours. A further two trips to Benghazi before getting a short run to Bardia. Another two trips to Benghazi took our total ops for the month of July 1941 to eight for a total of seventy-two hours thirty minutes, not bad going. Benghazi for another two trips then a great change: the Corinth Canal, decoys for Shallufa. The instructions were as follows:

> 'Distraction is the name of the game. The other boys will be down below you dropping mines in the canal. You will keep the Germans busy while 37 Squadron do their stuff.'

"Talk about fun and games. You have no idea until you fly with the RAF and get paid for it. Back to, yes – you know again – Benghazi and 206 hours ten minutes serious flying."

As can be seen, operations against Benghazi became more frequent and often very costly during 1941 and 1942, involving both bombing and minelaying; in the words of the 70 Squadron song (sung to the tune of 'Lily Marlene'):

'There's a certain squadron way out in the blue
Don't need anybody telling them what to do
They bomb Benghazi every night
and if they don't they all get tight
The boys who bomb Benghazi

Damaged by a CR.42, Mk.IC T2838 U of 148 Squadron made it back to a crash landing at Luqa, Malta 7 December 1940. (*Dave Underwood*)

The boys who bomb Benghazi'

On the night of 1/2 November 1941, 148 Squadron was once again on the receiving end of bad luck, writing off five aircraft which were forced to crash land in the desert, out of fuel due to their base at LG 104 Qotafiyah II west of Daba being fog bound; fortunately without loss of life. On 16 February 1942, 38 Squadron carried out a most interesting operation to drop dummy mines in the harbour, clearly intended to divert German resources onto a fruitless minesweeping exercise. Five aircraft were involved, operating from LG 09 Bir Koraiyim and all returned safely, while aircraft from other squadrons carried out diversionary attacks on the town. A further raid on the 25th, this time with live mines, proved costly, as one Wellington failed to return; the ORB recording:

> 'Four aircraft of the five which operated on the night of 24/25 returned to Shallufa safely. Aircraft "R" Z9108 Plt Off Knowles and crew did not return to LG 09. Upon investigation it was established that radio contact had been made with the aircraft as follows:
> 01:47 "R" called Malta and passed on a message for Mersa Matruh – 5 [message] groups unknown
> 01:55 Malta called "R" – "Mersa Matruh wants you to check". "R" answered "I will call you later".
> 02:34 "R" called Qotafiyah – "Please send your calls".
> 02:38 Qotafiyah did not answer but Kabrit called "R" and got no reply
> 03:30 SOS heard by Agir from unknown aircraft – bearing 270° – 3rd class.
> A search was organised by Sqn Ldr Mills of 231 Wing [part of 205 Group] between El Daba and Mersa Matruh but proved unsuccessful.'

The following day an army unit reported that two of the crew were safe at El Adem and the remaining four were uninjured and sleeping in the aircraft; eventually the crew were able to return to the squadron and report. The aircraft had been hit by ground fire and the two mines it was carrying were jettisoned. Knowles had been hit in the leg and only had altimeter and compass indications and, after two hours flying, it became more difficult to control the aircraft in the bumpy conditions so the order was given to bale out. Front gunner Sgt A White, second pilot Sgt E Hammett and WOp Flt Sgt Docherty abandoned the aircraft and the following morning White and Hammett found each other and searched for the aircraft. They were picked up by an army convoy late in the morning and eventually returned to Shallufa on 2 March 1942, Docherty being picked up separately. On 3 March the squadron received a letter from 121 Maintenance Unit in Tobruk, reporting the finding of Plt Off Eric Knowles outside the aircraft and the remains of two other bodies inside it on 26 February by a padre who had been taken to the scene by an Arab. The padre buried Knowles, navigator Sgt Kenneth Bevan and rear gunner Sgt Alan Durie at the site.

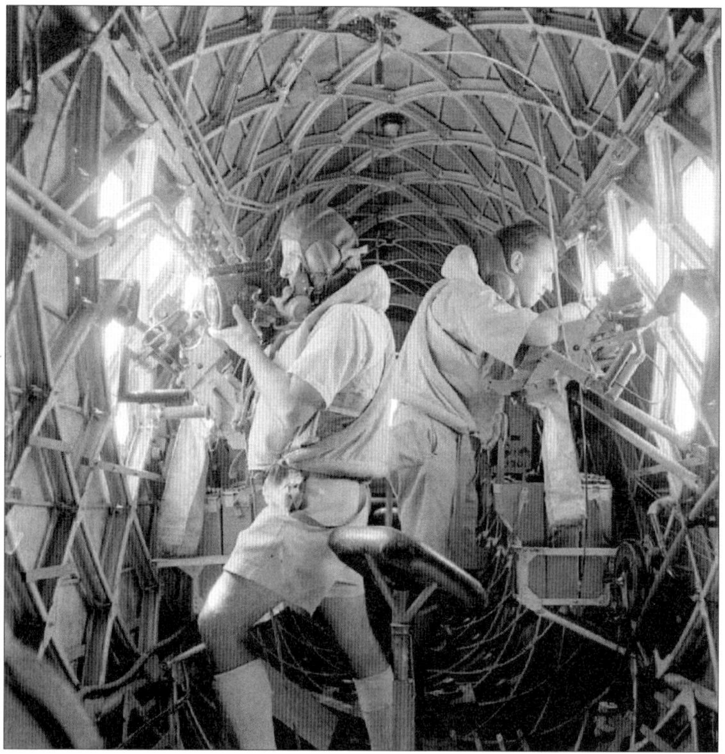

On board Mk.III Sea Rescue Flight Abu Sueir North. (*IWM CM3792*)

Fg Off John M Brennan DFC was a WOp/AG on 148 Squadron in the Canal Zone from November 1941 to August 1942 and among his operations were several to Greece during the German invasion of that country which commenced in April 1941:

> "When a target was selected we bombed up, fuelled up and took off in the early afternoon to a landing ground 250 miles up into the desert. On arrival there the tanks were topped up from four-gallon cans; we did not have jerry cans in those days. Our pre-operation meal consisted of tinned meat and veg with dog biscuits. Our flying rations were Horlicks tablets and 'wakey-wakey' tablets.
>
> "On 2 March 1942 we were detailed to drop supplies to troops who had been stranded in the mountains of Crete after the invasion of May 1941. The aircraft we used had a cover on the floor half-way down the fuselage. As usual we took off for the LG and after briefing we took off on the mission at about 20:30 hrs. On the way back we were still within sight of Crete when the starboard engine caught fire. The pilot managed to get the fire out and he feathered the prop to prevent drag. He instructed me to leave

the turret and to dump everything removable overboard. I removed the cover from the floor and then proceeded to remove the guns, ammunition, parachutes, flying gear, Elsan and oxygen bottles, but all to no avail. When I realised we were going to ditch I removed the astrodome and took up a crash position on the rest bunk.

"Our ditching was quite smooth and I was first out of the aircraft and the rest followed. The only pieces of equipment in the dinghy were a paddle and a heliograph. As we sat in the dinghy we realised we were going down with the aircraft as it was still attached to the wing by a lanyard. The pilot enquired if anyone had a penknife and it so happened that the WOp did. No sooner had he cut the lanyard than the aircraft disappeared. This was about 4 am on 3 March and we had ditched about eight miles from the Egyptian coast [off Daba Point]. After about eight hours we were picked up by an ASR [Air Sea Rescue] launch which took us to Alexandria and from there we returned to Kabrit by train. According to the squadron record book, 'The ditching was executed perfectly'. Our Mk.II aircraft was W5555 'D'."

Sgt James 'Ginger' Ware was a Cockney with an irrepressible sense of humour, an air gunner and a remarkable veteran of the earliest days of Wimpy operations with 99 Squadron. He was awarded the DFM in July 1941 for his action in shooting down an Me 110 on the night of 10 May that year while on his fifty-first operation, this time to Hamburg (in fact the German fighter must have only been damaged, since there was no Luftwaffe loss that night that fits in with this action). In February 1942, 99 Squadron was transferred to India and stopped off en route at Shallufa. At this point it was decided that he had already flown too many operations (around seventy by this time) and he was taken off flying and employed locally as an MT driver. This was too much for Ginger and he somehow wangled himself a posting onto 40 Squadron in June 1942 and started

Mk.IC BB464 D-Donald of 99 Squadron at Luxor 4 March 1942 en route to India. Taken over by 70 Squadron and crash landed at LG 140 4 December 1942. (*Robert Hails via 99 Squadron*)

Sgt Pilot 'Dixie' Dean & crew; top left Sgt James 'Ginger' Ware DFM 99 Squadron Waterbeach 1941. (*Norman Didwell*)

flying ops again.

He was on his eightieth operation on the night of 7/8 August 1942 – to Tobruk – when his aircraft (Flt Lt H Grant HX431), crash landed in the desert after a mid-air collision with DV663. All the crew survived except the navigator Plt Off Albert Hull who elected to bale out and did so too low (the entire crew in the other aircraft perished). This was the third time in his career he had landed without a serviceable aeroplane, and Ginger suffered a severe leg injury. "It sort of got tore off, like. Well, most of the foot and the ankle anyway, and the bones were smashed up all to tiny little splinters. I dare say it looked worse than it really was, because I went and bled right through all the bandages and it must have looked like somebody killed a pig." Rescued by a German patrol, his left leg was amputated and he spent the rest of the war in a POW camp, about which he said: "Well, I don't mind admitting there's a lot of places I'd sooner spend a couple of years in. The grub wasn't up to much."

Flt Lt Eric Barfoot DFC flew thirty-seven operations with 37 Squadron before transferring to South East Asia Command to fly Dakotas:

> "We were led on an op to Rhodes, and as we went along there was St.Elmo's Fire flashes around the guns and the cockpit, which frightened me to death, but no harm done. We had to bomb the airfield, which was behind the port. As we got to the port we could see the flak going up 'Wham!' a poor squadron got that. We got to the airfield round the back so we didn't go through it, we went round it. We were bombing the airfield and were attacked by a CR.42.
>
> "The only time we were really hurt was when (it wasn't called friendly fire then, it was something much more rude!), we were coming in to land after an op from Benghazi, and as we approached we saw this aircraft lit up with its lights on, going round and round getting a green light from the ground. By this time in 1942, I had never heard any voice on the RT, because it didn't work. But they gave this thing a green light and round and round it went, then suddenly we got a green. In we went, and this thing was an intruder, a Ju 88 it was. It sort of crept up behind us, and let us have it when we were at about 500 feet; he didn't do much damage. Both gunners and the army on the ground, who knew it was a Ju 88, had to ask 'When can we open fire?', but were told 'No, it was a Beaufighter in distress'. Well it was us that were in distress, but the gunners opened up and shot one of our elevators off. We scooted along the ground, but we all got out safely."

The constant threat posed by patrolling Luftwaffe night fighters operating initially out of bases in Sicily including Catania, before moving to the Libyan coast at Derna, caused a lot of problems for Wellington crews. Hptm Heinz Rökker, Knight's Cross with Oakleaves, became one of the highest scoring Luftwaffe night-fighter aces, flying the Ju 88 with Nachtjagdgeschwader (NJG)2. His first victory came in June 1942 against a Bristol Beaufort, following which his next five successes were all against Wellingtons of 205 Group:

> "In June 1942 Rommel and his Afrika Korps had taken Tobruk and were on the move eastwards. On the 25th I moved together with my crew and 1 Squadron from Catania to Derna for free night interceptions; due to the waxing moon one could see aircraft already from far away. On the night of 26/27 June we took off for our first mission of night interception. That night the English aircraft were bombing our arms stores on the Via Balbia and for better observation purposes they dropped flash bombs. This was a hint for me, because where flash bombs were dropped there must have been English aircraft.
>
> "When I was at an altitude of approximately 1,000 metres above the flash bomb I suddenly saw a Wellington about 300 metres away flying a little bit higher. In order not to lose sight of it I opened the throttle by which I approached the opponent very fast; the Wellington flew considerably slower than our Ju 88C-6. I approached it from behind at high speed and I could barely fire off a short burst from my machine gun. To avoid a collision with the Wellington I pushed my aircraft's nose down and flew below it with only a few metres to spare. After I turned I saw the burning Wellington crashing on the ground and exploding; this near-miss taught me a lesson. The victory was at 23:45 hours at Mersa Matruh."

The end of 104 Squadron Wellington E-echo whose bomb load blew up on the ground. (*Peter Fotherby*)

This Wellington was DV522 of 37 Squadron flown by Sgt I G Medwin RNZAF. The aircraft was belly landed in the desert but sadly one of the gunners, Sgt Jack Abson, misheard the pilot's instructions and jumped to his death. The rest of the crew walked for three hours to the British lines. Just over twenty minutes later Rokker also shot down DV564 L of 70 Squadron 40 km from Mersa Matruh, injuring the second pilot and WOp, and killing the rear gunner Flg Sgt Gordon Wagner RCAF in the process. This aircraft was flown by Flt Sgt Stewart RNZAF and another belly landing ensued back at their LG 104 base. Rökker's next victory came the following night:

"On 28 June we took off from Derna for the area of Mersa Matruh which in the meanwhile had been taken by German troops; it was a bright moonlit night. Already from a great distance we could again see the English flash bombs dropping. At 23:58 hours we discovered a Wellington and I attacked it at once from behind with a firing burst; the right engine started to burn. Due to its engine failure the Wellington suddenly flew very slowly and the pilot pushed the aircraft's nose far downwards. At once I reduced the throttles of my engines to stay behind the Wellington and to start a second attack. But my speed was too great so that I flew abeam the Wellington at the same altitude.

"At that moment we saw the muzzle flash of the front gunner and heard the bullets hitting our aircraft. One bullet shattered in our cabin on the weapons panel and I was hurt by splinters above my right eye and in my right thigh. My radio operator Carlos was hurt by a splinter in his foot. But I did not give up the chase. At the same time we drew much closer to the ground where I could clearly see vehicles in the bright moonlight. Some 100 metres further away the Wellington made a belly landing. I pulled my aircraft upwards again in order to look for more targets. But my flight mechanic told me that the temperature of the right engine was rising and I had to cut the engine in order to avoid a fire.

"After I had finally managed to feather the propeller and to cut off the engine the left engine suddenly started burning; I was up the creek without a paddle. There were two alternatives, either we had to jump or we had to risk a belly landing at night. I decided for the latter because we were just at an altitude of 300 metres. Shortly before ground contact I gave the order to drop the cabin roof panel; I pulled on the yoke so that we contacted the ground tail first."

The Wellington lost was R1029 of 108 Squadron flown by Sqn Ldr Donald Jacklin DFC, which force landed at Amriya, all the crew being safe, including the front gunner who had inflicted so much damage on the Ju 88. The next to fall to Rökker's guns was a month later:

"On 28 July we took off from El Qasaba in Ju 88 R4-EK, and at 23:10 hours we brought down a Wellington near Tobruk with two firing bursts from the lower aft side; the shoot down was confirmed by an 'archie' [flak] unit."

This time the Wellington was HX364 of 70 Squadron flown by Sgt H R Osborne who had been detailed to bomb Tobruk harbour and shipping. The aircraft was crash landed in the sea some 48 km from the target and, although all the crew were rescued by the Italian ship *Lino Bixo*, Sgts B K Hatch (gunner), E A Jones RAAF (gunner) and K S McDonald (WOp) subsequently drowned when the ship was sunk by a Royal Navy submarine off Greece on 17 August 1942. Rökker then had to wait some time for the next victory, but when it did come, the victim was yet another Wellington:

"On 18 April 1943 I received my take-off order from Castelvetrano in Ju 88 R4-CH for the area 'Mars' near Masala. At approximately 1 o'clock my fighter controller Oblt Knieriem guided me via R/T towards an aircraft captured on radar, and after fifteen minutes I recognised a Wellington flying ahead of me at an altitude of approximately

> 500 metres. I attacked it at once from behind. After a firing burst the left engine was burning and the aircraft crashed into the sea; the victory was confirmed by the fighter controller. It was the only shooting of mine within this area using the 'Himmelbett' night interception system."

What was to prove to be Rökker's final Wellington of his ultimately sixty-four victories was almost certainly HX487 'Y' of 221 Squadron based at Luqa, Malta. This aircraft was definitely lost on the same day – the only Wellington that fits – but curiously the 221 Squadron ORB does not show any operations on that date. However, a check of the Commonwealth War Graves Commission (CWGC) website shows the only possible casualties on that date to be nine men of 221 Squadron, including Sqn Ldr Michael Foulis DFC and bar (known on the squadron as 'Really Foul' after a popular cartoon character), who last appears in the ORB on 15 April 1943. Of the other men listed as killed on that day, four have been identified as having previously flown as crew with Foulis. Some sources claim that the aircraft was on a torpedo operation, and it is possible that it was flown out of Luqa and then continued on elsewhere, Berka II or Grottaglie perhaps, but never made it thanks to Heinz Rökker's intervention. If correct, this might explain why there were additional crew members aboard. They might have been part of a changeover of crew (air/ground), or the aircraft may have been going elsewhere for deeper servicing than that available on Malta.

COMMUNICATIONS JAMMING

A highly-unusual Wellington unit operating in North Africa was 109 Squadron which, as previously mentioned, had been formed at Boscombe Down in December 1940 for trials work on new equipment such as Oboe. In October 1941 instructions were received for the squadron to prepare for deployment to the Mediterranean to trial standard transmitters modified by Marconi-Ekco and code named Jostle. These were intended to jam the enemy's tank-to-tank very high frequency (VHF) communications in the light of an expected German offensive in Libya. Six 'tropical type' Wellingtons with provision for extra fuel tanks and engine air filters were allotted to the squadron which was tasked with designing, manufacturing and fitting the equipment, the aerial for which consisted of a 3-inch diameter brass tube about 7 feet in length, which could be let down during flight through a hole underneath the fuselage. Three aircraft left for Egypt on 18 October 1941 under the command of Wg Cdr W B S Simpson and was known locally as Special Flight, although it was officially referred to as 109 Squadron Detachment Middle East. Wg Cdr 'Arty' Ashworth DSO DFC AFC who flew with 75 & 38 Squadrons remembered them:

> "The Special Flight Wellingtons who interrupted the communications of the Afrika Korps and were flown by 'Scruffy' Williams and Co. were called 'Donkey's Prick' Wellingtons."

Having moved to a forward landing ground, the first operational flight was undertaken on the afternoon of 20 November 1941 in the Sidi Omar area, and captured enemy troops reported that the jamming had caused a breakdown of tank communications. The following day the aircraft were set upon by three Italian Macchi MC.202 fighters of 153º Gruppo, with one Wellington Z8907 being shot down and another claiming a fighter. The Wimpy pilot was Flt Sgt Herbert

Wolf RCAF and his crew of seven included Lieutenant Colonel (Lt Col) Roderick Denman, Royal Signals, who was a senior War Office specialist in radio countermeasures. Operations were continued and in January 1942, a brief interim report was issued discussing the results and was commented on by a senior staff officer at the controlling 80 Group as follows:

> "One is left with the impression that the results achieved, if any, did not justify the allocation of resources. There is no evidence to show that the Wellington operations had any decisive effect upon the operations of the enemy armoured forces. The fact that the enemy took no special steps to get rid of them is evidence that they were not even a serious nuisance.
>
> "I consider that the pilots and crews carrying out this duty had a most unpleasant task. To fly a Wellington up and down the battlefield during the day was asking for trouble, and we are fortunate that not more were destroyed. I do not know whether any awards have been made to any of these personnel, but I suggest that this action should be considered."

Despite this, jamming operations continued throughout 1942 and in December of that year a final report[3] was issued which clearly showed that the army remained unconvinced about the value of Jostle. They had requested operations be carried out by night and this enabled daytime operations to be abandoned due to the vulnerability of the aircraft. The report went on to say that night operations caused the loss of much of the value of Jostle, an odd statement, and that there was no requirement for it in the immediate future. However, six Jostle sets were retained should they be required in the future, with a recommendation that the Beaufighter would be a safer platform to use. In fact, despite its vulnerability, only one further Wellington was lost by the squadron on 22 November 1941, when X9988 flown by Sgt Richard Nicholson was another victim of Italian fighters with the loss of all six men on board.

RECONNAISSANCE

The second specialised Wellington unit in the desert war was 69 Squadron, which was established at Luqa in May 1942, flying a variety of aircraft including Wellington Mk.ICs and VIIIs on night reconnaissance operations over enemy ports and airfields ranging as far afield as Libya, Sicily and Italy (the work of the more conventional maritime reconnaissance Wellington units in the Mediterranean is discussed in Chapter Five). J R 'Eric' Cameron RCAF WOp/AG (W/AG):

> "My first tour was on Malta during the blitz (April or May '42 to November), during which I logged 300 op hours in Wimpys attached first to 221 Squadron, then as Special Duties Flight of 69 Squadron. 69 Squadron was a recce outfit with Marylands, Baltimores and a single photo-recce Spitfire. Its Wellingtons were used for shipping strikes in the Med using bombs and sometimes torpedoes, as well as flares for illuminating the targets. Those targets included anything that was at sea; MVs, destroyers, cruisers, etc. Two pilots and one of the navigators I flew with got 'gongs' for our exploits, such as hitting tankers bound for the Afrika Korps.
>
> "In August '42 during the very critical period for Malta, Operation Pedestal was a last-ditch attempt to rescue the island, and a large convoy set out from the UK via

Gibraltar. The 69 Squadron Wellingtons did night patrols around Tunisia and Sicily to shadow the Allied convoy and try to spot marauding Axis 'planes and naval battle units; quite a lot of excitement, to say the least, especially when the convoy rounded Cape Bon at night and was attacked by numerous enemy torpedo bombers and E-boats. We had to circle the convoy and observe the ships by taking a shellacking. We went too close to one destroyer that was illuminated by enemy flares and was under torpedo-bomber attack. They started shooting at us too, so we high-tailed it to a safer distance.

"The Wimpys operating out of Malta in summer '42 were very few in number and seldom were there more than three serviceable on a given night. Sometimes two aircraft would co-operate, whereby one loaded with flares and called a 'Flashington' would fly back and forth dropping parachute flares, while the attack Wellington armed with torpedoes would line up on the silhouetted ships and approach at 50 feet from the dark side – whence the enemy gunners expected them to come anyway.

"On 8 July '42 we had a hairy experience. Shortly after take-off for an op in HX391, the starboard engine caught fire. The field was under enemy air attack so we made an emergency landing without any flarepath lights. Loaded with parachute flares, the Wimpy went up like a fireworks display and the glare was probably visible from Sicily.

"In 1984 I met a German who had commanded a Staffel of Ju 88 night fighters operating from Catania in Sicily. He recollected that Goering and Kesselring were constantly hauling him and his fellow night fighter commanders on the carpet because of all the ships being damaged and sunk by the Wellingtons from Malta. The Ju 88s had a form of radar which seemed to 'glow' when switched on. So when we spotted one trying to make contact, our pilot throttled back, dropped the Wimpy's wheels and flaps and the aircraft sank like an elevator going down. The Ju 88 would pass overhead and lose the Wimpy on its radar. When I told the German our tactic for evading him and his boys, he seemed astonished. They had thought we were equipped with some kind of radar jamming device."

By this time the Afrika Korps was in full retreat following the battle of El Alamein in October and November 1942, and six Wellington squadrons pounded enemy armour concentrations. They were then able to follow the retreat and leave the desert landing grounds for more established airfields in Libya, before settling on bases in Tunisia from February 1943. The ground campaign was followed up by Operation Torch, the invasion of French North Africa in December. Axis forces in North Africa finally surrendered on 13 May 1943, enabling the RAF's attention to turn back towards the European mainland.

TUNISIA

As new bases in Algeria and Tunisia became established, the hard-pressed 205 Group Wellington squadrons were bolstered by the arrival of a number of additional units displaced from Bomber Command by the arrival of the four-engine heavies. These included 142, 150, 420 (RCAF), 424 (RCAF) and 425 (RCAF) Squadrons, all either fully equipped with, or in the process of receiving new Wellington Mk.X aircraft with improved Hercules Mk.XVI engines. This increase in strength needed the support of local OTUs to provide the necessary additional and replacement crews and accordingly four (Nos.75 to 78) were set up between December 1942 and January

Line-up of 70 Squadron aircraft at Kairouan, Tunisia 1943. (*Richard Stowers*)

Operations briefing for 70 Squadron crews at Kairouan in 1943. (*Richard Stowers*)

1944, 75 being based in Egypt and the other three in Palestine.

One of the largest concentrations of units in Tunisia was at Kairouan inland from Sousse, which actually comprised three separate airfields. Bob Stowers found conditions not much improved from the desert:

> "We had a couple of rain storms which turned the surface to sticky mud. If you started to move a Wellington about the earth clogged all the way round the wheels and made it impossible to taxi. I think one operation was cancelled because of this."

As the new focus of operations got under way, the principal targets in support of the forces advancing through Italy were German troop concentrations and supply routes, plus towns and cities including Naples, Salerno, Taranto and Turin. On the night of 1/2 March 1943, Bob Stowers was one of thirteen 70 Squadron crews briefed to attack Palermo and he successfully did so. This was his first raid as captain. However, on the way back they had crossed Sicily and navigator Cliff King started expressing concern about their dwindling fuel supply. Realising they could not make it back to Tunisia, Bob opted to head for Malta.

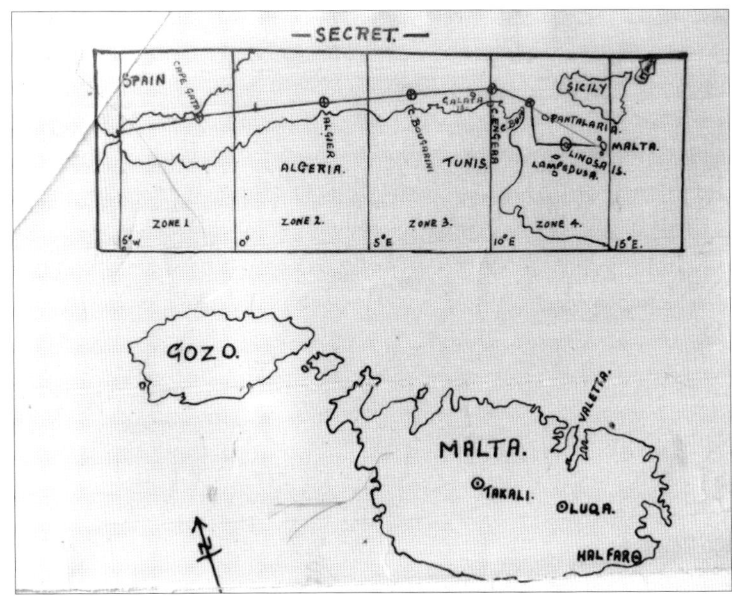

Crew map of Malta & North Africa en route airfields. (*Robert Hails via 99 Squadron*)

"We landed on Malta once only on an operation. You didn't go to Malta unless you had to, and we thought we had to. It turned out the gauges were just a bit funny in that particular Wellington. They [the Luqa airfield commanding officers] didn't like you taking petrol away from Malta, which was fair enough, as it was such a hard job to get it there, due to the convoys. We returned to base the next morning; Luqa had checked the fuel to make sure we had enough to get back with a couple of cupfulls to spare. We just had enough to get home; then we got a right bollocking for it!"

Flt Sgt Bill Burgess was a pilot on B Flight of 70 Squadron from July 1943 to May 1944, completing thirty-eight operations and he found that his reception from the retreating Germans was extremely fierce:

"On 24 November our target was the Turin ball-bearing works. The trip was undertaken through terrible weather, cloud obscured practically everything. Snow, rain and icing conditions were encountered. The target was totally obscured by cloud so it was not pranged. However on the return we dropped our bombs near or on a busy road near Savona. After they had exploded, some heavy guns opened up from the coast but the flak was easily evaded. The sack of nickels was scattered in the Turin area. On return to base we learnt that fifteen aircraft were missing of which five were from 70 Squadron.

"The next op, our twenty-third, was to the aerodrome at Ciampino. The weather for a change was reasonably good. Pinpoints in Italy were hard to pick up as cloud and haze were fairly abundant. The first flares were dropped well away from the target. We bombed the second lot of flares and hangars were identified as being those of the target detailed. Some dispute arose as to whether the target was the actual one. One aircraft was hit by flak and crashed in the target area; parachutes were reported. Reception was of light flak which was fairly accurate."

Mk.III HF742 W of 70 Squadron was flown by Bill Burgess on an op to Naples 1 August 1943. It was written off by 40 Squadron a month later. (*William Burgess*)

ITALIAN OPERATIONS

On the night of 9/10 July 1943 the Allied armies commenced Operation Husky, the invasion of Sicily, and by mid August they had successfully captured the whole of the island despite stiff resistance around the beaches along the Straits of Messina, resistance which brought a lot of attention from 205 Group Wellingtons over several nights. One 425 (RCAF) Squadron Wellington HE978 'Slow but Sure', set an unequalled record of completing every one of the unit's thirty-two operations during the Sicilian campaign, a result largely and quite rightly credited to the hard work and dedication of her ground crew, who not only recorded the ops tally on the nose of the aircraft, but added a DFC ribbon as well, since they felt the aircraft deserved it. This was one of the rare occasions when the ground crew were recognised by name; Cpl Andrew Lupien, and LACs Eric Merry, Yvon Monette and C Schierer. [4]

In August 205 Group squadrons finally began dropping 'Cookies', with the first being targeted on the 25th by Sgt Sykes and his 70 Squadron crew in Mk.X HZ135 on the railway marshalling yards at Taranto. Rear gunner Leslie Page noted with clear satisfaction, '1 x 4,000 lb with love'. Earlier that month his crew had attacked another railway target at Naples, dropping nine 500 lb bombs, and the photo flash dropped to take the bombing photograph went off immediately it left the aircraft, causing the gunner some difficulty:

> "I think it was this trip where I was blinded by premature firing of a 1,000,000 candle-power photo flash. I recovered my sight before we returned to base. Incident not reported."

Despite this, Leslie Page was able to continue operational flying and completed his tour of thirty-nine ops in early October. He did however, have to wear spectacles for the rest of his life as a result of the eye damage he had suffered.

By late October 1943 the Allied armies had crossed over onto the Italian mainland and, pushing up the east cost of Italy, captured the vital Foggia plain – a flat, almost featureless and mosquito-infested plateau which forms the 'spur' on the boot of Italy. This was a critical gain, for there were on the Foggia plain, some existing airfields. Airfield construction battalions of the USAAF and the RAF moved in to create more – scraping runways out of olive groves, then covering them with gravel and PSP (perforated steel planking) in order to create runways and taxiways, perimeter tracks and hardstandings.

WO Peter Fotherby, pilot with 104 Squadron. (*Peter Fotherby*)

When 205 Group moved to the Foggia area along with the day bombers of the USAAF 12th and 15th Air Forces, all of German-occupied Europe came under the threat of Allied bomber air power – either from the UK or from Foggia. This was a turning point in the air war. During the winter of 1943/44, and the following spring and summer, 205 Group came under the direct command of the 15th Air Force, the only RAF formation ever to come under the operational control of another country. The clutch of airfields on the Foggia plain became renowned for poor conditions and copious quantities of mud as well remembered by W/O Peter Fotherby who was a pilot with 104 Squadron operating from Foggia Main:

> "I had reached the ripe old age of twenty and was soon setting off on the first of forty bombing operations as a very green aircraft captain. Actually thirty-seven ops, but three particularly hazardous ones were counted as two each. The living conditions we endured for the whole of our operational life were dreadful. Our food was awful, no eggs and bacon after an op as our contemporaries in the UK enjoyed. Nor, of course, did we have a pub and the company of eager and not unwilling girls to return to! We even wore army khaki uniforms as no RAF blues were available. We were part of a forgotten air force as far as we were concerned. Our loos consisted of six buckets in a tent and each morning we would sit and speculate on the probable target for the night; we were nearly always right. Nor did we have any washing or shower facilities other than a water bowser at the end of our field, which was actually a vineyard."

Bill Burgess was now operating from Tortorella, another of the Foggia airfields:

> "Our thirty-third op on 11 March '44 took us to the Genoa marshalling yards. The target was again under 10/10ths cloud, but the boys bombed on the flak. On the return flak was encountered off Orbocella and ten minutes off the Volturno turn the starboard engine cut for lack of petrol. We made a forced landing at Marsenaisse and just after

Flt Sgt Bill Burgess in the cockpit and the crew of Mk.X LN317 W 70 Squadron Tortorella May 1944. Burgess completed 38 operations, this Wimpy completed a few more. (*William Burgess*)

landing the port engine cut causing the aircraft to swing off the runway, taking a Piper Cub with it. Our prop tip was bent and the flaps damaged."

The Wellington was Mk.X LN317, in which Bill and his crew had flown four of their ops. Although it was repaired after this dramatic arrival, it was written off in a crash landing in Algeria two months later. Four days after this raid, it was the turn of the railway marshalling yards at Sofia, Bulgaria. W/O Ken Hammond was flying Mk.X LN378, one of thirteen aircraft taking part from 150 Squadron, and his aircraft was the illuminator. Although the weather was bad en route, Hammond placed fifty-four flares over the target. He reported that street lights were visible in the city and were extinguished in sectors as the flares went down. There were inaccurate searchlights and light flak, but all aircraft identified the target and there was some good bombing; a 'Cookie' was seen to explode in the marshalling yards, and 132,000 Nickels were dropped. This particular raid was highly significant as it was the first time that the Pathfinder technique had been used in the Italian theatre, leading attacks on special targets. Much of the brilliant success achieved by the squadrons operating from airfields in the Foggia area, was due to 614 (Pathfinder) Squadron flying Halifax Mk.IIs, the only such unit in the Mediterranean war zone.

Flt Sgt Cliff Hobbs was a rear gunner in Peter Fotherby's crew on 104 Squadron, but did his first two ops with another crew:

> "When I got on the squadron in May '44 they gave us two trips as second gunner; I had no guns, just stood in the astrodome. My first one was with Flt Sgt Smith, an Australian and we went to the Tagliamento railway bridge. When they'd dropped their bombs, being Australian they wanted to go and see if they'd hit anything; I thought the object was to get out as fast as you can. The nose went down on the aircraft and they went down to about 1,000 feet to see if they'd had success.
>
> "One that really stands out in my mind is when we were bombing marshalling yards in Hungary on 20/21 September. We dropped our bombs and had been taking evasive action from a fighter on the way in and at the last minute the bomb aimer saw the tar-

104 Squadron ground crew with their charge, 'Elusive Eileen'. (*Peter Fotherby*)

get ahead and said 'Can we go straight?' Peter said yes and I kept my eyes skinned, the WOp was in the astrodome doing the same thing. We were the first to drop and went right across the marshalling yards blowing up a few trucks, and got away as fast as we could. Over a hundred miles away I could still see the fires burning.

"On 6/7 July we attacked Feuersbrunn aerodrome in Austria; that was an unpleasant one. The Yanks had gone out the day before and had been attacked by fighters, so we were sent out to bomb the airfield; it was quite a long trip. We had six 500 pounders on board but I don't know that we did a tremendous amount of damage. There was quite a lot of flak over Graz which stopped the fighters getting up at first, but whether we bombed them out of existence I don't know."

The squadron lost one aircraft when LP499 flown by Flt Sgt John McDonald, failed to return. Peter Fotherby remembered that raid vividly as they came uncomfortably close to not making it home:

"Full moon made night into day and the day fighters we were supposed to bomb took off and devastated our small force; seventeen missing out of fifty-one that reached the target. PFF marking was hopeless, indicators scattered widely and we searched for the target for fifteen minutes, and were then nearly blinded by a photo flash burst close ahead. We were dodging other aircraft, running fights all over the place. We went down to the ground and climbed to cross the mountains. Overflew Graz and were attacked by flak with a loud and heavy burst under the tail which made several holes. We were thrown into a vertical dive with negative G which stopped the engines. Loose fittings, ammunition and flares were all torn from their stowages and thick dust obscured my vision. I ordered 'prepare to abandon' and pulled out at 330 mph, quite near to the ground, the engines re-starting with positive G. Not a successful operation for the group."

In addition to continuing to harass the retreating German army, another prime target that came in for attention was the enemy's last remaining substantial oilfields at Ploesti in Romania. This had first been targeted on 1 August 1943 by USAAF B-24 Liberators flying from North Africa; the Americans had found, to their cost, just how heavily defended it was. Now that medium-range bombers were based within reach, Ploesti became the subject of repeated attacks. Flt Lt Harry Hacker went there as a bomb aimer with 40 Squadron based at Foggia Main:

Flt Lt Harry Hacker, bomb aimer with 40 Squadron at Foggia Main. (*Harry Hacker*)

"My first operation was the invasion of southern France, the docks at Marseilles. On the way in there, we had to watch the naval convoys and make sure you had your IFF switched on because, if you didn't, the navy boys wouldn't hesitate to blast you out of the bloody sky. Second operation was a bit livelier; it was the Ploesti oilfields. It was fortunate that I went in with an experienced crew; their bomb aimer had gone down sick and I was asked if I would go and, stupid as one was, I volunteered; green as grass and that was very exciting. Germany had lost the oilfields in the Caucasus so all they had left was Ploesti. They built a ring round all the oilfields. Most of the guns, the heavies and the light ones, were dug in on the hills around them so you had an umbrella over the target plus the fact that they also had searchlights that were radar-controlled, what we called master searchlights. If one of them got you he could hold you and then all the rest would converge on you and then they would throw everything at you. Also, we were told they had a crack squadron of Romanian night fighters; later research showed this was about 120 Me 109s defending the target and then about 200 aircraft defending the target approaches from all directions. On the bombing run in we had a bloke off our port quarter just blow up; he must have had a direct hit. He just went up in an orange flash. Quite chilling but by then there wasn't much time to worry; you were concerned with yourself and your bombing run. We could see the Pathfinders up ahead of us. We had 614 Squadron which were a mixture of Liberators and Halifaxes; they'd gone in and were receiving all the flak. They were replying with their guns as well. Going in was just hell let loose.

"I should think we were probably at about 12 to 15,000 ft. What we did then was to fly to Bucharest in the hope of drawing some of the mobile artillery south but, as soon as we turned off for the oilfields, that was it; they knew where we were going. They were waiting for us and the sky was just filled with flak, tracer fire all over the place. You concentrated on just staying alive and of course for the final thirty seconds to get your target in the bomb-sight. Whilst we were doing that we had all sorts of yells of fire coming in from night fighters but our West Indian air gunner was quite cool. He was hammering away with his guns while I was concentrating on staying straight and level because we had a rule of thumb, if you like. Never stay straight and level for more than twenty-five seconds because that's the time it would take for the master radar to get you, a shell in their gun and up to your altitude. So you're trying not to stay straight and level too long but you've still got to get the target in the tramlines of your bomb-sight.

"We'd just got rid of our bomb load when the gunner yelled that an aircraft was coming in from the starboard quarter up, a night fighter. He said, 'Stand by to corkscrew starboard' because we always turned towards it to try to tighten the circle. At the same time, the radio operator, standing in the astrodome because he'd got nothing to do except observe, just like the navigator, yelled 'One coming in from the starboard beam' so we had two fighters coming at us. Arthur was cool with the old four Browning machine guns. Although our armament wasn't heavy, if you coned it all in you had a heavy blast there and I think if I remember correctly the estimated range to the Ju 88s and Me 109s would be around 250 yards. So our gunner yelled, he kept his cool, he estimated 250 yards, based on the wingspan and the graticule and he opened up with everything and he hit this bloke, who just blew up. A great cheer went up from the wireless operator 'We got 'im, we got 'im'. The gunner always warns you to stand by port or starboard and then when he decides now is the time, when he thinks the enemy is just about to open fire, he would shout 'Now' and we up front would go into the corkscrew, or whatever. We did all that and when we thought the fighter had gone we had a moment to reflect.

"We looked at our air speed indicator and it was down to about 75 knots not far off the stalling speed, and we thought, 'Wow, we're just about to fall out of the sky here'. So we pushed the stick forward but after a second or two we realised we weren't stalling at all; we were second time round on the clock! We were in a steep dive. Oh shit! So both the skipper and I were pulling back on the bloody controls hoping to get it back up, hoping the wings would stay on. It took two of us to get it back. By the time we got the stick back, we were in Dante's Inferno; down to about 500 or perhaps 1,000 feet. Everything was going on around us, a whole mass of flames, gunfire and what have you. There was no time to worry about that anyway, we got it back to straight and level and we thought we'd stay down here for a bit, clear of the night fighters and clear of the target area and it was reasonably OK.

"We climbed back to our cruising altitude but on the way back we were still tormented by night fighters. We suddenly noticed, down on our starboard quarter, about 5,000 feet below us, navigation lights and we thought what the hell is this all about? We were in enemy territory; it couldn't be one of ours so we deduced that it had to be one of the night fighter bases with some of their blokes going in to land. So we thought, let's go in and give them a bloody treat so we went down, joined the circuit, hoping their identification was similar to ours; come in to land with green, hold off with the red Aldis lamp because there was no audio then. So we went in after two of theirs. We didn't see anyone behind us, hoping that our silhouette wouldn't divulge that we were a Wellington, as opposed to their night fighters. Everything was quiet, we had our nav lights on, going in as if to land and as we went along the runway we opened up. I went along to the front turret, the rear gunner put his guns to starboard, I put mine to port and we opened up the taps. We just sprayed for about thirty seconds and had tracer fire chasing our backsides. A quick turn to port with everybody yelling 'let's get the hell out of here' and that was it.

"We reached our cruising altitude safe and sound and headed back to Foggia Main. Then we thought, 'well, what do we do here? Do we say what we've done?' because we had a very blood-and-guts group captain, Gp Capt Harris. So we thought that, to be on the safe side, we wouldn't say anything at all. He always stood in at de-briefings, listening to what the crews had to say. He didn't pick us up or anything so we got away with it. The ground crew patched up all the bullet holes and we accounted for all the ammunition used as a night-fighter operation."

MINING THE DANUBE

As the Mediterranean Strategic Bomber Force continued its assault on the vital Hungarian and Romanian railway systems, the Germans began making increased use of the River Danube flowing 1,500 miles through Germany, Austria, Hungary, Yugoslavia, Romania and Bulgaria, and capable of carrying 10,000 tons of essential supplies daily. Disrupting this traffic would have a major effect on Germany's capacity to continue the war in south-east Europe. Consequently 205 Group commenced mining operations in April 1944 and over the next few months large numbers of mines were dropped, culminating in no fewer than 192 on the night of 1/2 July, dropped by a force of sixteen Liberators and fifteen Wellingtons. Harry Hacker summed up the difficulties surrounding these operations:

104 Squadron pilot's station in flight. (*Peter Fotherby*)

"Barges carrying supplies were numerous on the river and all were targets for our group. They were also used as flak barges so the enemy defences were strong along the river, and some sections, where the banks were high and where the river passed through gorges, meant these sections' defences actually fired down on us going very low in order to drop the mines. Casualties were high because if you were hit at these low levels it made recovery more difficult and of course parachute escape was out of the question."

W/O Bill Briton, rear gunner with 150 Squadron at Foggia Main:

"On 5 May '44 we were laying mines in the Danube, flying only 50 feet above the water. The hairy part of this was that at times we would be flying below the top of the river banks. In addition, the enemy strung trip wires from bank to bank, plus machine-gun emplacements to back up these devices. Luckily, other than light gunfire, all went well."

Peter Fotherby dropped two 1,000 lb mines into the river on the night of 30/31 July:

"We didn't much like the idea as two out of the six sent out last time failed to return – Holmes and Trevor Hunt; in fact we rather enjoyed it. A bright moonlit night (a necessity for a low-level drop) made flying a pleasure with clear views of the mountains. Our pinpoint on the Danube was clearly seen and we dived down to the required height of 150 feet, but reduced to low speed for the drop. Some light AA fire but Sid was unable to get into the front turret due to a fault so couldn't respond on the run in! A pleasant flight back but had trouble landing as the port engine flamed badly whenever I tried to throttle back, so we approached with lots of power on one side and made an 'arrival'."

2,000 lb bomb in a Wellington of 70 Squadron. (*Guy Sharp*)

The aircraft lost on 2 July were MF137 flown by Plt Off Edward Holmes RAAF aged twenty-one, and LP131 flown by Sgt Trevor Hunt who was just twenty. Michael Alvis completed sixty-eight operations in two tours:

"There were several minelaying sorties completed from Foggia, taking place when there was a full moon, and we were detailed to fly at 100 feet above the deck from the Yugoslav border to areas around Budapest and back at the same height. We were dropping two 2,000lb mines in the river at 25-50 feet. On one occasion we actually flew through some high-tension wires on the return, tearing off certain parts of the aircraft including the air intake below the starboard engine; how we missed the props is beyond my comprehension. I later heard that we were credited with having sunk 214 vessels."

The 205 Group Wellingtons were still being called upon for occasional raids against targets in Germany and Bill Briton found himself heading for Munich on the night of 13/14 June:

"The powers-that-be thought a surprise raid from Italy would really give the Germans something to think about. Unfortunately, it turned out to be a complete disaster. Firstly, we had to climb over the Swiss Alps (15,000 feet); this was more than the maximum height obtainable with a heavily-loaded Wellington; to achieve this height mean maximum climb from take-off. Our reliable old Wimpy struggled foot by foot from about 12,000 feet, but with careful coaxing we eventually skimmed the top of the Alps, so far so good. But when we arrived there were no markers. However, there was a huge corridor of searchlights about thirty miles long and one mile wide, just like a road leading into the target area. It was like daylight up there, with flak playing merry hell.

"As we flew down this searchlight path I saw about fifty fighters coming head on towards us, about 1,000 feet above; this didn't look too good! Luckily, they shot straight past us, evidently looking for the main stream of bombers. It turns out there was no main stream, as when we returned we learned that eighty percent of our aircraft could not climb over the Alps and had to return to base. The few that did get over became very ineffective as the enemy had managed to shoot down the Pathfinders. The situation was ridiculous, so we decided that the quicker we got rid of our bombs and got out, the better. So away went the bombs and away we went like rats deserting the ship. Not a very successful raid."

THE FINAL STAGES OF THE CAMPAIGN

By the late summer of 1944 the Wellingtons were ranging still further into Hungary, Greece, Romania and Yugoslavia, attacking German-occupied aerodromes, railway viaducts, marshalling yards, etc. In Hungary, the marshalling yards at Miskolc were attacked by Peter Fotherby on the night of 22/23 August, close to the end of his tour:

"Another six lost and several aircraft turned back due to the weather. We were all getting a bit worn out by now. The usual red lights and spooky things active were reported by many crews. Our GEE was U/S as was the intercom throughout the trip which made things difficult. No speech was possible so I used the call lights to signal the crew and passed messages on paper. We hoped no urgent situations would arise – they didn't, but everybody's nerves were on edge. A 614 Squadron Pathfinder Halifax was shot down near to us at the Danube."

A key role in Yugoslavia was dropping supplies to the partisan groups waging their own war on the occupiers. Harry Hacker:

"During a supply op in November '44 we flew over a village and in it was a bridge which either they'd blown up or the Germans had, but on the broken edge of the bridge was a whole load of partisans, from all the villages, waving to us. We were at about 500 to 900 feet, something like that. We'd dropped their supplies and they were still waving at us so we thought we'd give them a treat and flew between the two broken wings of the bridge and there were the people standing on the bridge edges and waving like mad."

The last pre-planned bombing raid of the war by a Wellington in any theatre took place five-and-a-half years after it had started, on 13 March 1945, when six aircraft attacked the marshalling yards at Treviso, Italy, in company with a force of Liberators. By that time the once mighty 205 Group Wellington force had been reduced to a single unit; 40 Squadron had begun re-equipping with Liberators in February, but kept some Wellingtons back long enough to carry out this final operation. Of the others, 37, 70 and 104 Squadrons had also switched to Liberators, while 148 Squadron had been disbanded as early as December 1942 before re-appearing at Gambut, Libya the following year, again with Liberators. 150 Squadron moved back to England and re-equipped with Lancasters, and the three RCAF units, 420, 424 and 425 also went home and changed over to the Halifax.

The final Wellington bombing operation was recorded by 40 Squadron thus:

> 'This proved to be the last operation carried out by Wellington aircraft on the squadron. Six attacked the marshalling yards at Treviso, five aiming for the Red TIs which were judged to have fallen close together on the yards. One crew claimed however, that the TIs did not fall until Z plus one and bombed visually. The crews aiming for the TIs also reported that bombing commenced before Z hour. The 4,000 lb bomb fell to the west of the TIs but near them; two crews claimed bursts at mean point of TIs, and the crew bombing visually claimed a stick across the yards. Incendiaries fell at the correct time during the attack but were scattered over a wide area round the target. A 4,000 lb bomb was seen to explode in the centre of the yards and bombing was judged to be reasonably well concentrated. An explosion was reported and fires, which commenced beneath the incendiaries, could be seen for fifty miles. Opposition: inaccurate heavy and slight inaccurate light in the target area, slight inaccurate light on the coast on the run in to the target.'

The six Mk.X aircraft and crews involved, all returning safely, were:

LP646 R	W/O J Webb, Sgt O Partington, Sgt A Bennett, Sgt A Atkinson, Sgt R Lysaght
LP718 G	Sgt D Argile, Sgt L Morris, Flt Sgt M McNeill, Sgt J Kemp, Sgt A Sturtin
LP720 T	Sgt J Whitter, Sgt O McParland, Flt Sgt R Weston, Sgt I Jones, Sgt C Enoch
LP362 Z	Flt Sgt M Lihou, Flt Sgt J McCabe, Flt Sgt C Blackstone, Flt Sgt F Edwards, Sgt A Oakes
LP331 B	Flt Sgt W Brookfield, Flt Sgt K Simpson, Flt Sgt P Harrison, Flt Sgt L Taylor, Flt Sgt R Harman
LP658 J	Plt Off J Burnett RAAF, Fg Off A Merrick, Flt Sgt T Radcliff, Plt Off T Faulkner RNZAF, Sgt R Turner

The last bomb dropped was the 4,000 lb carried by Maurice Lihou. In fact the squadron was briefed for what was intended to be the final Wellington operation for the following day, but this was cancelled because of fog at base, and the CO issued the following message to the unit:

> 'It has been an important month in the history of 40 Squadron. On the 13th the final operations on Wellington aircraft was carried out and thus passed the last of the Wel-

lingtons from 205 Group. Training was sufficiently well in hand to enable operations to be renewed on Liberators six days later. The conversion scheme involved large-scale re-organisation of aircrews, many personnel being put up for disposal to make way for an intake of trained crews from other directions.'

None of the aircraft involved saw any further service and all were struck off charge for scrapping in the spring of 1945.

Bill Briton summed up the way many crews must have felt as the war seemed to drag on interminably:

> "We had commenced our tour as a bunch of kids, our crew's average age being twenty years and four months. We were men living continually with death. It was a stark transition which stayed with us until our fortieth and final trip. We had become a very efficient, conscientious crew with luck on our side. I think the word 'death' became our way of life, right down to simple things like the trucks that picked us up and delivered us to our 'planes. I think of these trucks as 'vehicles of death' as they carried us like hearses to our kites. The sound of the engines, I shall never forget. They had a deep sinister gurgle, sounding sort of very confident, and one could imagine them saying: 'I've got them this time on a no-return trip, but if they do come back, I'll get them next time.' Upon entering these monsters, approximately three crews to each vehicle, everyone sat silent, deep in thought, thinking, planning the next step in our continuing drama. If one were to hear those engines even today, one would shudder with revulsion."

CHAPTER FIVE

HUNTING THE U-BOATS– MARITIME OPERATIONS

"We ambush the ambusher" *172 Squadron motto*

The first use of Wellingtons in a maritime role was in 1940 with the appearance of the DWI mine-sweeping variant discussed in Chapter Two, but it was the advent of effective Air-to-Surface Vessel (ASV) radar that saw the adoption of the Wellington in a maritime role in large numbers. ASV was first trialled from January 1941 by 221 Squadron using modified Mk.ICs operating from Limavady with detachments to Reykjavik in Iceland on so-called Bear Patrols covering a large area of the North Atlantic in search of submarines, while also monitoring icebergs and providing weather information. Over the ensuing twelve months before moving to the Mediterranean, the squadron had a rough time, losing seven aircraft and their crews:

An early maritime aircraft without ASV, Mk.IC DV597 T of 304 (Polish) Squadron taxiing at Dale, Pembrokeshire 1942. (*ww2images*)

10 April '41	Flt Sgt Frank Butterworth R1049 shot down over Norfolk by a Ju 88 during a training flight
11 April '41	Fg Off Alfred Cattley W5653 flew into a hill in cloud in County Donegal, Eire
12 May '41	Fg Off James Robinson W5615 crashed into Lough Foyle twenty minutes after take-off
22 June '41	Plt Off Alfred Johnson W5659 failed to return from a patrol
11 July '41	Fg Off Ian Sanderson W5631 shot down off the Scilly Isles

17 August '41	Flt Lt Cecil Cakebread W5730 failed to return from a patrol
28 November '41	Fg Off John Speak T2988 crashed into hills at Kolgrafafjordur, Iceland

Despite these losses the ASV concept had been proved, and Vickers produced the Wellington General Reconnaissance (GR) Mk.VIII which featured ASV Mk.II with the 'Stickleback' aerial arrangement and it began to enter service in the spring of 1942. The ASV Mk.II was developed by the Royal Aircraft Establishment at Farnborough and, under ideal conditions, it had an effective range of up to thirty-six miles and could guide the aircraft to about a mile from the target vessel.

The primary role of the Coastal Command Wellingtons was searching for U-boats in order to protect the Atlantic convoys – the Battle of the Atlantic – and this was quickly expanded to cover the Malta convoys with units being based in the Mediterranean theatre. The squadrons re-equipped with the new type were:

April '42	172 Squadron Chivenor formed out of 1417 Flt
April '42	304 (Polish) Squadron Lindholme from Bomber Command
April '42	311 (Polish) Squadron Aldergrove from Bomber Command
Sept '42	179 Squadron Skitten
Sept '42	458 (RAAF) Squadron Shallufa from Bomber Command
Oct '42	547 Squadron Holmsley South
Nov '42	612 Squadron Wick replacing Whitleys
Jan '43	407 (RCAF) Squadron Docking replacing Hudsons
Sept '43	415 (RCAF) Squadron Thorney Island
April '44	524 Squadron Davidstow Moor
Nov '44	14 Squadron Chivenor

In addition, 38 Squadron at Shallufa was transferred from a bombing to a primary maritime role in January 1942 to operate the torpedo-carrying Wellingtons as outlined in Chapter Four, while other squadrons were formed to provide maritime capabilities in South-East Asia and Africa and these are covered in Chapter Six. The main difficulty for the crews was locating the submarines at night, resolved by equipping the aircraft with a powerful retractable searchlight mounted under the rear fuselage.

Navigator Sgt Ricky Rickard 179 Squadron Gibraltar 1943. (*Diane Rickard*)

When Sgt 'Ricky' Rickard completed his navigator training, he was briefly sent to 53 Squadron which flew Lockheed Hudsons from St.Eval in Cornwall, then soon found himself being moved to the growing Wellington force:

"By the end of June '42 it was decided that 53 Squadron had too few serviceable operational Hudsons to use up the new crews, so off we went to Chivenor in Devon and Wellington aircraft, and so on 1 July 1942, we reported to 172 Squadron to convert to Wellingtons flying with ASV equipment. Apparently we needed two more in crew, so we picked up Second Pilot J O'Sullivan from Hull and an Australian flt engineer from Perth (Keith). We were a happy crew, all sergeants and no bull, but we had to go through local flying, circuits and bumps and bombing practice all over again.

"On our first hop local flying, we got off the deck OK thanks to lengthy runways and spent a good hour nipping in and out of the Cornish coves and generally admiring the scenery. On return to Chivenor however, we found the Wellington had different habits from the Hudson and we just couldn't get down. We made several uncertain approaches too high, too fast and finally lopped in from about 30 feet having just missed two or three armoury sheds. We did several kangaroo hops before coming to rest on the grass, having shot off the concrete runway. The flight commander tore off several strips and thankfully checked that the aircraft was still intact, and so we were well bloodied into 172 Squadron."

THE LEIGH LIGHT

The 24-inch diameter 22-million candle-power Leigh Light was the brainchild of Sqn Ldr Humphrey de Verde Leigh who was on the staff at Coastal Command headquarters, and who reasoned that this would considerably ease the problem of identifying and attacking surfaced U-boats at night. He was able to gain the support of the C-in-C Coastal Command, ACM Sir Frederick Bowhill and, in March 1941 Wellington DWI P9223 was the first to be fitted with a Leigh Light for trials. It was deemed suitable as it was already fitted with an auxiliary engine and generator, although later aircraft would use battery packs. The light was manufactured by Savage & Parsons and was installed in a retractable ventral 'dustbin' just to the rear of the wing trailing edge. Interestingly, the Leigh Light Wellington was referred to as the DWI Mk.III, which has caused some confusion; it had nothing to do with the magnetic mine role, and was so called simply because it had an auxiliary engine on board, as did the Marks I & II.

Mk.VIII HX379 WN-A of 172 Squadron Chivenor 1942. Note Leigh Light housing under the letter A. This aircraft was ditched off Gibraltar on 3 May 1943. *(via Richard Forder)*

Mk.VIII W5674 DF-D at Brooklands after fitting with ASV Mk.II for 221 Squadron Limavady 1942. It was damaged beyond repair on 1 April 1943. (*Brooklands Museum*)

Despite the success of early trials, the fitment to service aircraft was initially very slow as the Air Ministry favoured the alternative nose-mounted Turbinlite which had already been fitted to Douglas Havoc aircraft as a (not very successful) aid to night interceptions of enemy bombers. Despite this, Leigh Light work was allowed to continue and eventually won the day. 1417 (Leigh Light) Flight was formed at Chivenor on 8 January 1942 under the control of 19 Group with four Wellington Mk.VIIIs plus two reserves; Sqn Ldr Jeaffreson Greswell (later Air Commodore CB DSO DFC) commanded the flight. The first operational aircraft W5733 arrived on 8 February, with the first training aircraft – P9223 the original Leigh Light trials Wellington – arriving five days later. By the end of the month it had been decided to bring the flight up to full squadron strength with sixteen aircraft plus four reserves, when it would become 172 Squadron. Thus by the summer of 1942, Wellingtons fitted with Leigh Lights and ASV radar were patrolling over the Bay of Biscay looking for U-boats going out on, or returning from, North Atlantic patrols from their French bases.

Fairfield Aviation at Elstree aerodrome in Hertfordshire was a civilian organisation which carried out repair, overhaul and modification of Lysanders and Wellingtons. In all, 473 Wellingtons passed through their hands, with the final example being a GR Mk.XVIII which left on delivery back to Coastal Command on 10 October 1945. Bob Clarke worked there throughout the war:

> "I used to accompany Flight Lieutenant Tim 'Timber' Woods on test flights and sometimes go with him and an inspector to do a final check on a nearby airfield (Handley Page's at Radlett), to pick up a badly damaged Wellington to fly back to Elstree. The runway at Radlett was built for the Halifax, and more suitable for an inexperienced pilot to land a shot-up aircraft than our shorter runway. We tried several modifications to the Wellington, the most successful I believe, was the Leigh Light. The fuselage was festooned with aerials and the flight deck was equipped with sensitive instruments.

36 Squadron GR.XIV at Benbecula in spring 1945. (*Wg Cdr George Williams*)

Their job was to patrol over the sea at night where the U-boats were known to operate, they had to surface after dark to recharge their batteries. The Wellington would pick up emissions from the sub, and would dive down, switching on and lowering a retractable searchlight built into the belly amidships. Identification being made, an instant attack took place with depth charges, bombs or gunfire. We had some initial problems as the strain of lowering the searchlight stretched the geodetic frame and hatches would become loose and fall off."

Fg Off Graham Harrison was a two-tour pilot with 612 and 172 Squadrons:

"Initially the light was effective, especially in the Bay of Biscay where the U-boats were accustomed to surface at night to recharge the batteries used for underwater propulsion, in transit to or from their pens on the French coast. After the fitting of improved aircraft radar they took countermeasures such as staying submerged at night and fighting it out in daytime with improved armament.

"The absence of a front gun turret in the maritime marque of Wellington made of the aircraft's nose section a sort of retreat or bower that was enhanced by a long bench covering the accumulators for the Leigh Light. The retractable turret amidships containing the light would be lowered and raised hydraulically by one of the three WOp/AGs while the second dicky, flat out on the bench, would direct it onto the target by operating a sort of short joystick. The light would be lowered one mile from the target at 250 feet very precisely, of course we had a radio altimeter. The first attacks came in too high because they hadn't got the radio altimeter, and if you came in too high you missed the target. If you went round again they'd be waiting for you. Another crew member stood astride him firing the free-standing Brownings through the vengeful nose of the aerial Moby Dick."

The first successful attack came on the night of 3/4 June 1942 when Wellington Mk.VIII ES986

Fg Off Graham Harrison, pilot with 612 and 172 Squadrons. (*Graham Harrison*)

flown by Sqn Ldr Greswell of 172 Squadron based at Chivenor, Devon attacked and seriously damaged the Italian submarine *Luigi Torelli* which was caught on the surface. The attack was recorded by the squadron as follows:

> 'This aircraft opened the scoring for 172 Squadron at 01:44 hours in position 45 degrees twenty minutes North 6 degrees fifteen minutes West. It obtained a contact on homing aerials six-and-a-half miles to starboard. A run up to the contact was made and the Leigh equipment was switched on about one mile distant. A U-boat was sighted on the surface three-quarters-of-a-mile dead ahead. The aircraft was at 450 feet and the U-boat was lost to sight due to the steepness of the dive which caused the fuselage to obscure the target. The aircraft obtained another contact at a distance of three-and-a-half miles and two starred pyrotechnic signals were fired by a U-boat which gave a good idea of its position and it was illuminated at three-quarters-of-a-mile. The aircraft descended to 50 feet and four depth charges were dropped, three of which were seen to explode and straddle the U-boat. A further contact was obtained and a light observed flashing two miles ahead. A U-boat fired a rocket which exploded at 400 feet into five or six white stars, the aircraft passing over it at 150 feet. The Leigh equipment was trained to extreme deflection allowing the rear gunner to fire 200 rounds which were seen to ricochet from the conning tower and hull along the water line.'

Prevented from submerging by the damage inflicted on it and damaged again three nights later by 10 (RAAF) Squadron Short Sunderlands, the *Luigi Torelli* sought refuge in a neutral Spanish port.

CENTIMETRIC ASV

Following the successful introduction of the Pegasus-engined GR Mk.VIII, the aircraft was further developed to produce the GR Mk.XI and GR Mk.XII both fitted with Hercules engines, and the GR Mk.XIV which was generally similar to the Mk.XII but with uprated engines. However, the most important development common to all these later variants was the ASV Mk.III centimetric radar mounted in a chin radome giving a 60 degree field-of-view ahead of the aircraft and dispensing with the 'Stickleback' aerials. In late 1942 the Germans had introduced the Metox radio receiver which enabled them to detect ASV Mk.II transmissions, resulting in a significant increase in Allied shipping losses. The main advantage of ASV Mk.III was that the beam could be directed accurately, resulting in increased and better resolution. The new radar was trialled in Wellington Mk.VIII Z8902 of the TFU in late 1941. On 1 March 1943 a 172 Squadron aircraft flew the first patrol over the Bay of Biscay using the new radar and on the 17th they identified the first U-boat at a range of nine miles. From then on U-boat sightings increased dramatically, and shipping losses fell from a peak of 400,000 tons a month to around 100,000 tons. The German navy's senior submarine officer, Admiral Karl Dönitz, ordered his submarines to stay on the surface and fight it out with attacking aircraft.

COASTAL COMMAND OPERATIONS

Following the initial successes in 1942, operations were stepped up as more squadrons joined the fight. In March 1943 Coastal Command started Operation Enclose with patrolling over the Bay of Biscay increased to such an extent that U-boats were being sighted on average once every four sorties by 172 Squadron alone, sinking six of them between March and July.

The Wellingtons could carry a wide variety of armament to aid their attacks, including ether two 18-inch torpedoes or depth charges, the latter being the choice against U-boats. Late in 1943, 612 Squadron aircraft were the first to be fitted with underwing racks for the carriage of eight rocket projectiles.

Graham Harrison offered his thoughts about the maritime Wimpy and its operations:

> "Training in Canada seemed to promise a Spitfire, but after my return to the UK the growing U-boat crisis led to a Coastal Command posting. When standing, the Wimpy undoubtedly had a droopy-drawers appearance. Airborne in white maritime livery with undercarriage retracted, the tall tailfin and wide wingspan lent it a certain grace which, with the distinctive whistle of its engines, if not a swan, perhaps resembled a snow goose. Its gently undulating wings heightened this impression. Some, flying in it for the first time, were given to remark 'Jesus, the kite flies by flapping its wings!' Entry was on the underside of the nose by means of a ladder, stowed on the starboard side of the cockpit. Ground crew were known to break into the George Formby song 'When I'm Cleaning Windows' with fantasy ukulele accompaniment when aircrew ascended the ladder. It was heavenly after my stint at the controls to stoop down into the nose and stretch out on the bench after pouring coffee from the crew-size flask. On a clear night the dark sheen of the sea – surprisingly close and often with a waxy moon path – would be visible through the rounded perspex nose which even when blind with rain seemed protective. Weather is the worst enemy; humour the best friend. Since almost all our patrols took us over Biscay I thought of this transparency as my 'bay window', a reminder of one in the front bedroom at home.
>
> "There were six people in the crew; the skipper, second dickey, navigator and three WOp/AGs who would change from turret, wireless and radar. They tended to specialise a bit, the chap we mostly had on the radar was an expert on the centimetric, he was a wizard. The chap in the rear turret we tended to forget about; but they would turn and turn about. The indication from the centimetric radar was with the wireless operator. But then of course the Germans came up with a bit of kit that could pick up our radar at maybe thirty miles and they would dive before we got there. So that was quite a setback, but eventually it was solved.
>
> "612 would send out three, four or five aircraft a night; we only had twelve on the squadron. We also had a Canadian and a Polish squadron at Chivenor, so there would be, I suppose, ten aircraft covering the Bay each night. A typical sortie would last about nine or ten hours. In the Bay there were no surface vessels. We did come across Spanish

fishing boats; as far as we were concerned we didn't attack them but some people did, and it was pretty well OK because they might have been signalling the enemy. But we were pretty decent chaps, don't have a go at them, you might wake them up.

"The duties of a Coastal Command second pilot were not onerous, as the name 'second dicky' suggests, and it quickly became clear after crewing-up that our flight lieutenant captain was not of the press-on-regardless school of pilots, whose lust for distinction in action could turn a routine patrol into a series of dangerous attempts to seek out and engage the enemy at all costs. This was understandable as he had already completed a tour on Beaufort torpedo bombers and spent his 'rest' towing drogues for U/T air gunners to shoot at – 'far more dangerous than ops'.

"Sometimes our 612 Squadron box patrols ended near the Spanish coast, where U-boats passing between their French coastal bases and the Atlantic killing grounds were known to skulk under the protection of Spanish territorial waters, proof that Coastal Command's saturation patrols over the Bay of Biscay were having the desired effect. I remember often seeing the lights of Coruna shining in the dark land mass, disappearing as we wheeled back into the Bay towards the Stygian Kingdom. From then on my dreams, sleeping and waking, were of escape from the battered grey aircraft carrier which Britain had become to something shining with warmth, light and love.

"On 29 October 1943 we and another crew were briefed together and the large chart on the ops room wall featured a U-boat symbol in the search area. I was second dicky to Flt Lt Chappell in Wimpy 'O', and our patrol area was from Isle de Bas to Ushant. In the early hours of the 30th Fg Off Roy Yeadon [flying HF205 'C'] whose box patrol had started where ours terminated, attacked U-415 north of Cape Ortegal in the Bay, carrying out a strafing run before dropping four depth charges which did enough damage to the U-boat to send it back to Brest. The Wellington was hit by 20 mm fire and crashed 50 metres behind the U-boat killing all six crew members. It was their luck to find it, ours to return to a breakfast of bacon and eggs; minimal drama attended the failure of an aircraft to return from patrol, they just quietly disappeared.

"In February '44 we were detached to Limavady, Northern Ireland patrolling and carrying out escort duty over the North Atlantic, returning to Chivenor in March. In May '44 we only did one operation over the Bay, a nine-hour trip on the 7th. Between ops we did a vast amount of training flights, Link trainer sessions, aircraft recognition, etc. On 16 March 1944 in 'H' we were one of two aircraft that returned safely from a patrol when we were recalled due to bad weather. Flt Sgt Anthony Verdon (of the Avro aircraft company's Verdon-Roe family), disappeared having failed to respond to the recall signal; sadly he had married only two weeks before his last flight. The last verse of 'Wellington Pilot' a poem by wartime WAAF Pamela Gilligan[1] says it all."

'A college boy, fair-haired
Prankish to hold off fate.
I'd watched the ops board
For his name.
A night erased him –
Sweep of the duster,
Soft fall of chalk.'

ENCOUNTERS WITH U-BOATS

The Wellington proved to be an excellent anti-submarine aircraft, accounting on its own for twenty-five of the 220 U-boat sinkings credited to Coastal Command, and contributing to many more. Almost exactly one month after the attack on the Italian submarine, 172 Squadron was able to claim its first U-boat sinking when American Plt Off Wiley Howell sent U-502 to the bottom west of La Rochelle on 5 July '42, for which he received the DFC. Flt Sgt Eddie Goodman was a WOp/AG-SE (Special Equipment) with 172 Squadron, and was involved in the same attack[2]:

> "6 July '42 Wellington BB503 from Llandow; pilot Flt Lt Southall, co-pilot Plt Off Elisha. Flying at 400 feet, we sighted a U-boat on the surface three-quarters-of-a-mile away at 01:28 hours in the Bay of Biscay. The aircraft attacked from 100 feet dropping four 296 lb Torpex depth charges set at 25 feet and spaced at 36 feet while the U-boat was still on the surface and also fired sixty rounds from the rear guns. All the depth charges exploded and all were estimated to have straddled the U-boat's track about 20 yards ahead of the bows. Flame floats were dropped at the end of the stick, and were seen to ignite with the explosion of the depth charges, and a sheet of flame lasting about one second was seen in the position of the explosion. No further results were observed in two-and-a-half hours."

This same Wellington ditched 140 miles west of Brest on 12 August '42 while on an anti-submarine patrol flown by Plt Off Alan Triggs (later MBE DFC). Shortly after sighting some fishing vessels, the aircraft developed engine trouble and sank in two minutes after successfully ditching. The crew took to the dinghy and were rescued after almost six days at sea, having only sustained minor injuries in the ditching. The search for them had involved forty-two sorties by Beaufighters, Whitleys and Hudsons all operating from Chivenor and eventually a motor vessel was sent to rescue them. However, the Germans had the same idea and a number of Ar 196 seaplanes were seen escorting German motor vessels. Prior to the arrival of the British vessel a Sunderland had alighted on the sea to pick up the crew but had come to grief, only one crew member surviving to join the Wellington crew in their dinghy. 172 Squadron ORB:

> '22/23 December '42 Wellington LB150 from Chivenor; pilot Fg Off Peter Stembridge, co-pilot Plt Off Payne. The aircraft was flying at 1,600 feet when a contact was obtained six miles ahead, and two minutes later a dark object was seen two miles distant and one point on the starboard bow. The aircraft was then at 700 feet making a diving turn to starboard. The pilot switched on the searchlight which lit up a U-boat fully surfaced. The aircraft continued the diving turn and when at about 150 feet a stick of four depth charges was dropped at an angle of about 65 degrees to the U-boat's track. The U-boat had started to dive when the searchlight was switched on, but the conning tower was still visible at the time of release. The depth charges fell close together owing to the steepness of the dive, and were estimated to have exploded in the centre of the swirl, very close behind. The aircraft turned onto a reciprocal course but nothing further was seen.
>
> '21 March '43 Wellington MP539 from Chivenor; pilot Fg Off Stembridge, co-pilot

Fg Off Jim Boyd. Flying at 1,000 feet a contact was obtained at seven miles. The aircraft homed in losing height and switched on the searchlight at one mile and at a height of 350 feet. We sighted a U-boat, thought to be of the 517-ton type, in the act of crash diving, the conning tower and stern being still visible. The aircraft continued the dive and attacked at 60 degrees from port quarter to starboard dropping six depth charges set to 25 feet spacing 50 feet, from a height of 70 feet just ahead of the swirl of the conning tower, the stern still being visible. One large explosion was seen as the aircraft passed, and in the trough caused by the explosion the full length of the U-boat was visible. As the conning tower was not seen it was thought that the keel was uppermost. The rear gunner fired bursts of fifty rounds and the aircraft made a wide circle to port and three minutes later came over the flame floats with the searchlight switched on at 250 feet. Two separate patches of very large bubbles were sighted, but no part of the U-boat was seen. The Admiralty later confirmed the kill as U-665.'

304 (Polish) Squadron Mk.XIV HF448 QD-V with ASV III radome, loading depth charges probably at Benbecula in late 1944. It survived the war to be scrapped in June 1945. (*ww2images*)

After the war the Naval Historical Branch looked again at the actions against U-665 and decided that it had in fact been sunk by a Whitley Mk.V of 10 OTU flown by Sgt J A Marsden. It was also concluded that the Wellington crew had actually attacked U-488 which was undamaged. Flt Lt Peter Stembridge subsequently sank U-437 on 28 April, for which he was awarded the DFC; he later rose to the rank of group captain and received the AFC.

The aircraft by no means had things all their own way; the Bay of Biscay in particular was frequently patrolled by Ju 88s and a number of aircraft fell victim to them. One 304 (Polish) Squadron crew had a narrow escape on 4 February 1943 when patrolling in daylight off the Bishop's Rock lighthouse on the Scilly Isles. Sgt L Matjaszek and his crew were flying Mk.IC 5718 from their base at Dale in Pembrokeshire:

> "Front gunner sighted a silhouette at 11:00 hours. Silhouette, which was thought to be a ship, was three miles on the starboard beam. Captain turned to investigate and from 300/400 yards recognised two Ju 88s flying together. The Wellington took cover in cloud and when it emerged the enemy aircraft were seen fifteen to twenty miles away on a reciprocal course."

On the night of 28/29 January 1944, by which time the squadron had moved to Predannack, Cornwall, the same crew came under attack during a patrol in Mk.XIV HF121:

> "At 21:07 hours attacked by Me 110. Two short bursts of tracer passed under the tail. Rear gunner replied with four bursts, making a total of 800 rounds. No results observed and no claims made."

When caught on the surface, the U-boats could put up a stout defence, and it is believed that around twenty Wellingtons succumbed to their anti-aircraft fire, although with many aircraft simply failing to return, the exact number remains unknown. Some of the losses have been identified using information from the U-boat commanders' logs including[3]:

4 March 1943 172 Squadron Fg Off Gordon Lundon in MP505 (who had sunk U-268 on 19 February) caught U-333 on the surface in the Bay of Biscay and illuminated it with its Leigh Light, dropping four depth charges without causing any damage. The U-boat's fire succeeded in bringing it down and it crashed in flames after passing over the boat. It had dropped four depth charges, two of which hit U-333 but one broke up without detonating and the other bounced off.

8 September 1943 172 Squadron Fg Off Cyril Payne MP509. U-402 was located by Fg Off T Armstrong (MP791), also of 172 Squadron, in the Bay of Biscay and attacked with six depth charges using his Leigh Light. Ten minutes later they saw Payne's Wellington make an attack, but it was hit by anti-aircraft fire, caught fire and crashed into the sea. The other members of the crew who were lost were: WO Alan Brigden, Plt Off Richard Gerrett, Sgt Louis Vaughan-Harrison and Sgt Charles Moody; in common with so many of the Coastal Command crews who have no known graves, they are commemorated on the Runnymede Memorial in Surrey. Flt Sgt R E J Cooper apparently survived to be rescued, and the U-boat was undamaged.

25 September 1943 179 Squadron Sqn Ldr George Riddell MP722 was hit by flak dropping depth charges on U-667, and was seen to fly away with the Leigh Light still on. An SOS message was heard and the aircraft failed to return.

27 November 1943 172 Squadron Plt Off Thomas Wilkin flying HF153 attacked U-764 and was hit by anti-aircraft fire during a strafing run in his second attack. The aircraft crash was witnessed by U-262 and U-238 which picked up two survivors–Flt Sgt Nicholas Martin and Sgt Thomas Semple. Semple was the WOp and later convinced the Germans that the Allied aircraft were able to passively locate U-boats by homing in on their radar detection devices, a deception which led to the order to turn off their Naxos radar.

8 January 1944 36 Squadron Fg Off Richmond Bamford in HF245 attacked U-343 two days after it had entered the Mediterranean through the Straits of Gibraltar. The aircraft dropped five depth charges which fell astern and missed, but was hit by anti-aircraft fire in the port wing and caught fire. It ditched, killing the pilot and navigator, with the remaining four being picked up by a ship the next morning. The U-boat may well have been the same one sighted the previous day by Plt Off P Thrower in MP807 which opened fire on his aircraft and then dived before he could make his attack. U-343 was then attacked by two 179 Squadron aircraft, the second dropped six depth charges, but several anti-aircraft hits set the port wing of Fg Off W F M Davidson's Wellington on fire and it crashed killing five crewmen; only the pilot was thrown clear. U-343 passed close to his dinghy twice but did not take him prisoner because they had 'more important things to do'. He was picked up by *HMS Active* the next morning and later received the DFC.

31 January 1944 172 Squadron Flt Sgt Leighton Richards MP813. U-608 was attacked west of Bordeaux but no damage resulted and the U-boat scored hits on the aircraft which crashed shortly afterwards killing the crew. Witnessed by 304 (Polish) Squadron's Flt Sgt S Czekaski.

10 February 1944 612 Squadron Fg Off Roy Durnford in MP758 was fought off by U-283, suffered engine trouble and failed to return. In the early hours of the 11th 407 Squadron's MP578 flown by Fg Off Peter Heron RCAF (later DFC) also attacked the U-boat from a height of 60 feet and successfully sank it with depth charges.

24 May 1944 612 Squadron Fg Off Ken Davies in 'L' was shot down on his first operational sortie by U-736 which had been severely damaged by a 224 Squadron Liberator flown by Flt Lt E W Lindsay in the Bay of Biscay.

30 July 1944 172 Squadron Flt Lt Lionel Such in HF449 attacked U-618, was hit by AA fire and crashed, all crew lost.

14 August 1944 172 Squadron Fg Off Douglas Adams in 'P' shot down by U-445 on Brest-La Pallice route.

27 August 1944 172 Squadron Fg Off G E Whiteley in NB798 shot down by U-534. The squadron ORB recorded that the Wellington crew sighted a fully surfaced U-boat which immediately opened fire. It was attacked with six depth charges but no results were observed. The aircraft's port engine was feathered and the aircraft was ditched. Four of the crew found themselves in the water and two got into a dinghy while the other two clung on to it, one being the navigator Fg Off Roderick Gray RCAF who died during the night despite Whiteley holding on to him. They were picked up after fifteen hours by a 10 (RAAF) Squadron Sunderland and landed at Mount Batten, near Plymouth. Gray was posthumously awarded the George Cross, the citation reading:

> 'This officer was the navigator of a Wellington aircraft which was shot down into the Atlantic by a U-boat. Flying Officer Gray and three other members of the crew managed to extricate themselves from the aircraft. Despite a severe wound in the leg, Flying Officer Gray succeeded in inflating his own dinghy, and assisted into it his captain, who had also been wounded. Cries were shortly heard from another member of the crew, who had broken his arm; Flying Officer Gray helped him also into the dinghy. Although suffering intense pain, Flying Officer Gray refused to get into the dinghy, knowing that it could not hold more than two persons and for some hours he hung on

> to its side, aided by one of its occupants and by the fourth member of the crew. In spite of increasing pain and exhaustion, he steadfastly refused to endanger his comrades by entering the dinghy, and eventually lost consciousness and died. When it became light his companions, realising that he was dead, were forced to let his body sink. Flying Officer Gray displayed magnificent courage and unselfish heroism, thus enabling the lives of his comrades to be saved.'

Leslie Harrison (no relation to Graham) was a navigator on 172 Squadron and recalled that the CO at Chivenor arranged for some forward defensive armament to be fitted to his aircraft in an attempt to provide some additional protection:

> "Wg Cdr R G Musson introduced a light machine gun into the otherwise faired perspex nose of 172 Squadron's Leigh Light Wellingtons. As the crew member detailed to man this gun during a generally uneventful period of service in Coastal Command, I found it had a very effective role to play when attacking a surfaced and fighting-back U-boat. We always referred to it as a 'scare gun'; it fired 100 percent tracer as against one-in-three conventional spacing, and its sole purpose was to concern the U-boat gunners and hopefully, influence them to keep their heads down. As a morale booster it gave me (as an otherwise temporarily unemployed navigator) a definite feeling of doing something useful during an attack. I seem to recall that it was a .300 gun as against the other .303s, a very minor difference perhaps, but reflecting its non-offensive purpose in the sense of potentially structurally damaging."

Wg Cdr Roland Musson was killed flying MP624 on 24 August 1943 when the aircraft hit wires on high ground in a rainstorm following take-off from Chivenor. Another peril to Wellington operations came from what nowadays tends to be referred to as 'friendly fire' from vessels. At least two aircraft were lost this way, with 179 Squadron's Plt Off Ronald Bramwell and crew in

Surrendered U-boats in Derry harbour after being escorted in by Coastal Command May 1945. (*Graham Harrison*)

HX776 being shot down in error by an armed trawler off the Shetlands on 8 November 1942, and 172 Squadron's HX482 suffering a similar fate off Swansea, Glamorgan at the hands of a US oil tanker on 19 August 1942.

Having completed his first tour with 612 Squadron in July 1944, Graham Harrison was then sent to 6 (Coastal) OTU at Silloth as an instructor, before beginning his second tour in October with 172 Squadron at Limavady in Northern Ireland:

> "We were covering the North Western approaches. Why I don't know because a lot of the U-boats had got under-water breathing by then, therefore it was even more difficult to find them. The chance of picking up a couple of feet of periscope in a fairly rough sea was almost nil. But they were developing sono buoys which you drop in the water that could pick up the submarine, and we did some training on it. At the end of the war after the Germans caved in, the U-boats were told to surface on two lines, one in the North West approaches and one in the Bay of Biscay, and they did. We were surprised to see the number there were, just popping up and we escorted them to I think it was Ballykelly where they surrendered.
>
> "While we were in Chivenor the Canadians got one definite kill, the Poles got one definite kill, and one of our chaps got one kill. Apart from that, any attacks were not certain kills. You might have seen a drop of oil on the surface but of course the U-boats used to release that as a decoy. So the main job really was to keep them under; this was after the initial success of the Leigh Light when we killed quite a few, it panicked the Germans. For quite a period they started surfacing in the daytime. We thought we saw a German aircraft over the Bay once, but it was just a spot on the perspex!
>
> "When I became captain I spent a lot of time with the ground crew, which was unusual; they were tremendous chaps. A wise pilot always looks after his ground crew."

Mk.XIV NB814 RW-Q of 36 Squadron Benbecula, shadowing surrendered U-boats 14 May 1945. (*Graham Harrison*)

In the latter stages of the war, with the anti-U-boat campaign largely over, attention turned to the menace of E-boats and midget submarines operating against Allied shipping in the southern North Sea bringing supplies across from England to support the armies. 415 (RCAF) Squadron flew almost constant E-boat search operations, and were frequently frustrated due to the enemy's jamming. On 26 December 1944 Fg Off J F Paterson took off from Docking in aircraft 'H' just after six o'clock in the evening to patrol in co-operation with the Royal Navy. A contact was made just before midnight and a flare was dropped which caught in the aircraft's aerials. With the aircraft in danger of catching fire, an SOS was sent and course set for Catfoss; fortunately the flare burned itself out and the aircraft landed with only minor damage.

A brand-new GR Mk.XII MP684 awaiting delivery from Brooklands. It served with four squadrons to be scrapped in April 1945. (*Brooklands Museum*)

J R 'Eric' Cameron RCAF WOp/AG (W/AG):

> "I was posted to 407 RCAF Squadron, Coastal Command anti submarine Wellington Mk.XII, operating alternatively from Chivenor and Wick. Our crew never got a sub, but we had our share of malfunction scares. We were part of the special 407 Squadron Langham (Norfolk) detachment in May '45, hunting the German midget subs off the Dutch coast. On 4 May, just as the war was coming to an end, we returned one morning after a night patrol and our pilot made the error of landing downwind. We overshot the runway and would have demolished a nice little farmhouse if the co-pilot had not yanked up the undercart. We skidded around for a while, spewing shards of propellers, etc., but all got out OK and the Wimpy didn't burn. It was a brand new kite too!
>
> "During the spring of 1945, some 407 Squadron crews were sent down to Weymouth in Dorset to tour a U-boat that had surrendered to a Coastal Command Wellington. It was an interesting experience for Wimpy Coastal Command aircrew types to be able to visit a U-boat – one that had an aircraft painted on its conning tower!"

Even after the cessation of hostilities, patrolling aircraft finding U-boats on the surface heading home still had to be very careful. 304 (Polish) Squadron's ORB recorded one such event on the night of 11/12 May 1945 when patrolling the designated Blue Route for surrendering German vessels. Operating from St.Eval, Cornwall, the aircraft was MB806 which was scrapped just one month later, and it was flown on this occasion by Plt Off K Garstecki:

Mk.XIVs at Chivenor Devon, including MP774 P of 179 Squadron and HF127 2-C of 407 (RCAF) Squadron. (*IWM FLM 1995*)

"At 23:45 the aircraft was over a surfaced U-boat after having obtained a radar contact three minutes earlier. A message was sent at once to control and endeavours were made to discern the U-boat's number, first by Aldis lamp and then by Leigh Light, but both attempts were unsuccessful. The U-boat was seen to be flying what looked to be like a white flag with a black German cross. It responded to a request from control for the number of the U-boat, the aircraft replied that this was unknown and that a task force was near. This 'task force' however, turned out to be six fishing vessels. The aircraft shadowed the U-boat until 05:20, trying to establish contact with it by Aldis lamp. The U-boat replied only once, but only the letters N.T. were read. On reaching the limit of endurance, the aircraft returned to base.

"Note: This U-boat is now believed to be U-516 which already had an Allied boarding party aboard."

A unit that specialised in seeking and destroying the E-boats was 524 Squadron reformed on 7 April 1944 at Davidstow Moor with Mk.XIII and XIV Wellingtons which were put to use from 30 April patrolling the French coast to identify and illuminate targets, which were then attacked by other strike aircraft (usually Beaufighters), although the squadron did also carry out its own bombing operations against enemy shipping. In July 1944 it moved to Langham, Norfolk to be closer to the main area of activity, with sorties also being flown from Thorney Island, Hampshire, on Operation Purblind leading North Coates-based Beaufighters against German convoys. In April 1945 it took part in operations 'Taboo' and 'Physic' directing Royal Navy forces, and it continued in this role until its last sortie on 11 May, before disbanding on 25 June.

During its brief career 524 Squadron lost ten aircraft, including MF374 on 13 July 1944 during an anti-shipping patrol captained by Flt Lt The Honourable David Grimston DFC, a son of the 4th Earl of Verulam. His brother Brian was a squadron leader and DFC holder who was lost in April 1943 during a raid on Kiel in a 156 Squadron Lancaster. On 4 October '44 524 Squadron's MF319 under the command of Fg Off Michael Smith, fell foul of Oblt Walter Briegleb of 10./NJG3 just north of Borkum after a five-minute combat during which the rear gunner managed to disable Briegleb's starboard engine.

MEDITERRANEAN OPERATIONS

The role of GR Wellingtons in the Mediterranean was very much the same as it was in Coastal Command's home waters. Arriving at Blida, Algeria in June 1943, 36 Squadron shared the task of protecting convoys passing through the Straits of Gibraltar with 179 Squadron which arrived on the rock in November 1942. From September 1942 the eastern end of the sea was covered by 458 (RAAF) Squadron which was based at Shallufa in Egypt, before moving west to Tunisia and then to Foggia Main as the North African campaign came to a close. In addition to these, 38 and 221 Squadrons who worked so successfully in collaboration against surface vessels, also took their part in basic GR work. At the end of the war the SAAF established 17 and 27 Squadrons at Gianaclis, Egypt with a few GR Mk.XIIs pending receipt of Warwicks, but they took no part in operations and all the Wellingtons had left within a few months.

Ricky Rickard was the navigator in Flt Sgt John's crew on 179 Squadron, arriving in Gibraltar at the beginning of 1943. He kept a very detailed diary to complement the entries in his log book, which illustrate the very long hours of tedious searching, most often with no result:

> 'Jan 23. Up for breakfast as usual and reported at flights. Heard that one of our 'planes was missing and that another had crash landed on the 'drome, but luckily with no harm to the crew. We took off at 23:00 hours for a patrol east. This took ten-and-a-half hours, but luckily was uneventful. Drifts were checked by throwing out flame floats down the flare-chute. Use of the radio was strictly forbidden, so fixes were hard to come back, or took ages to work out!
>
> '29 Jan. Rather dull weather, flew a trip off SE coast of Spain groaning along at 120 knots – a lovely clear night and the Mediterranean sky is full of stars and the coastline is full of lights. This is a cushy trip for me as we are within reach of land most of the time and can get good fixes. Maybe I'll do some astro shots to while away the ten hours ahead. It is now midnight and we are due on patrol. We are turning in towards Algiers, we observe heavy ack-ack fire and what appears to be exploding bombs. Soon after, we were diverted by code to search for a U-boat sighted off Alborán. This involved a cross-over patrol in the suspected area, but obviously Jerry knows we are around and won't surface. Have just descended and lit up a terrified Spanish trawler, luckily with no barrage balloon and steel cables. After eleven hours and a final hectic quarter hour due to crosswinds and two attempts to land, we finally got down after a split-ass turn.
>
> '10 Feb. At 9:30 in the evening there was panic on the 'drome, as the petrol dump had gone up in flames. We turned out to push some of our Wimpys out of the way, although it was hinted that some had been pushed nearer.

'18 Feb. Made a very good landfall at 08:30 at Agadir in French Morocco and after breakfast and clean up had a wander round the camp, inspecting French aircraft. The camp itself and the quarters looked remarkably like a Foreign Legion camp. We were called up at 03:30 hours for 05:00 hours take-off to do a convoy patrol off the Canaries under the code name 'Teapot'. The convoy was in from the USA carrying supplies and equipment to support the Casablanca landings. We circled the convoy for several hours, receiving and transmitting Morse code messages by Aldis lamp. Not only was it difficult to keep up with their transmission speed, but it was tricky to keep them in view from the starboard wing of a constantly circling aircraft. However we managed to cope until it was time to leave.

'It being broad daylight, we thought we should have a good look at the Sahara Desert before returning to base, so inland we went down to 100 feet above the dunes. We came across what looked like a Foreign Legion fort, but as we got nearer it appeared to be a harem and we could see many heavily-garbed female figures dashing for cover (station orders subsequently posted said that the practice of low flying over Moroccan properties must cease forthwith). We carried on further to Dar Sibena in the Spanish Moroccan territory of Sidi Ifni and we came across what appeared to be a small flying strip. On closer inspection and still at only 100 feet, we saw several three-engined Junkers transports lined up on the tarmac and next thing we knew there was gunfire and the fabric of our 'plane was peppered in several places, one uncomfortably close to my ear.

'An all white 'plane against a pure blue sky and at very low level, we offered a sitting target and having broken rules by flying over neutral territory (so called) we had still to explain how we had incurred damage. We got out of this by claiming that when we took off in the dark, several loose stones and rocks had hit us (the runway was quite primitive), but we had decided that no serious damage was suffered so we proceeded with the patrol. Luckily this was accepted without question.

'21 Feb. The non appearance of "Y" for Yorker was giving some concern, as she had not returned to base, but her endurance time had not yet been reached so there was still hope. We learned that "Y" had force landed in Spanish Morocco and the crew had been interned for the duration of the war. [HX744 was brought down by Spanish flak near Ifni, and after force landing the crew destroyed the aircraft.]

'4 Mar. After something like forty operational trips since August '42, the strain was beginning to take its toll. Not only had we scooted around the upper North Sea, the Bay of Biscay, the North Atlantic and most parts of the Med and always at night, we had played as hard as possible. We hoped all this effort had done something to suppress U-boat activities. A 'blip' on the ASV would sometimes indicate a U-boat surfaced, but quite often after diving down and using our searchlight, it would turn out to be a small fishing boat or even a Royal Navy vessel. In any case a quick turn round and climb away to avoid trigger-happy sailors was always advisable. With such diversions three or four times each hour, and with variation of speed, height and direction, it made keeping a DR plot a full-time job and the navigator had no respite throughout the whole trip, with exception maybe of the last hour when familiar coastline has been picked up in the early dawn hours – and as the RAF saying went: "You shouldn't have joined..."

'7 Mar. Took off at 21:00 hours night flying over the Mediterranean for just over eleven hours and got as far as 6 degrees east. There was no evidence of any excitement, but to stay up so long in the dark and return to base safe and sound was enough in itself. We found out that Sgt Hodge and his crew, on the same trip as us, had failed to leave the deck on take-off and had ditched in the Bay. Naturally the kite was lost in the drink, but thanks to Air Sea Rescue all members of the crew were safe. This sort of thing occurred fairly frequently, with old Wellingtons, extra full tanks, 1,000 lbs of depth charges and a choice of one runway only 900 yards long. Quite often we only became airborne because the end of the runway was about 30 feet above the sea.

'29 Mar. I was duty NCO. Just after midnight some of the erks had been winding up one of the lads that he couldn't fly a Wimpy and with the beer talking wonders he accepted the challenge. Somehow they managed to start the engines on "C" Charlie and with the erk at the controls he opened up both engines to full boost. Only one thing was wrong – he was facing the Rock and taxiing at full speed and eventually crashed into four more transit Wellingtons and set all of them on fire. The flames could be seen across the bay at Algeciras and the Spanish consulate must have thought that Gibraltar was under a full-scale air raid. Strangely the erk was discovered unharmed, cowering in the rear gun turret of "C" Charlie and sure he must have been for the high jump!

'27 Apr. The Big Day has arrived and we are due to take LB156 "L" for Leather back to UK and with more than relief we finally get off the deck at 22:30 hours. With much singing of "Green Grow the Rushes O" over the intercom and nine hours flying, we finally touched down at Chivenor and our tour of ops was completed with no serious mishap – Praise Be! Devon at six in the morning, with its rolling mists and pleasing hills, is a joy at any time, but to our crew completing an ops tour it was heaven. We gathered up our kit, collected leave passes and travel vouchers and caught the first available train to Paddington. Having been together for a long time, we couldn't split up without celebrating. Somehow we found ourselves in a Marylebone Road pub, where we imbibed a few beers and toasted each other's health. I then went instructing at 105 (Transport) OTU at Bramcote and Nuneaton.'

Despite Rickard's lack of action, for two of his squadron's crews this was a very productive period. Flt Sgt Donald Cornish DFM RCAF and his crew accounted for three U-boats in quick succession in operations from Gibraltar and Lagens Field in the Azores during 1943, sinking U-431 on 21 October, U-566 on 24 October and U-542 on 26 November. Fg Off Donald McRae DFC RCAF and his crew sank U-134 on 24 August, U-211 on 19 November, and on 6 September damaged U-760 so severely that two days later she put into the Spanish port of Vigo and was interned.

By 1944 U-boats were becoming harder to find and there were other threats to counter; Master Navigator G P 'Tiny' Alborn of 38 Squadron:

Sgt Dennis Jackson, 36 Squadron air gunner. (*Dennis Jackson*)

"I was an Observer/Nav.B aboard 38 Squadron Wellington 'L' that carried out a search for an Italian midget submarine in co-operation with the navy on 3 April 1945. We found it off Cattolica, sank it in a position that I logged as just south of Rimini. The submarine was CB 6 which had been seized by the Germans when Italy surrendered and handed over to the reformed fascist Italian navy."

W/O Dennis Jackson, WOp/AG with 36 Squadron, stayed with the unit when it moved from India to North Africa:

"We followed the 8th Army all the way to Algeria, after which we got some new Mk.Xs and other marks with ASV radar. We were night flying over the whole of the Western Mediterranean on anti-submarine patrols, and it was at this time that I got my Goldfish [awarded to airmen who had suffered a ditching].

"On 16 May '44 in Mk.XIV HF272 we attacked and possibly sank a U-boat, although I think the navy claimed it. I was in the rear turret at the time and the trouble with the Leigh Light was that the U-boat gunners could just shoot up the beam and be fairly certain of hitting us. Anyway, we made a run over them and one depth charge went off with an almighty flash, so we were pretty sure we had hit it. When we got back to base, thinking we had escaped unscathed, the fitter told to us 'look at the tail'. There was a ruddy great hole just about a couple of feet from where I had been sitting. It was probably a piece of shrapnel caused by the depth charge explosion; any closer it could have ruined my manhood!"

The U-boat was U-616 and HF272 flown by W/O J M Cooke was the first to attack it. An hour later another 36 Squadron aircraft HF298 flown by Plt Off H R Swain RAAF made contact with the submarine again and it was forced to the surface, evacuated and sunk. At the end of May the German High Command issued orders that no further U-boats were to enter the Mediterranean due to the numbers being lost while passing through the Straits of Gibraltar. Dennis Jackson:

"We were carrying out a search in a Mk.XIV flown by the flight commander, Sqn Ldr Carmichael, for U-boats based at Marseilles, which used to be found around the Balearics and Corsica. It was 31 January '44, a beautiful night but as we headed back over the Algerian coast the weather clamped. We were based at Blida and we knew we would struggle to get back there. We still had 2,000 lbs of depth charges on board so we jettisoned them in the sea to lighten the aircraft, but still did not have enough fuel to make it back to any of the other airfields, all of which were just strips in the desert really, and none were less than an hour's flying time away. We had no other choice than to come down in the sea, so we lit the sea with flame-floats and ditched four miles off the coast. The aircraft broke its back in the ditching and sank after about ten minutes. We were all OK, no injuries, and were picked up by a French coastal launch after about forty-five minutes. The French hosted us very well and out came the wine. Then we were transferred to an RAF Air Sea Rescue launch and they gave us rum, so by the time we were landed in Algiers we were well gone.

"We flew a Special Duty from Corsica to cover the mock landings at Marseilles in August '44 and draw enemy troops away from the real landing site at Nice. There were three landing craft a mile apart from each other on spread-out approaches to the coast, and each of the three Wellingtons flew over one of them towards the coast, then did a 180-degree turn and flew back over them, dropping 'Window' the whole time. We carried on doing this until we got to within half-a-mile of the coast, when they started

Mk.XIV final assembly at Broughton. (*BAE via 99 Squadron*)

shooting and looking for us with searchlights so we scarpered. We flew another op after that looking for any subs. By this time we had been on ops for two years and we were told we were tour-ex. I had about 800 hours in my log book, of which 400 were operational."

Having already completed a Bomber Command tour with 75 (NZ) Squadron, Fg Off Jack Wakefield RNZAF then flew as rear gunner with Flt Lt Albert Wiggins DSO DFC RAAF on 38 Squadron:

"On my first trip, 24 October '42, we flew out over the Mediterranean from the border of Egypt and Libya and encountered atrocious weather with half a dozen waterspouts visible at one time. After being tossed around like a straw the captain decided to return to base. The approach seemed a bit staggering to me, heavy load, under-powered aircraft, dusk falling rapidly. I took out the astro hatch and lay down on the stretcher with my feet on the main spar. The undercarriage gave way on landing, one wing dug in, and the aircraft's back was broken. Two torpedoes had been torn out of the bomb bay and were lying under the wing, hissing compressed air. Later on we did mostly convoy protection as the 8th Army needed supplies; we moved up behind them. At El Alamein we could hear the gunfire from our desert strip. Quite often for a few days we would sleep in the aircraft, underneath the aircraft, on the ground in our clothes, meals were hours away.

"I did a course down the Red Sea exercising with *HMS Abdiel,* a fast minelayer; we dropped flares and picked her up easily on radar. We circled the convoy for eight hours after firing the colours of the day on our approach at a height of about 1,000 feet. I think that was the most satisfying part of my service, knowing that those men down below in the ships were sitting on fuel, ammunition, etc.; we were watching over them and they relied on us. In roughly the six months that I served in that area we never lost a ship."[4]

AIR SEA RESCUE

The increasing pace of air operations of all types that, of necessity, flew over the sea meant that more and more aircrew were finding themselves 'down in the drink'. It was realised that the loss of valuable aircrew, who had baled out and taken to their dinghies only to die of exposure waiting to be rescued, had to be addressed. Although the fleet of RAF-operated rescue launches had been doubled in 1940, there was a need for dedicated search aircraft, not least to relieve the pressure on other non-specialised flying units who were being called upon to conduct searches. In the UK a number of dedicated rescue squadrons were established from 1941 onwards, largely relying on aircraft such as the Anson and Lysander to carry out searches.

The situation in the Mediterranean was different as the much larger area to be covered demanded the use of longer-range aircraft. In Malta, an Air Sea Rescue & Communication Flight was formed at Hal Far on 1 March 1943, equipped with a variety of aircraft including Wellingtons to conduct searches and Westland Walrus amphibians to effect rescues. In August the unit moved across the island to Takali, returning to Hal Far in January 1944 prior to being redesignated Malta Communications Flight and ceasing its search and rescue role.

Meanwhile the Western Mediterranean was being looked after by 1 (North Africa) Air Sea Rescue Unit which was established in 242 Group under the command of Fg Off J W Roll at Sidi Ahmed, Tunisia in June 1943, moving to Protville, Tunisia in August and disbanding in December. During its brief existence its fleet consisted initially of four Wellington Mk.ICs and four complete crews, but in September the four original aircraft were declared unfit for further service and replaced by one Mk.X and one Mk.XIII. Search operations were flown with two pilots, a navigator and three WOp/AGs. Typical of the sorties flown out was a lengthy series of searches for a missing sailing boat recounted in the ORB:

'4 August. One sortie of three hours thirty mins made by Fg Off K P Cupper to search for sailing boat containing three men believed to be Italians or Germans. No sightings made.

'5 August. One sortie of eight hours twenty mins by Sgt K E George to continue search for sailing boat. A Marine Marker was dropped in DR position and the area in the vicinity thoroughly searched, without result. The aircraft then returned to the DR position and commenced square search of the area. At 09:53 hours the aircraft made a sighting of a sailing boat with three occupants and dropped a Marine Marker in the position. The behaviour of the men in the boat was suspicious, and at one time they were endeavouring to put out the Marine Marker but after several unsuccessful attempts they desisted and commenced to wave at the aircraft. The aircraft remained circling the boat pending the arrival of rescue aircraft or High Speed Launch. At 14:20 hours no relief aircraft had arrived and as the Wellington had reached the limit of endurance it was decided to return to base. A ration bag was therefore dropped for use of the occupants of the boat and the aircraft set course for base.

'6 August. One sortie of seven hours thirty-five mins flown by Fg Off K B Cupper. To continue searching for sailing boat and three occupants found on the previous day. A sighting was made but on investigation boat was found to be empty. The aircraft homed a High Speed Launch to the scene and then set out for base, sighting an empty aircraft dinghy on route which was sunk by gunfire. When forty-five minutes from base the aircraft developed engine trouble and the port engine failed. A distress signal was sent to base and the crew prepared for ditching. The aircraft however, continued to maintain height and limped home to base on the starboard engine where the pilot made a safe landing.

'7 August. Continuing the story of "The three men in a boat". It appears that a Walrus aircraft had been despatched from Palermo the previous day and had succeeded in rescuing them, after which nothing further was heard of the Walrus or its crew and occupants. No.1 Air Sea Rescue Unit was therefore instructed to fly a sortie to search for the Walrus."

Extensive searches over the next few days failed to find any trace of the Walrus. Most of the twenty to twenty-five sorties flown each month were similar, either responding to reported sightings of small boats or dinghies, or reacting to requests to search for aircraft known to have come down in the sea, with Beaufighters, Hudsons and B-17s being reported at various times. Most commonly nothing was found, although there were occasional successes, such as the 30 July search for the crew of a B-26 Marauder which found the five men in their dinghy. After dropping rations to them, the Wellington circled for two hours until the arrival of a Catalina which alighted on the sea and picked them up. Unfortunately it was unable to take off again and a High Speed Launch finally came to the rescue.

To replace these rather modest units, two full Air Sea Rescue squadrons were established in the autumn of 1943, with 293 Squadron being formed at Blida, Algeria in November with Warwicks to cover the Western Mediterranean. It was preceded, on 24 September, by 294 Squadron at Berka near Benghazi, commanded by Wg Cdr R G Walker, with a mixture of Walrus amphibians and Wellington Mk.ICs and XIs, under the control of the Aircraft Safety Centre – Persian

Gulf, which had its headquarters in Bahrain. This squadron moved to Amriya South (Egypt) the following month, Idku (also in Egypt) in March 1944 and finally Basra (Iraq) in June 1945, while maintaining detachments at various times in Cyprus, Greece, Libya, Palestine and further south at Sharjah, Masirah and Muharraq.

The squadron was certainly kept very busy as evidenced by Flt Sgt Lister's log for the month of February 1944. On the 16th he and his crew were airborne in W5620 for six-and-a-half hours searching for a missing Ventura crew north of Gambut. Two days later in HX510, they flew for almost eight hours looking for the crew of a 162 Squadron Wellington south of Crete. They went searching for a Marauder crew on the 21st, found a Beaufighter crew on the 25th, failed to find another on the 26th and successfully located yet another on the 29th during an eight-hour search. Although Warwicks joined 294 Squadron in November 1944, the Wellingtons soldiered on alongside them until the unit was disbanded on 8 April 1946.

CHAPTER SIX

THE FORGOTTEN AIR FORCES

"The bombing carried out by British Wellingtons...formed the background and the unceasing accompaniment to the land fighting"
Lord Mountbatten of Burma, Supreme Allied Commander South-East Asia

Three theatres of war in which the Wellington was involved but which little has previously been written about are South-East Asia and the maritime operations conducted by the French and South African Air Forces off the west coast of Africa, and the RAF in East Africa and Arabia.

SOUTH-EAST ASIA

When Japan began its attacks on Singapore in December 1941, the RAF bombing presence in the region comprised four squadrons of Blenheims in Malaya. Despite valiant efforts they were largely ineffective against an overwhelming force and Singapore surrendered on 15 February 1942. Thus began a long and bitter struggle which only ended with the Japanese surrender in August 1945. The spearhead of the British ground fighting efforts throughout this long time was the 14th Army, which came to be known as 'the forgotten army'; hence its blue uniform compatriots were the forgotten air force.

REINFORCEMENT

With Japanese forces rapidly advancing into Burma it was decided that a Wellington bomber force should be sent to the region with all speed, and two existing squadrons were chosen to join 225 Group; 99 and 215. A few short weeks after the collapse of Singapore, personnel from both units set out on the long sea voyage to India.

99 SQUADRON

99 Squadron had been gifted a complete squadron's worth of Wellingtons by the citizens of Madras, India; henceforth it officially became known as 99 (Madras Presidency) Squadron. Meanwhile, starting on 15 February 1942, their aircrews were flying six aircraft out to India via North Africa, where they were delayed in order to carry out some

99 Squadron Mk.IC B 'Madura I' named after an Indian district being unloaded of its bombs after a mishap at Digri March 1943. (*Norman Didwell*)

Wg Cdr Lucian Brett Ercolani DSO DFC. (*via Norman Didwell*)

ferrying work for the hard-pressed crews there. Lucian Ercolani unexpectedly found himself rejoining the squadron at this time:

"Air Chief Marshal Jackie Baldwin was AOC 3 Group when we were there and then when he went out to India, I was at the dinner when he made his last parting farewell speech. I had met him several times before and flown under his command, and he asked if I would like to go out on the India run. I said, 'Yes, very much.' I was posted out as his PA with instructions to call at his office in the Imperial Hotel. He didn't know when I was coming as they took us out by ship but it landed us in West Africa.

"We got fed up with hanging around then we went up to Kano, which is the crossroads of the desert. There happened to be an old Wellington on the side of the field, but very few people around. I decided that I would get into it. The ground crew were surprised and reluctant to come up with me, so I was the only one in it. Once in the air, I realised it probably wasn't a good idea to have gone up by myself, but fortunately it worked out all right.

"It was on the delivery run to Cairo so I hitched a lift. From there I managed to get on the ship into Bombay and on to Delhi and the AOC. We went to the C-in-C of India and rolled into his office where he pulls this drawer out and fishes out the tape with which you mark your rank. I was a flight lieutenant, so he fished in his drawer and pulled out a thin strip and said, 'There you are. Go and get that sewn on.' So I walked out having become a squadron leader! I arrived down with 99 when Jimmy Black was CO."

Sqn Ldr Ercolani, Wg Cdr Black, Flt Lt McDonald, Flt Lt Groves, WO Stanley, Digri Christmas Day 1942. (*Chota Ray via Norman Didwell*)

Mess Staff, Digri Christmas 1942 (*Norman Didwell*)

The Wellingtons eventually arrived at Pandaveswar in Bengal where they were left, the crews continuing by train to Ambala, north of Delhi where the squadron was re-established on 1 June 1942. Following a period of settling in and becoming familiar with the local situation, the squadron finally started operations on 18 November when eight aircraft attacked the airfield at Meiktila. By that time the unit had relocated to Digri, just east of Calcutta and closer to the intended area of operations. However the facilities there were still very basic to the extent that aircraft had to position to an advanced landing ground at Feni on the coast near Chittagong in order to bomb up. Lucian Ercolani:

Wg Cdr J B Black OC 99 Squadron, Digri November 1942. (*99 Squadron*)

> "We still had Wellingtons. Oh well we had very strong affection for them. One would take a hell of a lot of punishment! It was a wonderful aeroplane. I can't really compare it to others because I hadn't flown anything else. But I certainly have a lot of good memories of Wellingtons. Wonderful, good, old, tough geodetic construction; an amazing piece of work. We were flying over Burma obviously, and mostly still at night, over the Indian Ocean. Then we were going north – Mandalay and places like that. Seems an awful shame to think you go to bomb Mandalay – where the old flying fishes play."

W/O Tom Claridge flew as a captain on both the Wellington squadrons:

Mk.IC HD950 B of 99 Squadron burnt out at Digri after an oxygen bottle explosion and fire, 20 December 1942. (*Norman Didwell*)

"I did twenty ops with 99 Squadron, was then posted to 215 Squadron at Jessore, did more ops with them and after 280 hours of ops converted to Dakotas. Our front turrets were removed in the UK to reduce weight. 99 Squadron's first 'B' was destroyed at Digri on return from a raid with one 500 lb bomb hung up which exploded as the bomb doors were being opened. On one of several ops to Heho airfield (a long trip over ten hours), the target could not be located due to really bad weather so we returned with bombs on board and the undercarriage collapsed on landing."

99 Squadron line-up for first operation from Digri, India October 1942. (*99 Squadron*)

By the autumn of 1942 operations were in full swing and the 99 Squadron ORB records fierce attacks by Nakajima Ki.43 Hayabusa fighters of the 50th Sentai on the night of 23/24 November during a raid on Meiktila aerodrome by seven Wellingtons:

'Wellington G [HD977] Fg Off Brown. Primary target bombed from 8,000 feet and bursts seen on the runway. Intercepted by night fighter soon after bombing. Combat lasted about ten minutes during which eight attacks were made. No damage done to our aircraft or crew.

'Wellington F [DV875] Sgt Stanley. Primary target attacked from 7,000 feet. Results unobserved as combat with a night fighter started immediately. Many attacks were

Mk.IC HD977 S of 99 Squadron on arrival at Digri 28 October 1942. It was destroyed when a bomb exploded on landing there 5 January 1943. (*Robert Hails via 99 Squadron*)

Mk.IC of 99 Squadron at Digri, India November 1942. (*Norman Didwell*)

made during which the rear gunner [Flt Sgt William Austin] was mortally wounded and the aircraft severely damaged. A force landing was made at Chittagong when the aircraft immediately burst into flames and Flt Sgt Austin was killed. Plt Off MacDonald died the following day as a result of his injuries. Sgt Mercer went back into the flames in spite of his burns to rescue Plt Off MacDonald.'

Plt Off Robert MacDonald RCAF was the twenty-year-old observer. Four months later on 20 March '43, the now W/O Stanley again demonstrated superb skill when he managed to fly another Wellington, which had been crippled by anti-aircraft fire, to a crash landing at Chittagong with no further injuries to his crew (the rear gunner had been slightly wounded by shrapnel

Ground crew, 99 Squadron B Flt. (*99 Squadron*)

during their attack on the airfield at Toungoo).

A problem arose in December when a spate of engine problems caused all the aircraft to be declared operationally unserviceable until the fault could be remedied; on one occasion thrcc out of cight aircraft despatched had trouble. The investigation suggested that the use of 100 octane fuel was causing engine valves to stick. A change was made to 90 octane fuel which eventually solved the problem, but not before the ground crews spent three days and nights replacing the top five cylinders on every engine. Despite these huge efforts, Wellington serviceability continued to suffer due both to the climate and the difficult supply situation, such that only around half the fleet was available for operations in the early months of the campaign. The situation improved early in 1943 when the Bengal Maintenance Wing was set up to ease the pressure on the squadrons, and spare parts became more readily available.

Mk.IC of 99 Squadron at dispersal, Digri February 1943.
(*Chota Ray via Norman Didwell*)

In February 1943 Brigadier Orde Wingate led his Long Range Penetration Group, the Chindits, deep into Burma behind enemy lines, marking the first serious attempt to wrest the country from the Japanese. Throughout the ensuing months operations were focused on supporting the ground forces although the summer monsoons frequently led to operations being cancelled.

A raid on Heho airfield on the night of 1/2 April 1943 resulted in the loss of Flt Lt McDonald and his crew when they were forced to abandon their damaged aircraft over the enemy-occupied Chin Hills; the crew being taken prisoner. Over two years later in September 1945, the CO of 99 Squadron, which by that time was flying Liberators from the Cocos Islands, received a letter from Flg Off F E Townsend:

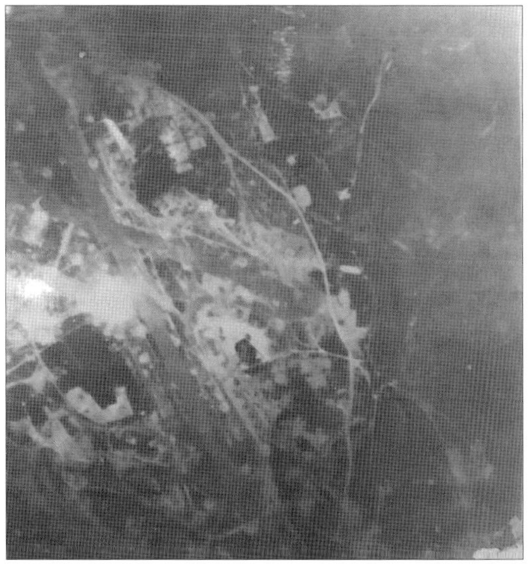

Japanese-occupied Heho airfield taken during an attack on 25 Jan 1943. (*99 Squadron*)

> "This is not in any way an official letter, but just an expression of the thanks of all the RAF personnel in Changi prison camp for all the messages of good cheer and happier times to come which were dropped along with all sorts of good things by the boys in the Liberators around the end of July.
>
> "It was a great pleasure to me as one of the squadron in March 1943, when Wellingtons were the order of the day. The Wellington I was flying in with Flt Lt McDonald didn't come back from Burma on 1/2 April. I have heard in a roundabout way that he and all the others except Sgt Griffiths got out of Rangoon on 1 May, but I heard no details whatsoever."

On the night of 7/8 September 1943, five aircraft were despatched to attack the vital port city of Akyab, but the four crews who arrived in the target area were unable to locate it due to cloud cover and returned to Jessore with their bombs. The fifth aircraft, captained by Fg Off David Allan DFC, suffered engine failure in HE663 one hour after take-off and turned back. Losing height rapidly, the bombs were jettisoned, and everything else that was loose was ditched overboard, including guns and ammunition. A ditching became inevitable and Sgt L Butler the WOp/AG sent out a distress message until the aircraft hit the sea. The captain, the injured navigator Sgt Chopping, and the wireless operator successfully escaped, but the bomb aimer and rear gunner, Sgts Alan Dacey and John Radmore, went down with the aircraft. The three survivors struggled to inflate the damaged dinghy and were eventually able to get it to support Sgt Chopping while the other two took it in turns to climb on board or cling to the side. They were eventually picked up by an Air Sea Rescue launch late in the evening of the following day.

The final year of Wellington operations saw little change, although aircraft serviceability had improved considerably allowing up to fourteen aircraft to be despatched at a time. The state of the ground war meant that operations largely switched to attacks on the Japanese supply routes attempting to deny them the use of trains by attacking marshalling yards, stations and railway junctions. On the night of 18/19 January 1944, the squadron attacked the marshalling yards at Mandalay and Flt Sgt Jim Cameron and his crew in LN331 had an incredible escape when their

WO E G Paterson RAAF during a daylight raid on Mandalay by 99 Squadron. (*Norman Didwell*)

A 4,000 lb 'Cookie' bomb awaiting loading. (*99 Squadron*)

port engine failed an hour into the return journey. Unable to maintain altitude, they were forced to fly lower and lower and navigate their way very gingerly through the Chin Hills since they were unable to fly over them. Once again the crew threw out everything they could to lighten the aircraft and they finally found a way up the last valley at around 500 feet and made it back to a safe landing after four hours on one engine. Both Jim Cameron and his navigator Flt Sgt Patrick Kearns were awarded the DFM for their superb airmanship.

At the beginning of 1944 the Japanese made a further attempt to break through into India and, by the end of February, the Japanese occupied the whole of Burma. Attention increasingly turned to harassing the enemy's positions wherever they were building strength for their planned assault. On 25 April a bold attempt was made in a daylight attack to cause a landslide on the Tiddim-Imphal road by the use of 4,000 lb 'Cookies', but the amount of dust thrown up by the explosions meant that the results could not be seen. The crucial Battle of Imphal which raged for several months called for considerable air support from the Wellington squadrons. By June the squadrons were almost fully engaged in ferrying bombs from Agartala and Kumbhirgram to the Hurricane airfields, where the easiest and quickest method of unloading was to simply open the bomb doors and allow the unfused bombs to fall to the ground. During that month 99 Squadron alone flew 171 such sorties carrying a total of 261 tons of bombs. On the 17th of the month the unit suffered what was to prove to be their last Wellington loss.

Wellington Mk.X HZ719 was captained by Sqn Ldr Anthony Ennis, a decorated 158 Squadron Halifax first tourist, who at the time was acting CO of 99 Squadron. Having already made three delivery flights to Palel that day, around mid-day he took off for the return trip to Agartala just as the local squadrons were engaged in repelling a Japanese attack by Ki.43 fighters. In his eagerness to get away quickly, he attempted to take the shortest direct route away rather than using the established air corridor, flew straight into the path of oncoming fighters and was immediately shot

down, falling in flames into Japanese-held territory. All of the crew were lost:
Sqn Ldr Anthony Ennis DSO DFC, pilot
W/O Donald Lindsay RCAF, second pilot
Flt Sgt William Griffin, navigator
Sgt David Rees, navigator
Flt Sgt Arthur Davison, WOp/AG
Flt Sgt Alwyne Atkin, WOp/AG

Mk.Xs of 99 Squadron Jessore en route to their target in Burma. (*IWM CI712*)

With the ground situation improving in July, the Wellingtons returned to more normal operations. This largely comprised reconnaissance and offensive patrols, with both day and night-bombing attacks on targets, including airfields and bridges. The squadron had the honour of flying the final operation in the theatre by Wellington bombers when, on 15 August '44, it sent eight aircraft in a daylight attack on enemy stores and dumps at Pinlebu. In ideal weather conditions, six aircraft succeeded in reaching the target and the bombing accuracy was good. One aircraft (Flt Sgt Appleby LN325) had a burst tyre and failed to take off, and this delayed the eighth aircraft (WO Sorohan LN747) for thirty minutes, so they dropped their 'Cookie' on the secondary target at Mawlaik. The aircraft and crews involved were:

LN666	Flt Sgt J W Reid, Flt Sgt R Price, Flt Sgt W J Rydhout, Sgt J L Longhurst, Flt Sgt A Coward
LN465	Fg Off P W Bowles, Flt Sgt K C Nutt, Fg Off J A Hickson, WO L W Neale, WO A B Pike
LN747	WO K F Sorohan, Flt Sgt J Willieson, Plt Off E R Garbutt, WO K B Younger, Sgt F G Lewis
HZ714	WO T S Sankey, Flt Sgt G H Power, WO G D Kenman, Sgt L D Butler, Flt Sgt J Labrecque
LN325	Flt Sgt A D Appleby, Flt Sgt G Knox, Flt Sgt J A Lawson, Sgt R A Skinner,

	Flt Sgt N M McCallum
LN462	Sqn Ldr E Trumper, Flt Lt W B Perry, Fg Off M T Simpson, WO A M Smith, Flt Lt P Crossley, Sgt J T Sim
JA467	Flt Sgt A M Draffin, Flt Sgt C McGlone, Fg Off B F Bennett, Sgt C F Kirby, Sgt A D Cox, Flt Sgt G R Gamble
LN331	Fg Off F G Barlegie, Flt Sgt R H Savage, Fg Off S J Duncan, Flt Sgt W Allen, Sgt A Fyle

Immediately after this raid the squadron stood down from operations to convert to the Liberator Mk.VI, with Lucian Ercolani taking over as commanding officer on 3 September 1944. The Wellingtons were all put into open storage before being struck off charge for scrapping between January and May 1945. Possibly the highest number of operations flown by any Wellington was the remarkable total of ninety believed to have been clocked up by 99 Squadron's Mk.X 'B', the identity of which is sadly unknown. Another aircraft that lasted a long time on the squadron was HZ950 which amassed thirty-five operations between February and May '44; it later continued flying with 3 Tactical Air Force (Burma) Communications Squadron Comilla, south of Dacca before being scrapped in March '45.

> "In record time 99 Squadron became the first bomber squadron in the Far East to complete 1,000 operational sorties."
> ACM Sir Thomas Kennedy GCB AFC DL, March 1944

215 Squadron

Although 215 Squadron had equipped with Wellingtons before the war, its role was primarily crew training, and it was disbanded on 22 May 1940 to become 11 OTU at Bassingbourn. It reformed on 9 December 1941 at Newmarket, moving to Stradishall the following month prior to taking over tropicalised Mk.ICs. These departed from St.Eval or Portreath in sections between 19 and 26 March 1942 and heading initially for Gibraltar. They arrived at Asansol from 14 April under the command of Wg Cdr James Sindall (later DSO), and with support from seconded 40 Squadron ground staff, were quickly ready for operations from Pandaveswar and detachments were maintained with A Flight at Dum Dum and B Flight at Alipore, both of which were on the outskirts of Calcutta and therefore much closer to the area of operations in Burma. The main base clearly had minimal facilities as the ORB records:

Mk.ICs of 215 Squadron dropping the 10th Ghurka Parachute Battalion over Rawalpindi February 1943. (*ww2images*)

'Pandaveswar at that time, consisted

> solely of one runway, there being no buildings whatsoever. A tented domestic camp was erected and gradually the squadron settled in; headquarters occupying the disused offices of a coal-mine which had been derelict for many years. Much discomfort was caused by excessive heat and an extreme shortage of water for drinking and washing purposes. It was here that the "Soya Link" was first met by the squadron and it figured prominently in every breakfast for several weeks.'

The first operation by 215 Squadron took place on 24 April 1942, and aircraft were prepared for bombing on many occasions, only to be prevented from operating by adverse weather conditions. South-East Asia Command (SEAC) daily summaries provide a good overview of the bombing campaign as it developed. In May aircraft began attacking Akyab and Magwe airfields in Burma which had been abandoned by RAF units two months earlier and were now home to significant numbers of Japanese aircraft. The first attempted raid failed however when, of the six Wellingtons despatched to Magwe, one diverted with a technical problem, one force landed in the sea near Kumina and the remainder returned to base due to poor weather. Akyab first received attention from just three Wellingtons on the night of 5/6 May, with follow-up raids taking place on the 11th and the 13th. The latter proved rather more successful with three of the five enemy aircraft caught on the ground being recorded as damaged.

May also saw the commencement of dropping food and medical supplies to both retreating troops and civilian refugees at locations including Malon, Homalin and Kangpat, but the numbers of aircraft involved remained small, generally three aircraft, although six were mustered for a raid on Japanese troop concentrations at Homalin on 6 June 1942. A raid on 2 June saw three aircraft dropping a total of twelve 500 lb bombs on Japanese positions at Oyster Island. One Wellington despatched to Homalin crashed at Gafargaon on 10 June 1943 having abandoned the operation because of poor weather.

Flying was considerably restricted when the monsoon started in mid-June '42; the runway at Pandaveswar became partially flooded and several aircraft were bogged down. On 18 August 215 Squadron moved to St.Thomas' Mount near Madras and re-started operations in earnest the following month, mainly flying patrols of the shipping lanes off the east coast of India. The squadron found these tedious:

> 'Of the thirty-four operational sorties flown this month, the majority of them consisted of sea patrols of the shipping lanes off the coast of India. Three escort sorties were flown and in two cases the vessel concerned was met while the other was abortive since a two-hour search failed to locate the vessel and the aircraft was forced to abandon the task due to an oil leak. Operationally it was a month of dull monotony, no enemy sightings were made and although all aircraft carried either depth charges or bombs, none were expended except on the 26th when a depth charge fell off an aircraft during take-off, but fortunately without damage to the aircraft or its occupants.'

By mid October 1942 the squadron had moved again, this time to Chaklala although it still maintained a detachment at St.Thomas' Mount. In November, a number of paratroop dropping flights were carried out, with men being dropped initially in sticks of two or four from the position originally built to house the ventral turret, but by the end of the month sticks of eight were trialled.

Aerial view of Chaklala airfield, north of Lahore, home to 99 Squadron in early 1943. (*Robert Hails via 99 Squadron*)

215 Squadron's final move while still operating Wellingtons was to Jessore on 12 March 1943. On the 1st of the following month Flt Sgt W B C Young made a forced landing near Asansol during a night cross-country. The aircraft was completely burnt out, although the crew were all safe. Operations continued against regular targets such as the airfield and villages on Akyab island and both operations and aircraft numbers had built up considerably. May proved to be a very difficult month for the squadron, beginning on the night of 17/18 May when Flt Lt John Guest RCAF and his crew were lost in BB456 during a raid by six aircraft on Kangaung. They were shot down in flames by a Ki.43 flown by Capt Miyamaru of 50th Sentai's 2nd Chutai. Two nights later WO Richard Clarke RNZAF and crew in LA988 failed to return from an operation to Taungup, and the following night Fg Off Peter Sykes and his crew were lost. This time the target was Kyaukpyu.

In September 1943 the squadron re-equipped with the Wellington Mk.X replacing the tired Mk.ICs. Throughout what was to be the final year of Wimpy operations, the unit continued its operations much as before, the most notable change being the introduction of flare-carrying aircraft for target illumination, which proved to be highly successful. As well as attacking Japanese airfields and supply dumps, during the critical siege of Imphal in mid 1944, 215 joined 99 Squadron to ferry 250 lb bombs to Hurricane units operating against the Tiddim-Imphal road from airfields on the Imphal Plain, and continued supply dropping in Burma and coastal patrols. They also loaned aircrews to relieve hard-pressed Dakota squadrons. By this time it was clear that the Wellington's days were numbered and, in June 1944, crews began conversion training onto the Liberator Mk.VI at 1673 Heavy Conversion Unit (HCU) Kolar east of Bangalore, with the aircraft arriving the following month. The last Wellingtons left in August, having flown their final operation early in the month.

Mk.X F of 99 Squadron with faint 'SNAKE' titling, meaning the aircraft must only be delivered to the Far East, Jessore 1942-43. (*99 Squadron*)

MARITIME OPERATIONS

The first maritime Wellington unit to be established in India was 36 Squadron which was re-formed at Tanjore in the south of the country on 22 October 1942, with five officers and 406 airmen, commanded by Wg Cdr Kenneth Mellor DFC. Prior to that it had operated outdated Vickers Vildebeest III torpedo bombers until being captured by Japanese troops at Tasikmalaja on the island of Java in March. The ORB recorded an understandably chaotic situation:

> '24 Oct '42. Arrival at Tanjore. Reception arranged by OC Golden Rock. Sufficient huts and beds to accommodate all personnel, also a small supply of cooking utensils and hurricane lamps. The squadron had no medical supplies, stationery or equipment, except for rifles, Sten guns and ammunition. All personnel inoculated against cholera by civil authorities because of epidemic in district.'

Difficulties were also encountered with the local labour force doing the construction work as there was little, if any, common language. The squadron was also completely devoid of any funds. The first Wellingtons arrived in December and were made up of a wide mixture of variants, the first torpedo bomber HX716 arriving in February. Operations commenced on 13 January 1943 with shipping and anti-submarine patrols and convoy escorts, carrying standard weapons loads of four or six 250 lb depth charges. On 5 February a detachment of four aircraft was established at Cholavarum, north of Madras, and was maintained for some time.

On 8 April 1943 the squadron moved to Dhubalia, north of Calcutta, three days after suffering its first loss on the 5th when Wellington Mk.IC HE114 caught fire during engine start-up at

Agartala and was completely burnt out, fortunately without injury to any of the crew. By now around forty-three sorties a month were being flown and Dennis Jackson flew with 36 Squadron in Sgt Burnett's crew:

> "I got my WOp/AG wing in 1942 and went to an overseas OTU. We ferried a Wellington from Portreath down to Gibraltar, but because of the threat from the Germans we had to fly way out over the Atlantic and then approach Gib from almost due west. Thereafter we went down the West African coast to Dakar, Takoradi and then Lagos, by which time the Wimpy was due its forty-hour inspection, so we were stuck there for two or three days, and it meant that the mossies took effect.
>
> "We then transited across Africa and started heading up the east side to El Obeid in Sudan where four of the crew went down with malaria, including me, so another crew took our aircraft on. We eventually got to Cairo just after Alamein and we started recovering aircraft that had been abandoned in the desert and patching them up with whatever spares were available to get them flying again.
>
> "Then we were sent to India to reform 36 Squadron. We were carrying out patrols over the Bay of Bengal along the Burma coast. We got some 'Stickleback' Wellingtons too, so I had some radar instruction. All the time we were having to rob parts from aircraft to keep others going, we had a lot of 'Christmas Trees'. We were there for nine months until late '43 when we moved to the jungle north of Calcutta and then eventually we were sent off on a troopship to Port Said."

After a comparatively uneventful few months in India, largely marked with frequent lengthy patrols off the Arakan coast, the squadron commenced its move to the Mediterranean theatre on 4 June 1943. Five aircraft, each carrying five aircrew and four ground crew, took off from Allahabad bound for Karachi on the first leg of their long journey. One of these, HX741, crashed on take-off due to engine failure, but Fg Off R Grenville and his crew all escaped. WOp/AG Flt Sgt Denis Fisher also made the move, his crew captained by Plt Off Ted Catley, taking seven days to fly Mk.VIII LP227 (which survived to be handed over to the French air force in 1946) to Blida, routeing Dhubalia – Allahabad – Karachi – Bahrain – Habbaniya – Cairo West – El Adem – Castel Benito – Blida in a total flying time of forty-one hours. They flew their first patrol exactly a week after arriving and thereafter flew twenty-seven anti-submarine and convoy escort sorties over the next four months without seeing any action.

To continue provision of maritime capability in SEAC, 203 Squadron, which had been flying Baltimores, was moved in the opposite direction. Seven newly-acquired Wellington Mk.XIIIs set out for Karachi via Habbaniya and Bahrain or Sharjah on 7 November 1943, followed the next day by a further seven, one of which was captained by the squadron CO Wg Cdr Cedric Masterman OBE DFC. On the 15th the squadron was established at Santa Cruz on the west coast of India, close to Bombay and the first operation was flown on 1 December when Sqn Ldr Kenneth Scotney DFM and his crew provided anti-submarine cover for the heavy cruiser *HMS Suffolk* which was engaged in firing exercises. Thereafter the familiar maritime tasks were conducted, with the principal area of operations being the shipping lanes between Bombay and Colombo, Ceylon and at the end of that first month the ORB commented:

> 'No sightings of U-boats or enemy forces were made during the month by aircraft of the squadron. Although sixteen Wellington aircraft Mk.XIII were on the strength of the squadron, operations were limited by the lack of serviceable aircraft due to the shortage of spares.'

Early in the new year a number of parallel detachments saw the squadron thinly spread, with aircraft operating on both Indian coasts from Cochin, Madras and Vizagapatam, plus Ratmalana in Ceylon (which also used the airfield at Sigiriya). In April an unusually large convoy of eleven merchant ships many of which were large troopships, together with five escorts, was covered on the Aden-Bombay route by several squadron patrols. On 12 July 1944 persistence finally paid off when Fg Off McKay and his crew located a submarine that had just sunk a merchant vessel; although they were able to attack and straddle it with depth charges, no further trace was seen. Occasional searches for missing aircraft were also made and on 8 August a total of five aircraft were despatched throughout the day from Santa Cruz to search for a Vultee Vengeance, but nothing was found. In October 1944 203 Squadron moved to Madura and re-equipped with Liberators.

AFRICA & ARABIA

Probably even more of a forgotten area of Wellington operations than South-East Asia was sub-Saharan Africa. The focus here was the need to protect the vital convoy route around Cape Horn against the U-boat threat in the event that the Suez Canal should be unavailable. The west coast saw considerable numbers of troopships in transit to and from South Africa, not least in support of the intense aircrew training carried out both there and in Rhodesia. On the eastern side of the continent it was decided to establish a number of units with some as far north as the Persian Gulf to also cover the Indian Ocean and approaches to the Suez Canal and relieve the pressure from other squadrons heavily involved in the Mediterranean campaign. Maritime Wellingtons were once again the chosen type. The primary equipment of each squadron was the GR Mk.XIII with a few other variants especially with 26 Squadron SAAF which had a mixture of five different marks. The squadrons established were:

May '43	26 Squadron SAAF Takoradi, Gold Coast and detachments at Pointe Noire, French Congo and Robertsfield, Liberia replacing Lockheed Venturas
Sept '43	621 Squadron Port Reitz, Kenya, later Mogadishu, Italian Somaliland, Khormaksar, Aden Protectorate and Mersa Matruh, Egypt
Nov '43	344 (French) Squadron Dakar, French West Africa
Dec '43	8 Squadron Khormaksar, Aden replacing Hudsons
Feb '44	244 Squadron Sharjah, Trucial States replacing Blenheims, quickly moved to Masirah, Muscat and Oman

WEST AFRICA

26 Squadron SAAF

Under the command of Lt Col D A du Toit, the first anti-submarine and convoy patrols by 26 Squadron took place on 29 May 1943 and on 15 July the first possible submarine contact occurred

South African Air Force Mk.XI N 'Nifty Nymph' with 26 Squadron aircrew. *(SAAF Museum)*

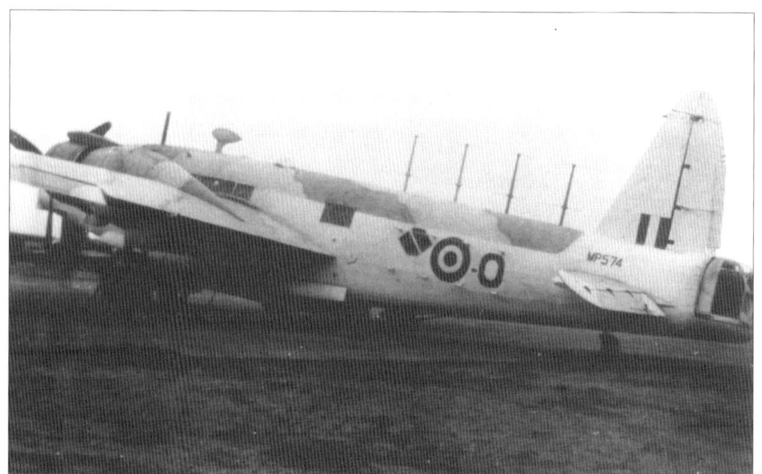

'Stickleback' Mk.XI MP574 O 26 Squadron South African Air Force, Takoradi, Gold Coast, was scrapped in August 1945. *(SAAF Museum)*

while Captain Paul Horsfield in Wellington '13' was escorting convoy WS31 at night. A large patch of oil was sighted and the aircraft homed onto two ASV blips eight miles from the oil. Although nothing was sighted Horsfield sent a 'suspect submarine' signal.

On 1 June '43 Wellington Mk.XI MP572 piloted by Lt Edward Baxter crashed off the seaward end of Takoradi aerodrome and caught fire; only the observer Lt Habergham escaped, although he died of his wounds later that day. This aircraft was delivered from the factory on 7 February 1943 and had flown just fifty-nine hours. The cause of the accident was never identified. On 16 August the squadron lost a second aircraft when Mk.XI MP592 flown by Lt Dessels on an anti-submarine sweep overshot the runway while landing at Robertsfield in appalling weather conditions and finished up partly submerged in a creek, fortunately with slight injuries to three of the crew. Salvage of the aircraft proved to be impossible and it was blown up where it lay, on the 22nd.

Despite these setbacks, the squadron settled into a routine of lengthy convoy escorts from three stations and for many months these passed without incident. An unusual task was carried out on 12 August when Captain Horsfield got airborne just before 9 am in Wellington 'B' and flew to the mouth of the Congo river to provide cover for a battleship being refuelled at anchor, shielded by five destroyers. The senior naval officer in the convoy had requested very close escort, so no sweeps up-river were carried out. At 4.30 that afternoon the battleship signalled visually to the aircraft 'Shall be here all tomorrow – shall require air cover'. The Wellington finally landed back at base after almost nine hours in the air; cover then continuing for a further four days before the convoy sailed.

A typical example from the ORB of the squadron's routine is dated 5 November 1943:

> 'There were six sorties from Takoradi today and in addition, aircraft "A" returned from Ikeja, carrying out an A/S sweep on the way. Convoys STL/5 and STL/4 were escorted all day without incident, the latter being augmented outside Takoradi by twelve motor vessels and two escort vessels, leaving a composition of sixteen vessels on their way west. Two "creeping line ahead" sweeps were carried out, east and west of Takoradi. Aircraft "Z" on one of these sweeps developed engine trouble about an hour after take off and was compelled to return. The crew (Captain Brown) transferred to "D" and were on their way again within eighteen minutes after landing. They completed their patrol, and altogether flew for ten hours twenty-five minutes. In the course of "D"s patrol, oil bubbles were seen covering an area five miles by half a mile and was duly photographed.'

The ORB also records that with effect from 7 November, the Wellingtons' bomb bays were being reconfigured to carry nine depth charges in the starboard bay and freeing up the port bay for the carriage of the 'Lindholme apparatus'. The Lindholme gear (or Air Sea Rescue Apparatus Mk.IV) consisted of five cylinder-shaped containers joined together by lengths of floating rope, and contained an inflatable nine-man dinghy and survival equipment. That same day saw another aircraft loss when MP591 piloted by Lt D N Campbell crashed into the sea off Takoradi just after getting airborne for a patrol, with the loss of the entire crew; the cause was never established. The others on board were second pilot Lt Morrison, navigator Lt Fell, WT/AGs Lt Shadwell, Flt Sgt A G Lamb and Flt Sgt Morland, plus Lt Janssens of the Belgian air force who was on attachment to the unit.

The squadron was never to achieve a successful attack against a U-boat. The closest it thought it had come, at least for a few moments, was on 17 November 1943:

> 'Convoy STL/6 was escorted all day. Aircraft "F" saw what appeared to be a submarine about twelve miles ahead of the convoy, and carried out an excellent attack with depth charges. It is not known whether the giant ray sunning itself on the surface was killed or not, although it was straddled by the depth charges.'

On the other hand Mk.XI HZ526 was believed to have been brought down by fire from a submarine on 18 December 1943 with the loss of Lt G S Bloyd and his crew, which included Plt

Mk.XIII MF582 of 344 (French) Squadron Dakar at Yundum, Gambia 3 Aug 1944. (*NK*)

Off Samuel Evans RAFVR. On 31 March 1944 commanding officer Lt Col Nash took eleven squadron aircraft to Ouakam, near Dakar, where they joined up with Sunderlands from 95 and 204 Squadrons plus Wellingtons from 344 (French) Squadron for a continuous parallel sweep by four aircraft at a time between Dakar and the Cape Verde Islands. From 4 to 7 April the efforts continued, without success, to find a U-boat known to be in the area. By the end of May 1944 the squadron had been operational for a year, in which time 1,232 sorties had been flown with the loss of ten aircraft and twenty-eight lives, and the same sortie patterns were set to continue unabated for a further ten months. All routine patrols ceased on 4 March 1945, although occasional random searches were made looking for U-boats. The squadron finally left for South Africa on 30 May and was disbanded on 12 June 1945.

344 (French) Squadron

Wellingtons were first used by the French air force's Groupe de Reconnaissance Maritime 'Artois' established at Pointe Noire on 27 February 1943 for coastal surveillance with Avro Ansons being added in May 1943.

After the Operation Torch landings in North Africa, some French air force and Aeronavale units based in Algeria and Morocco re-equipped with British and American aircraft and among these was Flotille 1E which had been flying anti-submarine patrols with a variety of aircraft. On 29 November 1943 it was re-numbered 344 Squadron in the sequence allocated to Free French units and brought under the operational control of the RAF's 295 Wing at Dakar until reverting to the French as Flotille 2FB on 27 November 1945. Starting in July 1943, 344 Squadron received Wellington Mk.XI and XIII aircraft to conduct maritime operations from Dakar/Ouakam. The

Wellingtons were ferried out from the UK by 3 Overseas Aircraft Despatch Unit (OADU) Hurn, Bournemouth and routed Ras El Ma - Dakar, with MP711 being the first to arrive. Although little is known about the squadron's operations, at least fifteen Mk.XIIIs have been identified as serving with them, of which the following were lost in accidents (the surviving aircraft were officially handed over to French control on 21 June 1945). No further details of the casualties are known:

5 August 1943	MP747 circumstances unknown
27 October 1943	HZ691 spun into the ground on approach to Ouakam
6 November 1943	HZ597 circumstances unknown
24 November 1943	HZ691 circumstances unknown, two killed
24 November 1943	MP691 Gorée near Dakar, two killed
19 December 1943	HZ710 caught fire and ditched off Ouakam, five killed
2 February 1944	HZ539 failed to return, seven missing
23 August 1944	HZ588 failed to return, seven missing

On 18 August 1943, the unit scored its only success against a U-boat when P M Chevanton and his crew in Mk.XIII HZ697 found U-403 on the surface which immediately began to dive. Six depth charges were dropped and shortly afterwards a large oil slick emerged accompanied by air bubbles and a considerable amount of debris. The destruction of the submarine was confirmed in January 1944.

EAST AFRICA AND ARABIA

On 18 September 1943 621 Squadron was established under the command of Wg Cdr P Green at Port Reitz, not far from the coastal town of Mombasa in Kenya. Its function was to provide general reconnaissance capability in the Indian Ocean under the control of the co-located 246 Wing. The unit establishment was 16 Wellington Mk.XIIIs divided into two flights, the first to arrive being HZ802 flown in by Plt Off J Grover on the day the unit formed. It was despatched to Mogadishu the following day to commence operations, which it did on the 24th with Grover and crew carrying out a 'creeping line ahead' search for a reported lifeboat or U-boat. After being airborne for nearly ten hours the aircraft requested a beacon and, after it had been flying for twelve hours, it ran out of fuel and crash landed inland, fortunately with only one injury – an inauspicious start to the squadron's operations. After three days of intensive searches by other aircraft, HZ808 flown by the CO, located the Wellington and dropped rations before landing alongside it and collecting the crew.

The squadron relocated to Mogadishu on 1 November 1943 to be nearer its principal area of interest, and on 5 December it moved again, this time to Khormaksar in Aden. Detachments to various locations around the Arabian coast were commonplace, with the usual mix of anti-submarine patrols, convoy escorts and air sea rescues. It was joined at Khormaksar by 8 Squadron, similarly equipped with Mk.XIIIs in addition to Hudsons, the last of which left in January.

The maritime force was further strengthened in February 1944 when 244 Squadron based at Sharjah in the Trucial States also began receiving Wellington XIIIs to start replacing its Blenheim Vs. It was noted by the squadron that there were some issues with bringing the Wellingtons on line, including corrosion and a general lack of equipment:

> 'Although there were numerous minor items of unserviceability, the ground crews, mostly inexperienced on this type of aircraft, did well in the absence of spare parts, and five aircraft have now left for Masirah ['Tin Can Island'] the squadron's new headquarters.'

This move took place on 17 March 1944, and the squadron also began operating detachments at Khormaksar and Mogadishu. On 9 May 1944, Wellington JA199 was lost off Perim Island off the south-west coast of Yemen during a convoy escort, taking the life of crewman Sgt James Greaves. Despite maintaining a constant stream of convoy escorts and anti-submarine patrols for the next seventeen months, no enemy shipping was ever sighted, which must have been most frustrating for the crews. The ORB commented in September 1944:

> 'U-boat activity in the area was at a minimum and at the end of the month for the first time on record since the outbreak of U-boat warfare in the Indian Ocean, the whole area was estimated free from threat. All convoy escort sorties from Santa Cruz were laid on primarily as exercises for the benefit of aircrews.'

On 13 March 1944 a search by 621 Squadron located several lifeboats and rafts containing seventy survivors from a sinking ship, and a few weeks later the unit had its sole success against a U-boat. On 1 May Fg Off H R Mitchell in JA107 found U-852, which had already been attacked by 8 Squadron's Fg Off J R Forrester RCAF in JA413, and attempted to finish it off. The following day, three further attacks were carried out by Fg Off E W Read JA184, W/O J P Ryall RCAF JA389 and the squadron commander in HZ940. Flt Lt J Y Wade in JA654 joined in and finally, on 3 May, U-852 was found to be ablaze and surrounded by wreckage and burning oil.

The squadron lost a number of aircraft in 1944 including JA315 which suffered engine failure and ditched off Socotra Island on 5 September with the loss of four crew members; Plt Off George Atkinson, Plt Off William Musgrave, Sgt Walter Smith, and LAC Alfred Swallow. Regular operations by both squadrons ceased in May 1945 with both 8 and 244 Squadrons immediately disbanding. Another role was found for 621 which changed over to transport flying, moving to Mersa Matruh, Egypt in November and re-equipping with Warwicks; the last Wellington leaving in December.

CHAPTER SEVEN

THE WIMPY IN OTHER ROLES

"I was posted to Lossiemouth to train Free-French aircrew in bombing and gunnery, flying Wellingtons. I decided this was rather dangerous so I volunteered for a second ops tour"
Fg Off Lyn Seabury 10 OTU

While the Wellington is justly renowned for its sterling work as a bomber and maritime reconnaissance aircraft, throughout its long service it proved to be a highly-versatile aircraft and was used in a wide variety of other roles, both operationally and in less hostile environments. These roles included transport, gunnery training, reconnaissance, special operations within Bomber Command's 100 Group and a very wide variety of experimental flying. Probably the best known of the secondary roles was that of crew training, which was to result in the Wellington's service being extended well into the post-war period, with the last RAF unit finally giving the type up as late as 1953.

The last Wellington bombing unit. Mk.XIII NC588 of 69 Squadron operating from Eindhoven in Holland July 1945, a month before disbanding. (*RAF Museum*)

SPECIALISED RECONNAISSANCE

In January 1942 the six-aircraft 109 Squadron detachment at Kabrit was renamed 162 Squadron under the command of Wg Cdr Douglas Rusher (later DSO) tasked with radar reconnaissance to locate and jam enemy radar stations in addition to continuing the jamming of tank radios. The first operation took place on 8 January when Plt Off Fenton captained Mk.IC X9986 and its crew of eight from LG 09 Bir Koraiyim to Crete and the Greek Islands on a signals investigation sortie. The Greek Islands were the initial area of focus, with night-time sorties assessing enemy defences by attempting to locate their radio direction finding (RDF) stations. In February a captured Savoia-Marchetti SM.79 torpedo bomber was added to the squadron strength for communication and wireless work in order to relieve the small Wellington fleet from non-operational duties. On 6 March the unit lost its first aircraft when Z8905 failed to return from a wireless investigation operation in the area of the Dodecanese Islands. The captain was Sgt M H Knowles and his crew included Lt Baker RN, and Sgts A F Murrel, R G Tregenza RAAF, K Westbrook RCAF, A Levy, J A Drever and R C Rawlins. Although the circumstances of the loss remain unknown, all the crew survived to be taken prisoner. A very lucky airman was one LAC Connor, who had been on the aircraft when it positioned forward to LG 09 but did not go on the operation.

By August the Wellington strength was down to just three aircraft, although it recovered to five by the end of the month. The squadron moved a number of times around the region and, in September '42, a detachment based on Malta carried out a detailed radar survey of Sardinia, Taranto and Tripoli. As the war swung in the Allies' favour, jamming activity continued at a reduced rate, and the Wellingtons found themselves being used for occasional bombing and 'Nickel' raids until the end of the war, finally disbanding in September 1944.

On 19 October 1942 544 Squadron was formed at Benson with a mixture of Ansons, Martin Marylands, Spitfires and two Wellington Mk.IVs with A Flight. They were tasked with experimental night photography, beginning on 4 November. The first operation was flown on 15 December when Sqn Ldr William Acott (who had been awarded the DFC for his work on 1 GRU) and second pilot Flt Lt John Loder DFC flew Z1418 on a two-hour-forty-minute sortie over northern France, during which they dropped two sticks of photo flashes, one from 10,000 feet and one from 8,000 feet. The proof of the concept came on 15 January 1943 when Z1417, this time with Flt Lt Loder as captain, achieved a series of overlap photographs of the harbour at St.Valery-en-Caux which were assessed to be comparable with pictures taken by day. Their job complete, the Wellingtons were disposed of in March when their role was taken over by Mosquitoes.

Once it had completed its tasks in Malta, 69 Squadron was re-located back to the UK where it set up home on 5 May 1944 at Northolt, Middlesex. It was part of 2nd Tactical Air Force's (TAF) 34 Wing for the purpose of night reconnaissance of enemy ground movements, Wg Cdr Terence Channon DSO commanding. The unusual nature of its forthcoming operations demanded some specialised training, as recorded in the ORB:

> 'The training programme was devised for pilots, navigators and air gunners and this, naturally, was intense, owing to the extreme change of flying conditions – from day – sea work on Coastal Command, to night – land work on TAF. Navigators were sent into the air in the worthy Anson to gain as much experience as possible in cross-country map reading exercises. In addition to this, they had to learn the mysteries of the 'GEE box', for which purpose two instructors were borrowed from Bomber Command. The theory, and a certain amount of ground practice was given, which was followed later by cross-countries in a specially-equipped Oxford aircraft. All navigators had the same training although some were later to act as Bombardiers, whose real operational job consists of map reading, visual reconnaissance, photography and flare dropping. Crews were encouraged to submit suggestions from their operational experience to enable a sound training for those to follow on in this specialised work.'

With nineteen Mk.XIII aircraft ready by the end of May 1944, the squadron's first operations took place on 5 June when two aircraft carried out a reconnaissance in the Beauvais region of France. The next day A Flight Commander Acting Sqn Ldr Alexander Dawson was killed when his Wellington JA619 crashed into a 75 (New Zealand) Squadron Stirling at Wratting Common, Cambridgeshire during an emergency landing in poor weather. Following the invasion, the bulk of the work comprised road and river reconnaissances and target illuminating using flares, the aircraft usually operating with a crew of four; pilot, two navigators and an air gunner. The first operational losses occurred on the night of 10/11 June when ME902 flown by Fg Off Russell White crashed near Evreux during a sortie along the Laval to Le Mans road; navigators Fg Off Dennis Davey RCAF and Fg Off John Grinde RCAF and air gunner Sgt Patrick McCarthy were buried locally alongside him. Four nights later MF231 flown by Fg Off C L Merrill RCAF failed to return while similarly engaged over the Seine river at Le Havre. In this case, however, all the crew survived. By September the ground situation in Europe was stable enough for the squadron to be moved initially to France, eventually settling at Melsbroek, near Brussels on the 26th of the month. Operations continued to increase and many enemy road convoys were successfully identified over the ensuing months with aircraft frequently descending as low as 1,000 feet to take photographs, and sometimes descending to as low as 50 feet to escape the area!

Despite being highly vulnerable during their night low-level operations, 69 Squadron's gunners acquitted themselves well when attacked by enemy fighters. During December, Sgt Fred Nichol (later DFM) claimed a Bf 109 on the 19th and remarkably, an Me 163 damaged on Christmas Day, although this seems unlikely since there is no record of any Me 163 action on that date – perhaps an Me 262 is more probable. That same day, Sgt W Gerlach claimed an Me 410. However, it was at Melsbroek that the squadron suffered its greatest loss, when their aircraft were caught on the ground during the Luftwaffe's Operation Bodenplatte (Baseplate), a last-ditch surprise strafing attack on Allied airfields in Belgium and Holland by large formations of fighters. The squadron ORB recorded the attack in some detail:

> 'To start the year the squadron suffered an extreme blow when eleven of its aircraft were completely destroyed and two seriously damaged, in the enemy's New Year's Day offensive. At about 09:30 hours on 1 January approximately forty Fw 190 and Me 109s attacked the airfield with little opposition, causing considerable damage and some casualties. Five of the ground crew of the Servicing Echelon (6069) were either killed, or died shortly after as a result of their wounds and twenty-five of the others were injured, for when the attack commenced they were at the dispersals working on aircraft and the nearest cover was too far away. Recovery from the effects of the attack was, however, speedy and had the weather been favourable, operations could have been carried out on 3 January, but it was not until the following night that operational sorties were made. 34 Wing Support Unit came to the rescue and ferried the new aircraft from England.'

Wg Cdr Mike Shaw was the CO at the time and recalled:

> "I remember that some of us were just coming out of our officers' mess, having just had breakfast, when low-flying aircraft started zooming about. We thought they were flown by RAF chaps who were giving us a New Year's 'beat-up' until we saw they had black crosses on the wings! Of my total strength of twenty-four Wellingtons I think fourteen were completely destroyed and another five or six were so badly damaged they would not fly again.[1]"

Despite this setback, operations were resumed after three days and the aircraft started carry-

Close-up of the nose art on a Mk.XIII of 69 Squadron at Eindhoven 1945 showing 23 operations symbols. (*RAF Museum*)

ing bombs in order to quickly attack any targets they located, thus ensuring that the Wellington continued to fulfil its design role throughout the war in Europe. By March 1945 all reconnaissance was being done visually and, in April, the number of operations quickly reduced with fewer targets to find. During that month, however, the squadron assisted a Royal Navy Swordfish squadron in locating and destroying enemy one-man submarines, with four Wellingtons positioned daily at B83 Knocke on the Belgian coast. The first such sortie was flown on 18 April by Wg Cdr Shaw, patrolling from the Scheldt estuary north to Ijmuiden, but no success was recorded. Aircraft continued to be lost however, with Sgt M A Hunt and crew in MP397 going missing on the night of 7/8 April in the Apeldoorn-Amersfoort area, plus Plt Off P T Wansborough and crew in NC539 on the night of 26/27th in the Pinnsburg-Itzehoe area. Operations ceased on 7 May and in July the squadron moved to Aalborg in Denmark to carry out survey work, moving again to Eindhoven, Holland to disband on 7 August 1945.

CREW TRAINING

In the early days of the Wellington's service, new crews were trained on the squadrons, regardless of their backgrounds. An appropriate example to illustrate this is Plt Off Gerry Stone whose first tour as a wireless operator was with 64 Squadron flying Hawker Demons from Martlesham Heath. In December 1938 he was posted to Bomber Command at 115 Squadron, Marham. At that time it was equipped with the Handley Page Harrow but, when Gerry arrived, plans were already well advanced to re-equip with Wellingtons. Consequently, Gerry's experience of the Harrow was limited to just ten flights, with the last one being recorded on 30 March '39.

The first time a Wellington appears in Gerry's log is 9 May and for the next year his flying became far more intense. For the first few months, aircraft familiarisation was followed by a variety of practice operations, cross-country and bombing exercises, air firing and so on. The longest trip recorded during this period was a mammoth ten hours and twenty-five minutes from Marham to Manston, Paris, Lyons, Marseilles and back to Manston. By the time war was declared in September, crewing seemed to have settled down, but it would still be another three months before Gerry and his crew started operations.

By early 1940 it became apparent that the need for increasing numbers of bomber crews required a significant change to the existing training system, not least to relieve the squadrons of the additional pressure of training. One key aspect of this change was the formation of OTUs whose primary role was to bring together aircrew who had completed their specialised training as pilots, navigators, wireless operators, air gunners, and later air bombers, to enable them to come together as crews whilst they learned the art of bombing operations, prior to joining a squadron. The first such units started forming in the spring of 1940, and for the next two years new OTUs continued to emerge, both at home and overseas, as the demand for new and replacement crews became ever greater (see Appendix 2).

The bulk of the units were based in the Midlands and northern Home Counties of England, well away from the areas further east reserved for operational squadrons and most prone to interference from enemy air activity. There was a particularly high density of Wellington operations in the area around north Buckinghamshire and Oxfordshire, with OTUs based at Silverstone, Upper Heyford, Westcott and Wing plus satellite aerodromes including Barford St.John, Cheddington, Chipping Warden, Enstone, Little Horwood and Oakley. With each unit having an establishment of between forty and sixty aircraft, the skies were very crowded indeed, as the use of Wellington OTUs as the providers of new crews for the four-engine heavies continued throughout the war.

Fg Off John Elliott joined 83 OTU at Peplow, Shropshire as a newly-fledged WOp/AG and recalled the crewing-up method:

> "Referring to my log book, that invaluable record (which incidentally, belongs to HM Government!), I recall that we spent three months at 83 OTU Peplow to become acquainted with the Wellington, or 'Wimpy' as it was known. I remember arriving at the airfield with brand new sergeant's stripes, all of us being NCOs now, much to the chagrin of the 'old sweats' ground staff who had spent many years getting their stripes. This was, of course, when we were gathered together in a large hangar and told to 'sort yourselves out' into a crew of pilot, navigator, bomb aimer, wireless op, and two gunners. This method of crewing-up was totally surprising, as normally, the RAF would have been expected to nominate people from each category to a crew. However, the system worked well most of the time except that we had to swap our first bomb aimer. He didn't fit in, and was replaced with a Canadian."

W/O Dave Fellowes and his crew started sorting themselves out even before they reached 30 OTU at Hixon. They went on to complete a full tour on Lancasters with 460 (RAAF) Sqn at Binbrook, Lincolnshire:

> "My skipper was Arthur Whitmarsh and we met first of all on a train. He'd finished his advanced flying unit up in the Scottish borders somewhere, where they'd been flying Oxfords with two others, Australian flight sergeants, and they were on their way down to Hixon. I met him at Crewe station and got on the same train because I was going to Hixon as well and in piled these three flight sergeants. We got chatting and I asked where they came from; I knew Australia was a big place. He said Sydney and I told him I had an aunt there in a suburb called Marrickville, and he said 'Well, that's where we live. What's her name?' So I said Evans and he said 'Well, I don't know what to say because my mother and your aunt go to the same chapel in Marrickville. Well, we're going to have to get crewed up so will you fly with me?' So I said yes and then, you know what it's like at OTUs, you've got to get crewed up. We then looked around for the navigator with the eyebrows, who was a studious-looking laddie called Dennis Collette and he

BK347 of 30 OTU preparing for a Nickelling sortie from Hixon (*IWM CH1841*)

was fantastic. The Australian wireless operator didn't know Arthur but that didn't matter, he fitted in and so did Jock Turnbull and so we formed a crew. That was the idea, we bonded together and stayed together right up to the end of the war."

Of course not everyone who found themselves at an OTU was necessarily pleased to be there. Sqn Ldr Jo Lancaster DFC was one such, who had harboured dreams of becoming a fighter pilot:

"I had finished EFTS on Tiger Moths. The Battle of Britain was on and I was recommended for training as a fighter pilot and went to Sealand, 5 FTS, where they had Miles Masters with Kestrel engines. It was a big course, there were about fifty of us; Neville Duke was on the same course. We were divided into four flights, and in December we were moved to Ternhill. At the end of this course, instead of being sent to a fighter unit, our flight, I think there were eleven of us, were all sent off to bomber OTUs.

"I went to Lossiemouth [20 OTU], Wellingtons and right next door is Kinloss, with Whitleys. I went to the group captain and suggested I should change to there, but he wasn't having any of that. So I was stuck with the Wellington and we were crewed up there. It was very strange, all the pilots stuck together and we didn't mix, but then one day we were all put in a hangar and told to make ourselves into a crew. We just wandered around, I didn't know anybody. I finished up with a Canadian navigator Len Leith, a Canadian front gunner/wireless operator, Bill Harris, a Welsh wireless operator, Jack Crowther, and a New Zealand rear gunner, Keith Crowther. We all arranged to meet in the Grand Hotel, pubs were in a bit of a short supply then, and the Grand Hotel was about the only place in Lossiemouth. We all got on very well, and remained as thick as thieves for the rest of our lives."

'Toddy' Knight RNZAF:

"During my period in the UK I did a tour and was then sent up to Lossiemouth for a so-called 'rest' period. Stone the crows, what a laugh. The first thing we did was to go out with some sprogs and fly into the side of a flaming great hill. Got out of that one and got back to 99 Squadron."

Dave Fellowes:

"We created mayhem at Hixon. We started off doing circuits and landings and when our skipper was qualified to go solo, that was it and then of course various different pilots would come with us; screen pilots. We even did a bit of formation flying, high-level bombing, straight and level, and we did a lot of gunnery. The first part was on the ground and the next part was daylight flying. We did twenty-eight hours fifty-five minutes: cross-country, air-to-sea and air-to-air firing, combat manoeuvres, everything really for gearing us up for operations, because that was what it was all about. The Wellington itself we rather liked: I think they had about thirty at Hixon, taking part in raids on enemy targets and they had Miles Masters for fighter affiliation, Martinets for pulling the drogue and Hurricanes were also used for that so there was a pretty good selection of aeroplanes there.

"One day we sat there, ready to take off, and we saw a B-17 come in. Our wireless operator said 'That's funny, listen to the radio boys' and 'In the Mood' was playing by Glenn Miller. He got a reprimand, actually, for improper use of the radio. Anyhow, that was the first half of the course and we then went on leave. When we got back, we started night flying, circuits and landings and all the cross-countries. We then had a special 'Bullseye' to Caen. You wouldn't count it as an operation but it was a hairy one; there was a lot of flak about. We did another couple of 'Bullseyes'; one got us across to France for five hours or so.

"The OTU was divided up into flights, and the flight sergeant in charge was one of the old-time ground staff. On the ladder going up into the aeroplane he had a mat and if you didn't wipe your feet before going up he'd have your guts for garters, on the grounds that the Wellington of course, being of geodetic construction, had the canvas sewn on. He maintained that if you went up there in your dirty flying boots, (there was only a little tiny gangway going up from the rear door to the front) you would take up grit, dirt and everything else. He said that all got in between the stringers and geodetic construction and it could cause wear and tear and rips. If we ever flew in one of his aeroplanes, we always wiped our shoes before going up into the aeroplane. After the OTU I went to 1481 Gunnery Flight at Ingham, still flying Wellingtons and all we used to do were exercises using a camera gun; total flying time three hours."

Initially, OTUs were equipped with different bomber types as appropriate, but once the four-engined heavies came into service it was recognised that putting newly-trained crews straight into a Stirling, Halifax or Lancaster was likely to present them with a significant challenge. So, coupled with the need to send all the factory output of the four-engined aircraft straight to operational squadrons, it was decided to retain twin-engined types at the OTUs and introduce an additional training step in the form of the HCU to transit to the larger aircraft. Fortuitously, this decision coincided with a reduction in the number of operational Wellington squadrons as the new types came in and so, for the remainder of the war, the Wimpy became by far the predominant OTU type.

John Elliott subsequently followed the OTU/HCU system, which then had an extra element, a Lancaster Finishing School (LFS) to convert from the Halifax they had used at HCU, before going on to complete a full tour of thirty operations with 550 Squadron at North Killingholme in Lincolnshire:

> "The first five weeks at OTU were spent doing circuits and bumps to familiarise our pilot Jim Lord with the aircraft – all flights varying between half-an-hour and an hour-and-a-half duration in daylight. Later on we did another week of circuits and bumps at night. Incidentally, the location of Peplow was very unfortunate, as it was close to the Wrekin, a small mountain rising to the height of 1,300 feet in Shropshire. This was a hazard at night as many crews came to grief approaching the airfield. I wonder who thought of the idea of putting an OTU filled with 'sprog' crews in such a place! The rest of the course involved cross-country flights and bombing exercises and enabled each crew member to become proficient in his particular task. It was during this period of 'circuits and bumps' that we, the rest of the crew, charged Jim a levy of sixpence a head for every bounce upon landing. Jim, being an accountant, soon smoothed out the landings! (The same thing applied later on when we were at a heavy conversion unit becoming familiar with the Halifax.)
>
> "The Wellington proved to be a sturdy, reliable aircraft which we liked, and only once during the three-month course did we experience an engine failure. This was a night exercise with an instructor pilot and we had to land at Middleton St.George, for some reason, weather probably, having to spend four days there before returning to Peplow. Access to the aircraft was by ladder up through the nose, and, as I remember, reasonably comfortable inside. It was an aircraft that served Bomber Command superbly throughout the war, reliable and able to withstand a lot of damage. The last flight of the OTU course was a 'Nickel' on 30 January 1944. This was an exercise designed to introduce us to flying into enemy-occupied territory. We didn't carry a bomb load, but I believe we dropped leaflets. The trip proved to be uneventful. I know that Jim Lord, as a pilot, liked the Wellington very much, as he became an instructor himself after completing our tour of operations.
>
> "A comparison of our two training courses – OTU at Peplow, and HCU at Sandtoft – will serve to confirm the superiority of the Wellington's reliability against that of the Halifax. We only had one engine failure on the Wellington compared with three on the shorter Halifax course."

In fact John's comment about the reliability of the engines on the Wellingtons he encountered is remarkable as the aircraft tended to be well-used by the time the OTUs got them, and engine problems figured largely in the tragically high numbers of accidents and incidents suffered by these units. Taking 11 OTU as an example, this unit was formed at Bassingbourn in April 1940, moving to Westcott in Buckinghamshire (with a satellite airfield at Oakley) in September 1942, from where it continued to operate until September 1945. A survey of just the aircraft lost in the vicinity of the home airfields[2] reveals that 11 OTU lost on average almost one aircraft a month during this period, with several others being lost while away from home or being written off on the airfield for various reasons.

Date	Aircraft	Circumstances & location
17 Nov '42	Wellington IC X9614	Engine failure on take-off, hit trees & crashed
10 Dec '42	Wellington IC DV916	Lost in low cloud, crashed at East Claydon
30 Dec '42	Wellington IC X9681	Engine failure, hit a tree at Ashendon in forced landing
31 Dec '42	Wellington IC DV764	Engine failure, crashed at Burcott Farm, Burcott
1 Feb '43	Wellington IC X9798	Lost control and crashed at Ashendon
5 Mar '43	Wellington IC DV923	Overshot approach crashed at Long Crendon
13 Mar '43	Wellington IC R1025	Handling problems crashed just short of runway
15 Mar '43	Wellington IC X9792	Stalled, crashed off NE end of SW/NE runway
14 May '43	Wellington IC DV826	Overshot after engine failure
16 Jul '43	Wellington IC DV720	Engine failure on take-off, ended up in railway cutting
17 Sep '43	Wellington IC DV608	Engine failure, crashed on high ground near Brill
22 Sep '43	Wellington IC DV815	Lost control hit wooded hillside 1 mile SE of airfield near Waddesdon Manor
27 Oct '43	Wellington IC R1790	Probable engine failure crashed into trees at Parrot's Field, Wotton Underwood
25 Nov '43	Wellington IC DV836	Lost propeller, crash-landed Manor Bridge near Westcott
30 Jan '44	Wellington X JA139	Lost power, crash-landed in a field at Mursley
4 Mar '44	Wellington X HE229	Engine failure on take-off, crashed Akeman Street station
15 Mar '44	Wellington X LN660	Mid-air collision with Stirling after take-off, crashed just E of Quainton
30 May '44	Wellington X LN741	Engine trouble crashed at Chetwode Grange S side of LNER railway
13 Sep '44	Wellington X HE227	Engine trouble on take-off, overshot, crossed Bicester road and ended up near DF station
28 Sep '44	Wellington X LP825	Hit trees on go-around at Oakley airfield
5 Dec '44	Wellington X LN226	Stalled and crashed on approach to Oakley
4 Jan '45	Wellington X HE740	Dived out of cloud into ground at North Marston
14 Jan'45	Wellington X LN403	Turned away on approach crashed near Wotton Underwood station
13 Feb '45	Wellington X LP396	Engine failure, force-landed 500 yds short of Oakley runway
16 Apr '45	Wellington X LP609	Collided with LP651 in Oakley circuit crashed 2 miles NNE in direction of Boarstall
16 Apr '45	Wellington X LP651	Collided with LP609 and came down in same area
25 Apr '45	Wellington X HE417	Engine failure, force landed near Waterstock, 4 miles W of Thame

In January 1943 Flt Lt George Dunn DFC found himself crewing up at 20 OTU at Lossiemouth

Flt Lt George Dunn DFC learned his Wellington skills at 20 OTU. (*George Dunn*)

(although in his case they flew from the satellite airfield at Milltown), and he echoed the impression that their aircraft were tired:

> "20 OTU was equipped with Wellington aircraft, many of them having seen better days and a little bit worse off for wear. This was not surprising as many of them had seen operational duties against the enemy. On closer examination, I thought how frail that fabric looked covering that geodetic construction. Most important were the two very fine Pegasus engines which were kept in good running order, but the aircraft were a bit clapped out. I thought it was a good aircraft. I mean, whilst there we did have an engine failure over the North Sea on one of the bombing and cross-country exercises but we got back on the one engine. The only snag was that we had to make a flap-less landing because we couldn't use the undercarriage controls. So then we had to wind down the undercarriage, which then prevented you from using your flaps but in the end it was OK because that was one of the things you were taught anyway."

Many other aspects of the training carried their elements of risk too, not least the need to be able to cope with crowded circuits, with fairly primitive aids, especially at night. Guy Sharp had a very narrow escape on 20 March 1943 when he was flying Wellington III X3368 'N':

> "I was instructing at 29 OTU North Luffenham. We had four stations: North Luffenham, Bitteswell, Bruntingthorpe and Woolfox Lodge. At Woolfox Lodge I had my nearest escape, I think. I landed, only going about five miles an hour, but it was thick fog, and at that moment we hit another Wellington. The front turret fell off, the undercarriage collapsed and I could hear the petrol just gushing out onto our hot engines. Why it didn't catch

21 OTU Wellington coded R at Moreton-in-Marsh December 1944. Note the faired-over front turret. (*ww2images*)

fire I shall never know; most of them did when they collapsed. This was a night landing, so we only had anti-collision lights, we didn't have Chance Lights or anything like that. I couldn't have missed him, even if I'd seen him."

Not all unexpected events had such a dramatic outcome, as W/O Jack Bromfield recalled from his time at 21 OTU at Moreton-in-Marsh, Gloucestershire:

"On a cross-country from Moreton we had two gunners in a Wimpy, but only one turret. Halfway round they would change over, and on that last long straight leg, they would tell the pilot, 'Ready for the exercise', and he would do gentle S-turns. Well one of the gunners reeled out the drogue, which was sort of fishtailing behind, and the other gunner shot at it – couldn't hit the side of a barn if he was in it! On this particular night, Robby [pilot Fg Off Arthur 'Robby' Robertson RCAF] had told the rear gunner to stream the drogue, because Doc Marion was in the turret.

"The skipper called me up, and said 'Have you got communication with Doc?' I said 'Yes', and he said 'I can't get anybody'. So I said I'd give him a shout and I called Doc in the rear turret and I said 'Has he streamed the drogue yet?' 'I can't see any drogue, he should have streamed it fifteen minutes ago.' Well what's going on now? The skipper said to me: 'Disconnect, walk down the back and have a look.' When I did I saw this little short man; he'd stepped back to admire his work and gone through the canvas; his legs were hanging outside the aircraft. We missed the best bit didn't we, Robby should have told me to go down and tell him when to start running as we landed!"

A similarly humorous but potentially very tricky situation occurred to Norman Nava when he was flying at 3 (Coastal) OTU at Cranwell, Lincolnshire:

"We took some ATC boys up on flight experience. The aircraft wouldn't level off and when we investigated we found a boy sitting on the elevator mass-balance and riding it like a see-saw; I had to knock him off quick!"

Those operational crews that were lucky enough to complete their tours frequently found themselves posted to an OTU as instructors on a 'rest tour' before ultimately rejoining the fray. One advantage of this for Bomber Command planners was that these units contained a core of staff who already had operational experience, which enabled them to be called upon occasionally to take part in operations, as we have seen was the case with the 1,000-bomber raids. There does not appear to have been a clear policy with respect to the use or otherwise of pupil crews during such operations, and this varied considerably between different OTUs. An example of the requirement for OTUs to support operations was the States of Readiness and Scales of Effort of Bomber Command Aircraft edict dated 16 March 1944. This denoted a normal readiness state calling for front-line squadrons only of 'Black' and scale of effort 'Goodwood'. Readiness states of 'White' and 'Emergency White' and scale of effort 'Grand National' meant that OTUs would be called upon to support operations and should be ready to take off within six hours.

Having completed a Wellington tour with 12 and 40 Squadrons, Jo Lancaster found himself as a reluctant instructor:

"I was posted to Wellesbourne Mountford, Wellington OTU [No.22], not that I enjoyed it very much at all, and there was no way you could call it a rest. I was on the conversion flight doing circuits and bumps, and in the winter we did night flying which was divided into four three-hour sessions. Obviously your turn came round to do 12 to 3 and 3 to 6 which was soul-destroying, I was far from happy. I did an OTU instructor's course at CFS Upavon; and I did a month's course on Oxfords. I didn't enjoy that either. Then they opened another OTU at Wymeswold [No.28 opened in May '42], near Leicester, and I was posted in to that. We sort of started it up from scratch. At OTU we got lumbered with 1,000-bomber raids. I was on the first two and I was going to be on the third one to Bremen, but the aircraft went U/S. The crew mix on those raids was variable. In my case I had a screened navigator Jo Hart, and a screened wireless op which turned out to be very fortuitous, and two pupil Canadian gunners. Over the top of Cologne, which was a sea of fire, one of the Canadians got very excited and asked if he could spray his guns about.

"So I did the OTU tour, and then one day in October '42 I went off with a pupil crew on a five-hour cross-country and came back sort of five or six o'clock-ish and found out I was detailed for a 'Bullseye' that same night. [A diversionary sortie by HCUs and OTUs to draw the attention of German early warning systems away from an actual raid.] There was no food or rest for me, and off I went; that time I had a completely sprog crew. I discovered that the wireless op had all his equipment in pieces on the floor, so they were going to be no help at all. Flying around the countryside at night with no wireless op and a sprog crew wasn't a very good idea I thought but we pressed ahead. I got into icing over the Solway Firth, and then we were supposedly going down to an island off the Welsh coast which was a popular turning point; it had an ultra-violet target there or something. Anyway, we got into icing, and the ice was bashing on the fuselage, so I decided to pack it in. We had to find our way back under cloud again, it was the only way we could see where we were going – the navigator and myself between us.

"On the next day I was on the carpet in front of the chief instructor; he hadn't done anything towards the war effort as far as I could see. He was a wing commander and he was telling me off for having turned back on this 'Bullseye', and he wanted to see my log book. I gave it to him and I had stuck a little cartoon in it which I don't think he liked very much. It was an aircraft engine with a chap sitting astride it with the caption: 'All the way from Hamburg on one engine.' He asked, 'Did you come back from Hamburg on one engine?' I started getting bloody rude to him, I didn't care anyway. I was fed up with this OTU stuff, it was just as dangerous as being on a squadron without the esprit. So I was quite insubordinate and he told me to take the cartoon out of my log book. I think I told him I wasn't going to. Very quickly, within a couple of days, I was posted."

Having completed his first tour on Halifaxes with 10 Squadron at Melbourne, George Dunn had similar feelings about his long rest stint instructing at OTU:

"I went to 18 OTU, Worksop in November '43. One night in January '44 I was officer-in-charge of night flying. This chap was actually one of my pupils and they were beginning to come in time from Flying Training Command, as far as flying was concerned, quite experienced. So it was just a question of converting them. On this particular night there was a bit of haze about and I thought 'Perhaps I'd better do a weather check before letting the pupils go up'. Well, it was only for ten minutes, so we took off, I did a circuit, the weather was quite OK and I had arranged for the lorry to pick me up at the take-off point so I could just nip down and the pupil could go straight off without having to go into dispersal. He took off again, did a circuit, for some reason he overshot, and that was the last we heard of him. He crashed somewhere down near Nottingham; and the whole crew were killed. I had to go to a Court of Enquiry the following day and it turned out eventually, that a prop blade had come off. I stayed there until December '44 and then volunteered to go on to Mosquitoes. I'd had enough! All that time!"

Briefing room murals, 16 OTU. (*TNA*)

Fg Off H E Fryer DFC AFC instructed at 16 OTU Upper Heyford and had a very lucky escape when his aircraft suffered a catastrophic wing failure:

The briefing room at 16 OTU Upper Heyford 28 March 1944. (*TNA*)

"On the morning of 6 July 1943 I was asked to air test Wellington IC BJ984 after it had completed a fifty-hour service. The test took about an hour and at its conclusion I was not satisfied with the aircraft as it kept dropping the port wing. It was taken back to the hangar and the engineering staff decided that the fault was probably caused by loss of power on the port engine, although the instrument readings did not bear this out. The aircraft eventually became ready for air-test at about 17:00 hours and I was accompanied by a ground staff fitter, Corporal Charles Hand. After being airborne about twenty minutes I decided that the aircraft was no better and that I would return to base. When over the aerodrome at approximately 3,500 feet the aircraft flipped onto its back and then started spinning on its own axis, and in addition doing what I can only describe as barrel rolls. It was decided to abandon the aircraft, not knowing at that point what was wrong (in fact the port mainplane had failed and broke off at 1,800 feet), and the lower hatch was opened as was the butterfly canopy over the cockpit.

"As soon as I released my Sutton harness I was thrown out through the top and managed to operate my 'chute at about 1,500 feet. I never saw the corporal again and he was killed in the subsequent crash. I can only assume that just as I had been thrown clear he was similarly thrown further into the aircraft. The main body of the aircraft crashed just beyond the perimeter of the aerodrome and the port mainplane came down feet away from the control tower. I landed in the station sports field breaking my ankle in doing so. Subsequently, all Wellington aircraft of this type were grounded and examined for cracks in the main spars. I know that at Upper Heyford more aircraft were found with such cracks. This was probably one of the earlier forms of metal fatigue."

A similar case of wing failure occurred a few weeks later on 29 August when, after just ten minutes in the air, Mk.III BK431 'J' of 29 OTU Bruntingthorpe, Leicestershire flown by Fg Off John Heath RNZAF suffered a near-identical event when its port wing folded upwards when pulling out of a dive and the aircraft disintegrated near Oakham, Rutland. The crew of six and Air Training Corps cadet J D Woodward, who was along for the ride, all perished. The investigation reported that the bolts securing the lower port wing spar had failed due to metal fatigue.

This was one of around twenty similar catastrophic wing failures over a two-year period, the earliest being 1483 Flight's T2802 on 24 May 1942 during a fighter-evasion exercise. An investigation by Vickers traced the problem to two primary causes, the detailed design of the main spar boom joint, and the material used in the manufacture of the spar tubes which had high levels of tensile stress, either of which could lead to fatigue cracking and structural failure. The solution was to use a modified spar boom joint using a different material, and this was approved in July 1944.

Charles La Force RCAF was a WOp/AG with the Royal Canadian Air Force (RCAF), who referred to the trade as W/AG, and recalled some exciting experiences during his OTU training:

"Donald R W 'Sandy' Saunders, sgt pilot (later flight officer, DFC), interviewed various trades, introduced us to one another, and we first flew as a crew in Wellington LN552 'A' on 2 July '44 at 82 OTU Ossington. After being airborne on twenty-one more or less uneventful flights (once we sneaked my visiting brother, a 425 Squadron armourer, on a cross-country exercise), we reached number twenty-two. It was a cross-country culminating in air-to-sea practice bombing over the North Sea; it was 8 August '44; we were busy and all was right with the world.

"Suddenly, someone said over the intercom 'look at that stupid clot coming straight at us!'; another spoke up 'it's a Mosquito, skipper'. Suddenly, tracer and bullets were flying by us and over us and our careless 'Mosquito' was a mean Ju 88. Immediately Sandy corkscrewed into a cloud below. I learned four things from that trip; first, we had better polish up our aircraft identification; second, the quick reaction of Sandy showed that we had the pilot we wanted. Third, cloud could be a bomber's friend and fourth, Wimpys came equipped with a skyhook for I swear, Sandy towed that cloud all the way home."

The Luftwaffe attempted to interfere with OTU operations in a very different fashion on 21 January 1945, when escaped POW Leutnant Kurt Ibling was apprehended on the airfield at

Bitteswell, Leicestershire, home to 105 OTU, after escaping from a prison camp near Crewe. At the time he was spotted he was paying close attention to Wellington X NC709, no doubt hoping to be able to gain entry and fly it home! Charles La Force continued:

"The next night, 9 August, we flew on a five-hour bomber diversion over northern France [a 'Bullseye']. This was close enough to see searchlights and imagine enough night fighters to keep the adrenalin flowing. On the 12th we went south of Paris; at the navigated point, the photo flash dropped (I stood at the 'chute with a sawn-off broom handle and made sure it did). The sky lit up and we had a picture; this was to photograph an aiming point as if we had bombed. Not long after, the aircraft filled with smoke and fumes and Sandy ordered ''chutes on'. We all had visions of a short tour and a long POW stay. The engines seemed OK, so the skipper told Andy to have a look in the nose of the aircraft. I kept at the radio set, although I wondered later what good an SOS or a 'Mayday' would have done there. Andy quietly reported 'the camera is on fire'; Sandy yelled 'well, kick it to hell out the side!' Andy did and soon the smoke and fumes cleared and the air was clean.

"On the night of 16 August we went back to France with another Wellington to drop leaflets; we came back, which is more than you can say about the other aircraft – a night fighter got them. Having seen the aircraft going down on fire, we thought they had all gone for a Burton [RAF slang for missing], but I think they all survived, some as POWs and I know the W/AG got out as I spoke to him a couple of weeks later. He said that his parachute drifted him over Free France and on landing, he was taken by the Maquis. They didn't understand his continued shouting of 'RCAF' and only took the knife away from his throat when one smiled and said 'RAF?' He then made a mistake that almost cost him a slit throat, he happily replied 'Yeah! Yeah!', which was too close to the German 'Ja! Ja!' With his identity at last established, it was food, cognac, champagne for days. When the hospitality began to wane, he opened his Pandora Box escape kit and used all the money to act as host for days, but soon, broke and exhausted, he hitch-hiked home, completely hung over."

The aircraft lost was Mk.III BJ590 skippered by Flt Lt J E Verge RCAF, and probably hit by flak. The whole crew baled out and survived although Verge broke a leg on landing. La Force continued:

"Then on 28 August we found out for sure what we had already assumed, we had the number one pilot. On a cross-country exercise our flying took us over the North Sea. Suddenly we were attacked by an Me 109. He made a couple more passes and I don't know if our guns hit him, but he hit us. Sandy was corkscrewing about the sky, guns were firing, and then we were in cloud. We were lucky to reach the cloud because now we had problems; the port engine quit. Either it controlled the hydraulics or we had a severed oil line; the rear turret stopped, the wheels dropped down and the bomb bay doors fell open. The cloud covered our escape and soon we sighted the English coast. Next, we found that the starboard wheel had taken some hits and the tyre was damaged. Sandy told us to bale out if we wanted but all voted to stay. Maybe the others thought as I did 'no way do I want to fly like a bird and land on that hard ground unless I was forced to'; I remembered jumping off those practice towers! Besides, if we go, we go as a crew.

"Shortly, the choice of parachuting was gone as we were losing height rapidly; we barely made it to Ossington. Sandy eased the Wimpy down superbly, with most of the weight on the port wheel. Finally the starboard wheel settled and we did an almost 90 degree of the runway. We tore around the grass, off the runway, but didn't upset or ground loop. Senior officers arrived from the control tower at almost the same time that we stopped. One jumped out of a car and immediately began shouting about the quality of the landing. I was too shaken to know whether he was talking tongue-in-cheek of whether he was acting true to his nature."

In Chapter Two the story of James Ward VC was told and, prior to arriving at 75 (NZ) Squadron, Ward had crewed up at 20 OTU Lossiemouth. While he was to become the only man to be awarded the Victoria Cross while flying Wellingtons, all the airmen listed below who were awarded the VC while flying other aircraft types, flew the Wimpy at various points during their careers, either while training, on earlier tours, or while instructing.

Arthur Aaron	26 OTU c.Jun 42-Mar 43
Ian Bazalgette	25 OTU Jan-Sep 42; 115 Squadron Sep 42; 20 OTU Sep 43-Apr 44
Norman Jackson	27 OTU Sep 42-Mar 43
Rawdon Middleton	23 OTU Oct 41-Jan 42
Andrew Mynarski	16 OTU Feb-Jun 43
Robert Palmer	15 OTU Sep-Nov 40; 75 Squadron Nov 40; 149 Squadron Nov 40-Feb 41; 20 OTU Feb 41-Nov 43
William Reid	29 OTU Sep 42-Jul 43
Edwin Swales	83 OTU Dec 43-Jun 44
George Thompson	14 OTU May-Aug 44

A further connection with notable airmen concerns Flt Lt John 'Hoppy' Hopgood DFC and bar, who lost his life on 17 May 1943 when his 617 Squadron Lancaster crashed during the attack on the Möhne dam. On 31 March, when the squadron was being set up, Hopgood was transferred from 1485 (Target Towing) Flight where he had been flying Wellingtons to give air gunners fighter affiliation practice.

TRANSPORTS

While extensive use was made of transport conversions of basic bomber variants, it is not possible to be precise about the numbers involved. Production conversions nominally for Transport Command included C Mk.IA, C Mk.IC, C Mk.IX, C Mk.XV and C Mk.XVI, of which fifty-nine examples have been identified. In addition to these there was an unknown number of conversions carried out in the field or at maintenance units to aircraft already delivered in bomber configuration, with a number of these being attached to communication flights as VIP transports for senior officers and their staff. It is believed that the total number of all transport conversions exceeded 100. L H Richards was a navigator who came across just such an ad hoc conversion:

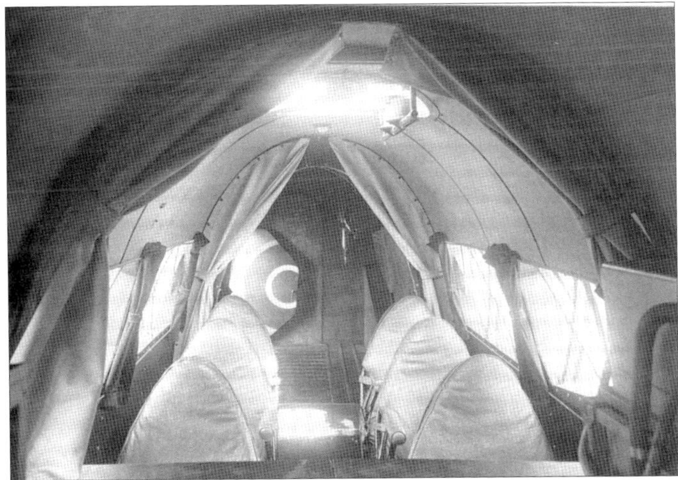

The cabin of a transport conversion by Fairfield Aviation at Elstree. (*Bob Clarke*)

"After a tour of ops on Bomber Command Lancasters, I was posted to 38 Group. Around the autumn of 1945 we became the personal aircrew to Air Vice-Marshal Ronald Ivelaw-Chapman the AOC, and my role was navigator. The AVM decided to have a special aircraft to be hauled about in and as a result we went to Brize Norton I believe [more likely to have been Lyneham as 6 MU at Brize Norton did not routinely handle Wellingtons] and chose one of about thirty Wellingtons. This new aircraft was then converted into a passenger aircraft and we flew the AVM and an assortment of air rank individuals as passengers all over the Continent."

C.Mk.I L4340 NQ-A 'Duke of Rutland' of 24 Squadron Hendon. (*Brooklands Museum*)

In August 1940, the Air Despatch Letter Service (ADLS) postal service to Malta previously operated by the British Overseas Airways Corporation (BOAC), was taken over by 24 Squadron based at Hendon just north of London, and three Wellington Mk.ICs joined the squadron's mixed fleet of types converted for transport use. The unit carried the lion's share of the communications burden throughout Great Britain. Flights were organised not only as required, but also to a quite complex schedule, with routes being started to Northern Ireland in July 1940, Gibraltar in April 1942 and Malta shortly thereafter. W K Knight served on the squadron at that time:

"The Wellington had all the bomb racks and wiring removed, and in their place was installed a long cylindrical petrol tank, so maximising its range to reach Malta. Two K

Mk.IC B.A.W.3 of BOAC with an unidentified pilot in the Western Desert 1942. (*ww2images*)

guns were fitted on each side of the fuselage. The day arrived for an air test, and on returning the starboard wing tip had been shot up. I think the officer was a squadron leader, how the problem was solved I don't know. Days ran into weeks as F.IIAs (fitters airframe) hand-drilled the rivets to release the damaged brackets and fit new ones. Returning from the cookhouse after dinner we found someone had put a few grass turves along the mainplane, this caused great laughter, but the flight sergeant didn't think so 'Get them off quick – end of joke'."[3]

The transport Wellingtons could carry up to nine passengers or eighteen troops, with Mk.IC P2522 of the Airborne Forces Experimental Establishment (AFEE) at Sherburn-in-Elmet being the first conversion, emerging as a Mk.IX. A more unusual conversion was Mk.I L4255 which was allocated to the Air Transport Auxiliary (ATA) at White Waltham, Berkshire for use as an air ambulance. In December 1944 and January 1945 Wellington XVIs were issued to two mainline Transport Command squadrons, 232 and 242, both at Stoney Cross, Hampshire. However, the type was considered unsuited to the route flying which was the units' bread and butter, and the Wellingtons only lasted until February '45 when their job was taken over by the Liberator VII and Stirling V respectively.

1680 (Western Isles Communication) Flight

This unit is an example of the kind of communications flying being carried out.The principal aircraft types used were the de Havilland Dominie, Fokker F.XXII and Walrus. Flights were regularly carried out to destinations such as: Abbotsinch, Prestwick, Port Ellen, Benbecula, Stornoway, Tiree and Coll plus a smattering of others. In December 1943 Wellington Mk.I L4263 was allocated to the flight from 24 Squadron, at Renfrew, Glasgow. However, it saw very little use and in January 1944 was only flown twice. Although the aircraft was retained largely unused, it did finally operate to Iceland on 19 April, returning the next day. On 8 July 1944 the Wellington was flown to Vickers at Shawbury, Shropshire for reduction to spares and produce in accordance with headquarters 43 Group signal TB8953.

COMMUNICATIONS FLYING OVERSEAS

The use of the Wellington bomber in a transport role had come about as a direct result of an urgent request, from RAF Middle East Command in 1941, for more transport aircraft and once again, with the acute shortage of such machines, necessity became the mother of invention.

Originally, MKs, I, II, III and IV were converted by simply removing all military equipment and fitting Valentia-type seats, but eventually Vickers themselves took on the task and well over 100 aircraft were modified. In some cases, in order to try to disguise their defencelessness, they had nose and tail gun turrets painted on the fuselage with a dummy gun fitted. The embryo Transport Command was still learning to make do with whatever equipment it could lay its hands on. W/O Jack Wade was a Wellington wireless operator in the Middle East:

> "People like myself on my section of Transport Command led a particularly cushy life, it was the luck of the draw but I sometimes have a twinge of conscience about it. I believe we tried to compensate by making the catchphrase 'press on regardless' a bit more than that, in fact one of the nicest compliments I ever heard was a casual remark in a briefing room, when a Bomber Command wireless operator, grounded by bad weather, complained to his skipper that we were going to fly while they waited for Met to come up with something better. His skipper replied, 'Stop whingeing, that's a transport crew – they'll fly in anything'. After that we'd have gone if we had had to taxi all the way!
>
> "In the Middle East and Italy, we invariably flew the Wellington X, with the odd XIII and occasionally a Warwick, but there was not an awful lot of difference. The aircraft could be fairly new out from the UK, or a patched-up fly-back to the knacker's yard at an MU. The first job my crew had was to take three has-been Wimpy ICs from Heliopolis in Egypt to Blida in North Africa. Pinching bits from the other two, the three wireless ops got one complete set in our Wimpy Mk.XVIII HX685 and my job was to get the messages and flash them by Aldis to the other two layabouts in their aircraft. We finally ran into a sandstorm south of Mersa Matruh and we never heard from them again.
>
> "We lost our port engine cowling climbing over the Atlas Mountains prior to letting down into Blida and arrived looking like something from the Oxfam shop. I remember thinking at the time that if it was always going to be like this, I hope my mum keeps up the insurance payments. It wasn't though, that sort of thing rarely happened. Considering what they had to work with, and some of the conditions in which they did their job, I don't think anyone can give the erks too much credit. The cynical flight sergeant with his standard remark 'It'll clear itself in the air sarge', or the other gem, 'It was all right on air test yesterday', was more of a cartoon character than a reality.
>
> "My crew was given the job of ferrying Air Vice-Marshal Ernest Cuckney [Senior Maintenance Staff Officer, HQ Mediterranean Allied Air Forces] around. His aircraft, Wellington X LP201 Sister Anna, was a standard aircraft converted for VIP use in '44. The aft section of the bomb bay was sealed, leaving a small forward section for luggage storage. The crew could enter as usual through the nose, but the AVM and staff made a more dignified arrival via a door let in on the starboard side. Turrets were removed and the holes faired over. The crew space was as normal, but aft of the navigator was a small compartment with three seats for the fitter and rigger who we always carried, and the third seat was used by the AVM's batman/driver. Aft of this area via a door in another bulkhead was the passenger compartment, with about a dozen seats for the AVM and staff. A most useful feature for me as wireless operator, was that the W/T call sign FALQK was known to all ground WOps, and when I was calling with position reports etc., any brash lad who attempted to break in was told smartly to shut up – it

made life very easy.

"The duties were straightforward; tours of inspection, conferences with other service personalities and so on. After a trip we would be given a date when the 'old man' would require us again and we would use the aircraft for normal passenger work in the meantime. Since the aircraft had to be serviced and air tested between each trip with the AVM, even if he had flown within the last twenty-four hours, those spare days were always busy. When not required, and on normal passenger work, we came into our own and eventually acquired the name of 'Cuckney's Private Airline', a fact which was not unknown to the boss, but thankfully he had a sense of humour. We opted for passengers not too high in rank, who were not in too much of a hurry; sociable types who would appreciate the red carpet treatment we laid on for them and who would respond when it came to their turn at the bar! It couldn't last of course, and eventually AVM Cuckney went home to a new appointment in Bomber Command, and we moved on to other flying units."

W/O Tom Claridge was a pilot on 3rd Tactical Air Force (Burma) Communications Squadron which flew Mk.Xs and Mk.XIIIs based at Comilla in 1943 and '44:

"These Wellingtons were used mainly for runs over the front line dropping urgent supplies and the daily papers (these were dropped from the flare 'chute). I had one very interesting flight in LN504 'X' [a Mk.X recently displaced from 99 Squadron by the arrival of Liberators] on 22 October 1944, when flying from Comilla to Allahabad with crew and six passengers. Stooging along at 8,000 feet the starboard engine suddenly gave a couple of coughs and stopped. Everything seemed OK until one of the crew said petrol was coming through the fuselage between the main spar and the rear turret. We feathered the prop and pressed the engine fire extinguisher. After settling down and going quite well on the port, it also decided to stop; luckily there was a landing strip

Mk.X HZ809 of the Balkan Air Force Communications Flight at Bari 1945. It caught fire starting up at Brindisi on 25 April that year and was burnt out. (*Peter Fotherby*)

> dead ahead. We couldn't raise anyone on R/T so we fired a good display of reds and just dropped in on them. The fault was found to be that the main fuel line to the starboard engine had come unscrewed, and the port engine eventually suffered from fuel starvation. We also discovered that air vents were blocked with wasps' nests! I got a Green Endorsement for that landing."

Following his tour on 104 Squadron, Peter Fotherby found himself flying a transport Wellington Mk.X with the Balkan Air Force Communications Flight at Bari from October 1944 to July 1945. One aircraft HZ809, had some local modifications done to it, finally coming to grief on 25 April '45 when it caught fire and was burnt out just after Peter had delivered it to Brindisi for an engine change:

Major A D D McKellar OC 28 Squadron SAAF.

> "These locally-converted aircraft were lashed together. This one had all its oxygen system and all the rows of oxygen bottles. I used to fly this thing and decided we didn't want that extra weight because we never flew high enough to use oxygen. So in taking them out we got in there with a spanner and there was a whistling sound and we ran for our lives! We should have got the engineers to do it.
>
> "It was nearly all ferrying people, although sometimes medical supplies. We had one trip where we ferried a load of rocket saddles for the fighters to somewhere in Yugoslavia. Randolph Churchill [the prime minster's son and a major in the 4th Queen's Own Hussars] used to fly around with us."

On 1 June 1943 28 Squadron SAAF was formed at Castel Benito under the command of Major A A D McKellar, as a passenger and cargo transport unit, equipped with Ansons plus four ex-BOAC Wellington Mk.ICs as stop-gaps pending the arrival of Dakotas. The first three Wellingtons were taken over on 19 July, with the fourth (Z8783) arriving on the 28th and the squadron was decidedly unimpressed, having a great deal of trouble maintaining them:

> 'The aircraft are pretty well clapped out and doubt is expressed as to whether they will be of much use. On 23 July Lt M J Lamb was forced down [by engine trouble] close to El Adem [Libya] and had quite a hair-raising experience taking off from a minefield partially cleared for the purpose.'

Some idea of the trials and tribulations of the operations can be gauged from the ORB entry for 28 July:

'Detailed to fly Wellington T2609 to Misurata and transport 113 Squadron personnel to Idku. Took off at 04:50, landed Misurata at 06:00. Took off with load at 07:20 and refuelled at Marble Arch [a landing ground on the Libyan coast]. Landed at El Adem at 13:45. Aircraft U/S because of tyre and throttle trouble. Spent the night at El Adem, took off at 06:55, and landed at Idku at 10:20. Lunched and took off at 12:05 and noticed that starboard magneto of starboard engine not too good. Landed at Almaza only to find that Wellington Z8783 which Lt Rall and his crew were to fly back had already been taken by an RAF pilot. Went on to Cairo West to pick up a load for return journey and reported various snags on aircraft. Starboard magneto of starboard engine, tailplane and Aldis lamp all U/S.'

As early as 13 August the unit's engineering report indicated that only two (T2609 and Z8783) remained on strength and that sixty-nine percent of unserviceability was caused by lack of spares. It was also pointed out that a large percentage of the squadron's mechanics had been away from home for twenty months and were now 'browned off and losing interest in their work'. Operations continued nonetheless, and detachments were maintained at Ras el Ma in Morocco, Oudna in Tunisia, Pachino in Sicily and Bari on the east coast of Italy until after the end of the war.

A conference was called on 19 October to discuss the continued use of the two remaining Wellingtons, at which it was stated that the aircraft were:

"Continually giving trouble and can never be relied upon to get a job done without some sort of hitch occuring. Although engine changes have been effected on both these aircraft, a considerable amount of maintenance is still required to keep them in a serviceable condition."

In the whole of November the two only flew a total of eight hours between them, and in December they were allotted away:

"To the relief of all. In their old age the Wellingtons required constant nursing and attention, and had proved a liability."

Neither aircraft saw any further service, with T2609 being stored and then struck off charge on 27 July 1944 and Z8783 following a similar fate, being broken up on 28 September.

FLEET AIR ARM

Between December 1942 and September 1945 the Royal Navy acquired a total of twenty-four Wellingtons of various marks for use in second-line squadrons. The largest user was 765 Squadron headquartered at Lee-on-Solent, Hampshire. The Wellingtons made use of the longer runways at Manston, Kent when crew training; the first example arriving in August '44, with the last of a total fleet of eight leaving in April '46. The primary role of the unit was as a travelling recording unit assessing the efficiency of radar units, but the aircraft were also employed on occasional long-range reconnaissance. In October 1945 it was redeployed to Hal Far, Malta where the Wellingtons were mainly used to position troops at Malta from various places around the Mediterranean prior to being embarked for home by sea.[4]

Other operators of numbers of Wellingtons included 758 Squadron, the Naval Advanced

Mk.X NC826 L8-F of the Fleet Air Arm's 765 Squadron detached to Manston in the summer of 1945. (*Fleet Air Museum*)

Instrument Flying School at Hinstock, Shropshire; 762 Squadron at Dale, Pembrokeshire for twin-engine conversion training; 783 Squadron at Arbroath for ASV training; and Yeovilton Station Flight. During their Fleet Air Arm service two Wellingtons were written off in accidents, both as a result of engine failure. Firstly Mk.XI MP564 on the charge of the RN Air Section at Eastleigh had a starboard engine failure on approach and crashed in a field 500 yards short of the runway, injuring the pilot Lt R Gardiner of the Royal New Zealand Navy and Artificer F R Horlick; secondly Mk.X HZ470 of 765 Squadron also suffered a loss of power from the starboard engine and crashed on take-off at Hal Far on 26 March 1946 while being flown by Sqn Ldr A G Sandison. Full details of the aircraft and their user units are shown in Appendix Two.

Low over The Fleet, Chesil Beach in Dorset Mk.III BJ895 drops a test spherical version of the dams weapon in March 1943. (*617 Squadron Association*)

TRIALS & EXPERIMENTAL FLYING

'Highball' Bouncing Ball

On 4 December 1942 'Mutt' Summers flew Wellington Mk.III BJ895 from Weybridge to Warmwell, Dorset, with Barnes Wallis acting as the bomb aimer, to conduct drop tests with an early prototype dams weapon (code named 'Highball') at Chesil Beach in Dorset. The aircraft had its bomb doors removed and two bombs were dropped, both breaking apart with the force of the impact causing the welded joints to fail. A fourth variation of 'Highball' known as 'The Heavy Type' (as distinct from the Mosquito 'Light Type') was designed for the Wellington and Warwick but never used. Summers' log book shows that he flew BJ895 on several occasions, but not all flights supposedly flown by him seem to have been recorded in his log book. The confusion may stem from the fact that Mutt's brother, Maurice, was also a Vickers test pilot and is also known to have flown BJ895, along with 'Shorty' Longbottom, Bob Handasyde and Tommy Lucke. Longbottom flew the aircraft from Turnberry, Strathclyde on four occasions in April 1943. This was the airfield where 618 Squadron Mosquitoes were detached from their base at Skitten to familiarise themslves with 'Highball' as the intended users of the weapon against the battleship *Tirpitz*.

In the early drops it is believed Vickers simply removed the bomb doors and bolted on the mine clamps; they may have added an air deflector at the front end of the bay. The well-known test drop sequence used in The Dam Busters film is one of the Chesil Beach trials. The Wellington was built at Chester and taken on charge by the company on 12 August 1943. The weapons carried by it, and dropped at Chesil Beach and later Reculver, Kent, were trial spheres only, to test the characteristics of the design, and were not filled with explosives. On 13 April 1943 BJ895 dropped two test weapons at Reculver from heights of 81 feet and 90 feet respectively; they were mid-sized between the small 'Highball' later carried by the Mosquito and the larger 'Upkeep' carried by 617 Squadron's Lancasters in May 1943.[5]

On completion of its trials work, BJ895 was de-modified back to the standard bomber configuration and issued to the Marine Aircraft Experimental Establishment (MAEE). It later went to the Central Gunnery School and was written off when it dived into the ground at Wykeham Abbey, Yorkshire during a fighter affiliation exercise on 24 July 1946.

JET ENGINE FLYING TEST-BEDS

In May 1942 Vickers were asked to modify a Wellington as a flying test-bed for the highly-secret jet engines being developed from Sir Frank Whittle's Power Jets prototypes and taken towards production. The aircraft selected was Mk.II Z8570 which had seen very little RAF service and,

Power Jets W.2B jet engine test-bed hybrid Mk.II-IV Z8570 at Rolls-Royce's test airfield Hucknall. (*Rolls-Royce Heritage Trust*)

following modification to carry a jet engine in the tail, it was despatched to the Rolls-Royce flight test airfield at Hucknall in Derbyshire. A W.2B engine was fitted by early August 1942, but concerns were expressed by Denis 'Dizzy' Drew of Rover and Wittold Challier, Hucknall's chief performance engineer, over the air intake design which delayed flight trials.

The Wellington was finally passed as fit for flight on 12 August, to be operated by a crew of four and was flown twice on the 14th, with the 'Squirter', as it was known even in formal reports, running satisfactorily throughout the second flight. During these flights the role of the observer was to be in the back end of the aircraft running the jet engine. The first altitude flight, lasting sixty-five minutes and reaching 23,500 feet, was undertaken on 1 February 1943. Due to the extreme aft centre of gravity, the handling of the aircraft was found to be particularly challenging to trim and in the landing configuration with full flap selected, with Chief Test Pilot Captain Ronald 'Shep' Shepherd remarking that they had to "push like hell" to get the nose down. Another issue with the aft weight distribution was a prevalence for tailwheel fork failures, with three occurring in twenty-seven hours flying early in 1943. Between September '43 and November '44, nine further W.2Bs were fitted for a total testing time of 456 hours in 302 flights; flights from April 1944 onwards being carried out from Church Broughton, Derbyshire. Z8570 was struck off charge in October 1945.

To cope with the increasingly demanding test programme, similarly modified Wellington W5797 was also allocated to Hucknall. By August 1942 it had flown 195 hours and had nine engine changes, making its last flight on or about 19 September 1942, thereafter being relegated to ground use only. It was replaced by W5389 (with wings from DR524) which had its first W.2B fitted in late June 1943, ultimately taking the engine up to 35,000 feet, without problem, on 13 March '44.

The aircraft came close to disaster on 28 December '44 when it suffered an oxygen system failure at 30,000 feet. After flying for an hour, the pilot Sqn Ldr Jim Heyworth felt the effects of oxygen starvation, warned observer D G T Harvey and began to black out. Harvey also started to black out, removed his oxygen mask, got an emergency bottle which he fitted to the unconscious pilot and then collapsed. They both became semi-conscious again to find the aircraft was at 28,000 feet in a shallow dive at 250 mph. By the time the pilot regained control the aircraft was down to 20,000 feet and was subsequently landed safely back at Hucknall.

The performance of the jet engine at altitude was generally found to be very good and provided the Wimpy with quite an enhanced turn of speed. Allegedly on one occasion the aircraft was descending and a Spitfire was spotted cruising along at 29,000 feet. The W.2B was relit and the Wellington set off in pursuit, the Spitfire pilot suddenly finding himself being overtaken by a diving Wellington with both propellers feathered! As engine advances began to demand higher performance test aircraft, W5389 was disposed of in June 1947.

A Mk.VI DR480 was to be have been fitted with a British Thomson-Houston built W.2B in November 1942, but these trials were delayed until 26 January 1943 and the aircraft was re allocated for use at TFU Defford without being converted.

On 11 September 1944 Power Jets (Research and Development) Ltd established a flight trials unit at Bruntingthorpe aerodrome in Leicestershire for engine testing. The first aircraft to arrive was a Lancaster B Mk.II and this was followed on 17 December, by a hybrid Merlin-powered Wellington Mk.II/VI W5518 fitted with a Whittle W.2/700 engine. This aircraft had previously seen service as a standard Mk.II with 405 Squadron, 15 OTU plus 1443 and 1446 Flights before

Mk.II prototype L4250 with a 40 mm Vickers cannon for trials in early 1942. The idea was not adopted and the aircraft relegated to ground training use. (*ww2images*)

being modified by Vickers at Wisley for its new role which included the fitting of Mk.VI wings taken from former 109 Squadron machine W5802. Three paraffin tanks for the jet engine, totalling 465 gallons, were fitted in the bomb bay, and the aircraft had made its first flight in this guise at Weybridge on 24 November. In May 1946 the flight was taken over by the National Gas Turbine Establishment (NGTE) and on 14 May the Wellington moved to its new home at Bitteswell. W5518 was to become the longest-lived of all the jet test-bed Wellingtons, finally being sold for scrap on 30 November 1948.

VICKERS' EXPERIMENTAL FLYING

Inspection of the Vickers flight test reports revealed a bewildering array of experimental work on almost all Wellington variants. Mostly these were the result of minor changes to equipment, but one programme that stood out was the proposal to fit the aircraft with a 40 mm 'S' gun for use offensively, and this was by far the heaviest weapon carried by any aircraft at that time. The idea was first mooted in 1938 and given the go-ahead early the following year. A Wellington Mk.II L4250 was selected for the trials as the Type 416, the centre fuselage being strengthened to take the large turntable and cradle necessary to support the weapon and the hydraulic motors needed to drive it. After the first flight in 1940 a decision was made to fit the aircraft with twin fins and rudders in an attempt to overcome severe vibration and control problems caused by the airflow over the gun and its mounting being disturbed as it impacted the standard single fin and rudder. On 13 December 1941 the aircraft was sent to the Air Gun Mounting Establishment (AGME) at Duxford near Cambridge for service trials and remained there until moving to A&AEE Boscombe Down on 24 January 1942. The gun was fired in the air for the first time on 8 March 1942 over Lyme Bay, Dorset and in subsequent firings the A&AEE report noted that firing the gun at low elevation to the beam tore fabric off the wing! Ultimately the requirement was not pursued and, later in 1942, the same aircraft was modified with a mid-upper turret carrying four 0.50 inch guns, after which it was scrapped at the end of the year.

A second Wellington Mk.II Z8416, which had seen service with 305 Squadron, trialled a nose-mounted 40 mm gun under the Type Designation 439. This first appeared at Vickers' Experimental Section on 3 November 1944 but, following general handling tests, this project was

T.XVIII ND129 ZQ-R1 of the Fighter Interception Development Unit at Ford, 10 April 1945. (*Official via M Chandler collection*)

also abandoned and the aircraft was eventually struck off charge two years later.

As late as 1946 the Wellington was still being used for some experimental work and on 5 July that year, Wg Cdr Roly Falk (later to achieve fame as a test pilot for the Avro Vulcan), had a narrow escape when coming in to land at Vickers's Wisley aerodrome in Mk.X LN817, which was testing experimental de Havilland reverse pitch propellers. During his final approach Falk selected reverse pitch which was intended to take six seconds to be achieved, but which actually took just a second-and-a-half. This caused an instantaneous nose-down pitch and the aircraft hit the roof of Cuckoo Farm (which had already been repaired after a previous encounter with a 'Highball' test weapon inadvertently dropped from a Mosquito!) Falk was thrown through the cockpit roof and into a hedge, escaping with serious injuries which kept him off flying for a year, after which he asked to go back to Avro! Needless to say, the Wellington was a total write off.

FIGHTER INTERCEPTION UNIT (FIU) TRIALS

The FIU was initially established to test new night-fighter equipment, but its role was later considerably expanded to cover many other areas, and for a number of trials it included Wellingtons in its varied fleet.

JU 88 NIGHT FIGHTER

On 9 May 1943 the RAF was gifted an intact Ju 88R-1 night fighter when 360043 'D5-EV' of IV./NJG 3 (now in the RAF Museum at Hendon) was flown by prior arrangement into Dyce, Aberdeen from its base in Norway by a defecting Luftwaffe crew. This was a major coup since it was equipped with FuG202 Lichtenstein BC airborne interception radar, and subsequent flight trials enabled assessment of the fighter and its equipment against all main bomber types.

Preliminary performance trials of the Lichtenstein radar were made at Farnborough with the Ju 88 flown by Wg Cdr Jackson DFC of HQ Fighter Command. Various forms of evasion were carried out by an identified Wellington, but the results were inconclusive, since the trials were made in daylight and the Wellington was more manoeuvrable than four-engined aircraft and the Ju 88 pilot found it was impossible to follow the Wellington's evasive actions.[6]

H2D Radar

On 12 June 1944 Wellington Mk.XIII NB823 was delivered from the TFU to the FIU for full trials of H2D surface-mapping radar; initial trials having been completed at Defford using sister aircraft NB822. H2D was a modified H2S, designed to detect movements of road traffic. For the trials the aircraft was required to fly in daylight at a minimum height of 3,000 feet along selected stretches of fairly straight roads. An observer in the nose of the aircraft kept a log of any observations in order that these could be compared with both the H2D operator's report and actual traffic movements, and sixteen such flights were conducted.

It was found that the maximum range at which vehicle movement could be detected was usually three miles, with just a few cases of detection at four miles. It was also found that it was necessary for the aircraft to be within 300 yards of either side of the road, otherwise no detection was possible. Overall the accuracy of the system when compared with real traffic movements was at best sixty percent and, in addition, there were significant false reports of vehicles generated by such things as trees alongside the road. As a result, it was assessed that there was no better than a fifty percent accuracy under ideal conditions of both weather and straight and level accurate flying, and the trial report concludes that there must be a considerable increase in accuracy before H2D could be used on operations.[7]

SPECIAL OPERATIONS

Despite the Wellington's withdrawal from Bomber Command main force operations in the autumn of 1943, that did not spell the complete end of the type's involvement with the strategic bombing campaign, largely thanks to the role of 192 Squadron at Foulsham, Norfolk which, as part of Bomber Command's 100 Group, continued with a variety of highly-specialised support operations.

On the night of 30/31 March 1944, the Bomber Command raid on Nuremberg proved to be the most disastrous night of the war for the bomber crews, with no fewer than ninety-six out of 795 bombers being lost, the vast majority falling to well-organised Luftwaffe night-fighter attacks. Raid Analysis Report No.44 produced by 100 Group specifically includes the squadron's role:

> "One Wellington took off from Ford to investigate 80 Wing countermeasures against the enemy navigational aids Knickebein 8 and Knickebein 10, operating on 31.5 and 31.2 Mc/s respectively. The aircraft confined its investigation largely to Knickebein 10. The beam was flown to a point twenty-five miles south of the English coast, after which countermeasures became effective and beam-flying was impossible."

GLIDER TOWING

The Airborne Forces Experimental Establishment at Sherburn-in-Elmet, Yorkshire conducted trials in 1942 using a Mk.IC DV942 as a tug aircraft for the General Aircraft Hotspur training glider. This was followed later in the same year by trials with the more powerful MK.III X3286 and MK.X HE731 which were able to tow the much larger and heavier Airspeed Horsa and Waco Hadrian gliders, and both marks were cleared for operational use as tugs. However, concern continued to be expressed that the inherent lack of rigidity in the geodetic construction could lead to it stretching when repeatedly subjected to such loads, and no further use was made of the type in this role.

LUFTWAFFE USE OF CAPTURED AIRCRAFT

The Luftwaffe Flight Test Centre Erprobungsstelle at Rechlin test flew a number of Wellingtons in the early years of the war, at least one of which was flown by the legendary pilot Ernst Udet, who was the Luftwaffe's Generalluftzeugmeister (Director-General of Equipment) and had been the second highest-scoring German fighter ace in World War I. He remarked that the aircraft was not very responsive in the turn and required some degree of effort. His somewhat energetic test flying led to noticeable rippling of the skinning on the upper-wing surfaces, which led him to return to a gentle landing!

Some publications have also linked Kampfgeschwader (KG) 200, the Luftwaffe's secret operations wing, with the Wellington. Although this unit did make extensive use of captured Allied aircraft including bomber types, for example up to eight B-17 Flying Fortresses and one or two B-24 Liberators, there is no evidence that Wellingtons were ever used.

Mk.IC Z8783 B.A.W.2 of BOAC in the Western Desert 1942. Passed to 28 Squadron SAAF it was scrapped in September 1944. (*ww2images*)

BRITISH OVERSEAS AIRWAYS CORPORATION

Four Wellington Mk.ICs, originally intended for the SAAF, were loaned to BOAC by the RAF from September 1942, and converted to carry passengers at Asmara in occupied Italian Eritrea. The conversion involved the removal of the front and rear turrets, bomb release gear, the oxygen system and auxiliary oil tanks. A detachable bulkhead was installed ahead of the pilot, with the nose space then being used for baggage, entry being via a hatch in the extreme nose. Provision was made for sixteen passengers on bench seating, with entry via a ladder through the hole in the forward fuselage adjacent to the pilot's position. However, due to the absence of any emergency exits, the aircraft did not qualify for a Certificate of Airworthiness (CofA), so they retained their military serials but were also marked as 'B.A.W.1' to 'B.A.W.4'. Initial flying was done using contracted captains, but legal problems arising from the lack of civilian registration led to seconded RAF Wellington pilots taking over.

Curiously, although BOAC had come into being on 1 November 1939 by the amalgamation of British Airways and Imperial Airways, the Wellingtons all carried British Airways titling. They were based at Almaza, Cairo as part of BOAC's No.5 Line and scheduled services commenced on 26 October 1942. The routes flown included a weekly Cairo – Lydda – Habbaniyah – Shaibah – Bahrain – Sharjah – Jiwani – Karachi service which operated until May 1943, and a weekly Cairo – Lydda – Basra (Shaibah) service which only lasted until 8 November 1942. After El Alamein, the aircraft were also used on sorties into the desert including to Mersa Matruh, El Adem and Marble Arch.

In May 1943 it was proposed to increase the fleet to twelve, but this was abandoned due to the poor performance being experienced with the initial four. All had previously seen RAF service with R1018 coming from 148 Squadron, T2609 from 3 Middle East Training School (METS), X9692 from 70 Squadron and Z8783 from 108 Squadron, and were consequently well-worn. There were also great difficulties maintaining them due to a lack of spares and suitable engineering facilities. Pilot F Tricklebank recalled:

> "I remember watching a Wellington which had been grossly misloaded, trying to get into Almaza. After some half dozen hairy efforts including hitting the boundary wall and various bounces, it eventually made it – just. The captain got out, very white and trembling, to be surprised by one of his passengers coming along and saying 'thank you captain for a delightful flight.'"[8]

The four Wellingtons stayed with BOAC until July of that year when they were replaced by Dakotas; they were then handed over to 28 Squadron SAAF.

CHAPTER EIGHT

POST-WAR TO RETIREMENT

"For the support you have always given me,
and for your tremendous personal contribution to the
achievement of the RAF in this war I can never adequately thank you"
Marshal of the Royal Air Force Sir Charles Portal to 'Bomber' Harris, 1945

In May 1945 the strength of the RAF stood at 9,200 aircraft and well over one million personnel, of which 193,000 were aircrew, and very quickly the services had to prepare for drastic reductions in aircraft strength and demobilisation of aircrew. One way in which this rapid change could be seen was the almost instant withdrawal of entire aircraft fleets, such as the Armstrong Whitworth Albemarle, Hawker Typhoon, and Lockheed Hudson, all of which had completely disappeared within a year. On the other hand, some older types were still considered to have useful service remaining, and the Wellington certainly fitted that category, flying on for a further eight years. Production of new aircraft ended with the delivery of Mk.X RP590 from Blackpool on 13 October 1945, this aircraft serving with 1 (Pilot) Refresher Flying Unit, later renamed the Flying Refresher School, before being struck off charge on 3 April 1950.

GR.XVIII NC606 FGEA of the Empire Air Navigation School at Lindholme 1947.
(*wwiivehicles.com*)

CREW TRAINING

With the end of hostilities, the reduced need for large numbers of bomber crews, which had already diminished substantially, removed the need for OTUs almost overnight. They were rapidly disbanded, with most having gone by the end of 1945, the last few lingering on until the autumn of 1946. The post-war rationalisation of flying training, to best suit the slimmed-down and ever-changing air force, resulted in advanced flying schools (AFS) plus conversion units for each major combat type replacing the old OTU system. The Wellington therefore carried on in the AFS role, with 201 and 202 AFS being established with the T Mk.X in 1947 at Swinderby and Finningley respectively. Furthermore, with large numbers of surplus aircraft available,

Flt Sgt Geoff Paine (*Geoff Paine*)

additional T Mk.X conversions provided another new role for the Wimpy, that of navigator trainer. In all, 270 were converted between January 1946 and March 1952 by Boulton Paul Aircraft at Wolverhampton.

At various periods between May 1945 and February 1952, six air navigation schools (ANS) were established with Wellingtons, with the rather late emergence of 5 ANS and 6 ANS in 1951/52 due to the increased training requirement to cope with the building up of RAF strength following the beginning of the Cold War and the Korean conflict. Flt Sgt Geoff Paine was an instructor on 2 ANS at Middleton St.George:

> "I really did enjoy that and I liked the Wellington. I had my own radio operator and we usually had a training navigator and up to four trainees on board. I relied on them entirely but kept an eye on them. I never had any trouble at all, they were well trained. Day and night, we did an awful lot of flying. We went off over the Highlands and down over the North Sea. I often used to go up over Scotland and then down between Wales and Ireland, for a bit of low-level experience. The nearest scrape I had was coming back one day to Middleton St.George when it was really thick cloud down to about 600 ft and I called up for a QGH, a controlled descent through cloud. You flew over the airfield and when they heard your engines overhead they would send you off in the downwind direction and then they would turn you left or right. Then they would tell you to let down and that was the scary bit because you were coming down completely through cloud. A U/T air traffic controller was on duty that day and he gave me the wrong course. I broke cloud, and I'm not kidding you, there was a hill no further away than the bottom of my garden. I screamed over the R/T: 'What the hell are you doing?' I stayed visual, came round and got back in, but that was a bit hairy. My CO climbed up into the tower after this was all over and the bloke got a rocket. It was very dangerous.
>
> "Once I heard this bloody noise…pop, pop, pop and I thought what the hell is that? I slid the little side window open; it was the port engine. I looked at all the instruments – everything was correct so I carried on and did a whole cross-country, five or six hours, and when I got down again one of the ground crew said, 'Here, you've nearly lost the end of one of your pots' on the radial engine and it was flapping about. Amazing actually, but it was generally a very reliable aircraft."

In late June and early July 1949 some relief came from the routine of flying around the country training navigators when Exercise Foil was held. This called for the Wellingtons to once

T.10 PG287 'A' of 5 ANS Lindholme 1952. (*Mike Bennison*)

again act as bombers in order to test the air defences, Geoff and the rest of his four-man crew flying lengthy sorties every day for a week waiting to be intercepted. Although nothing exciting came their way, the exercise was marred by the loss of a number of fighters including a Spitfire F.22 and a Vampire F.1. Sgt Michael Bennison was a National Serviceman who did his navigator training at 5 ANS Lindholme, Yorkshire;

Pupil navigator Keith Wallwork learning his trade with 5 ANS at Lindholme 1952. (*Mike Bennison*)

"Our main aircraft at Lindholme was the Wellington T Mk.X, an elegant aircraft in the air, although it looked clumsy on the ground. It was however very cold and draughty and at this period the aircraft were not too reliable. One night sortie of five aircraft had four aborted at various stages for engine problems (magneto drop) or brake failure on landing; I was in the fifth. The navigators' position was good, with a wide table just aft of the main spar and below the astrodome. A pipe dispensing warm air kept most of the chart table clear but it was possible to have ice forming on one's plot from breath condensing in your oxygen supply. We flew at 12,000 feet and a pair of us would take it in turns to be first and second navigator.

"Some of the pilots were Polish and, over the intercom they were sometimes hard to understand. Although some were non-commissioned there was never any question that they were in command as captain. On one occasion the Polish pilot said something incomprehensible to me. I nodded politely and the next thing I knew we were headed steeply towards the ground. He had said: 'What about trying a stall test now?' On another occasion we returned early because the distant reading compass (DRC) was malfunctioning, but the pilot was convinced that we were trying to get away early for the weekend and I had to do some quick talking to the wing commander flying on the Monday. We got away with it!

"We practised blind approaches using the Rebecca BABS [blind approach beacon system]; in skilled hands it was remarkably accurate. We also used GEE to a limited extent but it was thought to make navigation too easy and we were being trained to operate in adverse conditions. We practised bomb aiming and photography. For someone with mild vertigo the bomb aimer's position in a Wellington was somewhat exposed. Most of the top half of your body was stretched out above a perspex sheet with nothing below you for the next 12,000 feet. It was perfectly safe but one felt a bit nervous. Getting to the bomb aiming position was difficult as one had to climb over the main spar and inch past and below the pilot. In theory one should have had a portable oxygen bottle but I never saw anyone use one. Because of night blindness we were expected to be on oxygen at all times at night but for short periods at day time it was not a problem below 15,000 feet.

"The Wellington was fitted with a primitive autopilot, 'George'. George was also a bit unreliable and could cause a sudden loss of height when you switched it in. The aircraft's centralised compass system, the DRC, was also unreliable. Newer aircraft at this time were starting to come in with much better equipment but for most of our training it was very definitely WWII equipment and procedures. We were even using the old phonetic alphabet, Able Baker Charlie; I have never got to grips with Alfa Bravo Coca…"

One of only six T.XIX conversions completed, RP318 sits in storage at 24 MU Stoke Heath 1946. Never issued, it was scrapped in 1948. (*N C Parker*)

A second, more specialised, navigator training role was taken up by the Wellington with the T.XVII and T.XVIII being primarily used to train Mosquito night-fighter navigators, for which purpose they were fitted with Airborne Interception (AI) SCR720 radar behind a bulbous radome in the nose in place of the gun turret. Only the eighty T.XVIIIs were new-build aircraft, the nine T.XVIIs being in-service conversions of T.Xs. These variants first entered service from the latter stages of the war with 51, 54 and 62 OTUs, with 51 and 54 crews also being sent to 1692 Flight at Great Massingham for training on their Mk.XVIII. Two T.XVIIIs went to the Central Fighter Establishment (CFE) at West Raynham, Norfolk and the last seven examples of this mark saw out their service with 228 Operational Conversion Unit (OCU) at Leeming, Yorkshire.

The final version was the T.XIX, a 1946 Mk.X conversion to be used as a basic crew trainer. 24 MU at Stoke Heath, Shropshire was contracted to convert twenty-four aircraft during 1948 but only six were completed before the plan was cancelled and they were all flown from Ternhill to Little Rissington for storage in December that year and later scrapped without seeing any service.

The risk inherent in crew training continued to claim aircraft and crew, and the Wellington fleet suffered a number of accidents including two mid-air collisions. On 17 March 1948 two 1 ANS T Mk.Xs collided in the Topcliffe circuit. RP565 had just taken off and RP499 was joining the circuit, and with both aircraft in left turns they simply failed to see each other, with one coming down on the sergeants' mess. All eight airmen aboard lost their lives. The captain of RP499 was Flt Lt Franciszek Kula MM who had flown a tour with 305 Squadron and on the night of 28/29 August 1942 his aircraft Z1460 was badly damaged by night fighters and set on fire. Although three of the crew baled out – including the then Sgt Kula – the rear gunner was injured and could not do so, and the pilot was able to get back to a landing at Manston, Kent. Kula was able to evade capture and returned to England three months later. As a result of this accident, the investigation report recommended that in future the right-hand cockpit seat should always be occupied to provide a look-out.

T.10 RP567 FFKA of 1 ANS Topcliffe on exercise at Manston, Easter 1949. 1 Squadron Meteor F.4 in the background. (*Author*)

The second mid-air collision also involved a Polish pilot, Sgt Atanockovic, who was instructing two pupils in a 2 ANS T Mk.X NC925 on 20 June 1952 when it collided with a Meteor T.7 WA777 of 12 Group Communications Flight flown by Flt Sgt C Warner who was just breaking cloud over Calverton, Nottinghamshire. In this case all four crew members were able to parachute to safety.

THE FINAL DAYS

The longer-term requirement for improved navigator training to keep step with the more advanced front-line types entering service finally spelt the end of the Wellington's RAF service in 1953. It was quite quickly replaced at the ANSs by the Vickers Valetta and Varsity for basic and advanced navigation training respectively. Both had much in common with the Wimpy, using essentially the same wing in the case of the Valetta. The major change was a new fuselage, otherwise the tail undercarriage and engines were little different. Both new types offered much improved performance together with roomier and tailor made accommodation for pupils and instructor. R F Chandler flew as a staff pilot with 1 ANS Hullavington, right at the end of the Wimpy's service:

> "The RAF Museum Wimpy MF628 appears in my log book during my long tour at Hullavington. I carried out one or two air tests with it and a couple of cross-countries. It was not one of the many Wellingtons that I ferried across to Little Rissington [8 Maintenance Unit] during the whole of February 1953. They were all broken up, in fact demolition started before I had actually stopped both engines in two instances! The Hullavington ANS had switched over to the Varsity and Valetta and due to my long association with the Wellington aircraft, I had the honour to ferry them out and to beat up the airfield with full permission from OC Flying."

8 MU had been the major maintenance unit handling Wellingtons for some years and, by the end of 1945, it had no fewer than 1,388 of the type in storage at Little Rissington and its satellite aerodromes at Honeybourne in Herefordshire and Long Marston in Warwickshire. During a severe gale on 16 March 1947, no fewer than seventy-four Wellingtons were damaged with one being declared beyond repair.

The last Wellington in regular RAF service was LP806 which was retired from 1 ANS in March 1953. There are suggestions that two T Mk.Xs were taken from storage and flown out to Malta in November 1953 where the film Malta Story was being made; they were apparently

A grounded T.10 used for engineer training at 2 School of Technical Training Cosford 1954-55.

operated out of Luqa and Takali, and flown by RAF crews who also appeared as extras in the film. However, the aircraft reported as being involved, HF626 and NB113, were both scrapped in 1948, so the truth or otherwise of this story has proved elusive. What is certain though is that in April 1954 one of the two Wellingtons that survive today, T Mk.X MF628, was flown from storage at St.Athan to Hemswell, where it was attached to the station flight for its role in The Dam Busters film. It was flown extensively as a camera aircraft by Flt Lt 'Butch' Birch, Flt Lt Ken Souter and Czech pilot Joe Kmiejic, also appearing as the trials Wellington used for 'Highball' test drops over Chesil Beach. It was returned to St.Athan on 14 October 1954 and placed on non-effective strength.

Even this was not quite the end for the Wellington in the RAF. As early as 1940 Wellingtons were occasionally permanently withdrawn from flying, either because they were well-worn, an obsolete mark, or had suffered battle damage and were downgraded for use as ground instructional airframes at Schools of Technical Training (SofTT). The last of these lingered on until the mid 1950s and Charlie Harris did some of his practical Boy Entrant training on the type at 2 SofTT Cosford, near Wolverhampton:

> "During my Boy Entrant training in the summer of 1954, we spent about six weeks learning about airfield equipment. The classrooms for this comprised two large wooden huts on the airfield. In between them and the nearest hangar was a grass area on which about five World War 2 heavies were parked. The aircraft were there to give U/T engine mechanics practice in starting and running up, and the nearest to us was a Wellington IC. During NAAFI breaks, with our civvy instructor Mr Baldry holed up somewhere smoking his pipe, we would climb into the Wellington one by one by means of rotating the rear turret. Once inside we would fly it to the Ruhr, bomb the hell out of Krupps and shoot down whole Staffels of German night fighters on the way there and back.
>
> "One day a flight sergeant engines instructor thought he had caught one of his own trainees messing about and ordered him out of the rear turret. I can still see his face as the turret spun around and back, the doors opened and closed with a rhythm of their own and all sixteen of us erstwhile bomber crew spilled out! The Wellington was still there in January 1955 when I left."

Aeronavale 55S Wellingtons arriving at Agadir, Morocco from Port Lyautey in 1950. (*Aeronavale et Port-Avions*)

Aeronavale Mk.XIII MF742 K of 55S at Port Lyautey, Morocco c.1950. It originally served with the RAF at 78 OTU Ein Shemar. (*Gekho ww2aircraft.net*)

Armée de l'Air Mk.X LN374 first served with 26 (SAAF) Squadron passing to French ownership 29 May 1945. (*ww2images*)

'Stickleback' Mk.XIII of Aeronavale Flotille 2FB based at Dakar-Ouakam, Senegal. (*Aeronavale et Port-Avions*)

Ray Powell also did his Boy Entrant training at Cosford at that time:

> "While starting the Wellingtons engines they had to be primed with fuel via a Kygas pump in the undercarriage bay. On (I think) the starboard engine the exhaust pipe ran very close to one's head. If the priming was too vigorous there was often a large sheet of flame alongside one's ear-hole. Guess which one the instructors told newbies to prime!"

SERVICE WITH OTHER AIR ARMS

France

A total of 185 had been handed over from the RAF to the French air force [L'Armée de l'Air] by 1946, but little is known about what appears to have been their limited use post-war, although some Mk.XIVs were modified for use as transport aircraft and are believed to have seen service in French Indochina during 1947. The principal post-war user of these aircraft was the reformed Aeronavale which had first acquired Wellingtons in October 1944 for non-pilot and engineer training at the École de Premier Vol (EPV) school at Thiersville in Algeria. The later acquisitions were handed over from L'Armée de l'Air to the Aeronavale for a symbolic one franc. On 11 October 1948, EPV became 52S with a mixed fleet including Avro Ansons, Consolidated Catalinas, Junkers Ju 52/3Ms, Martin Marylands and Wellingtons based at Lartigue, Madaillan, moving to Agadir, Morocco in 1951.

Mk.XIII MF418 served with 344 (French) Squadron before going to the Aeronavale's 55S. Seen at Cuers, Provence. (*via Anciens cols Bleu*)

Wellingtons also served in the maritime reconnaissance role with Escadrille IS at Lanvéoc-Poulmic from November 1944, also operating from Lann-Bihoué. This was followed by Flotille 2F which was formed out of 344 Squadron RAF in November 1945 at Dakar-Ouakam, Senegal, then Port Lyautey, Morocco in June 1950. Along with 51S at Khouribga, formed in 1946 also in Morocco, these units were heavily occupied searching for any German mines remaining around the French coasts, and continued to do so until the end of 1951. Towards the end of that period, on 8 June 1951, Mk.XI MP696 '2F-8' was lost in an accident off Port Lyautey that claimed the lives of Flotille Commander Paul Brossier and his crew of five. This was the last of five Wellingtons lost in accidents post-war, and the event hastened the withdrawal of the remaining aircraft in 1952, their replacement being the Lancaster.

A total of about twenty GR.XIII and GR.XIV Wellingtons were on the strength of 52S/56S for crew training. The final users were 55S at Goeland and Port Lyautey and 56S in Agadir; the latter may have still had one or two serviceable aircraft on strength as late as 1955. During their in-service period the Aeronavale Wellingtons used included Mks.X, XI, XII, XIII and XIV.

Aeronavale's last Mk.XIV at Port Lyautey with 56S, believed to be in late 1955. (*Aeronavale et Port-Avions*)

Greece

Approximately nineteen Wellingtons, including a few Mk.Xs and sixteen Mk.XIIIs, were handed over to the Royal Hellenic Air Force in batches from November 1944 to April 1946. They were operated by 13 Squadron based at Hassani, near Athens, primarily on training and transport duties, although some crew training in the use of ASV took place. The Greeks found them to be in poor condition, having spent some time in open desert storage and they struggled to keep them airworthy, suffering two fatal accidents. On 10 April 1946 Mk.XIII MF188 spun into the sea while on an air test with the loss of all on board and, on 7 August 1936, Mk.XIII MF466 stalled during an overshoot at Eleusis. Several other aircraft suffered minor accidents but were deemed not worth repairing. The squadron was later renumbered 355 and remained at Hassani, but the Wellingtons were unloved and their replacement by ex-RAF Dakotas began in October 1946, with the last Wellington going for scrap in 1947.

Mk.XIII NC418 'X' of 13 Squadron Royal Hellenic Air Force, Hassani 1946. (*Markos Danezis*)

South Africa

The sole unit of the SAAF to operate Wellingtons after the end of the war in Europe was 17 Squadron, which was reformed at Gianaclis in May 1945 under the command of Captain Hulet in preparation for moving to the Far East. In addition to its primary equipment of eleven Warwicks, the unit received eight Wellington Mk.Xs and operated them as crew training aircraft until that September. Flying was severely restricted by poor weather, and on average only four Wellingtons were serviceable at any one time.

T.X LN715 Rolls-Royce Dart test-bed seen in 1948. Struck off charge April 1951. (*Brooklands Museum*)

ODDS AND ENDS

Wellingtons occasionally appeared in one-off roles well after the war. Mk.X LN715 served with 15 and 21 OTUs before being acquired by Rolls-Royce in 1948 as a flying test-bed for their new

Dart turbo-prop, which required substantial modifications to the aircraft and its systems. It was converted at Weybridge and made its first flight from there before being delivered to Rolls-Royce at Hucknall on 13 October 1948. Once the trials were completed, no further use was found for the aircraft and it was struck off charge in April 1952. Sister aircraft LN718 was flown by Bristols at Filton on a 100-hour test programme for the Hercules 100 engine intended for the Viking airliner and was distinguishable by its four-bladed propellers.

In 1949 T Mk.X RP468, which had no service history, appeared on the British civil aircraft register as G-ALUH and was fitted at Langley with a tail-boom radar for flights to the Norwegian coast. A Certificate of Airworthiness was issued on 22 July 1949 and the aircraft was returned to the RAF that same year, with its registration being cancelled on 11 October. Napier and Son at Luton acquired Mk.X NA857 for use as a flying test-bed of their Naiad turbo-prop engine, but in the event an Avro Lincoln was found to be more suitable and, although it is believed the Wellington had Naiads fitted, it never flew with them and was disposed of in November 1949.

WHAT WAS IT LIKE TO FLY?

To a man, everyone asked this question answered very positively; there was clearly great affection for, and trust in, the Wellington. Wg Cdr Jack Hoskins DSO DFC had a long tour with 221 Squadron, both in the UK and in the Mediterranean theatre:

T.10 G-ALUH formerly RP468, was used briefly by Airwork Ltd for radar trials, seen at Ringway on 8 September 1949. (*R A Scholefield*)

"The Pegasus-engined aircraft were by far the nicest to fly. The extra AUW [all-up weight] and speed of the Hercules variants considerably increased stick forces and lessoned manoeuvrability. Then perhaps our role called more for manoeuvrability, particularly in the 'Fishington' mode in the Med theatre.

"I must admit on the Mk.VIII we suffered from the lack of power given by the Pegasus engines. The extra drag of the 'Stickleback' aerials, heavy fuel loads for ten-plus hour sorties, and operating low down in hot conditions, caused many anxious moments. It was a constant concern to keep cylinder head temperatures down. Opening the cooling gills meant more drag and loss of speed, and produced a vicious circle. We were lucky to make much more than 100 knots for the first hour or so.

"Due to engine overhaul problems the limitation on engine oil consumption was raised to three gallons per hour – one always checked the F700 [aircraft servicing record] before the flight to see the consumption figures. On a ten-hour trip some 50 to 60 gallons of oil could be consumed, so we were obliged to carry five or six 4-gallon Jerrie cans of oil to top up the fuselage oil reserve stock (15 gallons). One crew member was kept busy pumping oil at forty-five strokes per gallon on the semi-rotary pump, and emptying the Jerrie cans to replace the losses.

"The wonderful geodetic construction was certainly strong. One of our aircraft hit the sea and bounced back into the air again, minus the bottom of the fuselage from the bomb bay to the rear turret. The rear gunner got a wet shirt and was obliged to stay put."

Don Bruce of IX(B) Squadron:

"I remember a very uneasy feeling I had when I made my first flight in a Wellington, looking out and watching the port wing flex and twist, something to which I was to become accustomed; also the general twitching of the tail. The close proximity of the flap and undercarriage levers to each other resulted in some very unpleasant incidents at 20 OTU when 'circuits and bumps' pupil pilots made errors on overshoots, retracting flaps instead of the undercart as they opened up for another circuit."

David Vandervord, 218 Squadron:

"It was easy enough to fly. On one occasion my brother, who was in the army, was on a bridge on the Norfolk coast which I beat-up at very low level not knowing he was there and my wireless operator came to me and said 'Do you realise our training area is out there?' I said, 'No, you never told me that.'"

Mk.IA N2887, Spitfire V and Mustang I of the Central Gunnery School, Sutton Bridge 24 June 1943. (*ww2images*)

THE SURVIVORS

Unsurprisingly, Wellingtons tended not to survive for very long in service, with operational losses, training losses and 'war-weariness' all taking their toll. Some aircraft had more luck and saw many years' service, with the longest-living being the Mk.Xs converted to T Mk.Xs and serving into the 1950s. Remarkably, there were also a few of the earlier variants that lasted for some time, including Mk.IAs N2867 and N2887, both delivered in 1939 and surviving the war – just. Their AM Form 78 aircraft movement cards show just how busy both aircraft were.

N2867 was awaiting collection on 1 August 1939 and was delivered to 149 Squadron on 1 September, subsequently serving with 214 Squadron, then back to 149, and finally Central Gunnery School before going into storage at 18 MU Dumfries in June 1944. It was struck off charge for scrapping on 27 December 1945.

N2980's instrument panel following restoration at Brooklands. (*Author*)

N2887 was ready on 9 August 1939 and went to 99 Squadron on 26 September, taking part in the Battle of Heligoland Bight on 14 December under the command of Fg Off John Dyer (later DFC). It then went on to 11 OTU, 15 OTU, 1 Air Armament School, and Central Gunnery School. Delivered to the Air Command South-East Asia in September 1944, any service it had from that point is not recorded, but it was struck off charge in theatre on 26 April 1945.

Today, of the 11,462 Wellingtons built, just two complete aircraft survive. In addition there are some fairly substantial remains of five others scattered around a number of locations in England and Norway.

Mk.IA N2980

Built at Weybridge and first flown on 16 November 1939, N2980 was first issued to 149 Squadron at Mildenhall, taking part in the Battle of Heligoland Bight on 18 December. It then moved to 37 Squadron at Feltwell where it flew a further fourteen operations before finally going to 20 OTU at Lossiemouth. In the late afternoon of 31 December 1940, it was conducting a navigation exercise towards Fort Augustus at the southern end of Loch Ness in the Scottish Highlands, with the following crew on board, which included five trainees:

Sqn Ldr N W D Marwood-Elton, pilot
Plt Off J Slater, second pilot
Plt Off Lucton
Sgt C Chandler
Sgt E Ford

Mk. IA N2980 'R' after restoration at Brooklands Museum. (*Author*)

The remains of N2980 emerging from Loch Ness 21 September 1985. (*Norman Didwell*)

Sgt R Little
Sgt W Wright
Sgt John Fensome, rear gunner

When overhead Inverness at 8,000 feet, the aircraft ran into heavy snow showers and the starboard engine began to fail. Marwood-Elton gave the order to bale out and then ditched the aircraft into Loch Ness just off shore from Urquhart Castle, as this was the only flat area he could make out in the snow and creeping darkness. Regrettably Sgt Fensome's parachute snagged on the structure as he escaped, failed to deploy properly and he was killed. The survivors got out onto the wing of the still-floating Wimpy, got into the dinghy and paddled to the shore, where they were picked up by a passing lorry which took them into Inverness in time for the New Year celebrations!

After the accident, the seven surviving members of the crew continued their service, but Plt Off Slater and Sgts Chandler, Ford and Little all lost their lives. Marwood-Elton was shot down in a 578 Squadron Halifax in March 1944 while on an operation to Hamburg and was taken prisoner (by which time he had reached the rank of group captain and was the station commander at Burn).

In 1976 a search of Loch Ness, by a team from the American Academy of Applied Science led by Marty Klein, located the wreckage of the Wellington on sonar. Naval diving teams were sent down and established that it was lying at a depth of 70 metres. In 1981 Robin Holmes of Heriot-Watt University in Edinburgh, working with the team that discovered the aircraft, completed a full survey that confirmed the belief that its recovery was possible. N2980 finally broke the surface again at Lochend on 21 September 1985, with the wings and fuselage as far back as the mid-point between the wings and tail coming up first, followed later by the tail section with rear turret, and the front turret, all of which had broken away. There to see it were David Marwood-Elton and Sqn Ldr Paul Harris who had flown it on an operation to Wilhelmshaven in December 1939. Remarkably, when a new battery was connected to the tail, the aircraft's lights came on. British Aerospace transported the aircraft to the Brooklands Museum in Surrey on 27 September 1985, and over the next almost twenty years it was carefully conserved and reassembled. This task required the manufacture of a substantial new geodetic structure to replace the damaged nose and the sections where the centre and rear halves of the aircraft had parted. N2980 remains on display at Brooklands; a truly remarkable survivor.

T Mk.X MF628

This aircraft was built at Blackpool and first flown on 9 May 1944, but it was little used until converted to a T Mk.X by Boulton Paul in March 1948. It was issued to 1 ANS at Hullavington in April 1949 and served there until 28 October 1952 when it was sent to 19 MU St.Athan, Glamorgan for storage. It was maintained in airworthy condition and is known to have made two air show appearances, the Royal Aeronautical Society (RAeS) Garden Party at Hatfield in June 1953 and a brief flying appearance at the Aston Down Battle of Britain display on 19 September 1953.

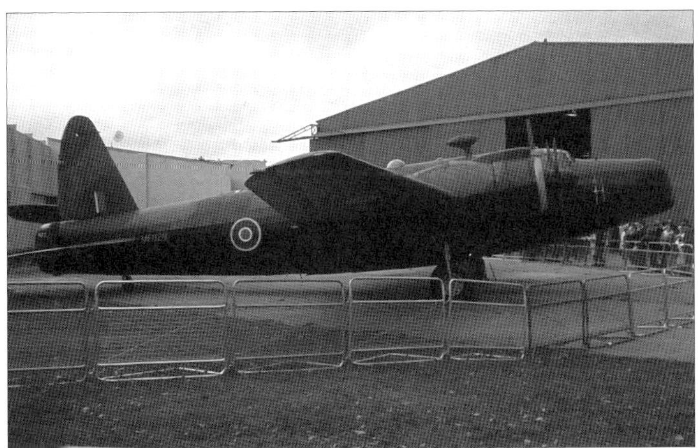

Before going to Hendon, the RAF Museum's T.10 MF628 spent many years stored at Biggin Hill, seen here on 18 September 1965. (*Author*)

On 5 April 1954 it was flown to Hemswell for film work and, following its return to St.Athan on 14 October 1954, the aircraft was stored for three months before being sold to Vickers at Weybridge. On 24 January 1955 it was flown from St.Athan to Wisley by Flt Sgt 'Herbie' Marshall, accompanied by Master Flight Engineer Jim Pickersgill. Its departure from St.Athan was marked by two very low flypasts and some air-to-air filming from an Airspeed Oxford, before touching down after a flight time of one hour and ten minutes. A modest reception party duly saluted the aircraft as it taxied in and shut down for the final time. This flight is still credited as being the last ever by any Wellington; however, rumours persist that France's Aeronavale may have still had one or two on strength capable of flight until at least later in 1955, based on reported sightings of what appeared to be one or two airworthy machines at Agadir in Morocco where Escadrille 56S was based.

T.10 NA831 'K' of 1 ANS Hullavington visiting Cranwell. Like so many of its type it was broken up in the mass cull of late 1953. (*Author*)

Apart from a brief appearance in the static park at the RAeS Garden Party at Wisley in July 1956, the Wellington languished in outside storage until it was moved to under-cover storage at Hendon in November 1957. By late 1959 it had moved again, this time to the British European Airways (BEA) hangar at Heathrow airport, where some restoration work was carried out by the Historic Aircraft Maintenance Group. Then in 1961 it was taken to 71 MU at Bicester for repair and repainting prior to allocation in the historic aircraft collection housed at Biggin Hill, Kent that March, becoming a regular static display attraction at the annual Battle of Britain 'At Home' days.

In early 1968 MF628 went back to St.Athan for a more substantial refurbishment before appearing at the RAF's fiftieth anniversary display at Abingdon in June, where it suffered some substantial damage. Repaired and back in storage at Henlow, the aircraft finally arrived at the new RAF Museum at Hendon in October 1971 where it remained on display until the summer of 2010 when it was dismantled and taken to the Michael Beetham Conservation Centre at Cosford for a lengthy full restoration.[1]

The partial remains of five other Wellingtons include:

Mk.I L4288 a 9 Squadron aircraft which had a mid-air collision with L4363 over Honington on 30 October 1939 and crashed near Sapiston Rectory, Suffolk killing both crews. The centre section, engine nacelles, cowlings and engines were recovered in 1982-83 and now form the centre piece of the Bomber Command display building at the Norfolk & Suffolk Aviation Museum, Flixton.

Mk.IA L7775 which flew into a hill at Bruach Moor near Braemar, Aberdeenshire on 23 October 1940 while operating with 20 OTU at Lossiemouth when the pilot apparently mistook snow-covered ground for cloud; all the crew survived. The remains were recovered in the summer of 1986 and parts of the nose and the tail section eventually found their way to the Wellington Museum at Moreton-in-Marsh until 2013 when it was relocated to become part of the Stratford Armouries Museum, Warwickshire. Strangely the same aircraft's wings and parts of the forward fuselage are displayed at the Lincolnshire Aviation Heritage Centre at East Kirkby, while its restored turrets are with the North Yorkshire Aircraft Recovery Centre who retrieved all the wreckage in 1985. It can only be hoped that one day all these widely dispersed remains can be reunited.

Mk.IV Z1206 a 104 OTU machine from Nutts Corner, Belfast which ran out of fuel and force landed just off the beach at Uigg on the Isle of Lewis in the Outer Hebrides on 26 January 1944. Washed up onto the beach and buried in the sand, the forward fuselage was recovered in 2002 by the Midland Aircraft Recovery Group at Kenilworth, Warwickshire.

Mk.III BK309 of 150 Squadron Kirmington crashed into a lake on a minelaying operation to Norway on 24 October 1942. Three of the crew were taken prisoner and two lost their lives. The substantial remains of the rear fuselage and tail section are displayed at the Flyhistorisk Museum at Sola Airport, Stavanger, Norway.

THE LAST WORDS

Although just two complete Wellingtons have survived, far more important are the brave men and women who built, flew, maintained and supported the aircraft in so many ways throughout its lengthy and illustrious service career, a great many of whom did not survive to see the end of

The remains of Mk.III BK309 of 150 Squadron at the Flyhistorisk Museum, Sola, Norway. (*Flyhistorisk Museum*)

the war. Of the 11,462 Wellingtons built no fewer than 1,727 were lost on operations alone, leaving over 9,000 men killed, wounded, taken prisoner or evading. The dwindling band still with us retain tremendous affection for the Wimpy and justified pride in their achievements, although few can accept that their contribution amounted to much. This feeling was beautifully summed up by the late Bill Briton who passed away, aged eighty-nine years, at Victor Harbour, South Australia in August 2013.

> "As we were taxiing back to our dispersal after our fortieth and last raid the skipper was told 'It's all over for you boys, you've done your share'. In some ways this seemed unreal as one never believed this way of life would end. We climbed out, shook hands and kissed the ground. When I look back I realise that we needed to be stood down, we had battle fatigue. Looking back, it was sad to be one of only two crews to survive our complete tour of ops on our squadron during the time we operated. With an average of three aircraft out of twenty being lost per raid, it meant that after about seven raids the whole squadron was wiped out. Forty raids under our belt meant we should, on statistics, have been killed at least six times. We never discussed raids, problems, successes etc. as a crew, but all simply got on with the job.
>
> "I can cry easily now just remembering, as I had never cried for myself, our crew, the hundreds of young men who gave their lives from our squadron, also for our enemy in the air and on the ground. Man needs to cry, it is never too late."

'And now you have heard the story,
Of our Wimpy, brave and bold,
For she is the greatest Wellington
That Vickers ever sold.
In time we'll go to Heaven – we hope!
With happiness to spare,
But Heaven won't be nothing unless,
Our Wimpy is also there.'

The final verse of the 75 (New Zealand) Squadron song – Anon.

Wellington Variants & Production

Variants and Vickers type numbers

Note: All British military aircraft mark numbers used Roman numerals until 1948 when Arabic numerals were adopted. However, for purposes of clarity Roman numerals are used throughout this book regardless of the period.

B.9/32 Type 271 – 1 built
Prototype K4049 first flown 15 Jun 1936

Mk.I Type 285, 290, 403 – 181 built
Wing span 86 ft length 61 ft 3 in height 17 ft 5 in, gross weight 24,850 lb, service ceiling 21,600 ft, range 3,200 miles at 180 mph at 15,000 ft. Pegasus XVIII 1,050 hp. Vickers nose and tail turrets, Nash and Thompson ventral turret. Type 403 for RNZAF. DWI (Directional Wireless Installation) Type 418, 419.Converted Mk.I for anti-magnetic mine purposes and fitted with 51 ft, later 48 ft diameter degaussing ring powered by Ford V8 or DH Gipsy Six engine

Mk.IA Type 408, 412 – 187 built
Pegasus X. Frazer Nash nose and tail turrets. Strengthened landing gear with larger wheels. Conversions to C.Mk.IA for Transport Command. One example modified as Type 451 with Frazer Nash mid-upper turret as test-bed for Short R.14/40 flying boat installation. Type 412 for RNZAF

Mk.IB Type 409
Alternative variant to replace Mk.I. Not built in favour of Mk.IA

Mk.IC Type 415, 416, 435, 452 – 2,685 built
Wing span 86 ft 2 in length 64 ft 7 in height 17 ft 5 in, gross weight 28,500 lb, service ceiling 18,000 ft, range 2,550 miles at 180 mph at 15,000 ft with 1,000 lb bomb load. Pegasus XVIII 1,050 hp. Ventral turret replaced by two Vickers K or Browning beam guns; improved hydraulics and electrical systems. Conversions to C.Mk.IC for Transport Command. Type 435 one aircraft for Turbinlite tests. Type 452 minelayer

Mk.II Type 298, 406, 416, 439, 445, 450, 470, 486 – 402 built
Wing span 86 ft 2 in length 64 ft 7 in height 17 ft 5 in, gross weight 33,000 lb, service ceiling 23,500 ft, range 2,200 miles at 180 mph at 15,000 ft. Merlin X 1,145 hp. Prototype L4250 first flown 3 March 1939. Type 416 experimental dorsal 40 mm Vickers S gun. Type 439 experimental version with nose-mounted 40 mm cannon. Types 445, 450, 470 and 486 W5389, W5518 and Z8570 used as test-beds for Whittle jet engines, mounted in the tail

Mk.III Type 299, 417, 452 – 1,519 built
Dimensions as for Mk.IC, range 2,200 miles with 1,550 lb bomb load, 1,540 miles with 4,000 lb bomb load Hercules XI 1,590 hp. Frazer Nash 20A four-gun rear turret. Prototype L4251 first flown 16 May 1939. Type 452 was BJ895 used for 'Highball' weapons tests

Mk.IV Type 410, 424 – 220 built
Pratt &Whitney Twin Wasp R-1830 1,050 hp, otherwise similar to Mk.III. Type 410 prototype R1220

Mk.V Type 407, 421, 426, 436, 440, 443 – 3 built
Hercules III 1,425 hp. High-altitude bomber to operate up to 40,000 ft. Prototypes R3298 & R3299 first flown August 1940. One further aircraft W5766. Type 443 one aircraft for Hercules VIII tests

Mk.VI Type 431, 439, 442, 443, 449 – 64 built
Wing span 86 ft 2 in length 61 ft 9 in height 17 ft 8 in, gross weight 30,450 lb, service ceiling 38,500 ft, range 2,275 miles with 1,500 lb bomb load. Merlin 60 1,600 hp. High-altitude bomber. Prototype W5795 plus 63 production aircraft, some used as GEE trainers by one flight of 109 Squadron which received 4 aircraft

Mk.VII Type 430 – none completed

Intended as improved Mk.II with Merlin XX engines. Single prototype only, passed to Rolls-Royce uncompleted and used as a Merlin test-bed

GR Mk.VIII Type 429 – 394 built
Wing span 86 ft 2 in length 64 ft 7 in height 17 ft 8 in, gross weight 30,000 lb, service ceiling 19,000 ft, range 2,550 miles at 144 mph. Pegasus XVIII. Mk.IC variant for Coastal Command. Initially referred to as DWI Mk.III and fitted with ASV Mk.II radar with four aerials on the rear fuselage and a searchlight. Some fitted with Leigh Light

Mk.IX Type 437
Converted Mk.IA for Transport Command, total number unknown

Mk.X Type 440, 478, 602, 619 – 3,803 built
Wing span 86 ft 2 in length 64 ft 7 in height 17 ft 6 in, gross weight 36,500 lb, service ceiling 22,000 ft, range 1,885 miles at 180 mph with 1,500 lb bomb load. Improved Mk.III with Hercules VI or XVI 1,675 hp. Final bomber variant. Type 478 one aircraft for Hercules 100 tests. Type 602 T Mk.X LN715 Roll-Royce Dart test-bed. Type 619 post-war T Mk.X variant for navigator training

GR Mk.XI Type 454, 458, 459 – 180 built
Hercules VI or XVI. Torpedo bomber variant of Mk.X. Later fitted with ASV Mk.III scanner in nose radome

GR Mk.XII Type 455 – 58 built
Hercules VI or XVI variant of GR Mk.XI with ASV Mk.III and retractable Leigh Light. Front turret deleted

GR. Mk.XIII Type 466 – 845 built
Wing span 86 ft 2 in length 64 ft 7 in height 17 ft 8 in, gross weight 31,000 lb, service ceiling 16,000 ft, range 1,750 miles Hercules XVII 1,735 hp variant of GR Mk.XIII optimised for low-level maritime patrol and fitted with ASV Mk.II or Mk.III

GR. Mk.XIV Type 467 – 840 built
Hercules XVII variant of GR Mk.XII specifically for anti-submarine work. ASV Mk.III and retractable Leigh Light

C.Mk.XV – 18 conversions
Transport Command variant of Mk.IA. Re-designated from C.Mk.IA

C.Mk.XVI – 54 conversions
Transport Command variant of Mk.IC. Re-designated from C.Mk.IC

T.Mk.XVII Type 487 – 9 conversions
Hercules XVII. Service conversion of Mk.XI for AI radar training fitted with SCR720 radar in place of the nose turret

T.Mk.XVIII Type 490 – 80 built
Hercules XVII. Night-fighter crew trainer with radar scanner in the nose and accommodation for an instructor and four pupils

T.Mk.XIX no type number allocated – 6 conversions
Training variant of Mk.X for bomber crews. Six produced in 1946 by in-service conversion, including NA851 and RP318. 18 further conversions cancelled

Total built 11,462

Production Breakdown

Vickers production lines were at Squires Gate Blackpool, Hawarden Chester, and Weybridge

Cancelled batches are not listed, but included 889 Blackpool Mk.X, 145 Chester Mk.XIV, and 150 Blackpool Mk.XIV

Prototype K4049. Built Weybridge

180 Mk.I L4212-L4311, L4317-L4391, R2699-R2703 ordered 15 Aug 1936. Built Weybridge. Conversions to DWI

100 Mk.I, IA & IC L7770-L7789, L7790-L7819, L7840-L7874, L7885-L7899. Built Chester

100 Mk.IC N2735-N2784, N2800-N2829, N2840-N2859. Built Chester. Conversions to Mk.XVI

120 Mk.IA N2865-N2914, N2935-N2964, N2980-N3019. Built Weybridge. Conversions to Mk.XV

100 comprising 50 Mk.IA P2515-P2532, P9205-P9236; 50 Mk.IC P9237-P9250, P9265-P9300. Built Weybridge. Conversions to DWI Mk.III, Mk.XV, Mk.XVI

550 Mk.IC R1000-R1049, R1060-R1099, R1135-R1184, R1210-R1254, R1265-R1299, R1320-R1349, R1354-R1414, R1435-R1474, R1490-R1539, R1585-R1629, R1640-R1669, R1695-R1729, R1757-R1806. Built Chester. Conversions to Mk.IV, Mk.XVI

100 Mk.IC R3150-R3179, R3195-R3239, R3275-R3299. Built Weybridge. Conversions to Mk.II, Mk.IV, Mk.XVI

300 Mk.IC T2458-T2477, T2501-T2520, T2541-T2580, T2606-T2625, T2701-T2750, T2801-T2850, T2873-T2922, T2951-T3000. Built Weybridge. Conversions to Mk.II, Mk.VIII, Mk.XVI

300 comprising 74 Mk.IC W5612-W5614, W5616-W5618, W5620-W5622, W5624-W5630, W5644, W5646, W5648, W5650, W5652, W5654, W5656, W5658, W5660, W5663-W5670, W5673, W5675, W5677, W5679-W5690, W5703-W5724, W5726, W5727, W5729, 199 Mk.II W5352-W5401, W5414-W5463, W5476-W5500, W5513-W5537, W5550-W5598, W5611, 27 Mk.VIII W5615, W5619, W5623, W5631, W5645, W5647, W5649, W5651, W5653, W5655, W5657, W5659, W5661, W5662, W5671, W5672, W5674, W5676, W5678, W5725, W5728, W5730-W5735. Built Weybridge. Conversions to Mk.XVI

1 Mk.V W5795, & 20 Mk.VI W5796-W5815. Built Weybridge

500 comprising 50 Mk.IC X3160-X3179, X3192-X3221, 450 Mk.III X3222-X3226, X3275-X3289, X3304-X3313, X3330-X3374, X3387-X3426, X3445-X3489, X3538-X3567, X3584-X3608, X3633-X3677, X3694-X3728, X3741-X3754, X3784-X3823, X3855-X3890, X3923-X3957, X3984-X4003. Built Blackpool. Conversions to Mk.X, Mk.XVI

710 comprising 378 Mk.IC X9600-X9644, X9658-X9707, X9733-X9757, X9784-X9834, X9871-X9890, X9905-X9954, X9974-X9993, Z1040-Z1054, Z1066-Z1115, Z1139-Z1181, 195 Mk.IV Z1182-Z1183, Z1202-Z1221, Z1243-Z1292, Z1311-Z1345, Z1375-Z1424, Z1459-Z1496, 137 Mk.III Z1562-Z1578, Z1592-Z1626, Z1648-Z1697, Z1717-Z1751. Built Chester. Conversions to Mk.XVI

200 Mk.II Z8328-Z8377, Z8397-Z8441, Z8489-Z8538, Z8567-Z8601, Z8643-Z8662. Built Weybridge

250 Mk.IC Z8702-Z8736, Z8761-Z8810, Z8827-Z8871, Z8891-Z8910, Z8942-Z8991, Z9016-Z9045, Z9095-Z9114. Built Weybridge. Conversions to Mk.VIII, Mk.XVI

50 Mk.IC AD589-AD608, AD624-AD653. Built Weybridge

50 comprising 43 Mk.IC BB455-BB460, BB462-BB465, BB467-BB470, BB472-BB475, BB477-BB480, BB482-BB484, BB497-BB502, BB504-BB512, BB514-BB516, 7 Mk.VIII BB461, BB466, BB471, BB476, BB481, BB503, BB513. Built Weybridge

600 Mk.III BJ581-BJ625, BJ642-BJ675, BJ688-BJ730, BJ753-BJ801, BJ818-BJ847, BJ876-BJ922, BJ958-BJ991, BK123-BK166, BK179-BK214, BK234-BK281, BK295-BK315, BK330-BK358, BK385-BK408, BK425-BK471, BK489-BK517, BK534-BK564. Built Chester

150 comprising 145 Mk.III DF542-DF579, DF594-DF608, DF610-DF642, DF664-DF685, DF687-DF700, DF702-DF709, DF727-DF729, DF731-DF739, DF741-DF743, 5 Mk.X DF609, DF686, DF701, DF730, DF740. Built Blackpool

44 comprising 9 Mk.VIA DR471-DR479, 35 Mk.VIG DR480-DR504, DR519-DR528. Built Weybridge

415 Mk.IC DV411-DV458, DV473-DV522, DV536-DV579, DV593-DV624, DV638-DV678, DV694-DV740, DV757-DV786, DV799-DV846, DV864-DV898, DV914-DV953. Built Chester. Conversions to Mk.XVI

16 Mk.IC ES980-ES995. Built Weybridge. ES986 converted to Mk.VIII

1,125 comprising 85 Mk.IC HD942-991, HE101-HE134, HE136-HE146, 1 Mk.III HF112, 242 Mk.IV HF121-HF155, HF167-HF208, HF220-HF252, HF264-HF312, HF329-HF363, HF381-HF422, HF446-HF495, HF513-HF545, HF567-HF606, 789 Mk.X HE147-HE184, HE197-HE244, HE258-HE306, HE318-HE353, HE365-HE398, HE410-HE447, HE459-HE508, HE513-HE556, HE568-HE615, HE627-HE667, HE679-HE715, HE727-HE772, HE784-HE833, HE845-HE873, HE898-HE931, HE946-HE995, 8 Mk.XII HF113-HF120. Built Chester

153 comprising 123 Mk.III HF609-HF613, HF615-HF621, HF623-HF625, HF627-HF629, HF631-HF633, HF635-HF637, HF639-HF641, HF643-HF645, HF647-HF649, HF666-HF668, HF670-HF703, HF718, HF719, HF721,HF722, HF724, HF726-HF728, HF730, HF731, HF734, HF736-HF738, HF740-HF742, HF744-HF746, HF748-HF750, HF752-HF754, HF756-HF758, HF760-HF762, HF764, HF791, HF792, HF794-HF796, HF798-HF802, HF806, HF807, HF809, HF810, HF812-HF816, 27 Mk.X HF614, HF622, HF626, HF630, HF634, HF638, HF642, HF646, HF650, HF669, HF723, HF725, HF729, HF732, HF735, HF739, HF743, HF747, HF751, HF755, HF759, HF763, HF793, HF797, HF805, HF808, HF811, 3 Mk.XI HF720, HF803, HF804. Built Blackpool

84 comprising 62 Mk.IC HF829-HF837, HF839-HF849, HF851-HF853, HF855, HF856, HF858, HF859, HF861, HF862, HF864, HF865, HF867 HF868, HF881, HF822, HF884, HF885, HF887, HF888, HF890, HF891, HF893, HF894, HF896-HF900, HF902, HF903, HF905, HF906, HF908, HF909, HF911, HF912, HF914, HF915, HF917, HF918, HF920, HF921, 22 Mk.VIII HF828, HF838, HF850, HF854, HF857, HF860, HF863, HF866, HF869, HF883, HF886, HF889, HF892, HF895, HF901, HF904, HF907, HF910, HF913, HF916, HF919, HF922. Built Weybridge

300 serials HX364-HX403, HX417-HX452, HX466-HX489, HX504-HX538, HX558-HX606, HX625-HX656, HX670-HX690, HX709-HX751, HX767-HX786 comprising 124 Mk.IC HX364-HX371, HX373-HX375, HX377, HX378, HX380, HX382, HX384, HX385, HX387, HX389, HX390, HX392, HX393, HX395, HX397, HX399, HX400, HX402, HX417, HX421, HX423, HX425, HX429, HX431, HX433, HX435, HX438, HX440, HX442, HX445-HX447, HX449, HX451, HX468, HX470, HX472, HX475, HX478, HX480, HX483, HX484, HX486, HX488, HX506, HX508, HX510, HX514, HX516, HX518, HX521, HX523, HX525, HX527, HX529, HX533, HX536, HX558, HX560, HX564, HX567, HX569, HX571, HX573, HX577, HX580, HX583, HX585, HX589, HX591, HX594, HX597, HX601, HX603, HX606, HX627, HX631, HX633, HX635, HX637, HX639, HX643, HX645, HX648, HX651, HX655, HX670, HX673, HX676, HX680, HX682, HX685, HX688, HX710, HX712, HX714, HX716, HX718, HX722, HX724, HX727, HX730, HX734, HX736, HX739, HX742, HX746, HX748, HX750, HX767, HX769, HX773, HX775, HX778, HX781, HX785, remainder of this batch 176 Mk.VIII. Conversions to DWI. Built Weybridge

850 serials HZ102-HZ150, HZ173-HZ209, HZ242-HZ284, HZ299-HZ315, HZ351-HZ378, HZ394-HZ439, HZ467-HZ487, HZ513-HZ554, HZ570-HZ604, HZ633-HZ660, HZ689-HZ727, HZ752-HZ770, HZ793-HZ820, HZ862-HZ897, HZ937-HZ981, JA104-JA151, JA176-JA210, JA256-JA273, JA295-JA318, JA337-JA363, JA378-JA426, JA442-JA481, JA497-JA539, JA561-JA585, JA618-JA645 comprising 301 Mk.X HZ102, HZ105, HZ108, HZ111, HZ114, HZ117, HZ120, HZ123, HZ125, HZ129, HZ132, HZ135, HZ138, HZ141, HZ144, HZ147, HZ175, HZ181, HZ187, HZ193, HZ199, HZ205, HZ243, HZ249, HZ255-HZ273, HZ277-HZ282, HZ300-HZ305, HZ304-HZ314, HZ353-HZ358, HZ362-HZ367, HZ371-HZ376, HZ398-HZ403, HZ410-HZ415, HZ422-HZ427, HZ434-HZ439, HZ457-HZ487, HZ513-HZ521, HZ528-HZ533, HZ540-HZ545, HZ552-HZ554, HZ570-HZ572, HZ579-HZ582, HZ713-HZ720, HZ809-HZ818, HZ941-HZ950, JA111-JA140, JA185-JA194, JA341-JA352, JA448-JA481, JA497-JA512, JA519 JA534, 72 Mk.XI HZ142, HZ143, HZ178, HZ184, HZ190, HZ196, HZ202, HZ208, HZ246, HZ251-HZ254, HZ274-HZ276, HZ283, HZ284, HZ299, HZ306-HZ308, HZ315, HZ351, HZ352, HZ359-HZ361, HZ368-HZ370, HZ377, HZ378, HZ394-HZ397, HZ404-HZ409, HZ416-HZ421, HZ428-HZ433, HZ522-HZ527, HZ534-HZ539, HZ546-HZ550, 415 Mk.XIII HZ551, HZ573-HZ578, HZ583-HZ604, HZ633-HZ660, HZ689-HZ712, HZ721-HZ727, HZ752-HZ770, HZ793-HZ808, HZ819, HZ820, HZ862-HZ897, HZ937-HZ940, HZ951-HZ981, JA104-JA110, JA141-JA151, JA176-JA184, JA195-JA210, JA256-JA318, JA337-JA340, JA353-JA363, JA378-JA426, JA442-JA447, JA513-JA518, JA525-JA539, JA561-JA585, JA618-JA645, remainder of this batch 62 Mk.III. Built Blackpool

150 serials LA964-LA998, LB110-LB156, LB169-LB197, LB213-LB251 comprising 16 Mk.IC LA965, LA968, LA973, LA978, LA984, LA988, LA994, LB110, LB116, LB120, LB126, LB131, LB141, LB148, LB152, LB174, remainder of this batch Mk.VIII. Built Weybridge

1,382 Mk.X LN157-LN189, LN221-LN248, LN261-LN303, LN317-LN353, LN369-LN409, LN423-LN458, LN481-LN516, LN529-LN571, LN583-LN622, LN633-LN676, LN689-LN723, LN736-LN778, LN791-LN823, LN836-LN879, LN893-LN936, LN948-LN989, LP113-LP156, LP169-LP213, LP226-LP268, LP281-LP314, LP328-LP369, LP381-LP415, LP428-LP469, LP483-LP526, LP539-LP581, LP595-LP628, LP640-LP686, LP699-LP733, LP748-LP788, LP802-LP849, LP863-LP889, LP901-LP930, LP943-LP986, LR110-LR142, LR156-LR164, LR168-LR183, LR195-LR210. Built Chester

600 serials ME870-ME914, ME926-ME960, ME972-ME999, MF113-MF156, MF170-MF213, MF226-MF267, MF279-MF320, MF335-MF377, MF389-MF424, MF439-MF480, MF493-MF538, MF550-MF596, MF614-MF659, MF672-MF713, MF725-MF742, comprising 299 Mk.X ME870-ME883, ME951-ME960, ME972-ME999, MF113-MF124, MF131-MF144, MF193-MF202, MF236-MF249, MF281-MF288, MF311-MF316, MF346-MF351, MF367-MF372, MF399-MF404, MF421-MF424, MF439-MF441, MF452-MF459, MF468-MF479, MF500-MF538, MF550-MF572, MF583-MF597, MF614, MF615, MF624-MF635, MF644-MF655, MF676-MF687, MF695-MF706, MF728-MF739, 4 Mk.XIV MF450, MF451, MF726, MF727, remainder of this batch 297 Mk.XIII. Built Blackpool

250 serials MP502-MP549, MP562-MP601, MP615-MP656, MP679-MP724, MP738-MP825, comprising 50 Mk.XII MP503, MP505-MP515, MP536-MP542, MP575, MP578, MP581, MP584, MP587, MP590, MP593, MP596, MP599, MP615, MP618, MP620, MP622, MP624, MP626, MP628, MP630, MP632, MP634, MP636, MP638, MP650, MP652, MP654, MP656, MP680, MP682, MP684, MP686, MP688, MP690, 42 Mk.XIII MP704-MP709, MP711, MP713, MP715, MP717, MP719, MP721, MP723, MP738, MP740, MP742-MP749, MP751, MP753, MP755, MP757, MP759, MP761, MP762, MP764, MP765, MP767, MP768, MP770, MP771, MP773, MP790, MP793, MP796, MP800, MP804, 53 Mk.XIV MP710, MP712, MP714, MP716, MP718, MP720, MP722, MP724, MP739, MP741, MP750, MP752, MP754, MP756, MP758, MP760, MP763, MP766, MP769, MP772, MP774, MP789, MP791, MP792, MP794, MP795, MP797-MP799, MP801-MP803, MP805-MP825, remainder of this batch 105 Mk.XI. Built Weybridge

27 Mk.X MS470-MS496. Built Blackpool

263 Mk.X NA710-NA754, NA766-NA811, NA823-NA870, NA893-NA937, NA949-NA997, NB110-NB139. Built Chester

296 Mk.XIV NB767-NB783, NB796-NB841, NB853-NB896, NB908-NB952, NB964-NB999, NC112-NC160, NC164-NC209, NC222-NC234. Built Chester

500 serials NC414-NC459, NC471-NC517, NC529-NC576, NC588-NC632, NC644-NC692, NC706-NC750, NC766-NC813, NC825-NC870, NC883-NC929, NC942-NC990, ND104-ND133 comprising 90 Mk.XIII NC414-NC418, NC433, NC440, NC453-NC459, NC471, NC482-NC489, NC503, NC510, NC534-NC541, NC555-NC562, NC571-NC576, NC588, NC589, NC602-NC609, NC626-NC631, NC656-NC663, NC741-NC747, 84 Mk.XIV NC419, NC420, NC441, NC442, NC490-NC493, NC511-NC513, NC542-NC544, NC590, NC591, NC610-NC613, NC622-NC625, NC632, NC644-NC647, NC672-NC677, NC771-NC776, NC785-NC788, NC797-NC800, NC828-NC835, NC848-NC855, NC870, NC883-NC889, NC902-NC907, ND129-ND133, 30 Mk.XVIII NC868, NC869, NC926-NC928, ND104-ND128, remainder of this batch 296 Mk.X. Built Blackpool

400 serials PF820-PF866, PF879-PF915, PF927-PF968, PF979-PF999, PG112-PG157, PG170-PG215, PG227-PG269, PG282-PG326, PG338-PG379, PG392-PG422 comprising 162 Mk.XIV PF820-PF822, PF831-PF838, PF847-PF854, PF863-PF866, PF879-PF882, PF889-PF893, PF902-PF911, PF931-PF940, PF949-PF958, PF967, PF968, PF979-PF986, PF995-PF999, PG112-PG116, PG125-PG134, PG139-PG148, PG153-PG157, PG170-PG174, PG183-PG192, PG197-PG206, PG211-PG215, PG227-PG231, PG240-PG245, PG266-PG269, PG282-PG285, PG298-PG293, 30 Mk.XVIII PG236-PG239, PG246-PG249, PG254-PG257, PG349, PG356, PG367-PG370, PG395-PG400, remainder of this batch 208 Mk.X. Built Blackpool

226 comprising 206 Mk.X RP312-RP329, RP336-RP347, RP352-RP358, RP373-RP391, RP396-RP411, RP430-RP469, RP483-RP526, RP538-RP590, 20 Mk.XVIII RP330-RP335, RP348-RP351, RP392-RP395, RP412-RP415, RP428, RP429. Built Blackpool

Total production 11,462 including 3,406 at Squires Gate who made the final Wellington delivery (RP590) on 13 October 1945

Wellington Operating Units

Notes:
Variants are listed in the order in which the unit received them
Dates refer to Wellington operating period(s)
Main bases only are listed; many squadrons had frequent detachments to other stations
Unit codes, where carried, are shown in parentheses

Royal Air Force & Allied Air Forces
The groups which controlled Wellington units included the following. Note that some units came under different groups at different times.

1 (Bomber) Group Benson, Hucknall, later Bawtry Hall. 12, 101, 103, 142, 150, 166, 199, 300, 301, 304, 305, 460 Squadrons
3 (Bomber) Mildenhall, Harraton House Exning near Newmarket. 9, 15, 37, 38, 40, 57, 75, 99, 101, 109, 115, 149, 156, 192, 214, 215, 311, 419 Squadrons
4 (Bomber) Heslington Hall York. 104, 196, 405, 429, 458, 466 Squadrons
5 (Bomber) St.Vincents Grantham, Morton Hall Swinderby. 57 Squadron
6 (Operational Training) Abingdon. 75 Squadron, 11, 12, 15, 18, 20 OTUs
6 (RCAF) Linton-on-Ouse, Allerton Park Knaresborough. 420, 424, 425, 426, 427, 426 Squadrons
7 (Operational Training) Brampton Grange Hunts, Winslow Hall Winslow, St.Vincents Grantham. 11, 18, 25, 26, 27 OTUs
15 (General Reconnaissance) Derby House, Liverpool. 36, 172 Squadrons
16 (General Reconnaissance) Black Lion Fields Gillingham. 407, 415, 524, 544, 612 Squadrons
17 (Training) Mackenzie Hotel, Edinburgh. 1, 3, 5, 6, 7 OTUs
18 (General Reconnaissance) Pitreavie Castle Rosyth. 547 Squadron
19 (General Reconnaissance) Mount Wise, Plymouth. 14, 172, 179, 304, 311, 407 Squadrons. 1417 Flt
91 (Operational Training/Bomber OTU) Abingdon. 10, 15, 19, 20, 21, 22, 23, 24, 27, 30 OTUs
92 (Operational Training/Bomber OTU) Winslow Hall, Bucks. 11, 12, 14, 16, 17, 26, 27, 28, 29, 84, 85 OTUs
93 (Operational Training/Bomber OTU) Egginton Hall, Derby. 18, 27, 28, 30, 82, 83 OTUs
100 (Special Duties) Bylaugh Hall East Dereham. 192 Squadron
205 (Heavy Bomber) Shallufa, followed by frequent moves around North Africa and Italy. 37, 38, 70, 104, 108, 148, 150, 420, 424, 425, 462 Squadrons
216 (Ferry) Heliopolis, with frequent moves around North Africa and Italy
225 (Composite) Bangalore

Bomber Squadrons

9 (KA,WS)	Mk.I, IA, IC, II, III. Stradishall Jan 39, to Honington Jul 39, Lancaster Sep 42
12 (PH)	Mk.II, III. Binbrook Nov 40, Wickenby Sep 42. Lancaster Nov 42
15 (LS)	Mk.IC. Wyton Nov 40. Stirling Apr 41
37 (LF)	Mk.I, IA, IC, III, X. Feltwell May 39, Luqa Nov 40, Fayid Dec 40, Shallufa Dec 40, LG 09 Apr 42, LG 224 Nov 42, LG 106 Nov 42, LG 140 Nov 42, Benina Jan 43, El Magrun Jan 43, Gardabia East Feb 43, Gardabia West Feb 43, Kairouan May 43, Djedeida Nov 43, Cerignola Dec 43, Tortorella Jan 44. Liberator Oct 44
38 (NH, HD)	Mk.I, IA, IC, II. Marham Nov 38, Ismailia Nov 40, Fayid Dec 40, Shallufa Dec 40. Warwick Jul 45. Last Wellington left Dec 46
40 (BL)	Mk.IC, III, X. Wyton Nov 40, Alconbury Feb 41, Luqa Oct 41, disbanded Feb 42, reformed Abu Sueir May 42, Shallufa Jun 42, Kabrit Aug 42, LG 222A Nov 42, LG 104 Nov 42, LG 237 Nov 42, Heliopolis Jan 43, LG 237 Jan 43, Gardabia East Feb 43, Gardabia South Mar 43, El Adem East May 43, Hani West Jun 43, Oudna No.1 Nov 43, Cerignola No.2 Dec 43, Foggia Main Dec 43. Liberator Feb 45. Last Wellington left Mar 45
57 (DX)	Mk.IA, IC, II, III. Feltwell Nov 40. Lancaster Sep 42
70	Mk.IC, III, X. Kabrit Sep 40, LG 75 Jan 42, LG 104 Feb 42, LG 224 Jun 42, Abu Sueir Jun 42, LG 224 Nov 42, LG 106 Nov 42, LG 140 Nov 42, Benina Jan 43, El Magrun Jan 43, Gardabia East Feb 43, Gardabia West Feb 43, Temmar May 43, Djedeida Nov 43, Cerignola Dec 43, Tortorella Dec 43. Liberator Jan 45

75 (FO, AA)	Mk.I, IA, IC, III. Honington Jul 39, Stradishall Jul 39, Harwell Sep 39. Reformed as 75 (New Zealand) Sqn Feltwell Apr 40, Mildenhall Aug 42, Newmarket Nov 42. Stirling Nov 42
99 (LN)	Mk.I, IA, IC, II, III, X. Mildenhall Oct 38, Newmarket Sep 39, Waterbeach Mar 41, Ambala Jun 42, Pandaveswar Sep 42, Digri Oct 42, Chaklala Apr 43, Jessore Jun 43, Dhubalia Aug 44. Liberator Sep 44
101 (SR)	Mk.IC, III. West Raynham Apr 41, Oakington Jul 41, Bourne Feb 42, Stradishall Aug 42, Holme-on-Spalding Moor Sep 42. Lancaster Oct 42
103 (PM)	Mk.IC. Newton Oct 40, Elsham Wolds Jul 41. Halifax Oct 42
104 (EP)	Mk.II, X. Driffield Apr 41, Luqa Oct 41, Kabrit Jun 42, LG 224 Nov 42, LG 104 Nov 42, LG 237 Nov 42, Soluch Feb 43, Gardabia Main Feb 43, Cheria May 43, Hani West Jun 43, Oudna Nov 43, Cerignola No.2 Dec 43, Foggia Main Dec 43. Liberator Feb 45
108	Mk.IC. Kabrit Aug 41, Fayid Sep 41. Liberator Nov 41, last Wellington left Nov 42
109 (HS)	Mk.IC, I, VI. Boscombe Down Dec 40, detachment to Egypt Oct 42-Dec 42, Tempsford Jan 42, Stradishall Apr 42, Lancaster and Mosquito from Jul and Aug 42, last Wellington left Dec 42
115 (BK, KO)	Mk.I, IA, IC, DWI, III. Marham Mar 39, Mildenhall Sep 42, East Wretham Nov 42. Lancaster Mar 43
142 (QT)	Mk.II, IV, III. Binbrook Nov 40, Waltham Nov 41, Blida Dec 42, Kirmington Dec 42 (UK echelon only), Fontaine Chaude May 43, Kairouan May 43, Oudna Nov 43, Cerignola No.3 Dec 43, Amendola Feb 44, Regina Jul 44. Disbanded Oct 44
148	Mk.I, IC, II. Stradishall May 39, Harwell Sep 39, disbanded Apr 40. Reformed Luqa Dec 40, Kabrit Mar 41, LG 106 May 42, Kabrit Jun 42, LG 237 Aug 42, LG 106 Nov 42, LG 09 Nov 42, LG 167 Dec 42, disbanded Dec 42
149 (OJ)	Mk.I, IA, IC. Mildenhall Jan 39. Stirling Dec 41
150 (JN)	Mk.IA, IC, III, X. Newton Oct 40, Snaith Jul 41, Kirmington Oct 42, Blida Dec 42, Fontaine Chaude May 43, Kairouan West May 43, Oudna No.2 Nov 43, Cerignola No.3 Dec 43, Amendola Feb 44, Regina Jul 44. Disbanded Oct 44
156 (GT)	Mk.IC, III. Alconbury Feb 42, Warboys Aug 42. Lancaster Jan 43
158 (NP)	Mk.II. Driffield Feb 42, East Moor Jun 42. Halifax Jun 42
166 (AS)	Mk.III, X. Kirmington Jan 43. Lancaster Sep 43
192 (DT)	Mk.IC, III, X. Gransden Lodge Jan 43, Feltwell Apr 43 (plus Halifax and Mosquito), Foulsham Nov 43. Last Wellington left Jan 45
196 (ZO)	Mk.III, X. Leconfield Dec 42, Witchford Jul 43. Stirling Jul 43
199 (EX)	Mk.III, X. Blyton Nov 42, Ingham Feb 43, Lakenheath Jun 43. Stirling Jul 43
214 (UX, BU)	Mk.I, IA, IC, II. Feltwell May 39, Methwold Sep 39, Stradishall Feb 40, Honington Jan 42, Stradishall Jan 42. Stirling Apr 42
215 (LG)	Mk.IA, IC, X. Honington Apr 40, Bassingbourn May 40. Disbanded May 40. Reformed Newmarket Dec 41, Stradishall Jan 42, Asansol Apr 42, Pandaveswar Apr 42, St.Thomas Mount Aug 42, Chaklala Oct 42, Jessore Mar 43. Liberator Jul 44, last Wellington left Aug 44
218 (HA)	Mk.IC, II. Oakington Nov 40, Marham Nov 40. Stirling Jan 42
300 (BH)	Polish. Mk.IC, IV, III, X. Swinderby Dec 40, Hemswell Jul 41, Ingham May 42, Hemswell Jan 43, Ingham Jun 43, Faldingworth Mar 44. Lancaster Apr 44
301 (GR)	Polish. Mk.IC, IV. Swinderby Oct 40, Hemswell Jul 41. Disbanded Apr 43
304 (NZ, QD)	Polish Mk.IC. Bramcote Nov 40, Syerston Dec 40, Lindholme Jul 41. To Coastal Command Apr 42.
305 (SM)	Polish. Mk.IC, II, IV, X. Bramcote Nov 40, Syerston Dec 40, Lindholme Jul 41, Hemswell Jul 42, Ingham Jun 43. Mitchell Sep 43 at Swanton Morley
311 (KX)	Polish. Mk.IC. Honington Aug 40, East Wretham Sep 40. Transferred to Coastal Command Apr 42
405 (LQ)	RCAF. Mk.II. Driffield May 41, Pocklington Jun 41. Halifax Apr 42
419 (VR)	RCAF. Mk.IC, III. Mildenhall Jan 42, Leeming Aug 42, Topcliffe Aug 42, Croft Oct 42. Halifax Nov 42
420 (PT)	RCAF. Mk.III, X. Skipton-on-Swale Aug 42, Middleton St.George Oct 42, Kairouan Jun 43, Hani East Sep-Oct 43. Halifax Dec 43 at Tholthorpe
424 (QB)	RCAF. Mk.III, X. Topcliffe Oct 42, Leeming Apr 43, Dalton May 43, Kairouan Jun 43, Hani East Sep-Oct 43. Halifax Dec 43 at Skipton-on-Swale

425 (KW) RCAF. Mk.III, X. Dishforth Aug 42, Kairouan Jun 43, Hani East Sep-Oct 43. Halifax Dec 43 at Tholthorpe

426 (OW) RCAF. Mk.III, X. Dishforth Oct 42, Linton-on-Ouse Jun 43. Lancaster Jul 43

427 (ZL) RCAF. Mk.III, X. Croft Nov 42, Leeming May 43. Halifax May 43

428 (NA) RCAF. Mk.III, X. Dalton Nov 42, Middleton St.George Jun 43. Halifax Jun 43

429 (AL) RCAF. Mk.III, X. East Moor Nov 42, Leeming Aug 43. Halifax Aug 43

431 (SE) RCAF. Mk.X. Burn Dec 42, Tholthorpe Jul 43. Halifax Jul 43

432 (QO) RCAF. Mk.X. Skipton-on-Swale May 43, East Moor Sep 43. Lancaster Oct 43, last Wellington left Nov 43

458 (MD) RAAF. Mk.IV, IC. Holme-on-Spalding Moor Aug 41-Mar 42. To maritime operations

460 (UV) RAAF. Mk.IV. Molesworth Nov 41, Breighton Jan 42. Halifax Aug 42, last Wellington left Sep 42

466 (HD) RAAF. Mk.II, X. Driffield Oct 42, Leconfield Dec 42. Halifax Sep 43

Maritime Squadrons

8 Mk.XIII. Khormaksar Dec 43. Disbanded May 45

14 (CX) Mk.XIV. Chivenor Nov 44. Disbanded May 45

36 (RW) Mk.IC, VIII, X, XI, XII, XIII, XIV. Tanjore Dec 42, Dhubalia Apr 43, Blida Jun 43, Réghaia Apr 44. Tarquinia Sep 44, Chivenor Sep 44, Benbecula Mar 45. Disbanded Jun 45

38 Mk.IC, VIII, XII, XIII, XIV. Transferred from bombing to primarily maritime role at Shallufa Jan 42, Berka III Feb 43, Kalamaki Nov 44, Grottaglie Dec 44, Foggia Main Jan 45, Falconara Apr 45, Luqa Jul 45. Warwick and Lancaster from Jul 45 and Jul 46. Last Wellington left Nov 46

172 (OG, WN, 1) Mk.VIII, XII, XIV. Chivenor Apr 42, Limavady Sep 44. Disbanded Jun 45

179 Mk.VIII, XIV. Skitten Sep 42, Gibraltar Nov 42, Predannack Apr 44, Chivenor Sep 44, Benbecula Sep 44, Chivenor Oct 44, St.Eval Nov 44. Warwick Nov 44

203 Mk.XIII. Santa Cruz Nov 43, Madura Oct 44. Liberator Oct 44

221 (DF) Mk.IC, VIII, XI, XII, XIII. Bircham Newton Nov 40, Limavady May 41, Reykjavik Sep 41, Docking Dec 41, LG 39 Jan 42, LG 87 Feb 42, LG 89 Mar 42, Shandur Jun 42, Shallufa Satellite Aug 42, Shallufa Aug 42, Luqa Jan 43, Grottaglie Feb 44, Kalamaki/Hassani Oct 44, Idku Apr 45. Disbanded Aug 45

244 Mk.XIII. Sharjah Feb 44, Masirah Mar 44. Disbanded May 45

294 Mk.IC, XI, XIII. Rescue sqn, Berka Sep 43, LG 91 Oct 43, Idku Mar 44, Basrah Jun 45. Disbanded Apr 46

304 (2) Polish. Mk.IC, X, XIII, XIV. Lindholme Apr 42, Tiree May 42, Dale Jun 42, Talbenny Nov 42, Dale Dec 42, Docking Apr 43, Davidstow Moor Jun 43, Predannack Dec 43, Chivenor Feb 44, Benbecula Sep 44, St.Eval Mar 45. To Transport Command Jul 45

311 (KX) Polish. Mk.IC. Aldergrove Apr 42, Talbenny Jun 42, Beaulieu May 43. Liberator Jun 43

344 French. Mk.XI, XIII. Dakar Nov 43. Disbanded to French control Nov 45

407 (1, 2) RCAF. Mk.XI, XII, XIV. Docking Jan 43, Skitten Feb 43, Chivenor Apr 43, St.Eval Nov 43, Chivenor Dec 43, Limavady Jan 44, Chivenor Apr 44, Wick Aug 44, Chivenor Nov 44. Disbanded Jun 45

415 (NH) RCAF. Mk.XIII. Thorney Island Sep 43, Bircham Newton Nov 43, East Moor Jul 44. Halifax Jul 44

458 (MD) RAAF. Mk.IC, VIII, XIII, XIV. Shallufa Sep 42, LG 91 Mar 43, Protville Jun 43, Bone Oct 43, Alghero May 44, Foggia Sep 44, Gibraltar Jan 45. Disbanded Jun 45

524 (7R) Mk.XIII, XIV. Davidstow Moor Apr 44, Docking Jul 44, Bircham Newton Jul 44, Langham Oct 44. Disbanded May 45

547 Mk.VIII, XI, XIII. Holmsley South Oct 42, Chivenor Dec 42, Tain Jan 43, Chivenor Apr 43, Davidstow Moor May 43, Thorney Island Oct 43, Aldergrove Oct 43. Liberator Nov 43

612 (8W, WL, 3) Mk.VIII, XIII, XIV. Wick Nov 42, Davidstow Moor Apr 43, Chivenor May 43, St.Eval Nov 43, Chivenor Dec 43, Limavady Jan 44, Chivenor Mar 44, Limavady Sep 44, Langham Dec 44. Disbanded Jul 45

621 Mk.XIII, XIV. Port Reitz Sep 43, Mogadishu Nov 43, Khormaksar Dec 43, Mersa Matruh Nov 45. Warwick Dec 45

Radar Reconnaissance Squadrons

162 Mk.IC, III, DWI (with other types). Kabrit Jan 42, Shallufa Jan 42, Bilbeis Apr 42,

	Benina Apr 43, LG 91 Aug 43, Idku Apr 44. Disbanded Sep 44

Night Reconnaissance Squadrons

69	Mk.IC, VIII. Luqa May 42-Feb 43. Mk.XIII Assigned to 2nd TAF No.34 Reconnaissance Wing. Northolt May 44, A 12/Balleroy Sep 44, B 48/Amiens/Glisy Sep 44, B 58/Melsbroek Sep 44, B 78/Eindhoven Apr 45. Disbanded Aug 45
544	Mk.IV. Benson Oct 42-Mar 43 (with other types)

Transport Command Squadrons

24 (NQ, ZK)	Mk.IA, XVI. Hendon Feb 43. Wellingtons left Jan 44
232	Mk.XVI. Stoney Cross Dec 44. Liberator Feb 45
242	Mk.XVI. Stoney Cross Jan 45. Stirling Feb 45
304 (QD)	Polish. Mk.XIV. North Weald Jul 45, Chedburgh Sep 45. Warwick from Jul 45, last Wellington left Jan 46

Other Squadrons

138	Mk.DWI. Stradishall, Tempsford. A squadron operating for the Special Operations Executive (SOE) had a single DWI Wellington, later passed on to 161 Squadron
141	Mk.XVIII. Fiskerton Feb 45. This Mosquito VI fighter unit operated a single Wellington on loan from 1692 Flight for a short period
161	Mk.DWI. Tempsford. See 138 Squadron above
169	Mk.XVIII. Great Massingham 45. This Mosquito VI fighter unit operated a single Wellington on loan from 1692 Flight for a short period

Operational Training Units

Note: The many satellite airfields used by OTUs to relieve congestion at their main station are not shown

1 (Coastal)	Mk.IC, VIII. Silloth Nov 40. Wellingtons left Jul 41
3 (Coastal) (4J)	Mk.IA, IC, III, VIII. Silloth/Kirkbride, Cranwell Jul 41. Haverfordwest Jun 43. Disbanded Jan 44
5	Mk.XIII, XIV. Turnberry May 44. Disbanded Aug 45
6 (K7, OD)	Mk.IC, III, VIII, IX, XI, XII, XIII, XIV. Thornaby Oct 42. Silloth Mar 43. Kinloss Jul 45
7	Mk.IC, VIII, X, XI, XIII. Limavady Apr 42. Haverfordwest Jan 44. Disbanded May 44
10 (RK, UY, ZG)	Mk.X. Stanton Harcourt Jun 44. Abingdon Nov 44. Disbanded Sep 46
11 (KJ, LG, OP, TX)	Mk.I, III, X. Bassingbourn Apr 40. Westcott Oct 42. Disbanded Sep 45
12 (FQ, JP, ML)	Mk.IC, III, X. Benson Nov 40. Chipping Warden Aug 41. Disbanded Jun 45
14 (AM, GL, VB)	Mk.IC, III, X. Cottesmore Sep 42. Market Harborough Aug 43. Disbanded Jun 45
15 (EO, FH, HR, KK)	Mk.IA, IC, II, III, X, XVIII. Harwell Apr 40. Mount Farm Jul 41. Harwell Feb 42. Disbanded Mar 44
16 (GA, JS, XG)	Mk.IC, III, X. Upper Heyford Apr 42. Barford St.John Mar 42. Upper Heyford Dec 42. Disbanded Jan 45
17 (AY, JG, WJ)	Mk.IC, II, X. Silverstone Apr 43. Became 201 AFS Mar 47
18 (EN, VQ, XW)	Mk.I, III, IV, X. Bramcote Nov 40. Finningley Mar 43. Disbanded Jan 45
19 (UO)	Mk.III, X. Kinloss Aug 44. Disbanded Jun 45
20 (AI, HJ, JM, XL, YR, ZT)	Mk.IA, IC, III, X, XIV. Lossiemouth May 40. Disbanded Jul 45
21 (ED, SJ)	Mk.IC, III, X. Moreton-in-Marsh Jan 41. Finningley Nov 46. Became 202 AFS Mar 47
22 (DD, LT, OX, XN)	Mk.IC, III, X. Wellesbourne Mountford Apr 41. Disbanded Jul 45
23 (BY, FZ)	Mk.IC, III, X. Pershore Apr 41. Disbanded Mar 44. Code WE may also have been used
24 (FB, TY, UF)	Mk.III, X. Honeybourne Apr 44. Disbanded Jul 45
25 (PP, ZP)	Mk.IC, III, X. Finningley May 41. Disbanded Feb 43
26 (EU, PB, WG)	Mk.IC, III, X. Wing Jan 42. Disbanded Mar 46
27 (BB, UJ)	Mk.IC, III, X. Lichfield Apr 41. Disbanded Jun 45
28 (LB, WY)	Mk.IC, III, X. Wymeswold May 42. Ossington Jun 43. Wymeswold Jun 43. Disbanded Oct 44
29 (NT, TF)	Mk.III, X, XIII. North Luffenham Apr 42. Bruntingthorpe May 43. Disbanded May 45
30 (BT, KD, TN)	Mk.IC, III, X. Hixon Jun 42. Gamston Feb 45. Disbanded Jun 45
51	Mk.XI, XVII, XVIII. Cranfield Mar 44. Disbanded Jun 45. Codes BD, PF may have been used
54 (ST)	Mk.X, XI, XVII, XVIII. Charterhall Mar 44. East Moor Nov 45. Leeming Jun 46. Became 228 OCU May 47. Codes BF, LX, ST, YX may have been used
62	Mk.XVII, XVIII. Ouston Mar 45. Disbanded Jun 45

63 Mk.XI, XVII. Honiley Sep 43. Disbanded Mar 44. Code HI may have been used
75 Mk.XIV. Gianaclis Dec 42. Shallufa Feb 45. Disbanded Jun 45
76 Mk.IC, III, X. Aqir Oct 43. Disbanded Jul 45
77 Mk.IC, III, VIII, X, XIV. Qastina Jan 44. Disbanded Jul 45. Code AX may have been used
78 Mk.III, VIII, X, XII, XIII, XIV. Ein Shemer Jan 44. Disbanded Jul 45
81 (EZ, KG) Mk.X. Sleap Nov 44. Became 1380 (Transport) CU Aug 45
82 (9C, BZ, KA, TD) Mk.III, X. Ossington Jun 43. Disbanded Jan 45
83 (GS, MZ) Mk.III, X. Peplow Aug 43. Disbanded Oct 44
84 (IF) Mk.III, X. Desborough Sep 43. Disbanded Jun 45
85 (9P) Mk.III, X. Husbands Bosworth Jun 44. Disbanded Jun 45
86 (Y7) Mk.III, X. Gamston Jun 44. Disbanded Oct 44
104 (Transport) Mk.IV. Nutts Corner Mar 43. Disbanded Feb 44
105 (Transport) (7Z, 8F) Mk.IC, X. Bramcote Apr 43. Dakota Apr 44. Became 1381 CU Aug 45
107 (Transport) (CM) Mk.III. Leicester East May 44. Became 1333 CU Mar 45
111 (Coastal) (X3) Mk.XIII, XIV. Lossiemouth Aug 45. Disbanded May 46

Air Gunners Schools

1 Mk.III,X. Fulbeck Nov 44. Disbanded Jun 45
2 Mk.III,X. Dalcross Nov 44. Disbanded Nov 45
3 Mk.III,X. Castle Kennedy Oct 44. Disbanded Jun 45
10 (FFA, FFD) Mk.III,X. Barrow May 45. Disbanded Jun 46
11 (FFF) Mk.III,X,XIV. Andreas Nov 44. Jurby Sep 46. Disbanded Oct 47
12 Mk.X. Bishops Court Nov 44. Disbanded May 45
Air Gunnery & Bombing School Mk.X. El Ballah 45
I Air Gunnery School (India) Mk.IC. Bairagarh (Bhopal)

Air Navigation Schools

1 (FFJ, FFK) T Mk.X. Topcliffe Apr 47. Hullavington Jul 49. Disbanded May 54
2 (FFO) T Mk.X. Bishops Court Jun 47. Middleton St.George Oct 47. Thorney Island May 50.
5 (FFJ, FFK) T Mk.X. Jurby May 45. Topcliffe Sep 46. Became 1 ANS Apr 47. Reformed Lindholme Mar 51. Disbanded Nov 52
6 T Mk.X. Lichfield Feb 52. Disbanded Dec 53
7 (FFO) T Mk.X. Bishops Court May 45. Became 2 ANS Jun 47
10 (FFS) T Mk.X. Dumfries Jun 45. Chipping Warden Jul 45. Swanton Morley Dec 45. Driffield Sep 46. Disbanded Mar 48
Air Navigation School Mk unknown. Willingdon
Air Navigation & Bombing School Mk.III,X. Jurby Jan 45. Became 5 ANS May 45

Other Units

Aden Communication Flight Mk.IC,X. Khormaksar
Advanced Bombing & Gunnery School (Middle East) Mk.X. El Ballah
201 Advanced Flying School (FMA, FMB) T Mk.X. Swinderby Mar 47. Varsity Oct 51
202 Advanced Flying School (UH, FME) T Mk.X. Finningley Mar 47. Disbanded Dec 47
1 Air Armament School Mk.I,X,XIII. Manby Jun 41. Disbanded Oct 44
Airborne Forces Experimental Establishment Mk.IC,III,IX,X. Sherburn-in-Elmet
Airborne Forces Tactical Development Unit Mk.X. Tarrant Rushton Dec 43 Became ATTDU Jan 44
Airborne Transport Tactical Development Unit (ATTDU) Mk.X. Netheravon Jan 44. Became Transport Command Development Unit Aug 45
Aircraft Gun Mounting Establishment Mk.II, Duxford Dec 41-Jan 42
Aircraft Torpedo Development Unit Mk.XVIII. Gosport
Aircrew Transit Pool Mk unknown. Poona
Air Fighting Training Unit Mk.IC. Amarda Road
Air Headquarters Eastern Mediterranean Communication Flight Mk.IC, XI. Mariut
Air Headquarters Greece Communication Flight Mk.X Kalamaki/Hassani
Air Headquarters Italy Communication Squadron Mk unknown. Marcianise
Air Headquarters Levant Communication Flight Mk.IC. Lydda
Air Headquarters Malta Communication Flight Mk.VIII, X. Hal Far

Air Headquarters Middle East Communication Flight Mk.IC. Heliopolis
Air Photographic Development Unit Mk.X. Benson
Air Sea Rescue & Communication Flight Mk.IC,VIII,X. Hal Far, Takali
1 (North Africa) Air Sea Rescue Unit Mk.IC. Sidi Ahmed Jun 43, Protville Aug 43. Disbanded Dec 43
Air-Sea Warfare Development Unit (P9) Mk.XIV. Thorney Island Jan 45
Air-Sea Warfare Development Unit (ACSEA) Mk.XIII. Ratmalana
Air Transport Auxiliary Mk.IA ambulance. White Waltham
Air Transport Auxiliary Advanced Flying Training School Mk.I. White Waltham
26 Anti-Aircraft Co-Operation Unit Mk.X. El Firdan
21 Armament Practice Camp Mk.IC. St.Thomas Mount, Yelahanka, Cholavarum
ASV Training Flight/Unit Mk.XII,XIII,XIV. Chivenor
Balkan Air Force Communication Flight Mk.X Blida 1945
2/1502 Blind/Beam Approach Training Flight Mk.I. Driffield
3/1503 Blind/Beam Approach Training Flight Mk.I,IA,IC. Mildenhall Dec 40. Holme-on-Spalding Moor Sep 42. Lindholme Jan 43
4/1504 Blind/Beam Approach Training Flight Mk.I,IA,IC. Wyton Dec 40. Graveley Aug 42. Honington Aug 42
5/1505 Blind/Beam Approach Training Flight Mk.I,IA,IC. Honington Dec 40. Mildenhall Sep 42
8/1508 Blind/Beam Approach Training Flight Mk.IC. Wattisham Dec 40. Ipswich Feb 41. Watton Dec 41
9/1509 Blind/Beam Approach Training Flight Mk.I,IC.XI. Thornaby Dec 40. Dyce Jul 41
10/1510 Blind/Beam Approach Training Flight Mk.I,IC. Leuchars Dec 40
Bomber Command Instructors' School (ZQ) Mk.III,X. Finningley Dec 44
1688 (Bomber) Defence Training Flight (6H) Mk.X. Feltwell, Wyton
1690 (Bomber) Defence Training Flight (9M) Mk.X. Syerston
Bomber Development Unit Mk.IC. Boscombe Down Nov 40. Disbanded May 41
2 British Airways Repair Unit (Middle East) Mk.II,III. Heliopolis
Centaurus Flight Mk.II, X Filton 1943 for test-bed trials of Bristol Centaurus engines
Central Fighter Establishment Mk.X,XIII,XIV,XVIII. Wittering, Tangmere, West Raynham
Central Gunnery School (VD, FJS) Mk.I,IA,IC,III,X,T Mk.X,XIII. Warmwell, Castle Kennedy, Chelveston, Sutton Bridge, Catfoss, Leconfield
Central Navigation School (FGE post-war) Mk.VIII,X,XII,XIII,XIV,T Mk.X. Cranage, Shawbury
Central Navigation & Control School (FGE) T Mk.X. Shawbury
Central Signals Establishment (4S,V7) Mk.X. Watton
Coastal Command Development Unit Mk.IC,VIII,XI,XII,XIII,XIV. Dale, Angle
Coastal Command Flying Instructors' School Mk.X. St.Angelo, Turnberry, Tain
Coastal Command Preparation Pool Probably Mk.XIII or XIV. Bircham Newton
1 (Coastal) Engine Control Demonstration Unit Mk.XIII. Longtown, Great Orton, Aldergrove, Angle
Communication Flight Iraq and Persia Mk.III,X,XIII,XIV. Habbaniya
Communication Flight Khartoum Mk.VIII,X,XIII. Khartoum
1331 Conversion Unit Mk.XVI Mauripur, Risalpur
1380 Conversion Unit (EZ) Mk.X. Tilstock
1381 (Transport) Conversion Unit (7Z) Mk.X. Bramcote
Czechoslovak Flight Mk.IC,VIII. Thornaby
Empire Air Armament School (FGB post-war) T Mk.X,GR.13,GR.14. Manby
Empire Air Navigation School (FGE post-war). T Mk.X,GR.13. Shawbury
Empire Central Flying School Mk.III,X. Hullavington
Empire Flying School (FCT to FCX) T Mk.X. Hullavington
Empire Test Pilots' School Mk.III Boscombe Down Jul 44-Oct 45
1 Engine Consumption Unit Mk.III. Weybridge, Mildenhall
1 Engine Control & Demonstration Unit Mk.II,III,X. Bassingbourn, Westcott
Engine Control Instructional Flight Probably Mk.XIII or XIV. Thorney Island, Harwell
21 Ferry Control Mk.IC. Mauripur
22 Ferry Control Mk.X. Allahabad (Bamhrauli)
1 Ferry Crew Pool Mk.III. Lyneham, Melton Mowbray
4 Ferry Pilots Pool Mk.IC Prestwick
5 Ferry Pilots Pool Mk.XVI Hatfield, Luton
3 Ferry Pool (U5 Lichfield only) Mk.XIV. Lichfield, Polebrook, Henlow
Ferry Training Unit Mk not known. Honeybourne

301 Ferry Training Unit Mk.IC. Lyneham
303 Ferry Training Unit Mk.IA,IC,VIII,X,XIII,XIV,XV,XVI. Stornoway, Talbenny
304 Ferry Training Unit Mk.IC, X,XI,XIII. Melton Mowbray Jan 44. Disbanded Oct 44
307 Ferry Training Unit Mk.XIII. Melton Mowbray. Became 304 FTU Jan 44
310 Ferry Training Unit Mk.II,X. Harwell
311 Ferry Training Unit Mk.I,III,X. Moreton-in-Marsh
312 Ferry Training Unit Mk not known. Wellesbourne Mountford
3 Ferry Unit Mk.XIII. Oujda, Blida
8 Ferry Unit Mk.IA. Mauripur
11 Ferry Unit Mk.X,XIII. Talbenny, Dunkeswell
12 Ferry Unit Mk.X. Melton Mowbray Oct 44
Fighter Interception Development Unit/Sqn (ZQ) Mk.XIII. Ford, Sep 44. Tangmere, West Raynham
3 Film Production Unit Mk.X. Calcutta, Alipore
1302 Meteorological Flight Mk.IC. St.Thomas Mount 44
1417 (Leigh Light Trials) Flight Mk.I,IC,VIII. Chivenor
1418 Flight (GEE Development Unit) Mk.IC,III. Marham, Tempsford, Gransden Lodge
1420 Flight Mk.I,IC. Christchurch, Middle Wallop
1422 (Night Fighter) Flight Mk not known. Heston
1425 (Communication) Flight Mk.IA,IC. Prestwick, Lyneham
1429 (Czech) Operational Training Unit/Flight (KV) Mk.IC,IV,VIII. East Wretham, Woolfox Lodge, Church Broughton, Thornaby
1443 (Ferry Training) Flight Mk.IC,II,VIII. Harwell
1446 (Ferry Training) Flight Mk.I,IA,IC,II,III. Bassingbourn, Moreton-in Marsh
1473 (RCM) Flight (ZP) Mk.IC,III,X. Feltwell, Little Snoring, Foulsham
1474 (Special Duties) Flight Mk.IC,III,X. Stradishall, Gransden Lodge
1481 (Bombing) Gunnery Flight Mk.IA,IC,III,IV,X. Lindholme, Binbrook, Ingham
1483 (Target Towing) Flight Mk.IA,IC,III,X. Newmarket, Marham, Newmarket
1485 (Target Towing/[Bomber] Gunnery) Flight Mk.IA,III,X. Coningsby, Dunholme Lodge, Fulbeck, Skellingthorpe, Syerston
1572 (Ground Gunnery) Flight Mk.IC. St.Thomas Mount Jul 43. Became 21 APC Jan 44
1577 (Glider Development) Flight Mk.X. Mauripur, Chaklala
1680 (Western Isles Communications/Transport) Flight Mk.I. Abbotsinch, Prestwick
1689 (Ferry Pilot Training) Flight (9X) Mk.X. Aston Down
1692 (Bomber Support Training) Flight (4X) T.Mk.XVIII. Great Massingham Dec 44
7 Flying Instructors' School Mk not known. Upavon
11 Flying Instructors' School Mk.X. Shallufa, El Ballah, Deversoir
12 (Operational) Flying Instructors' School Mk.X. St.Angelo
Flying Refresher School T Mk.X. Finningley Jun 49. Became 101 FRS Apr 51
101 Flying Refresher School (O) T Mk.X. Finningley Apr 51. Disbanded Feb 52
104 Flying Refresher School (U) T Mk.X. Lichfield Jul 51. Disbanded Feb 52
2 French Technical Liaison Unit Mk.X, XIII, XIV. Blida Jun 44. Disbanded Jul 45
General Reconnaissance Aircraft Preparation Pool Mk.XIV. Haverfordwest May 44. St.Davids Oct 44. Disbanded Jan 46
1 General Reconnaissance Unit DWI. Manston Dec 39. Combined with 2 GRU Mar 40. Ismailia May 40. Disbanded Mar 44
2 General Reconnaissance Unit DWI. Bircham Newton Mar 40. Combined with 1 GRU May 40
3 General Reconnaissance Unit DWI. Manston Apr 40. Thorney Island May 40. Disbanded Jul 40
38 Group Communication Flight (5N) Mk.X. Netheravon, Upavon
60 Group Communication Flight Mk.X, XIII. Halton Dec 44. Wing Jan 45
87 Group Communication Flight (P8) Mk.XV, XVI. Buc May 45, Le Bourget, Buc
92 Group Communication Flight Mk.X. Bicester, Little Horwood
205 Group Communication Flight Mk.X. LG 20, Bardia, Ismailia, Birel Gardabia, Kairouan, El Aouina, Bari, Tortorella, Foggia Main, Kasfareet, Fayid
216 Group Communication Flight Mk.X. Heliopolis
218 Group Communication Flight Mk.X. Hussein Dey, Maison Blanche
224 Group Communication Flight Mk.III. Willingdon, Dum Dum, Cox's Bazaar, Akyab, Chittagong, Maunubyin, Comilla, Yelahanka, Baigachi, Kalemang, Kallang

2 Group Disbandment Centre Mk.XIII. Fersfield Aug 45. Disbanded Dec 45
92 Group Instructors' Course/School/Flight Mk.II, X. Upper Heyford Dec 42. Silverstone Mar 44.Disbanded Jul 45
60 Group Radar Navigation Aids Test Flight Mk.X. Wing Feb 45. Disbanded Oct 45
93 Group Screened Pilots' School Mk.X. Church Broughton May 43. Leicester East Apr 44. Disbanded Oct 44
93 Group Servicing Section/Flight Mk.X. Church Broughton Dec 42. Disbanded Oct 44
5 Group Target Towing Flight Mk.IA, IC. Driffield
3 Group Training Flight Mk.IC. Stradishall Feb 41. Newmarket May 41. Disbanded Feb 42
5 Group Training Flight Mk.I. Finningley, Coningsby, Scampton
205 Group Training Flight Mk.IC, III. Shallufa Feb 42. Disbanded Apr 42
Gunnery Research Unit (HP) Mk.I, III, X. Exeter Jun 40. Collyweston Apr 44. Disbanded Mar 45
Handling Flight/Squadron Mks unknown. Upavon. Boscombe Down Nov 40. Hullavington Aug 42
Headquarters RAF Austria Communication Flight Mk.X. Klagenfurt
1 Heavy Glider Maintenance Unit Mk.X. Netheravon. Reported use not mentioned in ORB
Hemswell Station Flight T Mk.10 Apr-Oct 54
High Altitude Flight (A&AEE) Mk.V, VI. Boscombe Down
18 Maintenance Unit (W6) Mk.XVI. Dumfries
30 Maintenance Unit Mk.IC. Sealand
46 Maintenance Unit Mk.IA. Lossiemouth
Marine Aircraft Experimental Establishment Mk.III. The unit was based at Felixstowe which had no provision for landplanes, so its Wellington was probably kept at Martlesham Heath
Mediterranean Allied Coastal Air Forces Communication Flight Mk.XIII. Blida, Réghaia, Pomigliano, Marcianise
Mediterranean and Middle East Communication Squadron Mk.X. Maison Blanche, El Aouina, Capodichino, Marcianise
Metropolitan Communication Squadron (ZA) Mk.X. Hendon
Middle East Communication Squadron Mk.III, X. Heliopolis
1 Middle East Training School Mk.VIII. El Ballah, Muqeibila, El Ballah
2 Middle East Training School Mk.IC, II, III. Kabrit May 42. Aqir Aug 42. Disbanded Jun 43
3 Middle East Training School Mk.IC. Amman
4 Middle East Training School Mk.IC. Kabrit May 42. Ramat David Mar 43. Disbanded Apr 44
5 Middle East Training School Mk.IC, VIII. Shallufa May 42. Wellingtons left Nov 43
2 (Middle East) Ferry Control Mk.I. Wadi Seidna
Mk.X (AI) Conversion Flight Mk.X, XVIII. Pomigliano Sep, Baigachi Mar 45. Disbanded Nov 45
New Zealand Flight Mk.I, IA. Marham Jun 39. Hemswell Sep 39. Stradishall Jan 40. Feltwell Feb 40. Became 75 (NZ) Squadron Apr 40
Night Fighter Leaders School (ZQ) GR.18. West Raynham Oct 45
1 (North Africa) Air Sea Rescue Flight Mk.IC, X, XIII. Sidi Ahmed, Protville, Blida 1943
2 Officers Advanced Training School Mk.X. Hal Far Nov 44. Amman Feb 46. Disbanded Sep 46
228 Operational Conversion Unit (ST) T Mk.XVIII. Leeming May 47
Overseas Aircraft Despatch Unit Mk.IC. Kemble, Portreath 41-42. Became 1 OADU
1 Overseas Aircraft Despatch Unit Mk.XV, XVI. Portreath Jan 42. Disbanded Oct 45
1 Parachute Training School Mk.X, XI. Ringway Feb 45. Upper Heyford Mar 46. Code 7M may have been used
4 Parachute Training School Mk.X. Gioia del Colle May 44. Disbanded Apr 45
Photographic Reconnaissance Development Unit Mk.X. Benson
Photographic Reconnaissance Unit Mk.I. Heston
3 Photographic Reconnaissance Unit (LY) Mk.IC. Oakington Oct 40 with other types. Last Wellington left Apr 41 by which time it was 1 PRU
1 (Pilot) Refresher Flying Unit (FDB) T Mk.X. Moreton-in-Marsh Aug 47. Finningley Jan 48. Became Flying Refresher School Jun 49
15 (Pilots) Advanced Flying Unit Mk.IV. Babdown Farm
20 (Pilots) Advanced Flying Unit Mk.IV. Kidlington
Polish Flight Mk.IC, III, VIII, X, XI. Thornaby Oct 42 Haverfordwest Oct 43. Became part of 6 (C)OTU Silloth Jan 44
1 Radar Training Flight Mk.XIV. Chivenor May 44 disbanded 20 Jun 45
Radio Warfare Establishment Mk.X. Swanton Morley, Watton
3 Refresher Flying Unit Mk.IC, II, X. Poona Feb 44. Bairagarh Sep 45
4 Refresher Flying Unit Mk.III, X, XI, XIII, XIV. Haverfordwest May 44. Mullaghmore Sep 44. Disbanded Oct 44
108 Repair and Salvage Unit Mk.XV, XVI. Bone Oct 42, then multiple moves, disbanded Miramas Feb 46

Royal Air Force Bengal/Burma Communication Squadron Mk.III, XIII. Baigachi
Royal Air Force College Mk.IA Cranwell
Royal Air Force Flying College (FGB, FGE) T Mk.X, GR.14. Manby Jun 49
Royal Air Force Training Delegation (France) Communication Flight Mk and location unknown
2 School of General Reconnaissance Mk.IC. Squires Gate May 40
Sea Rescue Flight/Unit Mk.IC. Kabrit Aug 41. Burg El Arab Sep 41. El Adem Jan 42. Gambut Jan 42. Fuka Feb 42. Abu Sueir Jul 42. Burg El Arab Nov 42. Berka Mar 43. Became 294 Sqn Sep 43
Signals Development Unit Mk.XIII. Hinton-in-the-Hedges
Signals Flying Unit (7N, 9T) Mk.XIII, XIV. Honiley Jul 44. Disbanded Sep 46
Signals Squadron Mk.IC. Kabrit Jan 42. Redesignated 162 Sqn Mar 42
Special Duties Flight Mk unknown. Boscombe Down
Special Duty Flight Mk.I, VIII. St.Athan, Christchurch
Special Signals Flight Mk unknown. Shallufa Jul 41 to at least Dec 41
Staff Pilot Training Unit Mk.X. Cark
Station Flight Chivenor Mk.XIII, XIV
Station Flight Christchurch Mk.II
Station Flight Finningley Mk.X
Station Flight Hemswell T Mk.X
Station Flight Khormaksar Mk.IC
Station Flight Kunming Mk.X
Station Flight Netheravon Mk.III
Station Flight Northolt Mk unknown
Station Flight St.Mawgan Mk.X
Station Flight Stradishall Mk.IC
2nd Tactical Air Force Communication Flight/Squadron/Wing Mk.III. Northolt, then various bases on the Continent
Tactical Air Force (Burma) Communication Squadron/3rd Tactical Air Force Communication Squadron. Mk.III, X, XIII. Comilla
Technical Training Command Communication Flight Mk.III. White Waltham, Wyton
Telecommunications Flying Unit Mk.IC, III, VI, IX, XI, XII, XIV, T Mk.XVII. Defford
Test Pilots' School Mk.III Boscombe Down Feb 44 Part of A&AEE. Became Empire Test Pilots' School Jul 44
Torpedo Development Unit Mk.IC. Gosport
Torpedo Training Flight Mk.VIIITB. Limavady Mar 43. Absorbed into 1 TTU Mar 43
Torpedo Training Unit Mk.VIII. Abbotsinch, Turnberry
1 Torpedo Training Unit Mk.VIII, IX. Turnberry Mar 43. Wellingtons left Sep 43
1380 Transport Conversion Unit (EZ, KG) Mk.X. Sleap Aug 45
1381 Transport Conversion Unit (7Z, I5) Mk.X. Bramcote Aug 45
Wellington Attachment Mk.IC Luqa Oct 40
Wellington Conversion Flight Mk unknown. Cranfield
Wellington Development Flight (attached to 99 Squadron) Mk.IA, IC. Mildenhall, Newmarket
235 Wing Mk.VIII. Benghazi and various other North African stations
247 Wing Communication Flight Mk.IC. Gianaclis, Berka
334 Wing Communication Flight Mk.XIII. Castel Benito, Brindisi, Foggia Main, Gainaclis
34 Wing Support Unit Mk.XIII. Northolt Jul 44. Blackbushe Oct 44. Mount Farm Jul 45. Disbanded Aug 45
Wireless (Intelligence) Development Unit Mk.IC Boscombe Down Oct 40. Became 109 Sqn Dec 40

Maintenance Units

There were many RAF maintenance units (MU) that included Wellingtons in the aircraft types for which they were responsible for repair and overhaul, and/or storage, including:

4	Ruislip	30	Sealand
5	Kemble	32	St.Athan
8	Little Rissington	33	Lyneham
10	Hullavington	37	Burtonwood
13	Henlow	38	Llandow
18	Dumfries	44	Edzell
20	Aston Down	45	Kinloss
23	Aldergrove	46	Lossiemouth
24	Stoke Heath, Ternhill	48	Hawarden

51	Lichfield	168	Heliopolis
60	Church Fenton	273	Polebrook

Government units
Aeroplane & Armament Experimental Establishment. All Mks. Boscombe Down
National Gas Turbine Establishment. Mk.II/IV Bruntingthorpe, later Bitteswell
Research Department Flight (part of RAE, unofficially known as Balloon Barrage Flight)
Royal Aircraft Establishment. Farnborough

Fleet Air Arm
Total of 24 aircraft; 2 Mk.I, 3 Mk.II, 4 Mk.X, 10 Mk.XI, 5 T.XVII
Squadrons

716	Mk.XI. Eastleigh Jul 44 with other types. Disbanded Sep 45
758	Mk.XI. Hinstock Sep 43 with other types. Last Wellington left Dec 43
762 (P1)	Mk.XI. Dale Aug 44 with other types. Last Wellington left Apr 45
765 (L8)	Mk.X, XI. Lee-on-Solent Aug 44 with other types. Hal Far Oct 45. Disbanded Apr 46
778	Mk.II. Crail Oct 43 with other types
782	Mk.I. Donibristle Dec 42
783	Mk.I, II. Arbroath Feb 44. Last Wellington left Jun 45

Other units
RN Air Section Mk.XI. Eastleigh May 44
Station Flight (Y9) Mk.XI. Yeovilton Feb 45. Last Wellington left Dec 45
TFU (RN Section) Mk.II, XI. Defford Dec 43 to at least Nov 45

French Air Force – L'Armée de l'Air
Total of 185 aircraft have been identified as being handed over to France, all but a few initially to the air force. Most were later passed to the Aeronavale

69 Mk.X HZ120, HZ941, JA526, JA529, LN374, LN383, LP469, LP704, LP750, LP809, MF119, MF131, MF348, MF368, MF369, MF372, MF404, MF422, MF453, MF456, MF459, MF470, MF474, MF677, MF733, MF734, NA710, NA770, NA925, NA926, NA927, NA934, NA956, NA970, NA984, NA985, NA986, NB796, NB812, NB826, NB876, NB913, NB919, NB927, NB942, NB943, NB947, NB971, NB975, NB977, NB980, NB983, NB998, NC122, NC123, NC124, NC421, NC517, NC545, NC564, NC566, NC567, NC864, NC922, NC923, PG181, PG290, PG291, PG316

8 Mk.XI HZ143, HZ420, HZ538, HZ539, MP691, MP695, MP696, MP698

80 Mk.XIII HZ585, HZ588, HZ595, HZ597, HZ691, HZ696, HZ697, HZ704, HZ710, HZ770, HZ806, HZ816, HZ881, HZ891, JA272, JA302, JA391, JA404, JA416, JA419, JA562, JA567, JA568, JA578, MF170, MF187, MF251, MF266, MF279, MF293, MF297, MF298, MF304, MF320, MF344, MF355, MF362, MF365, MF409, MF411, MF416, MF418, MF448, MF493, MF495, MF573, MF578, MF580, MF582, MF619, MF659, MF688, MF691, MF694, MF707, MF708, MF741, MF742, MP709, MP711, MP747, MP751, MP761, MP770, MP771, NC414, NC415, NC416, NC417, NC434, NC435, NC436, NC437, NC438, NC454, NC455, NC456, NC457, NC483, NC504

13 Mk.XIV MP741, MP756, MP774, MP807, MP818, MP825, NC492, NC647, PF837, PF996, PF997, PG183, PG230

Groupe de Reconnaissance Maritime 'Artois' Mk. Feb 43 Pointe-Noire, with Ansons

French Navy – Aeronavale
Mk.X, XI, XIII, XIV see above

CEPA 10S	St.Raphael 47
Escadrille 1S	Lanvéoc-Poulmic 44
Escadrille 10S	Hyères 45
Flotille 2FB	Mk.XIII, XIV. Formed from 344 Sqn RAF Nov 45. Dakar-Ouakam (Sénégal). Port Lyautey Jun 50. Wellingtons left 52. Constituent units were:
Escadrille 51S	Mk.XIII or XIV. Khouribga
Escadrille 52S	Mk.XIII or XIV. Lartigue Oct 48. Agadir 51
Escadrille 55S	Mk.X. Goeland, Port Lyautey, Agadir 50. Lancaster 52
Escadrille 56S	Mk.XIII or XIV. Agadir. Lancaster 52. Last unit to operate Wellingtons, possibly until 1955

L'Ecole du Personnel Volant (EPV) Thiersville Oct 44

Royal Hellenic Air Force

A total of at least 19 aircraft were handed over from RAF stocks between November 1944 and April 1946 including 16 Mk.XIII and a small number of Mk.X, the last being withdrawn from use in 1947. Mk.XIIIs identified are: HZ981, JA392, JA582, ME890, ME907, ME940, MF181, MF183, MF188, MF190, MF206, MF254, MF466, MF643, NC418, NC433

Squadrons

13	Mk.XIII, T Mk.10. Hassani Nov 44, with Baltimores. Renumbered 355 Squadron
355	Mk.XIII. Renumbered from 13 Squadron. Replaced by C-47 from Oct 46

Luftwaffe

At least three and perhaps as many as seven Wellingtons force landed in enemy territory were repaired for test-flying, primarily at 2/V.OKl at Rechlin. Known aircraft include:

Mk.IC L7788 KX-E 311 (Czech) Squadron force landed in Holland during op to Berlin 24 Sep 40; Flt Lt K Trojacek and crew taken prisoner. Tested at Rechlin from Nov 40 carrying the code 5-1

Mk.IC L7842 KX-T 311 (Czech) Squadron missing from a raid to Boulogne 7 Feb 41; Plt Off F Cigos and crew taken prisoner. Tested at Rechlin

Mk.IC T2501 LN-F 99 Squadron shot down by flak near Vitry-en-Artois returning from Dusseldorf 4 Dec 40; Fg Off F H Vivian and crew taken prisoner. Tested at Rechlin carrying the code 5-4

Mk.IC R1379 115 Squadron shot down by a night fighter flown by Lt Eckhart-Wilhelm von Bonin of II./NJG 1 near Tonning, Germany returning from Hamburg 10 May 41; Pilot Sgt J Anderson killed, remainder of the crew taken prisoner

Others quoted as captured include aircraft from the following squadrons:
15 Squadron LS-A
101 Squadron SR-P

Royal New Zealand Air Force

30 Mk.I aircraft ordered, first 18 comprising Mk.I NZ300-NZ305 and Mk.IA NZ306-NZ317. Six received prior to 3 September 1939, after which they and the remainder of the batch reverted to RAF serials for service initially with 75(NZ) Squadron. Balance of order diverted to RAF

Portuguese Air Force

Reports persist that the Portuguese air force may have operated a Wellington Mk.X interned when it landed on their territory. A candidate aircraft has not been identified, but is probably one that landed near Cape St.Vincent in April 1943 while en route to the Mediterranean

South African Air Force

Total of 48 known aircraft; 4 Mk.IC including Z8783, 3 Mk.X HE708, HE711, LN374,, 26 Mk.XI HZ299, HZ522, HZ523, HZ524, HZ525, HZ526, MP567, MP568, MP570, MP572, MP573, MP574, MP576, MP586, MP591, MP592, MP594, MP595, MP601, MP639, MP681, MP687, MP692, MP693, MP694, MP699, 1 Mk.XII MP743, 6 Mk.XIII HZ889, HZ890, MF258, MP709, MP753, NC454, 8 Mk.XIV none identified

Squadrons

17	Mk.X. Gianaclis May 45 with Warwicks. Last Wellington left Sep 45
26	Mk.III, X, XI, XII, XIII. Takoradi May 43. Disbanded May 45
27	Mk.XIV. Gianaclis Feb 45. Warwick Mar 45. Last Wellington left Mar 45
28	Mk.IC. Castel Benito Jul 43 with other types. Last Wellington left Dec 43

British Overseas Airways Corporation (BOAC)

Four Mk.ICs R1018, T2609, X9692 and Z8783 1942-1943. Operated from Almaza as B.A.W.1-B.A.W.4 but the allocations to which aircraft are not known beyond B.A.W.2 which was probably Z8783

The Vickers-Armstrongs Warwick

Types 284/413/422/460/462/468/483

Vickers Warwick C Mk.III HG248 used by Napier at Luton as a Sabre engine flying test-bed. (*Cliff Minney*)

The Warwick is frequently referred to as a Wellington replacement, but this is incorrect as it was a parallel and somewhat larger design, with the prototype making its first flight in 1939. Originally intended as a heavy bomber complement to the Wellington and sharing many of its design and structural features including geodetic construction, the prolonged development of the Warwick ultimately proved to be its undoing as by the time it was nearing readiness for service, the four-engine heavies had arrived and it was destined never to see operation as a bomber. Originally intended to be powered by the disastrous Rolls-Royce Vulture, the problems with these being significant in delaying the Warwick's service entry and production aircraft were fitted with Bristol Centaurus or Pratt and Whitney Double Wasp engines. The bulk of the 845 Warwicks built were issued to Coastal Command for general reconnaissance and Air Sea Rescue duties, for which latter purpose many were equipped to carry an airborne lifeboat. Others were used for transport duties, including fourteen which were delivered to BOAC.

RAF squadrons wholly or partially equipped with Warwick ASR Mks I, GR Mk.II and GR Mk.V, or C Mk.I and C Mk.III transports included:

38, 167, 179, 251, 269, 276, 277, 278, 279, 280, 281, 282, 283, 284, 292, 293, 294, 301, 304, 353, 520, 525 and 621.

Warwicks first entered service with 280 Squadron at Langham, Norfolk in August 1943 and the last examples were withdrawn from use 1946; 621 Squadron at Aqir near Tel Aviv, being the final user giving up its aircraft in August.

REFERENCES

Chapter One

1 Flying log book of Joseph 'Mutt' Summers, Brooklands Museum
2 *British Flight Testing* by Tim Mason, Putnam 1993
3 Vickers flight test reports, Brooklands Museum
4 *Wellington Crash Log* by David J Smith
5 *The Right of the Line* by John Terraine, Macmillan 1985
6 *Action Stations Revisited* by Michael JF Bowyer, Crécy 2000

Chapter Two

1 Sqn Ldr Richard James, IX(B) Squadron Association
2 Ibid
3 Ibid
4 Letter to John Maynard via Norman Didwell
5 *Diary of a Bomber Pilot* by Christopher Jary
6 Anon via Robin Barnes

Chapter Three

1 *No Flight From The Cage* by Calton Younger, Fighting High 2013
2 HQ Bomber Command Interceptions/Tactics Report 115/42
3 Geoff Mann
4 Sqn Ldr Richard James, IX(B) Squadron Association
5 *The Second World War Royal Air Force 1939-1945 Signals Volume VII,* Centre for Air Power Studies, MLRS books

Chapter Four

1 *Wellingtons Over the Med* by Richard Stowers, Stowers 2012
2 Wg Cdr Thomas Vickers, Old Comrades Association
3 Headquarters RAF Middle East MS.54202/Ops 21 Dec 42
4 *RAF & RCAF Aircraft Nose Art in World War II* pp 180 by Clarence Simonsen, Hikoki 2001

Chapter Five

1 *The All-Steel Traveller* Bloodaxe Books 1994
2 Via Brooklands Museum
3 U-Boat.net website
4 *An Air Gunner's Story* by Jack Wakefield

Chapter Seven

1 *Bodenplatte – The Luftwaffe's Last Hope* pp 208/209 by John Manrho and Ron Pütz, Hikoki 2004
2 *Bomber Command Losses – Vol 7* by W R Chorley, Midland 2002
3 24 Squadron Association
4 *The Squadrons of the Fleet Air Arm* by Ray Sturtivant, Air Britain 1994
5 'Wellington BJ895 Highball/Upkeep Trials' Brooklands Museum
6 FIU Report No.209 dated 12 July 1943
7 FIU Report No.249 dated 3 July 1944
8 Via Keith Hayward British Airways

Chapter Eight

1 Andrew Simpson, Royal Air Force Museum

THE NATIONAL ARCHIVE REFERENCES

Air 14 Bomber Command
Bomber Night Interceptions Air 14/658
Correspondence with the Prime Minister Air 14/1926
Correspondence with the Vice Chief of the Air Staff Air 14/1812
Director of Bomber Operations Air 14/1934
Information on Prisoners of War Air 14/1470
Missing Aircraft Register Air 14/2791

Air 23 Overseas Commands
Deployment of RCM Wellingtons against German tanks Air 23/1195
South-East Asia Command Daily Summaries Air 23/1918 et al

Air 24 Coastal Command
Coastal Command Strategy Air 24/various

Air 25 Groups
1 Group ORB Air 25/1
3 Group ORB Air 25/52

Air 26 Wings
80 Wing ORB Air 26/580

Air 27 Squadron ORBs
9 Sqn Air 27/126
17 Sqn SAAF Air 27/241
24 Sqn Air 27/295
26 Sqn SAAF Air 27/322
27 Sqn SAAF Air 27/331
36 Sqn Air 27/383 & 384
38 Sqn Air 27/397
40 Sqn Air 27/414
57 Sqn Air 27/538
69 Sqn Air 27/606, 607,608 & 609
70 Sqn Air 27/617
75 (NZ) Sqn Air 27/645
99 Sqn Air 27/788, 789, 790 & 791
104 Sqn Air 27/822
108 Sqn Air 27/849
109 Sqn Air 27/853
115 Sqn Air 27/888
149 Sqn Air 27/1000 & 1001
162 Sqn Air 27/1070 & 1071
172 Sqn Air 27/1105 & 1106
179 Sqn Air 27/1127
192 Sqn Air 27/1156
203 Sqn Air 27/1199 & 1200
214 Sqn Air 27/1319 & 1320
215 Sqn Air 27/1329
221 Sqn Air 27/1368
232 Sqn Air 27/1429
242 Sqn Air 27/1472
244 Sqn Air 27/1477
300 (Polish) Sqn Air 27/1656
304 (Polish) Sqn Air 27/1670
311 (Polish) Sqn Air 27/1687 & 1688
407 Sqn Air 27/1794 & 1795
415 (RCAF) Sqn Air 27/1812
458 (RAAF) Sqn Air 27/1902
466 (RAAF) Sqn Air 27/672
544 Sqn Air 27/2028
612 Sqn Air 27/2115 & 2116
621 Sqn Air 27/2135

Air 29 Other unit ORBs
201 Advanced Flying School Air 29/2143
1 Air Armament School Air 29/588
10 Air Gunnery School Air 29/597
1 Air Navigation School Air 29/1433
1 Air Sea Rescue Unit Air 29/449
Air Sea Warfare Development Unit Air 29/913
Air Transport Tactical Development Unit Air 29/
2 British Airways Repair Unit Air 29/458
Central Gunnery School Air 29/605
Communications Flight Lydda Air 29/
1 Ferry Crew Pool Air 29/458
303 Ferry Training Unit Air 29/629
Fighter Interception Unit Air 29/27
1417 Flight Air 29/868
1418 Flight Air 29/868
1422 Flight Air 29/868
1473 Flight Air 29/870
1481 Flight Air 29/870
1483 Flight Air 29/870
1485 Flight Air 29/870
1577 Flight Air 29/878
1680 Flight Air 29/881
1692 Flight Air 29/882
5 Group Training Flight Air 29/871
1 General Reconnaissance Unit Air 29/32 & 196
11 Operational Training Unit Air 29/642 & 643
15 Operational Training Unit Air 29/654
16 Operational Training Unit Air 29/657
17 Operational Training Unit Air 29/659
20 Operational Training Unit Air 29/664
22 Operational Training Unit Air 29/666
26 Operational Training Unit Air 29/669
29 Operational Training Unit Air 29/672
30 Operational Training Unit Air 29/672
1 Overseas Aircraft Despatch Unit Air 29/471
Special Duty Flight Air 29/859
Telecommunications Flying Unit Air 29/
Torpedo Development Unit Air 29/770B
1 Torpedo Training Unit Air 29/70

ABBREVIATIONS

A&AEE	Aeroplane & Armament Experimental Establishment
AC	Air Commodore
AC1	Aircraftman First Class
AC2	Aircraftman Second Class
ACM	Air Chief Marshal
AFC	Air Force Cross
AFDE	Air Fighting Development Establishment
AFM	Air Force Medal
AFS	Advanced Flying School
AGME	Air Gun Mounting Establishment
AI	Airborne Interception
AID	Aeronautical Inspection Department
ADLS	Air Despatch Letter Service
AM	Air Marshal
AM	Air Ministry
ANS	Air Navigation School
AOC	Air Officer Commanding
AOC-in-C	Air Officer Commanding-in-Chief
ASV	Air-to-Surface Vessel
ATA	Air Transport Auxiliary
ATC	Air Training Corps
AVM	Air Vice-Marshal
BABS	Blind Approach Beacon System
BEA	British European Airways
BOAC	British Overseas Airways Corporation
CAS	Chief of the Air Staff
CB	Companion of the Order of the Bath
CBE	Commander of the British Empire
CFE	Central Fighter Establishment
CFS	Central Flying School
CGS	Central Gunnery School
CO	Commanding Officer
CofA	Certificate of Airworthiness
Cpl	Corporal
CWGC	Commonwealth War Graves Commission
DF	Direction Finding
DFC	Distinguished Flying Cross
DFM	Distinguished Flying Medal
DI	Daily Inspection
DR	Dead Reckoning
DRC	Distant Reading Compass
DSO	Distinguished Service Order
DWI	Directional Wireless Installation
EFTS	Elementary Flying Training School
EPV	L'Ecole du Personnel Volant
ETA	Estimated Time of Arrival
Fg Off	Flying Officer
FIDS	Fighter Interception Development Squadron
FIU	Fighter Interception Unit
Flt Lt	Flight Lieutenant
Flt Sgt	Flight Sergeant
Fw	Feldwebel (equivalent to Sergeant)
GP	General Purpose
Gp Capt	Group Captain
GR	General Reconnaissance
GRU	General Reconnaissance Unit
HCU	Heavy Conversion Unit
HFDF	High Frequency Direction Finding
HMS	His Majesty's Ship
HMT	His Majesty's Troopship
hp	Horsepower
Hptm	Hauptmann (equivalent to Flight Lieutenant)
HQ	Headquarters
IFF	Identification Friend or Foe
JG	Jagdgeschwader (Fighter Wing)
KG	Kampfgeschwader (Bomber Wing)
kW	Kilowatt
LAC	Leading Aircraftman
lbs	Pounds
LFS	Lancaster Finishing School
LG	Landing Ground
LNER	London & North Eastern Railway
Lt	Leutnant (equivalent to Pilot Officer)
Lt Cdr	Lieutenant Commander
Lt Col	Lieutenant Colonel
MAEE	Marine Aircraft Experimental Establishment
Maj	Major (equivalent to Squadron Leader)
MBE	Member of the British Empire
MC	Military Cross
METS	Middle East Training School
Mk	Mark
MO	Medical Officer
Mph	Miles per Hour
MV	Motor Vessel
NAAFI	Navy Army and Air Force Institute
NCO	Non-Commissioned Officer
NFT	Night Flying Test
NGTE	National Gas Turbine Establishment
NJG	Nachtjagdgeschwader (Night Fighter Wing)
OADU	Overseas Aircraft Despatch Unit
OBE	Order of the British Empire
Oblt	Oberleutnant (equivalent to Flight Officer)
OCU	Operational Conversion Unit
OR	Operational Requirement
ORB	Operations Record Book
OTU	Operational Training Unit
PAF	Polish Air Force
PFF	Pathfinder Force
Plt Off	Pilot Officer
POW	Prisoner of War
PRU	Photographic Reconnaissance Unit
PSP	Perforated Steel Planking
RAAF	Royal Australian Air Force
RAE	Royal Aircraft Establishment
RAeS	Royal Aeronautical Society

RAF	Royal Air Force
RAFVR	Royal Air Force Volunteer Reserve
RCAF	Royal Canadian Air Force
RDF	Radio Direction Finding
RN	Royal Navy
RNZAF	Royal New Zealand Air Force
R/T	Radio Telephony
SAAF	South African Air Force
SBA	Standard Beam Approach
SCI	Smoke Curtain Installation
SE	Special Equipment
SEAC	South-East Asia Command
Sgt	Sergeant
SOE	Special Operations Executive
SofTT	School of Technical Training
Sqn Ldr	Squadron Leader
St.Fw	Staffel Feldwebel
TAF	Tactical Air Force
TFU	Telecommunications Flying Unit
TI	Target Indicator
UK	United Kingdom
USAAF	United States Army Air Force
U/S	Unserviceable
U/T	Under Training
VC	Victoria Cross
VHF	Very High Frequency
VIP	Very Important Person
W/AG	Wireless/Air Gunner
WAP	Western Air Plan
Wg Cdr	Wing Commander
WO	Warrant Officer
WOM	Wireless Operator Mechanic
WOp	Wireless Operator
W/T	Wireless Telephony
ZG	Zerstörergeschwader (Destroyer Wing)

SELECT BIBLIOGRAPHY

Andrews, C F, *Vickers Aircraft Since 1908,* Putnam 1969.
Boiten, Dr Theo, *Nachtjagd War Diaries,* Red Kite 2008, two volumes
Chorley, W R, *RAF Bomber Command Losses,* Midland Counties, 7 volumes 1992-2007
Collier Webb, Derek, *UK Flight Testing Accidents 1940-71,* Air Britain 2002
Cornwell, Peter, *The Battle of France Then and Now,* After The Battle 2007
Flintham, Vic & Thomas, Andrew *Combat Codes,* Airlife 2003
Halley, James, *The Squadrons of the Royal Air Force & Commonwealth 1918-1988,* Air Britain 1988
Holmes, Robin, *The Battle of Heligoland Bight 1939,* Grub Street 2009
Jefford, Wg Cdr C G *RAF Squadrons,* Airlife 1988
Mackay, Ron, *Wellington in Action,* Squadron/Signal Publications 1986
Mason, Tim, *British Flight Testing – Martlesham Heath 1920-1939,* Putnam 1993
Maton, Michael, *Honour the Air Forces,* Token Publishing 2004
Meecoms, K J & Morgan, E B *The British Aircraft Specifications File,* Air Britain 1994
Middlebrook, Martin & Everitt, Chris *The Bomber Command War Diaries,* Midland Counties 2011
Rökker, Heinz *Ausbildung und Einsatz eines Nachtjagers im II. Weltkrieg,* VDM 2006
Shores, Christopher et al, *A History of the Mediterranean Air War 1940-1945, Volume I* Grub Street 2012
Sturtivant, Ray & Burrow, Mick *Fleet Air Arm Aircraft 1939 to 1945,* Air Britain, 1995
Sturtivant, Ray & Hamlin, John *RAF Flying Training & Support Units since 1912,* Air Britain 2007

INDEX

PLACE NAMES

UNITED KINGDOM

OVERSEAS